MEGUMI OSUGA

One of our assistants went to a maid café for the first time in his life while suffering from a 102-degree fever. The maid poster he bought is hanging in our work office.

It is glorious.

Megumi Osuga

Born December 21 in Chiba Prefecture, Megumi Osuga made her debut with *Tonpachi*, which ran in *Shonen Sunday R*, and had a short series in *Shonen Sunday Super* called *Honou no Ana no Yomi*. In 2007, her serialization of *Maoh: Juvenile Remix* started in *Shonen Sunday*.

Kotaro Isaka

Born in 1971 in Chiba Prefecture, Kotaro Isaka is one of the most popular Japanese novelists and has received numerous awards. He has many titles under his belt, most of which have been

MAOH: JUVENILE REMIX
Volume 08

Shonen Sunday Edition

Original Story by **KOTARO ISAKA**
Story and Art by **MEGUMI OSUGA**

Logo and cover design created by Isao YOSHIMURA & Bay Bridge Studio.

Translation/Stephen Paul
Touch-up Art & Lettering/James Dashiell
Design/Sam Elzway
Editor/Alexis Kirsch

The rights of the author(s) of the work(s) in this publication to be so identified have been asserted in accordance with the Copyright, Designs and Patents Act 1988. A CIP catalogue record for this book is available from the British Library.

The stories, characters and incidents mentioned in this publication are entirely fictional.

Printed in the U.S.A.

Published by VIZ Media, LLC
P.O. Box 77010
San Francisco, CA 94107

10 9 8 7 6 5 4 3 2 1
First printing, December 2011

MAOH
JUVENILE REMIX

ORIGINAL STORY BY
KOTARO ISAKA

STORY AND ART BY
MEGUMI OSUGA

08

CONTENTS

Chapter 68 Joining Up

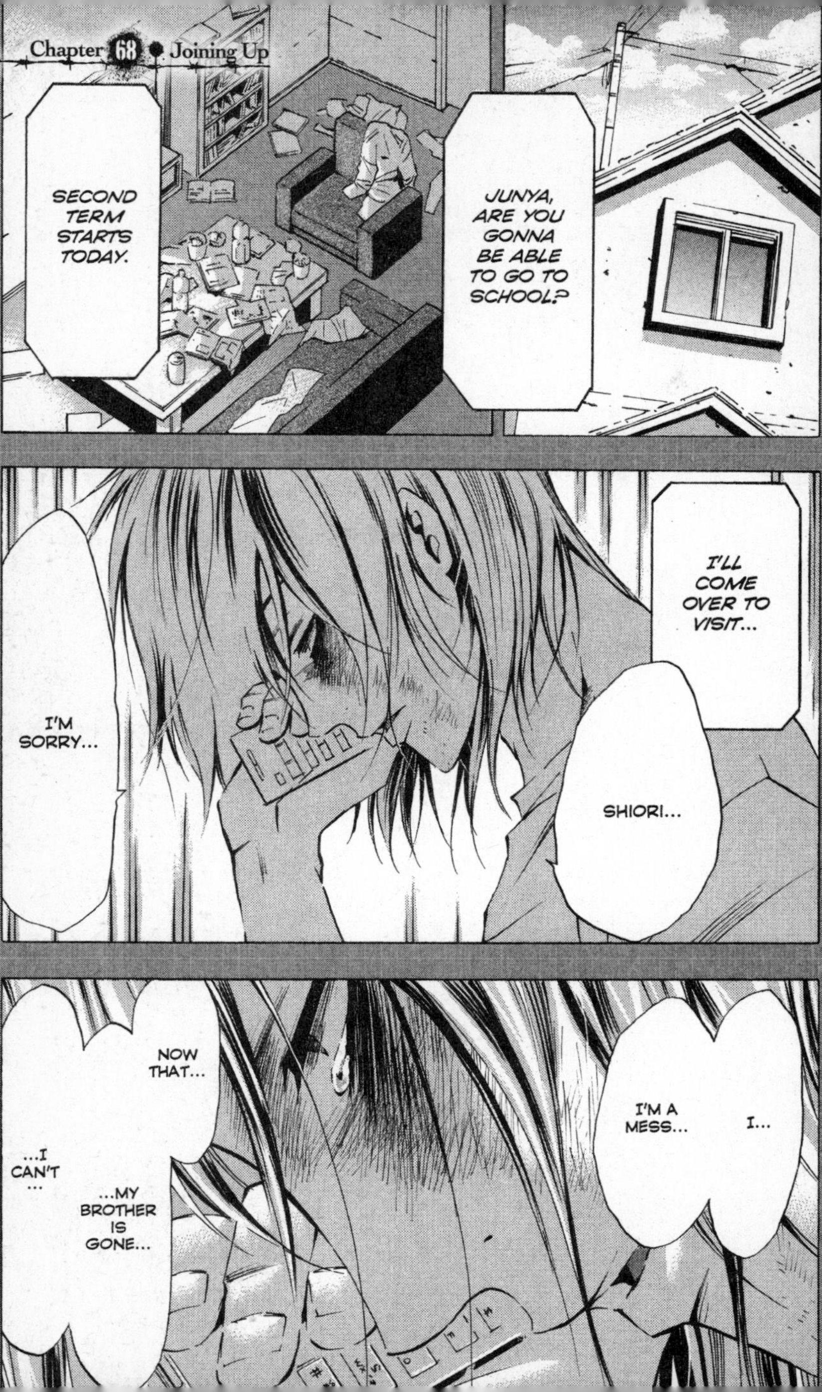
JUNYA, ARE YOU GONNA BE ABLE TO GO TO SCHOOL?
SECOND TERM STARTS TODAY.
I'LL COME OVER TO VISIT...
SHIORI...
I'M SORRY...
I...
I'M A MESS...
NOW THAT...
...MY BROTHER IS GONE...
...I CAN'T ...

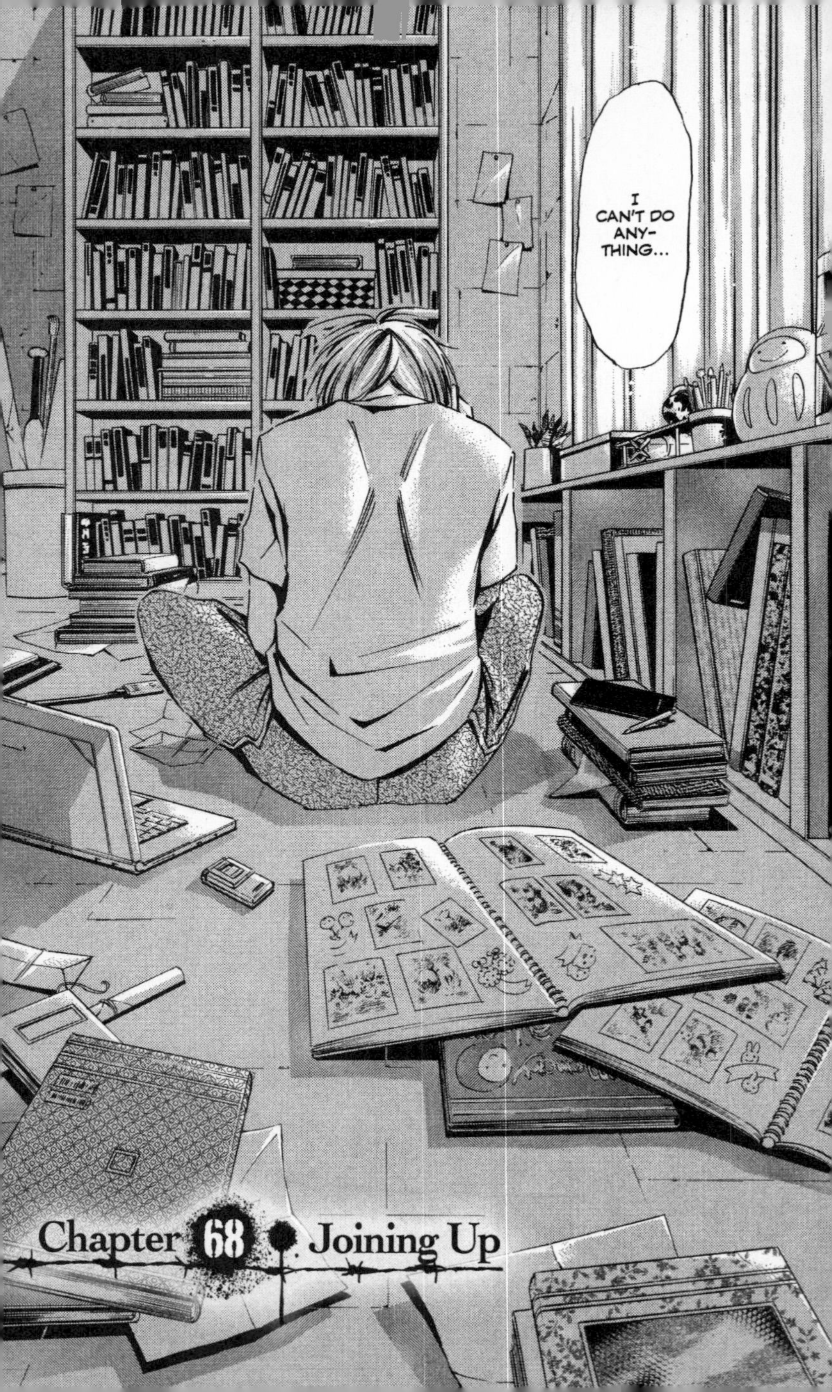
I CAN'T DO ANY-THING...
Chapter 68 Joining Up

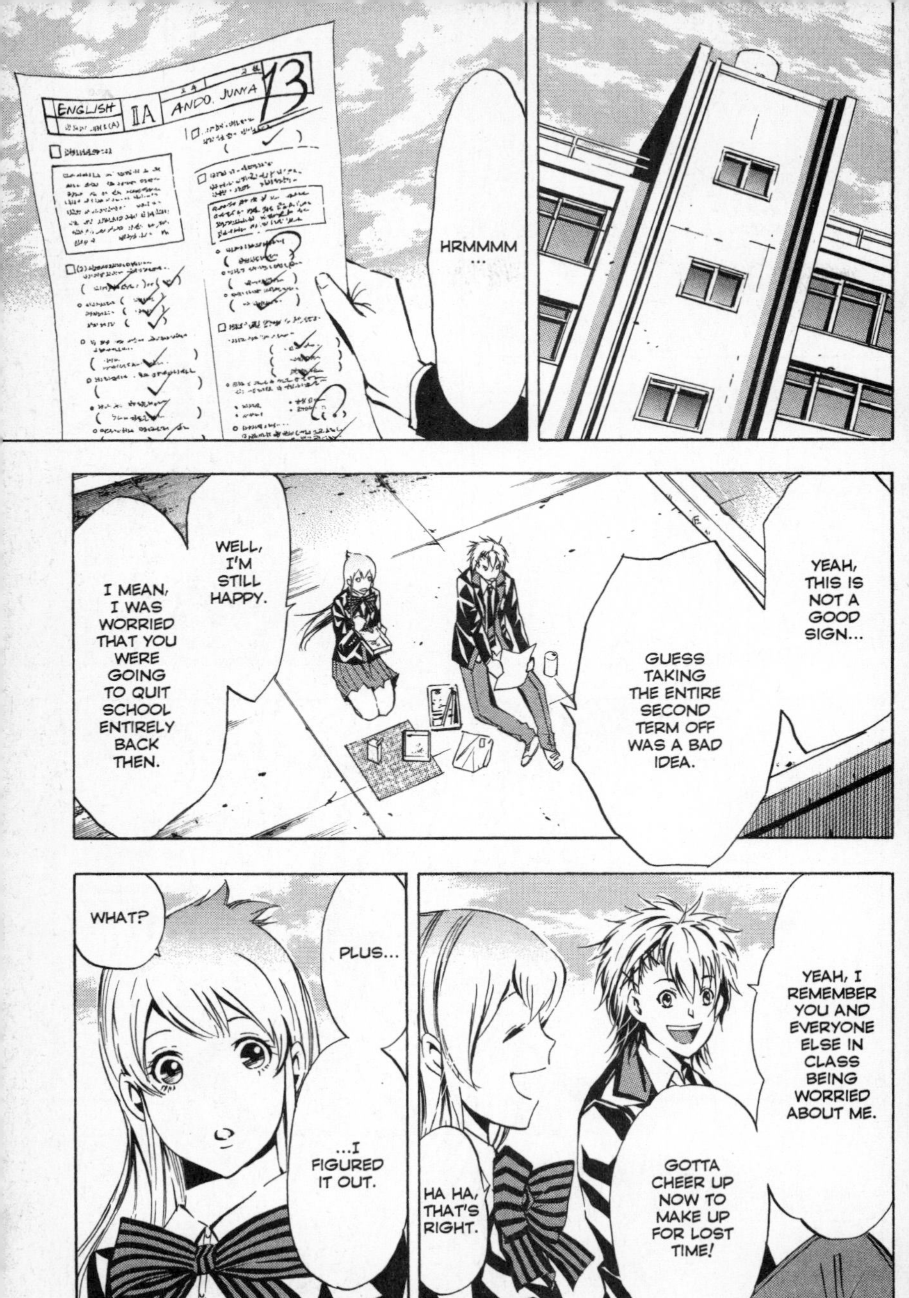
HRMMMM ...
ENGLISH
IIA
ANDO, JUNYA
13
YEAH, THIS IS NOT A GOOD SIGN...
GUESS TAKING THE ENTIRE SECOND TERM OFF WAS A BAD IDEA.
WELL, I'M STILL HAPPY.
I MEAN, I WAS WORRIED THAT YOU WERE GOING TO QUIT SCHOOL ENTIRELY BACK THEN.
YEAH, I REMEMBER YOU AND EVERYONE ELSE IN CLASS BEING WORRIED ABOUT ME.
GOTTA CHEER UP NOW TO MAKE UP FOR LOST TIME!
HA HA, THAT'S RIGHT.
PLUS...
WHAT?
...I FIGURED IT OUT.

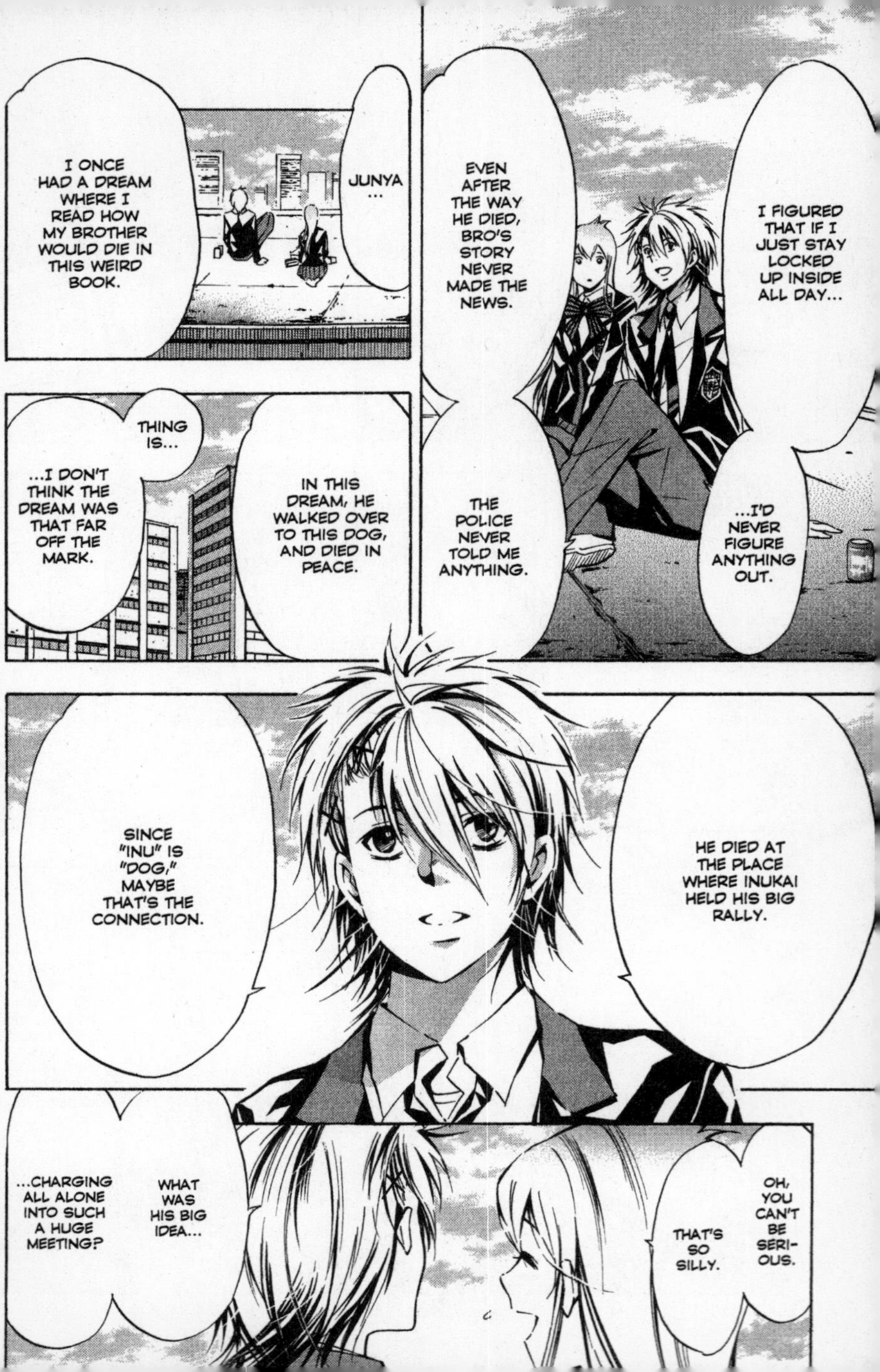
I FIGURED THAT IF I JUST STAY LOCKED UP INSIDE ALL DAY...
...I'D NEVER FIGURE ANYTHING OUT.
EVEN AFTER THE WAY HE DIED, BRO'S STORY NEVER MADE THE NEWS.
THE POLICE NEVER TOLD ME ANYTHING.
JUNYA...
I ONCE HAD A DREAM WHERE I READ HOW MY BROTHER WOULD DIE IN THIS WEIRD BOOK.
IN THIS DREAM, HE WALKED OVER TO THIS DOG, AND DIED IN PEACE.
THING IS...
...I DON'T THINK THE DREAM WAS THAT FAR OFF THE MARK.
HE DIED AT THE PLACE WHERE INUKAI HELD HIS BIG RALLY.
SINCE "INU" IS "DOG," MAYBE THAT'S THE CONNECTION.
OH, YOU CAN'T BE SERI-OUS.
THAT'S SO SILLY.
WHAT WAS HIS BIG IDEA...
...CHARGING ALL ALONE INTO SUCH A HUGE MEETING?

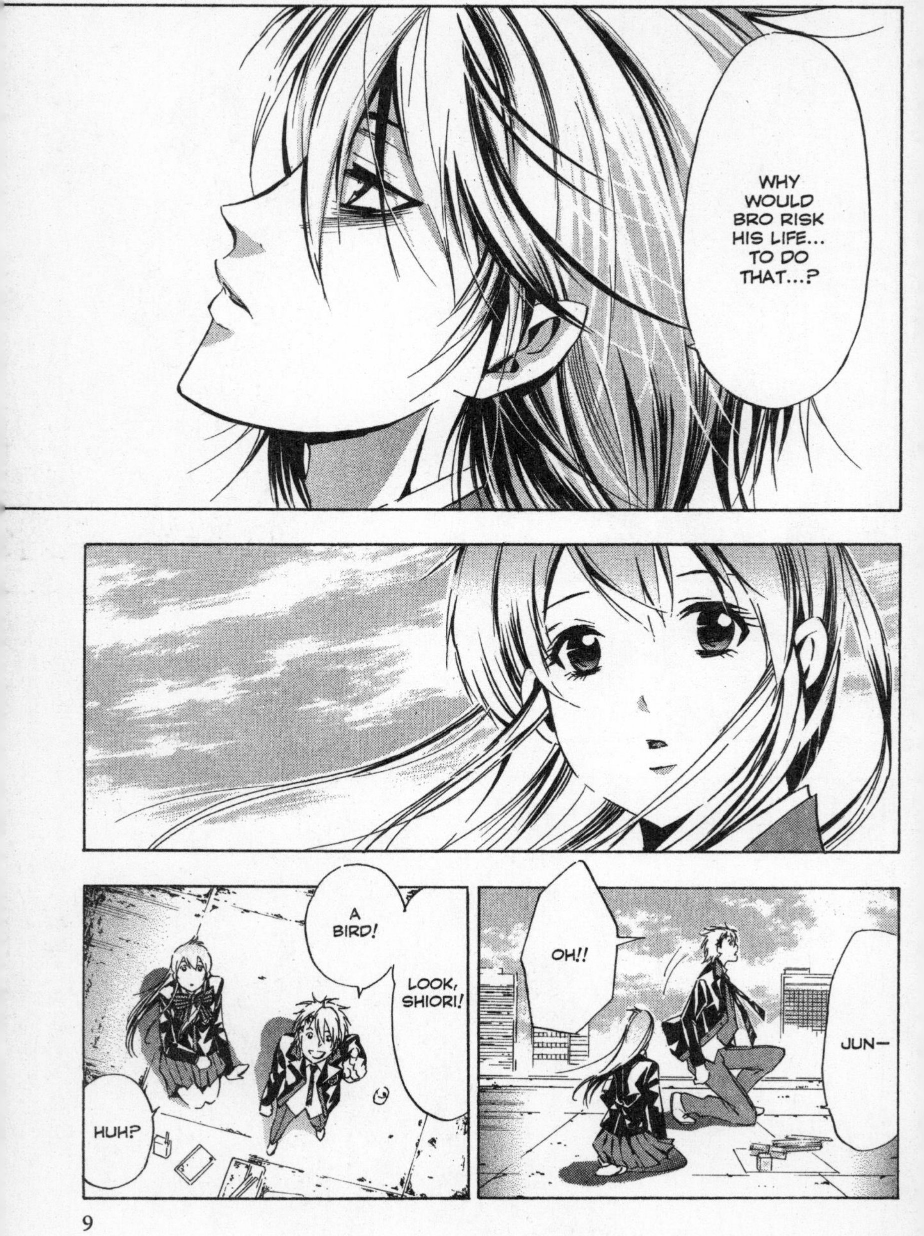

WHY WOULD BRO RISK HIS LIFE... TO DO THAT...?
JUN—
OH!!
A BIRD!
LOOK, SHIORI!
HUH?

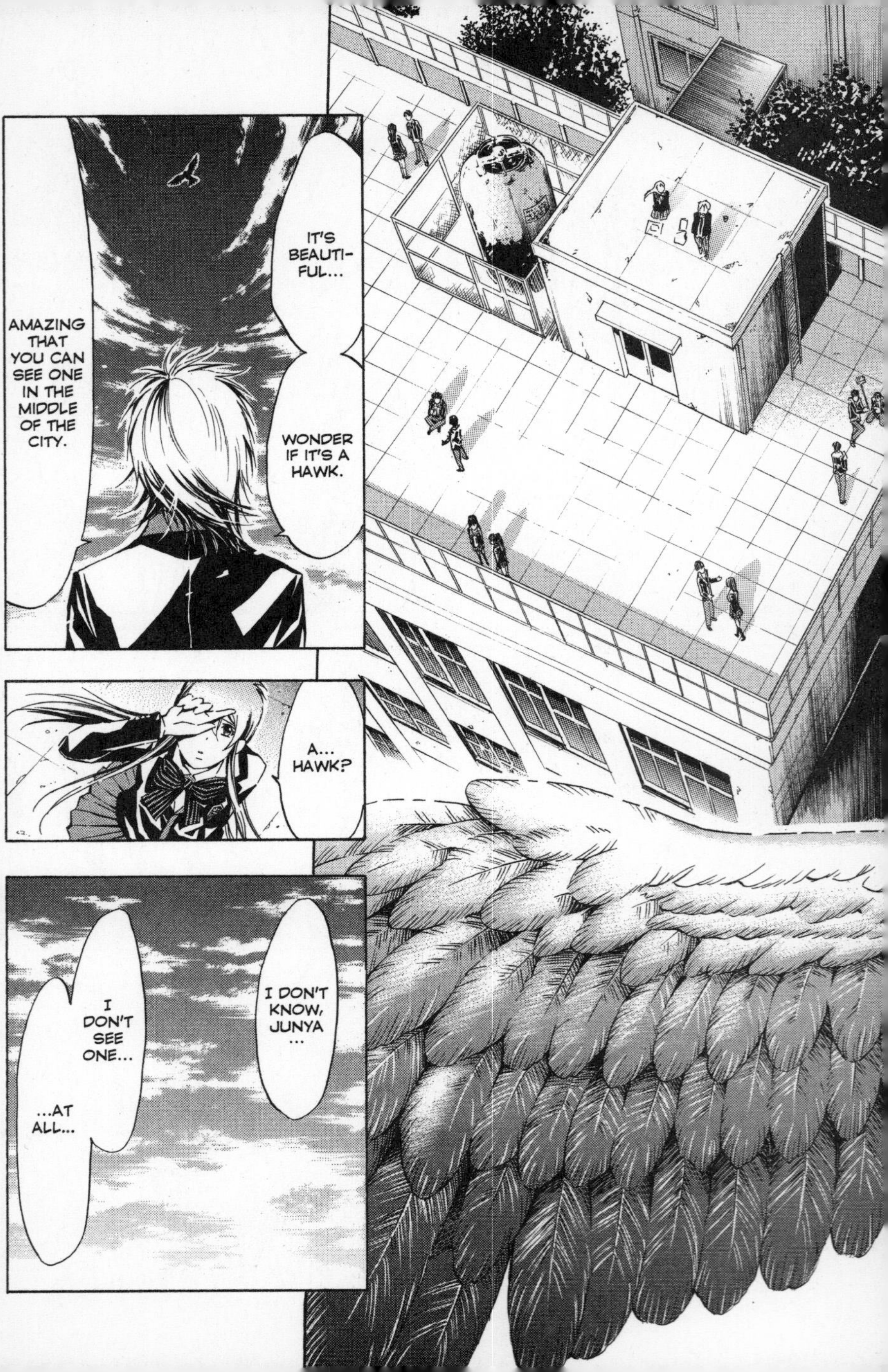
IT'S BEAUTIFUL...
AMAZING THAT YOU CAN SEE ONE IN THE MIDDLE OF THE CITY.
WONDER IF IT'S A HAWK.
A... HAWK?
I DON'T KNOW, JUNYA...
I DON'T SEE ONE...
...AT ALL...

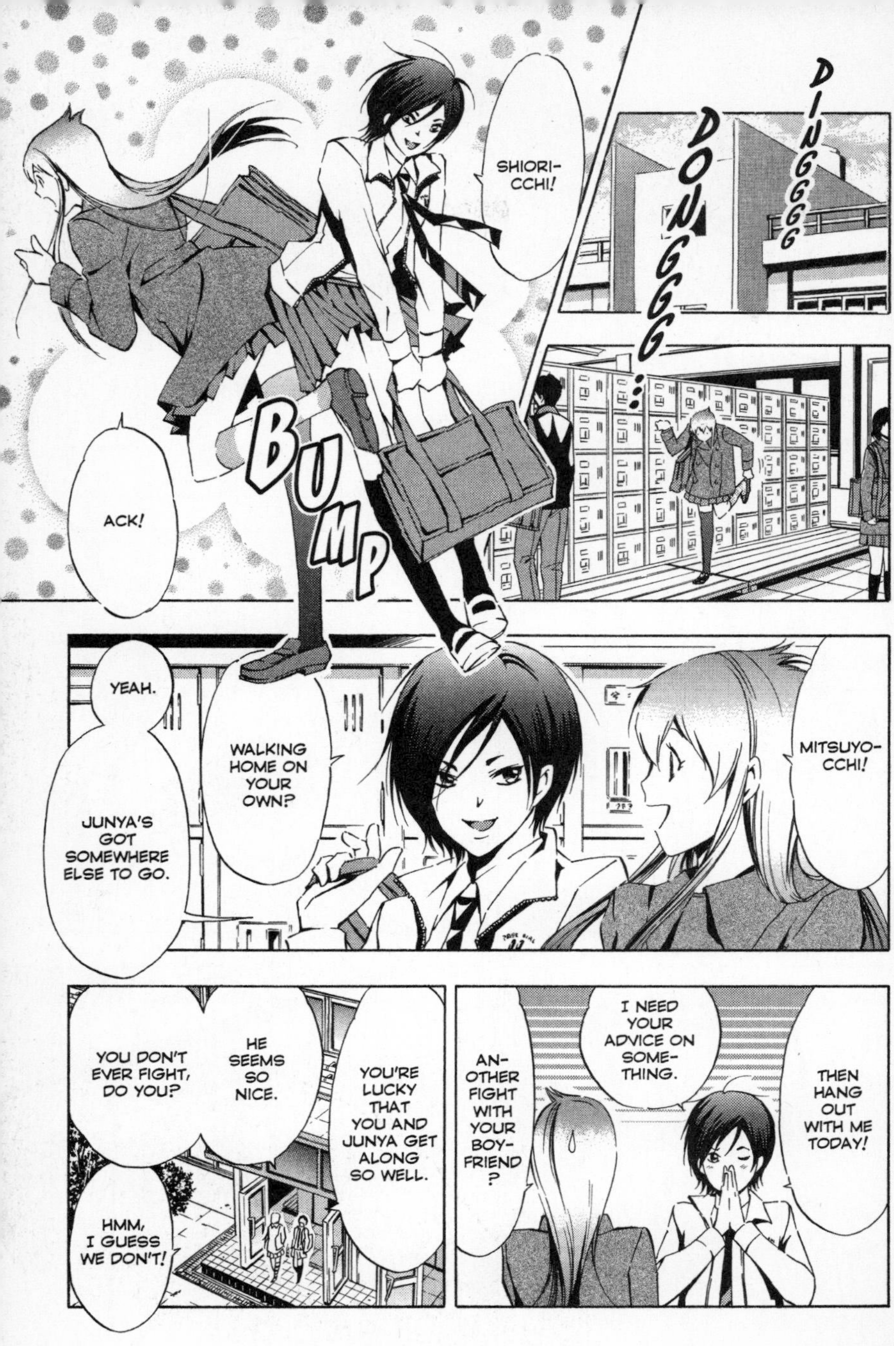
DINGGGG
DONGGGG...
SHIORI-CCHI!
BUMP
ACK!
MITSUYO-CCHI!
WALKING HOME ON YOUR OWN?
YEAH.
JUNYA'S GOT SOMEWHERE ELSE TO GO.
THEN HANG OUT WITH ME TODAY!
I NEED YOUR ADVICE ON SOME-THING.
AN-OTHER FIGHT WITH YOUR BOY-FRIEND?
YOU'RE LUCKY THAT YOU AND JUNYA GET ALONG SO WELL.
HE SEEMS SO NICE.
YOU DON'T EVER FIGHT, DO YOU?
HMM, I GUESS WE DON'T!

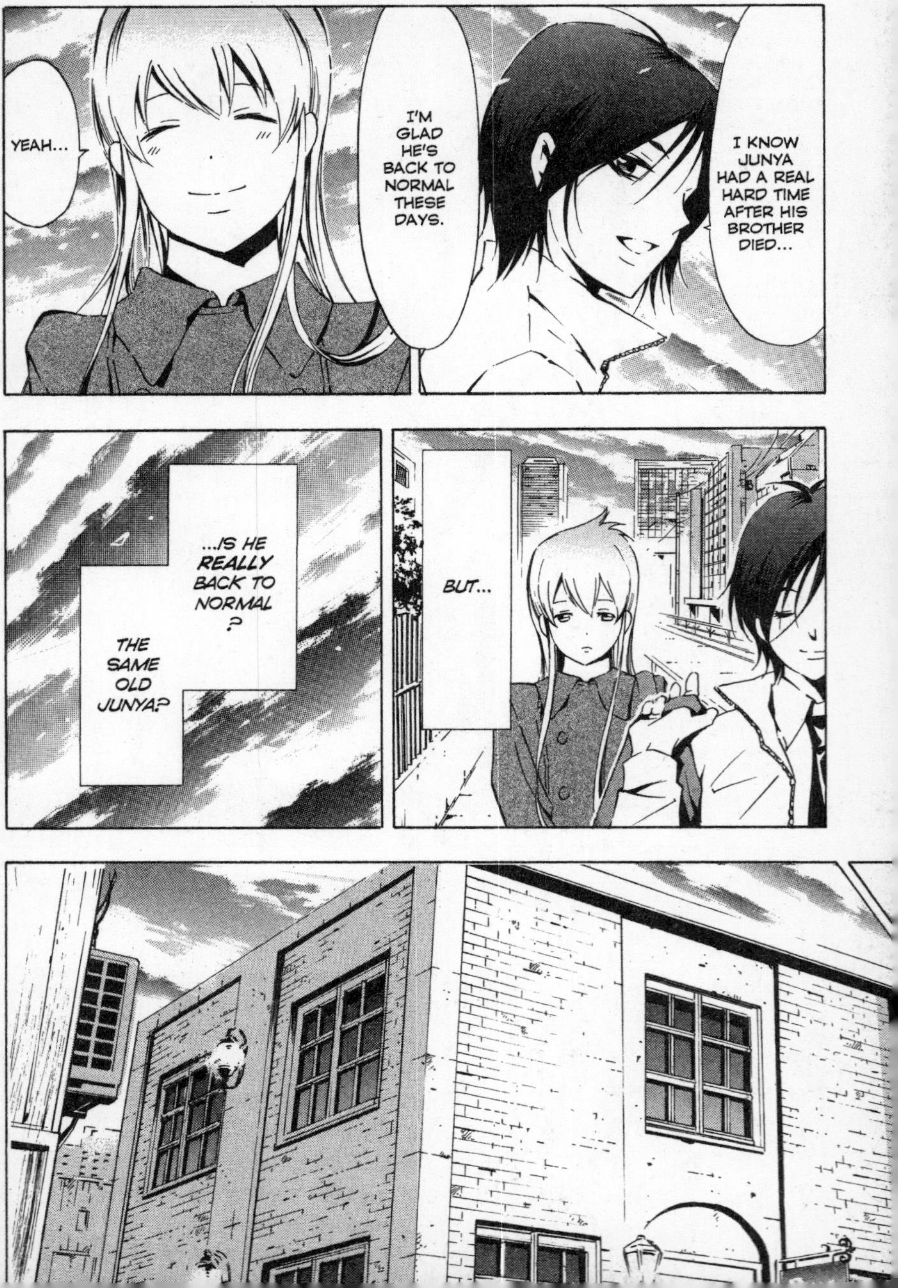
I KNOW JUNYA HAD A REAL HARD TIME AFTER HIS BROTHER DIED...
I'M GLAD HE'S BACK TO NORMAL THESE DAYS.
YEAH...
BUT...
...IS HE *REALLY* BACK TO NORMAL?
THE SAME OLD JUNYA?

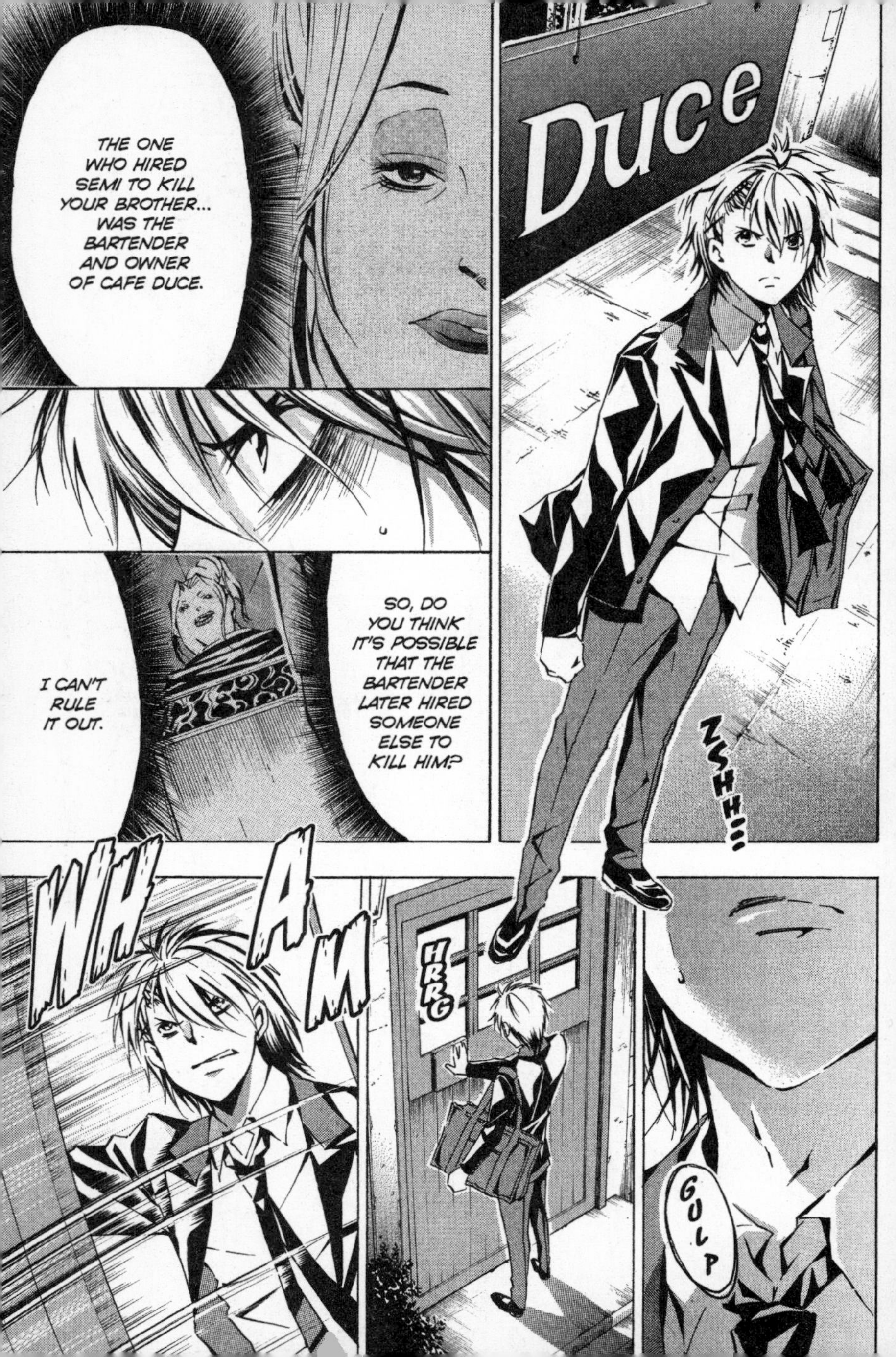
Duce
ZSHHH!!
THE ONE WHO HIRED SEMI TO KILL YOUR BROTHER... WAS THE BARTENDER AND OWNER OF CAFE DUCE.
SO, DO YOU THINK IT'S POSSIBLE THAT THE BARTENDER LATER HIRED SOMEONE ELSE TO KILL HIM?
I CAN'T RULE IT OUT.
GULP
HRRG
WHAM

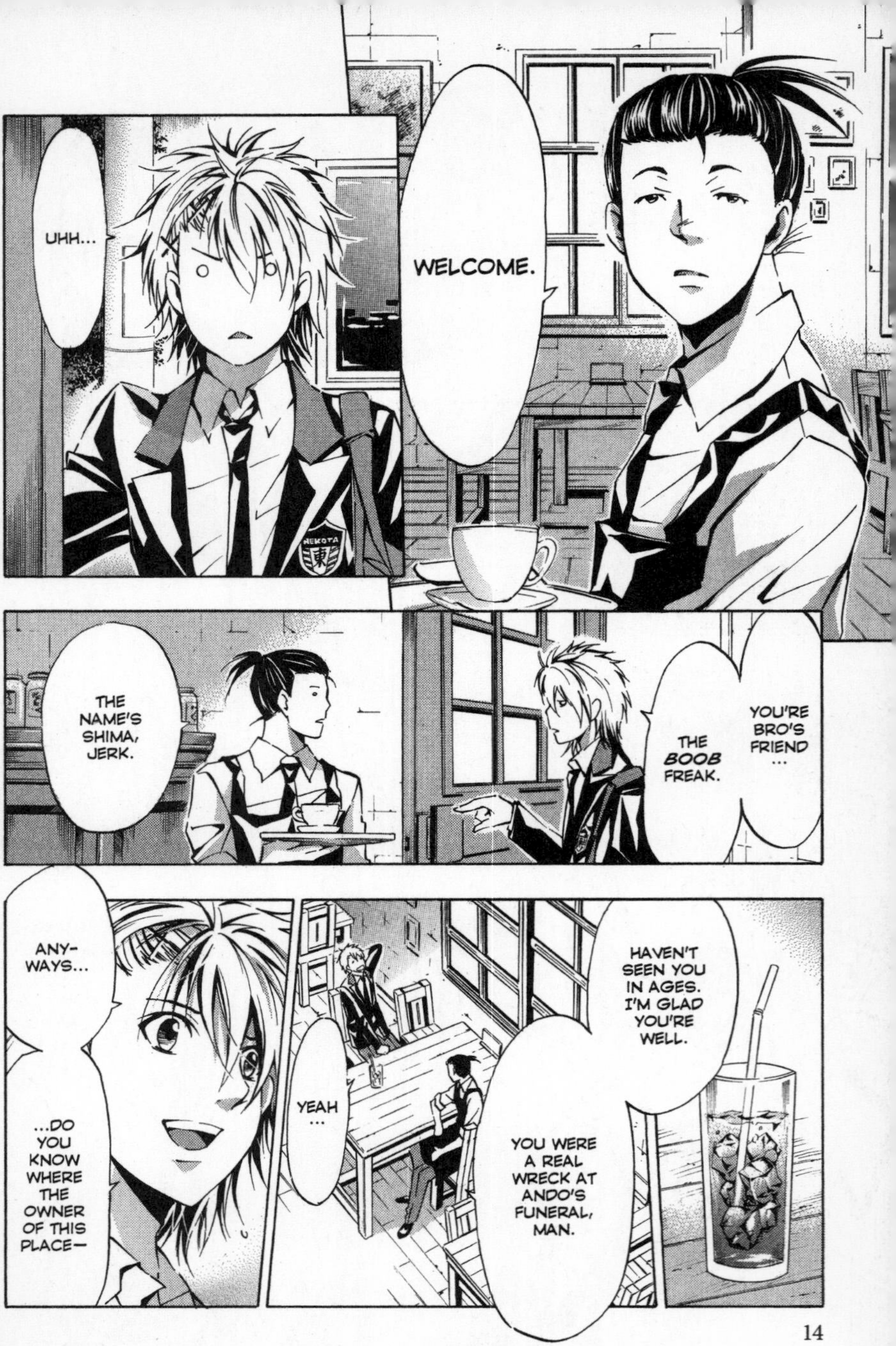
WELCOME.
UHH...
YOU'RE BRO'S FRIEND ...
THE *BOOB* FREAK.
THE NAME'S SHIMA, JERK.
HAVEN'T SEEN YOU IN AGES. I'M GLAD YOU'RE WELL.
YOU WERE A REAL WRECK AT ANDO'S FUNERAL, MAN.
YEAH ...
ANY-WAYS...
...DO YOU KNOW WHERE THE OWNER OF THIS PLACE—

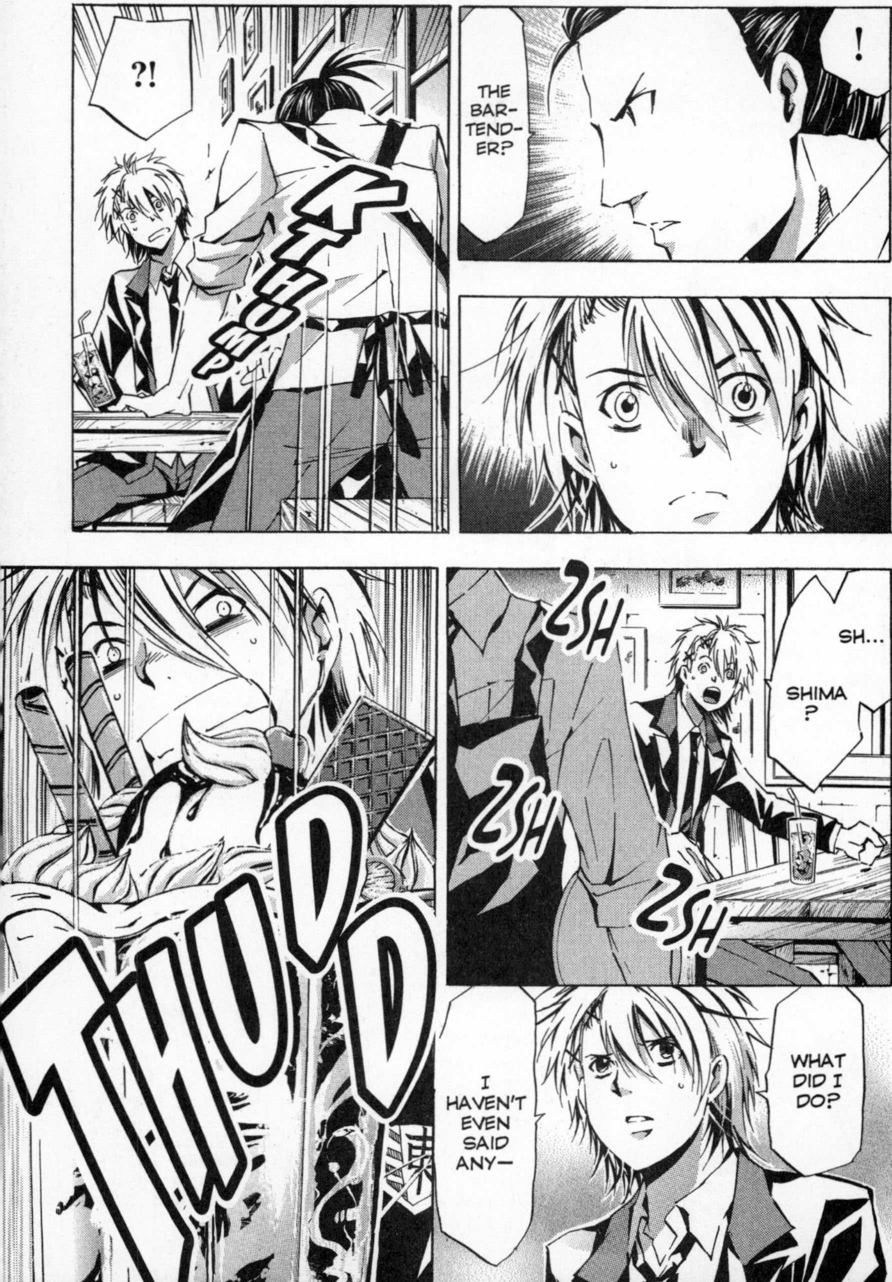

!
THE BAR-TEND-ER?
?!
KTHUMP
SH...
SHIMA?
ZSH
ZSH
ZSH
WHAT DID I DO?
I HAVEN'T EVEN SAID ANY—
THUDD

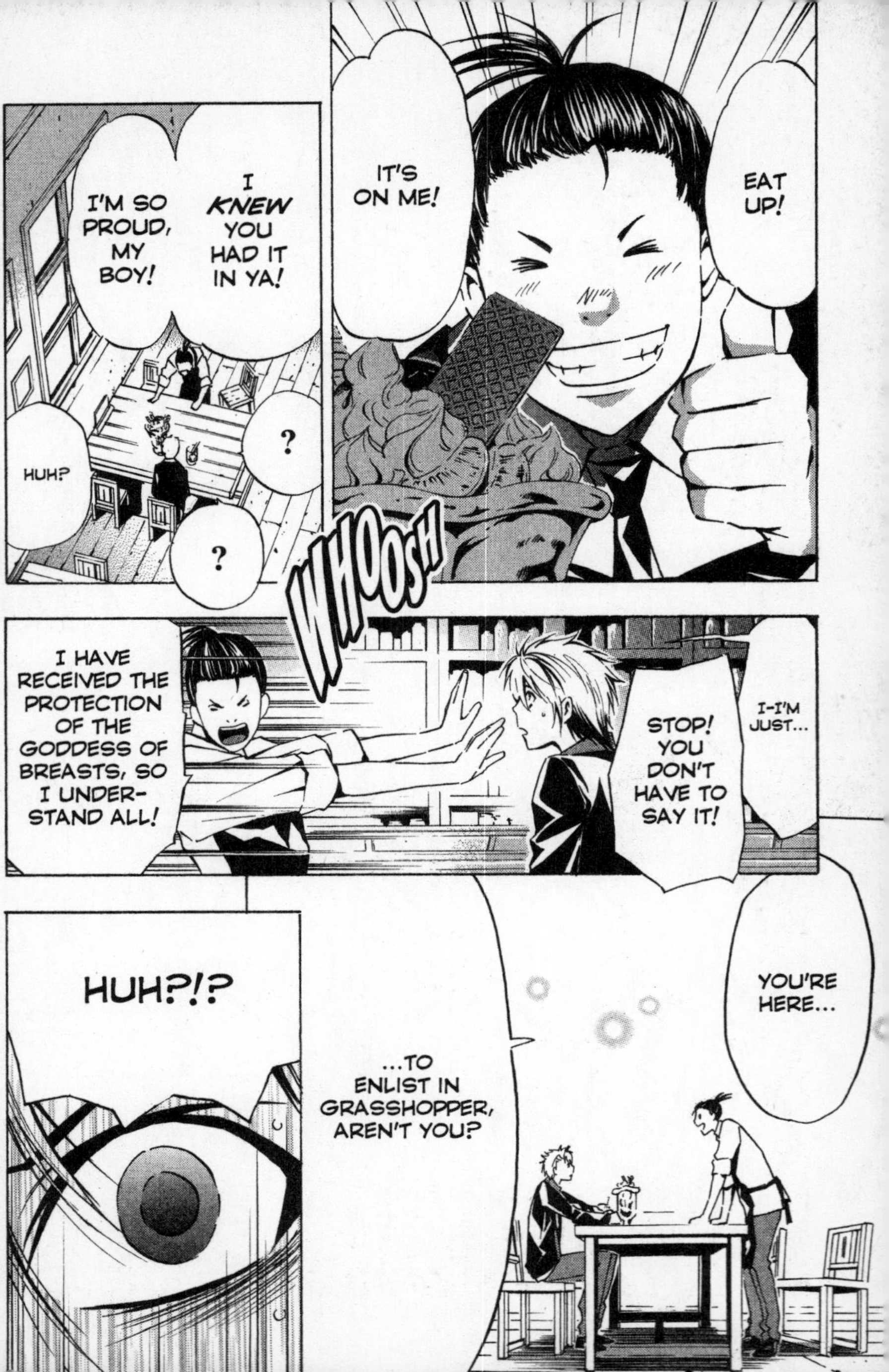
EAT UP!
IT'S ON ME!
I *KNEW* YOU HAD IT IN YA!
I'M SO PROUD, MY BOY!
?
?
HUH?
WHOOSH
I-I'M JUST...
STOP! YOU DON'T HAVE TO SAY IT!
I HAVE RECEIVED THE PROTECTION OF THE GODDESS OF BREASTS, SO I UNDER-STAND ALL!
YOU'RE HERE...
...TO ENLIST IN GRASSHOPPER, AREN'T YOU?
HUH?!?

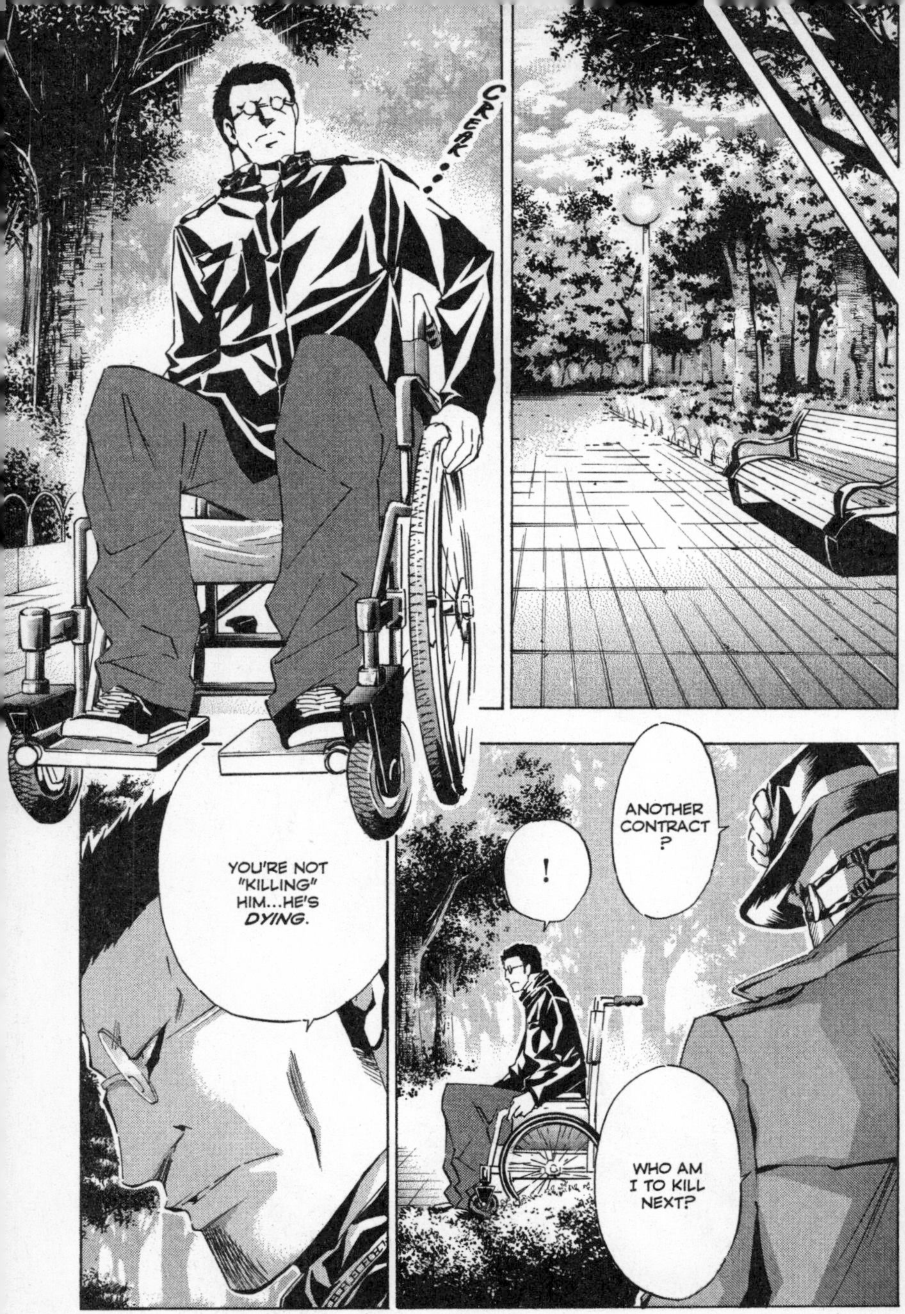
CREAK...
ANOTHER CONTRACT?
!
WHO AM I TO KILL NEXT?
YOU'RE NOT "KILLING" HIM...HE'S *DYING*.

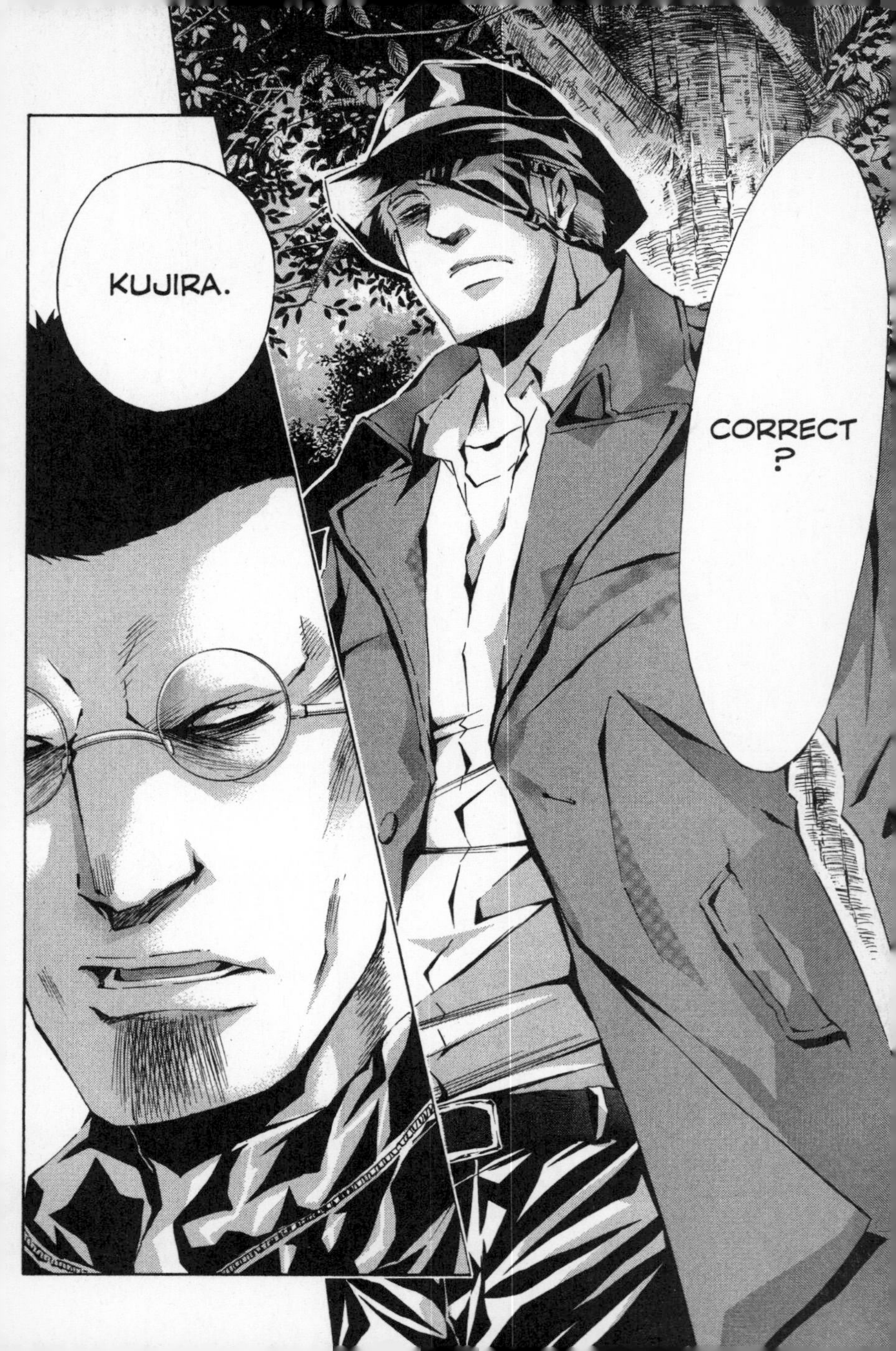
CORRECT?
KUJIRA.

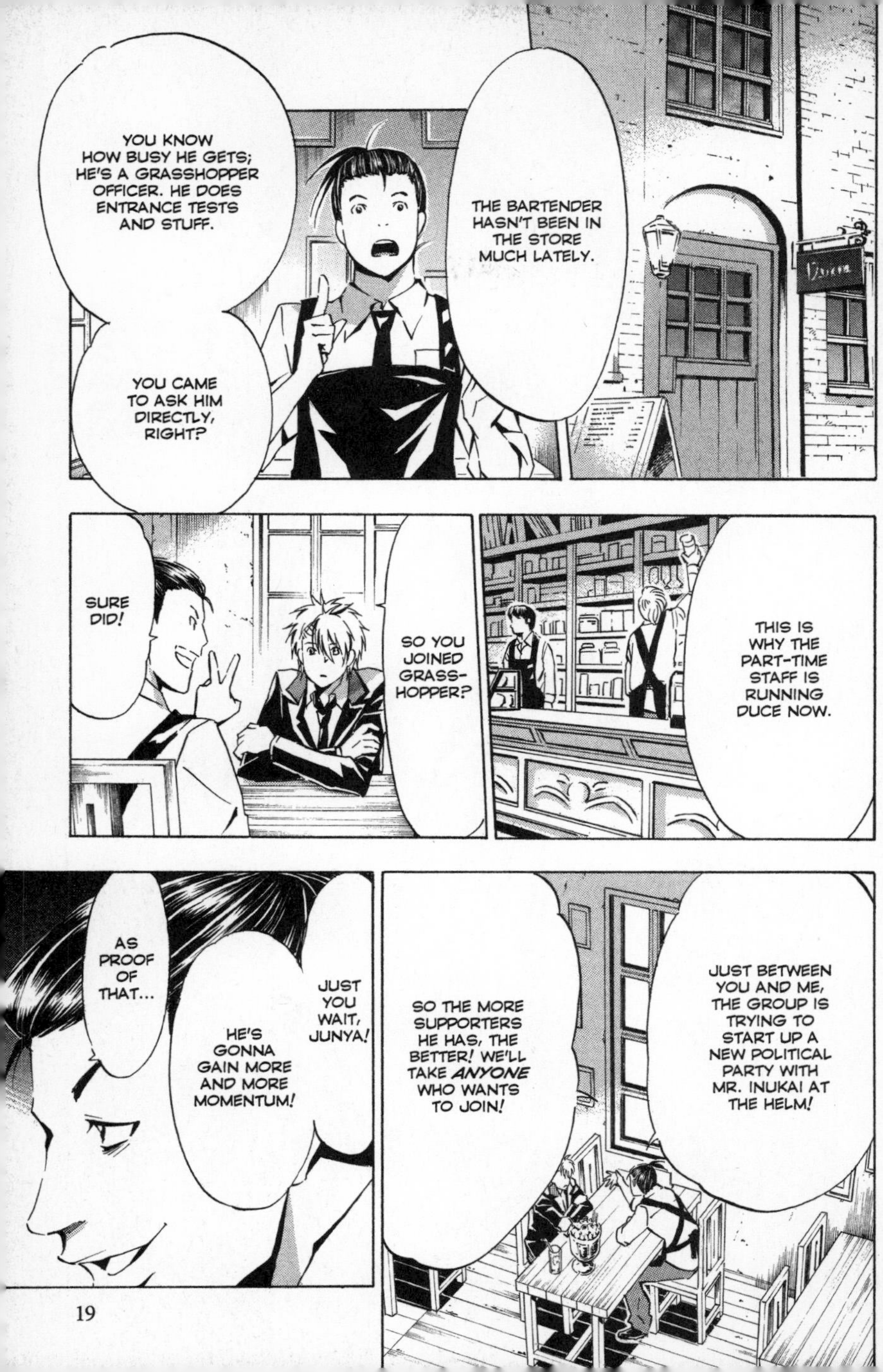
THE BARTENDER HASN'T BEEN IN THE STORE MUCH LATELY.
YOU KNOW HOW BUSY HE GETS; HE'S A GRASSHOPPER OFFICER. HE DOES ENTRANCE TESTS AND STUFF.
YOU CAME TO ASK HIM DIRECTLY, RIGHT?
THIS IS WHY THE PART-TIME STAFF IS RUNNING DUCE NOW.
SO YOU JOINED GRASS-HOPPER?
SURE DID!
JUST BETWEEN YOU AND ME, THE GROUP IS TRYING TO START UP A NEW POLITICAL PARTY WITH MR. INUKAI AT THE HELM!
SO THE MORE SUPPORTERS HE HAS, THE BETTER! WE'LL TAKE *ANYONE* WHO WANTS TO JOIN!
JUST YOU WAIT, JUNYA!
HE'S GONNA GAIN MORE AND MORE MOMENTUM!
AS PROOF OF THAT...

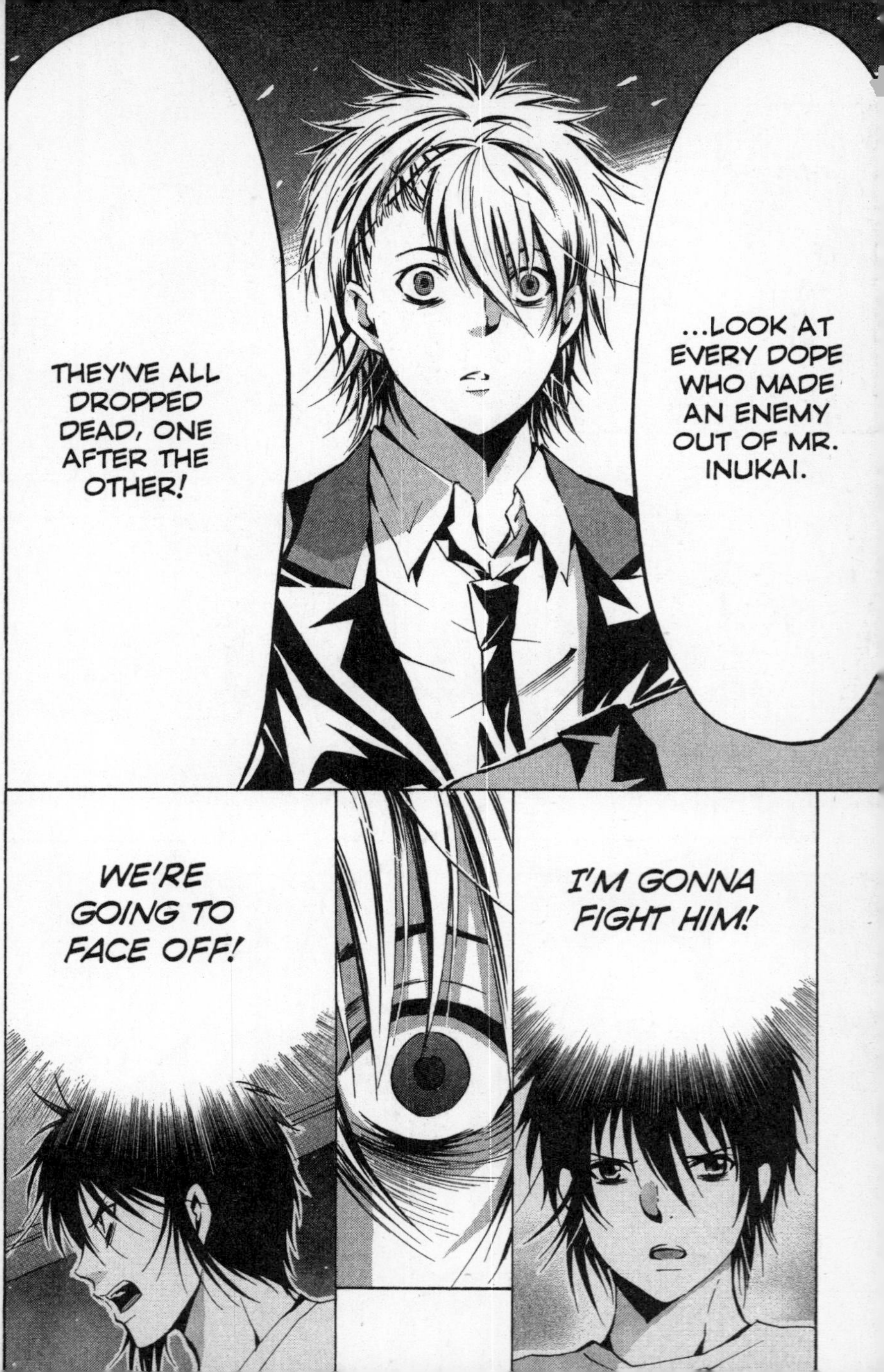
...LOOK AT EVERY DOPE WHO MADE AN ENEMY OUT OF MR. INUKAI.
THEY'VE ALL DROPPED DEAD, ONE AFTER THE OTHER!
I'M GONNA FIGHT HIM!
WE'RE GOING TO FACE OFF!

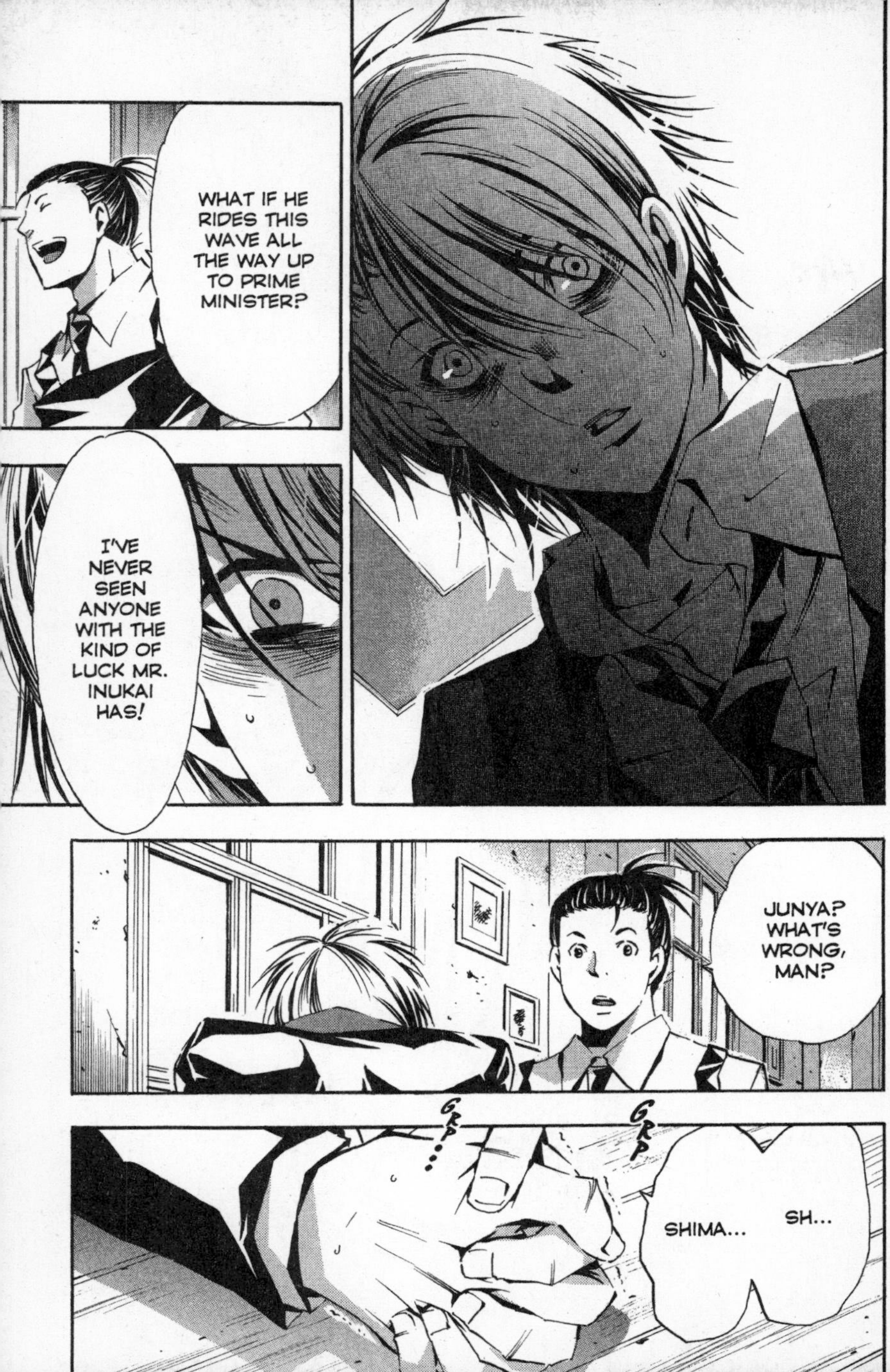
WHAT IF HE RIDES THIS WAVE ALL THE WAY UP TO PRIME MINISTER?
I'VE NEVER SEEN ANYONE WITH THE KIND OF LUCK MR. INUKAI HAS!
JUNYA? WHAT'S WRONG, MAN?
GRP
GRP...
SH...
SHIMA...

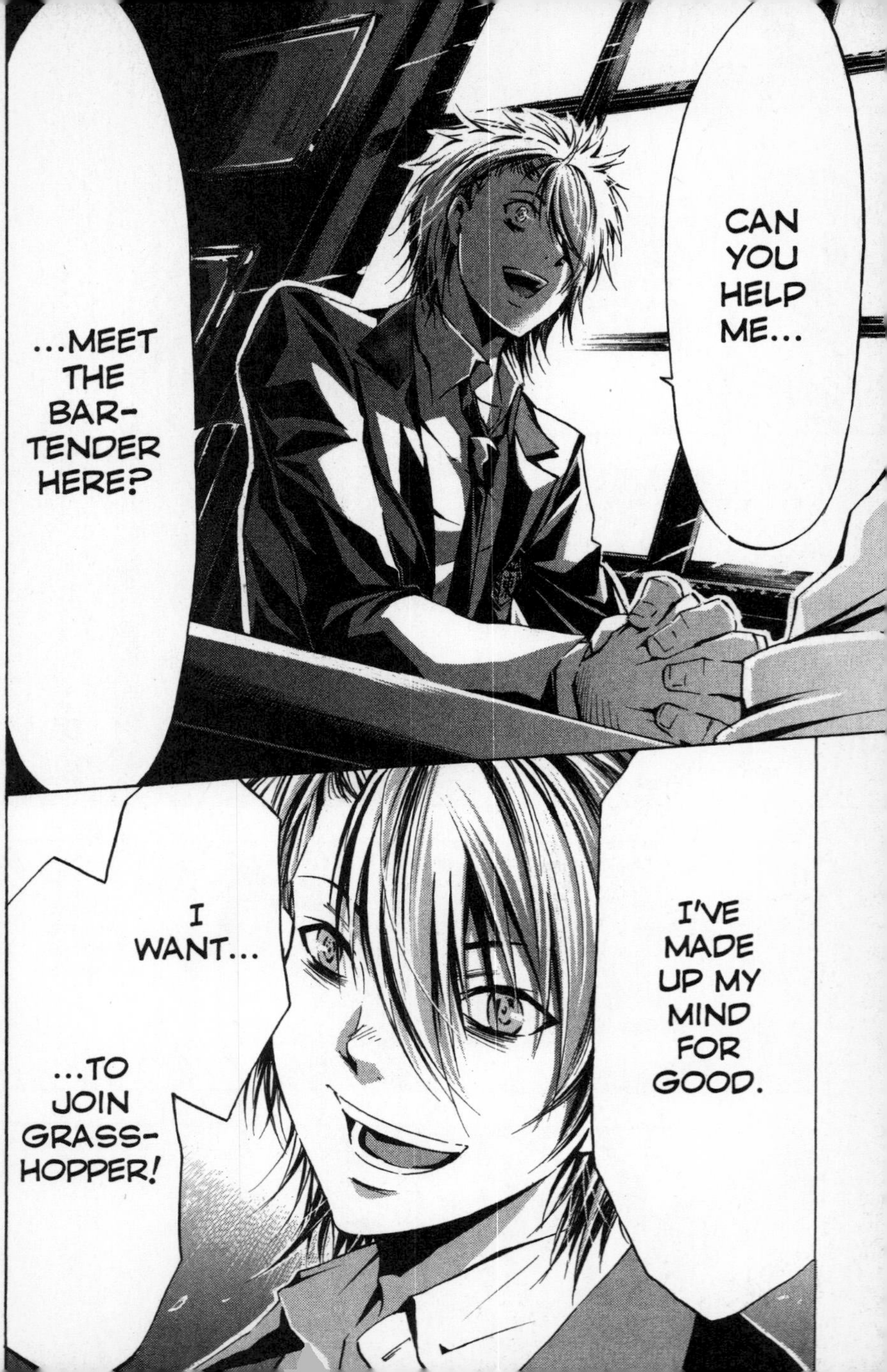
CAN YOU HELP ME...
...MEET THE BAR-TENDER HERE?
I'VE MADE UP MY MIND FOR GOOD.
I WANT...
...TO JOIN GRASS-HOPPER!

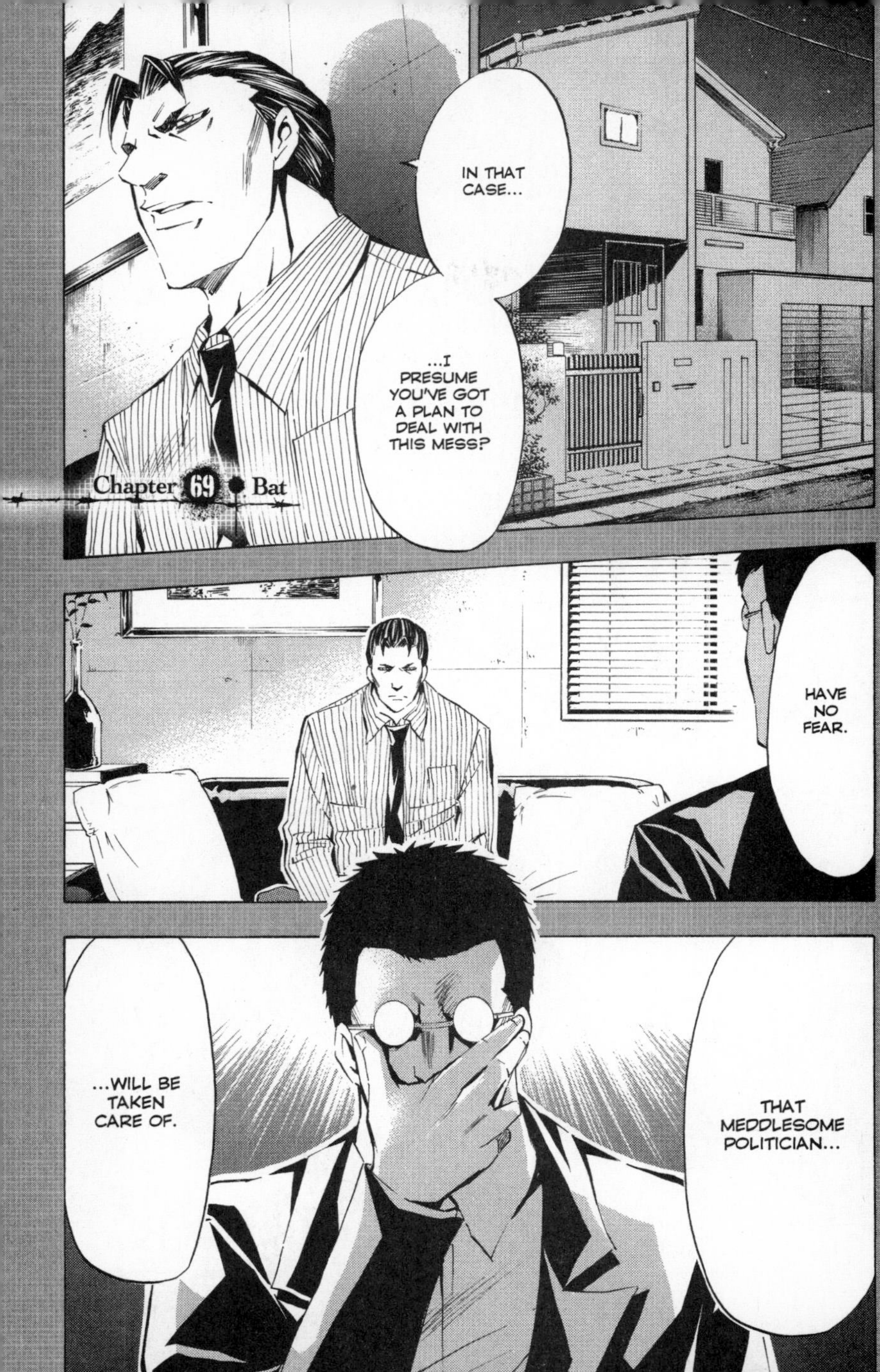
IN THAT CASE...
...I PRESUME YOU'VE GOT A PLAN TO DEAL WITH THIS MESS?
Chapter 69 Bat
HAVE NO FEAR.
THAT MEDDLESOME POLITICIAN...
...WILL BE TAKEN CARE OF.

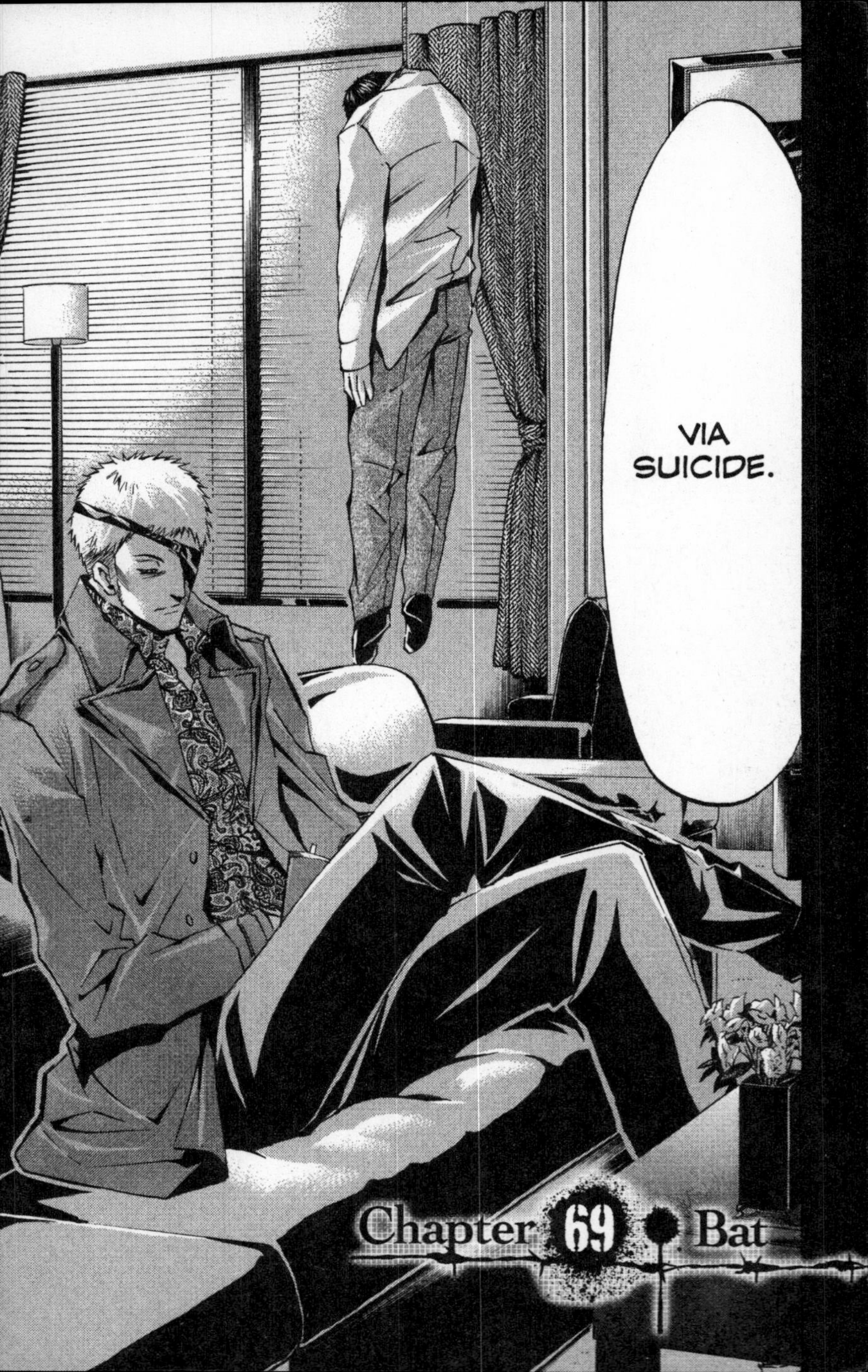
VIA SUICIDE.
Chapter 69 Bat

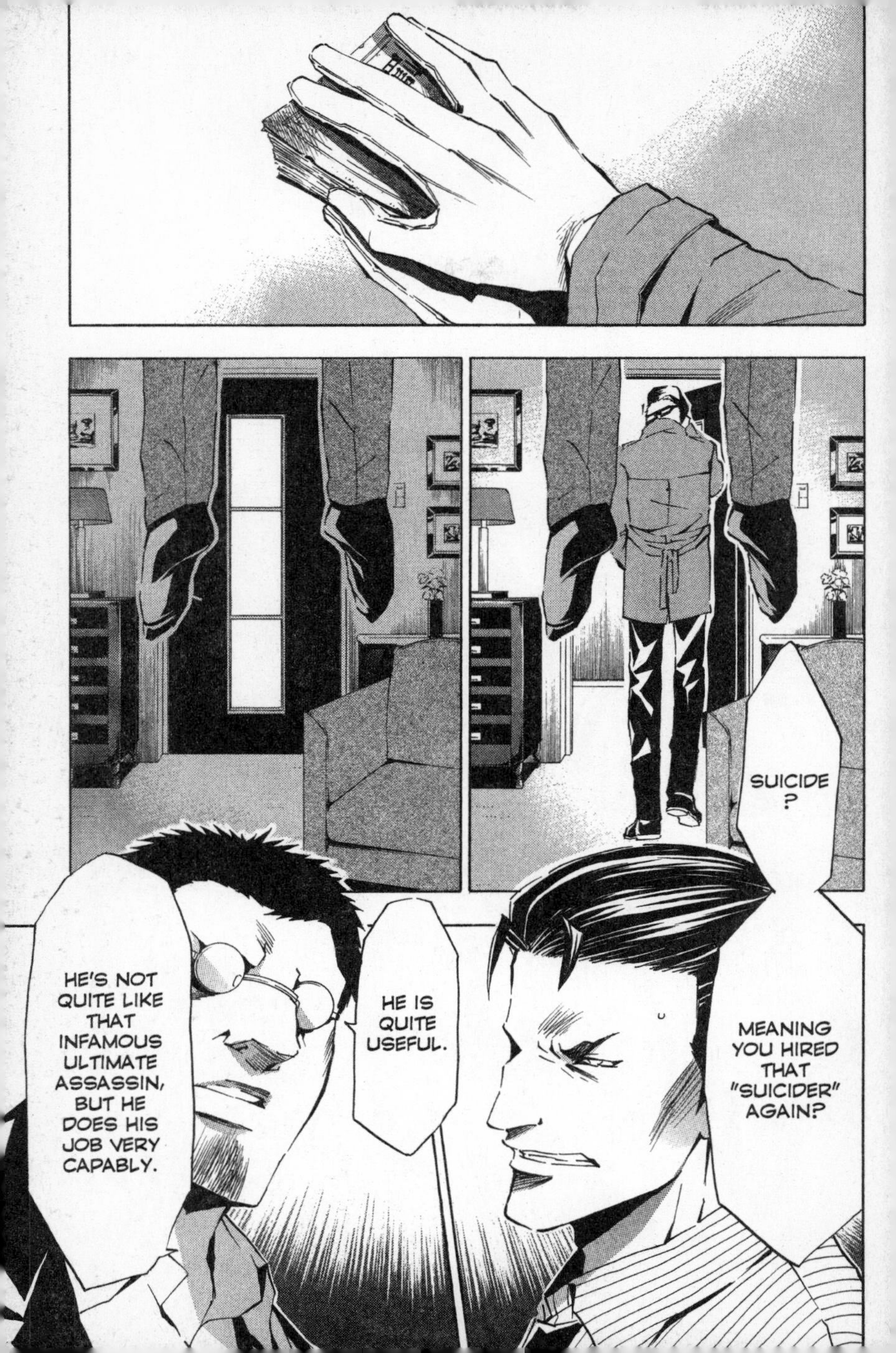
SUICIDE?
MEANING YOU HIRED THAT "SUICIDER" AGAIN?
HE IS QUITE USEFUL.
HE'S NOT QUITE LIKE THAT INFAMOUS ULTIMATE ASSASSIN, BUT HE DOES HIS JOB VERY CAPABLY.

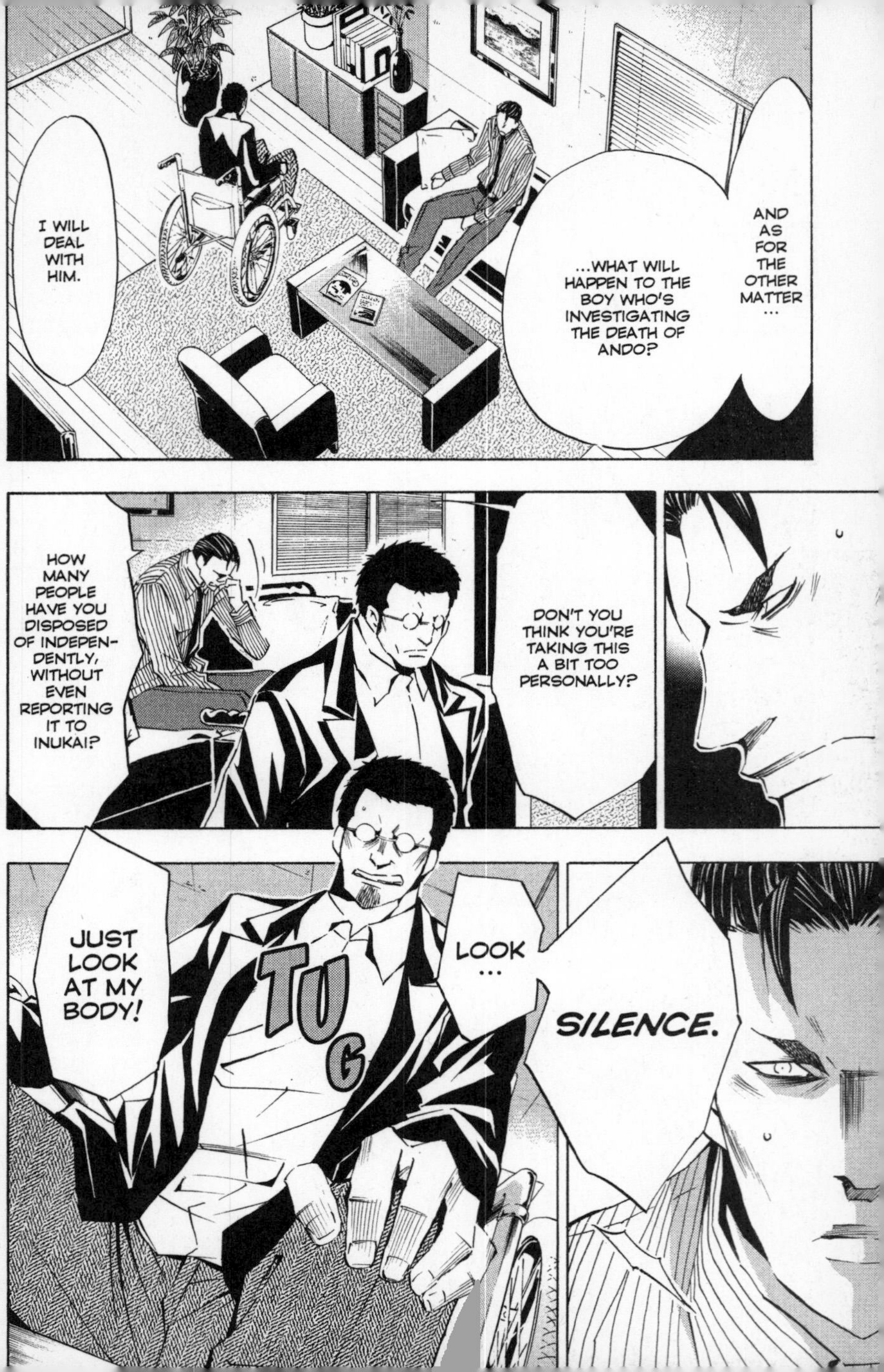
AND AS FOR THE OTHER MATTER...
...WHAT WILL HAPPEN TO THE BOY WHO'S INVESTIGATING THE DEATH OF ANDO?
I WILL DEAL WITH HIM.
DON'T YOU THINK YOU'RE TAKING THIS A BIT TOO PERSONALLY?
HOW MANY PEOPLE HAVE YOU DISPOSED OF INDEPENDENTLY, WITHOUT EVEN REPORTING IT TO INUKAI?
SILENCE.
LOOK...
TUG
JUST LOOK AT MY BODY!

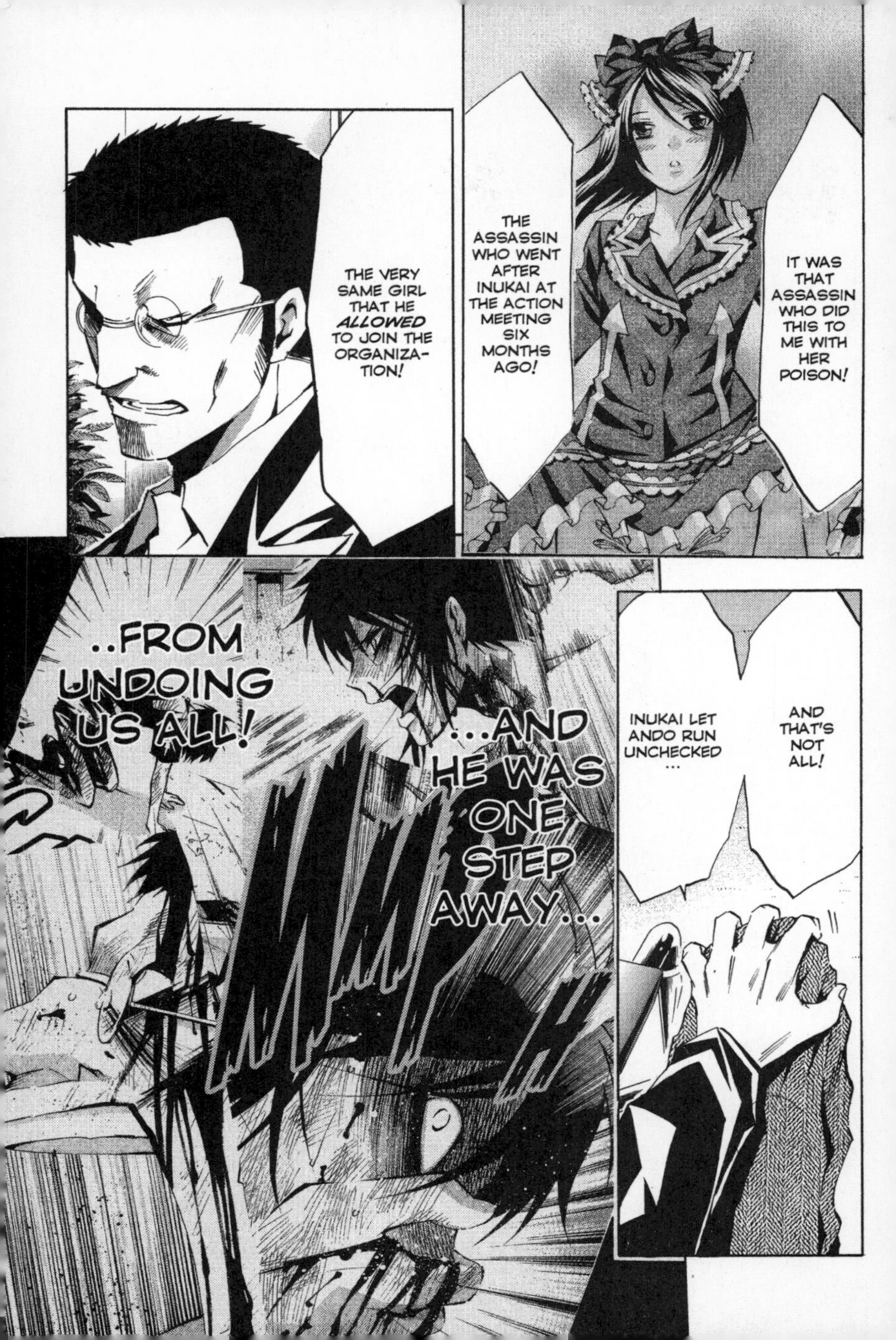
IT WAS THAT ASSASSIN WHO DID THIS TO ME WITH HER POISON!
THE ASSASSIN WHO WENT AFTER INUKAI AT THE ACTION MEETING SIX MONTHS AGO!
THE VERY SAME GIRL THAT HE *ALLOWED* TO JOIN THE ORGANIZA-TION!
AND THAT's NOT ALL!
INUKAI LET ANDO RUN UNCHECKED ...
...AND HE WAS ONE STEP AWAY...
..FROM UNDOING US ALL!

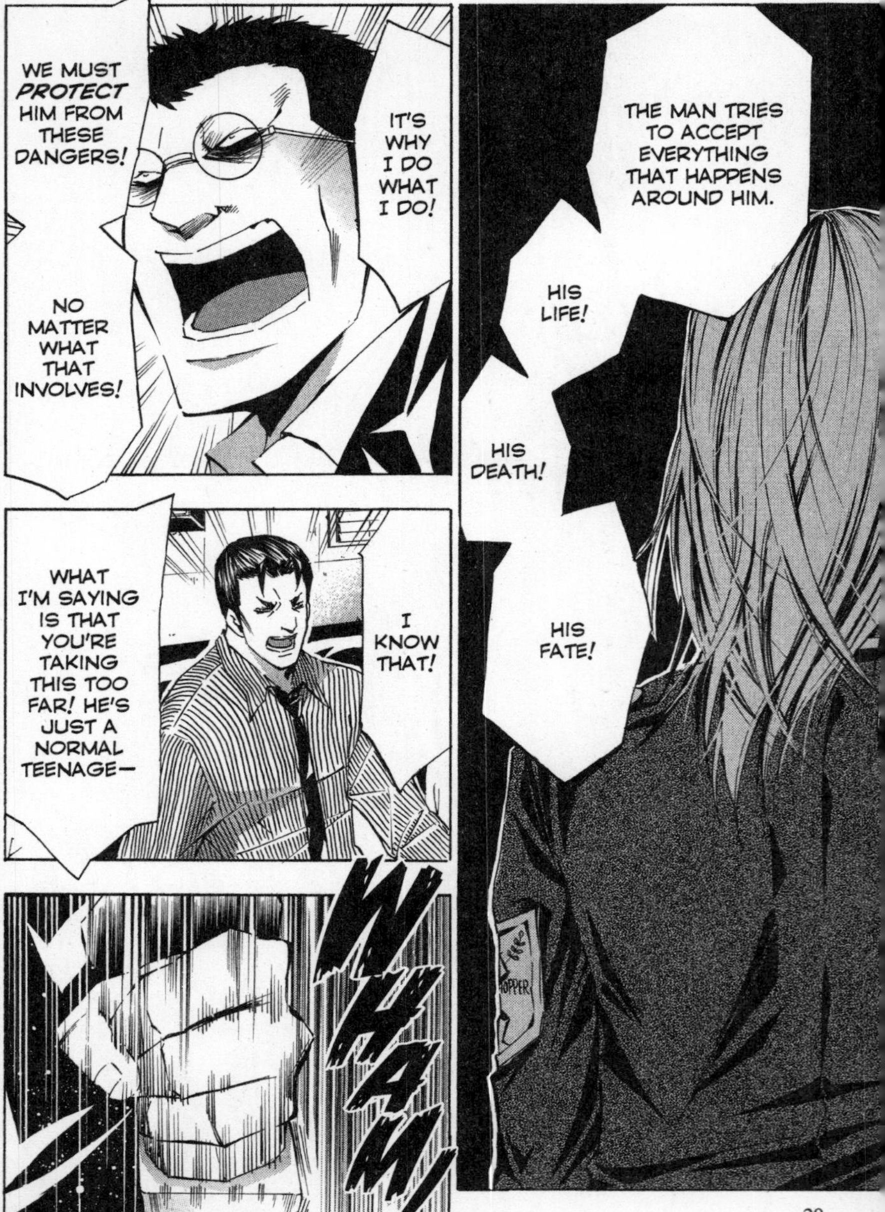
THE MAN TRIES TO ACCEPT EVERYTHING THAT HAPPENS AROUND HIM.
HIS LIFE!
HIS DEATH!
HIS FATE!
IT'S WHY I DO WHAT I DO!
WE MUST *PROTECT* HIM FROM THESE DANGERS!
NO MATTER WHAT THAT INVOLVES!
I KNOW THAT!
WHAT I'M SAYING IS THAT YOU'RE TAKING THIS TOO FAR! HE'S JUST A NORMAL TEENAGE—
WHAM!

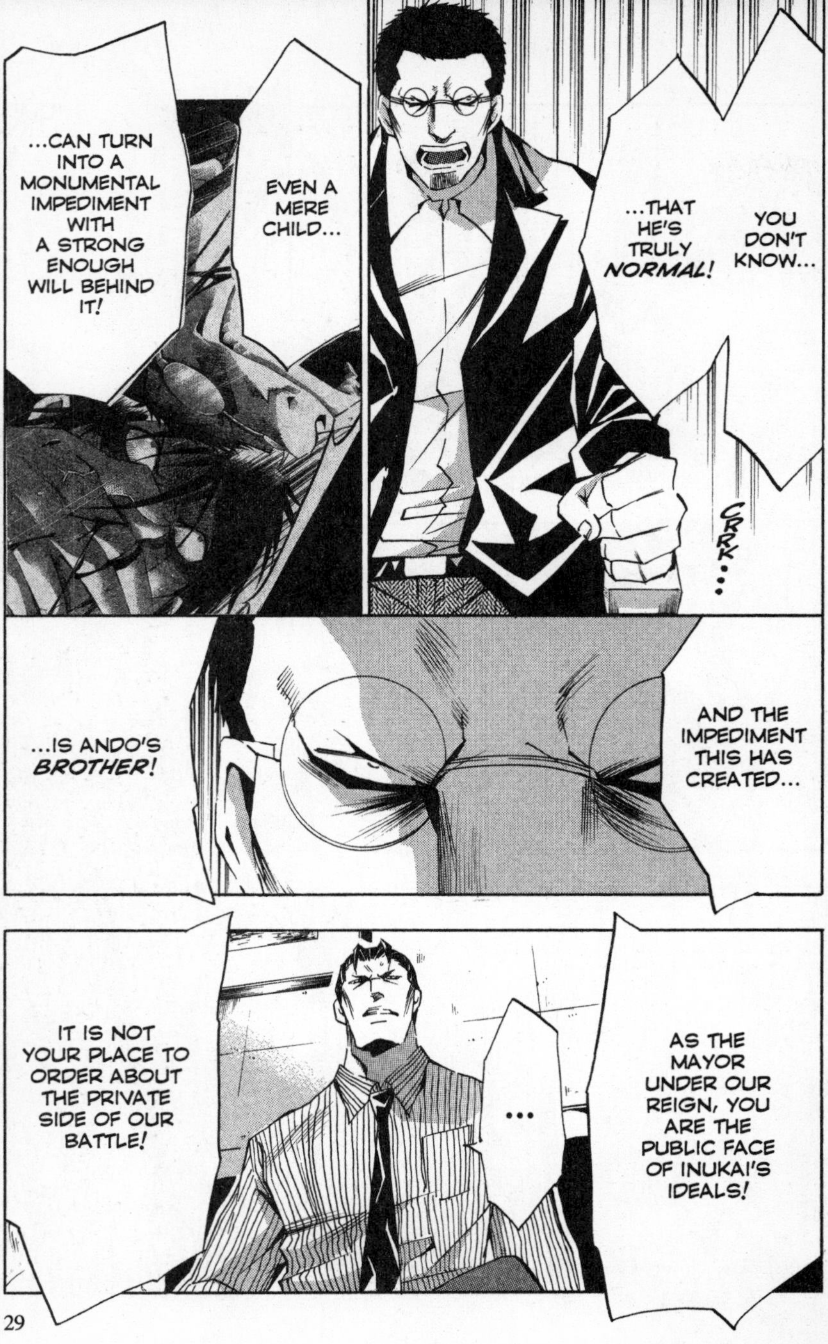
YOU DON'T KNOW...
...THAT HE'S TRULY NORMAL!
CRRK...
EVEN A MERE CHILD...
...CAN TURN INTO A MONUMENTAL IMPEDIMENT WITH A STRONG ENOUGH WILL BEHIND IT!
AND THE IMPEDIMENT THIS HAS CREATED...
...IS ANDO'S BROTHER!
AS THE MAYOR UNDER OUR REIGN, YOU ARE THE PUBLIC FACE OF INUKAI'S IDEALS!
...
IT IS NOT YOUR PLACE TO ORDER ABOUT THE PRIVATE SIDE OF OUR BATTLE!

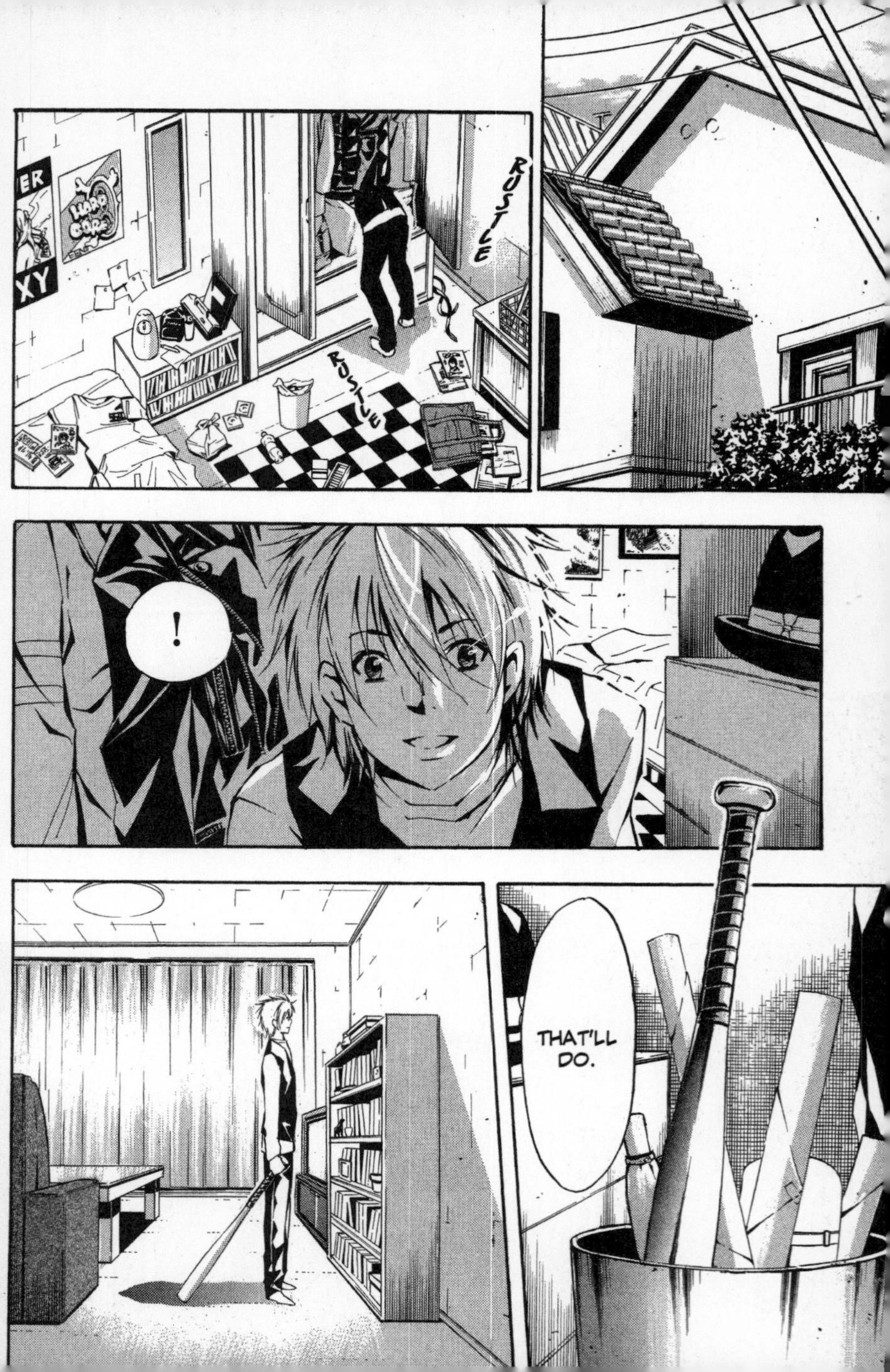
RUSTLE
RUSTLE
!
THAT'LL DO.

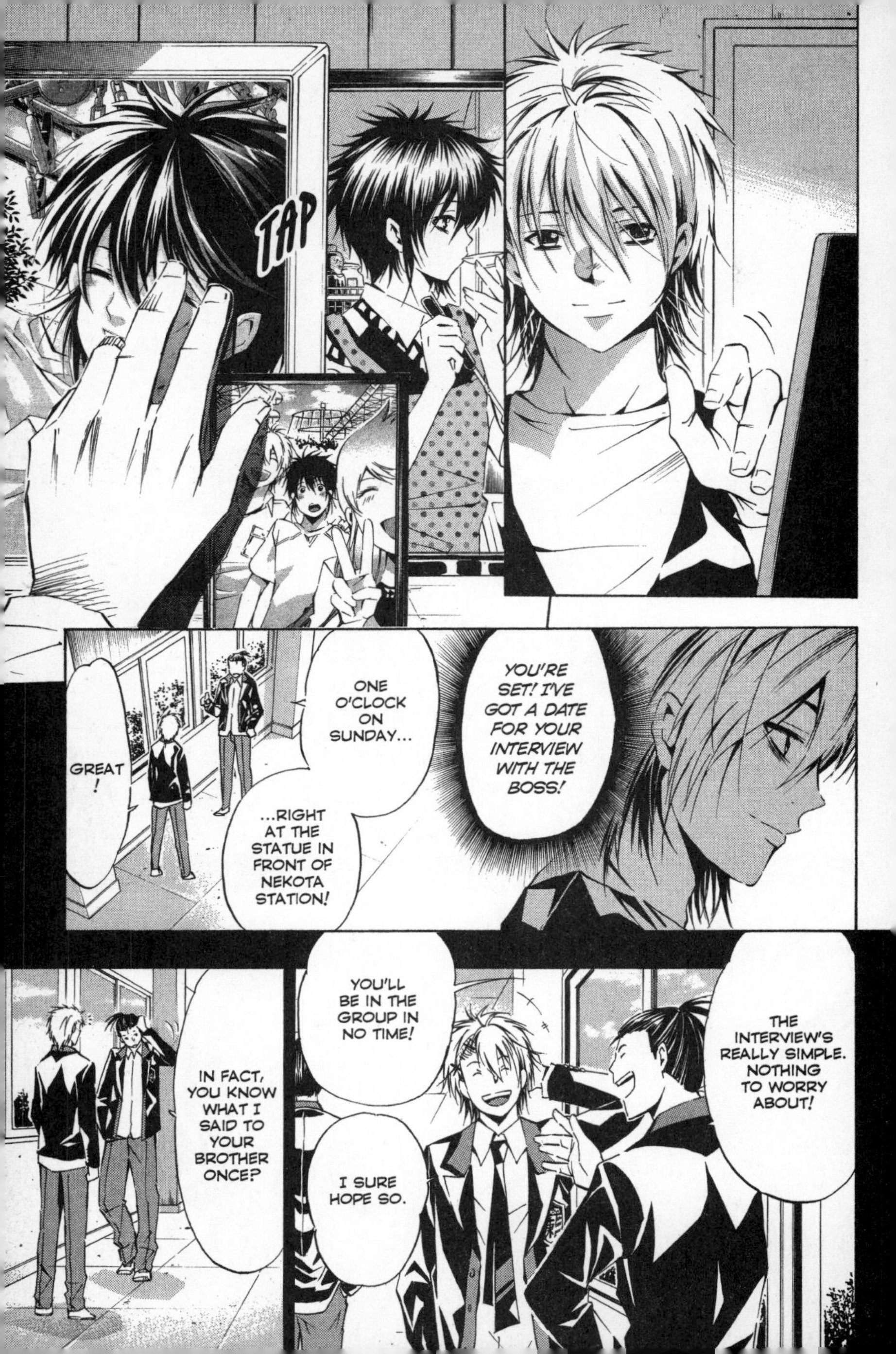
TAP
YOU'RE SET! I'VE GOT A DATE FOR YOUR INTERVIEW WITH THE BOSS!
ONE O'CLOCK ON SUNDAY...
...RIGHT AT THE STATUE IN FRONT OF NEKOTA STATION!
GREAT!
THE INTERVIEW'S REALLY SIMPLE. NOTHING TO WORRY ABOUT!
YOU'LL BE IN THE GROUP IN NO TIME!
I SURE HOPE SO.
IN FACT, YOU KNOW WHAT I SAID TO YOUR BROTHER ONCE?

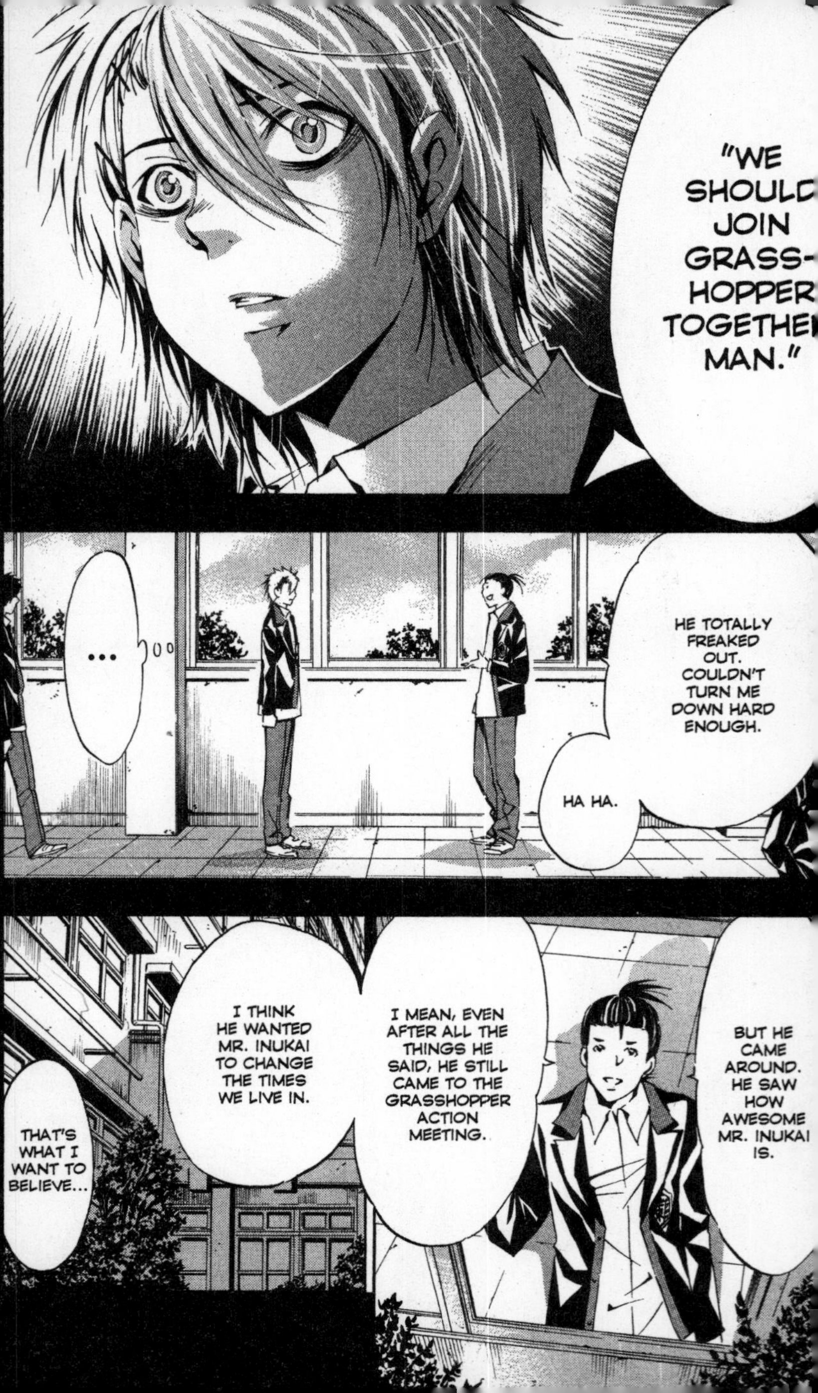
"WE SHOULD JOIN GRASS-HOPPER TOGETHER MAN."
HE TOTALLY FREAKED OUT. COULDN'T TURN ME DOWN HARD ENOUGH.
HA HA.
...
BUT HE CAME AROUND. HE SAW HOW AWESOME MR. INUKAI IS.
I MEAN, EVEN AFTER ALL THE THINGS HE SAID, HE STILL CAME TO THE GRASSHOPPER ACTION MEETING.
I THINK HE WANTED MR. INUKAI TO CHANGE THE TIMES WE LIVE IN.
THAT'S WHAT I WANT TO BELIEVE...

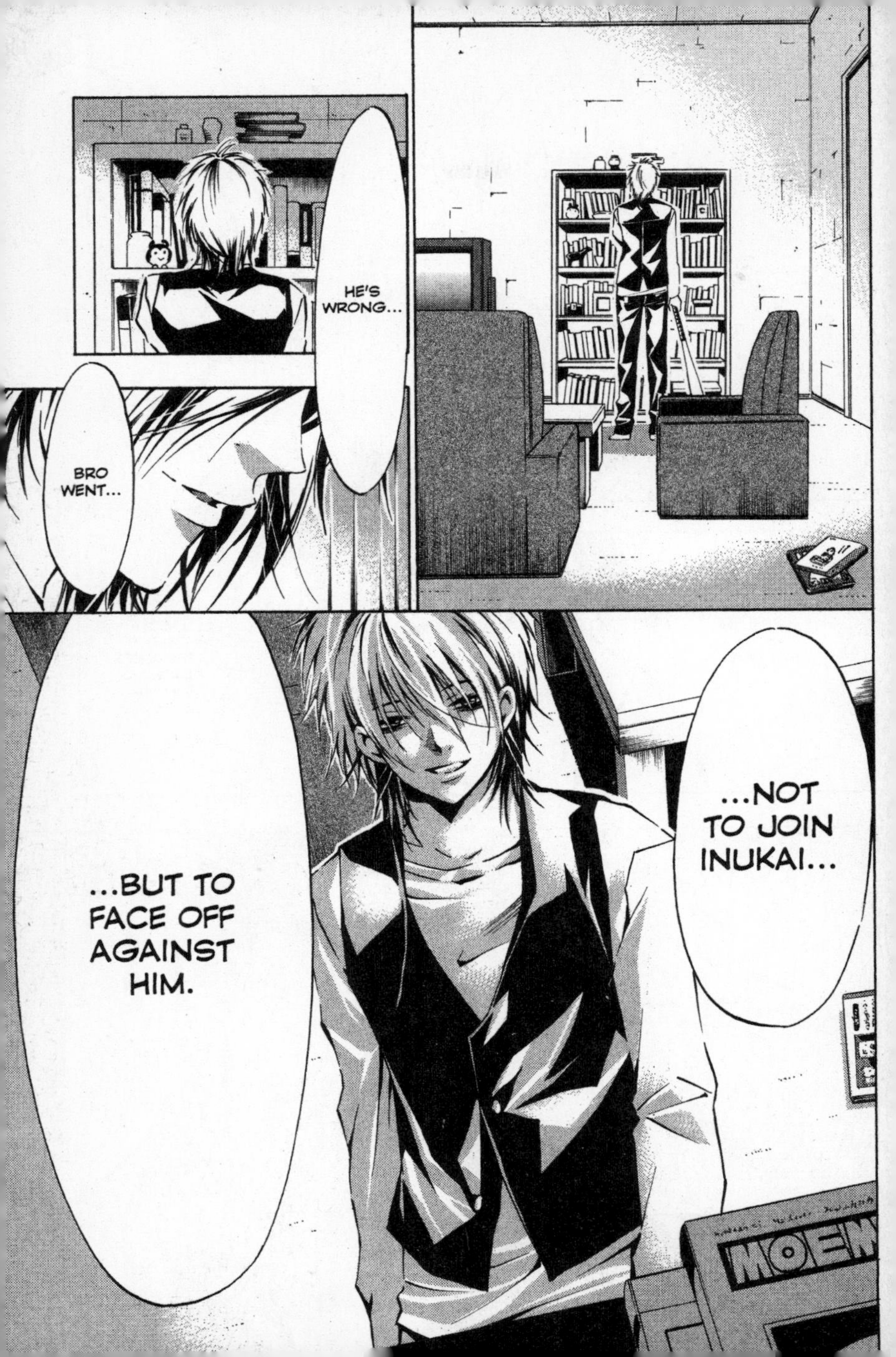
HE'S WRONG...
BRO WENT...
...NOT TO JOIN INUKAI...
...BUT TO FACE OFF AGAINST HIM.

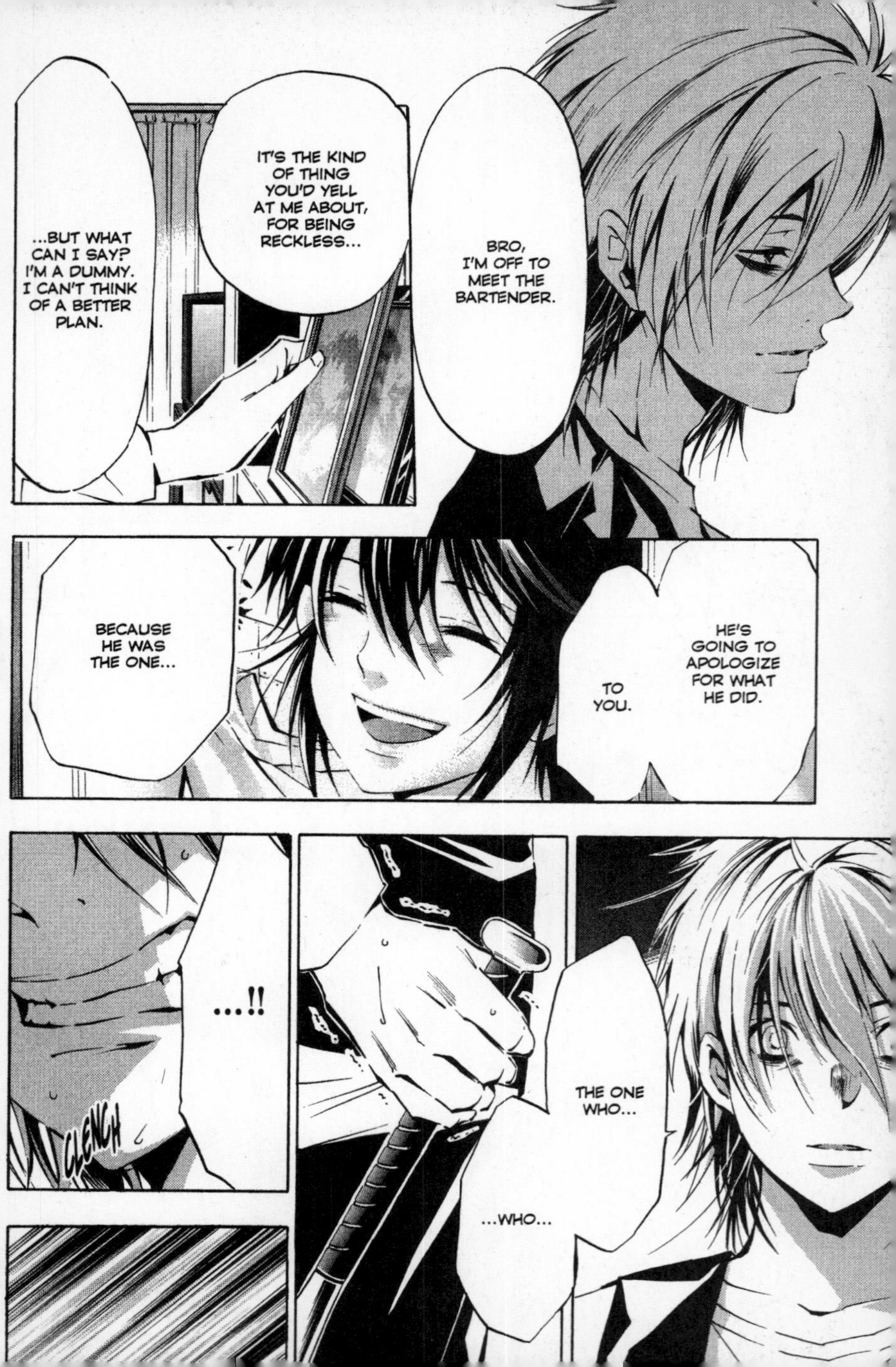
BRO, I'M OFF TO MEET THE BARTENDER.
IT'S THE KIND OF THING YOU'D YELL AT ME ABOUT, FOR BEING RECKLESS...
...BUT WHAT CAN I SAY? I'M A DUMMY. I CAN'T THINK OF A BETTER PLAN.
HE'S GOING TO APOLOGIZE FOR WHAT HE DID.
TO YOU.
BECAUSE HE WAS THE ONE...
THE ONE WHO...
...WHO...
...!!
CLENCH

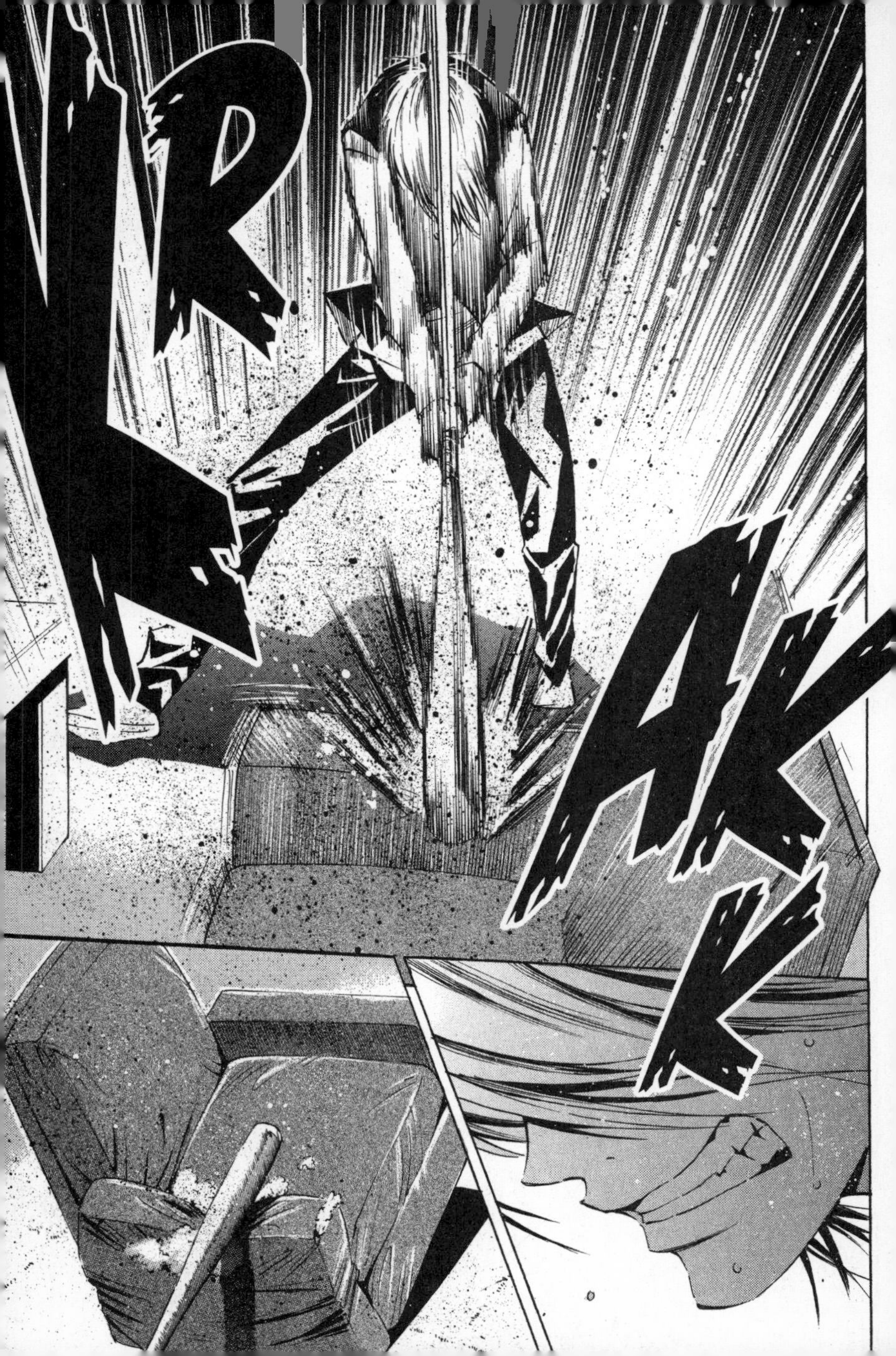
KRAKK

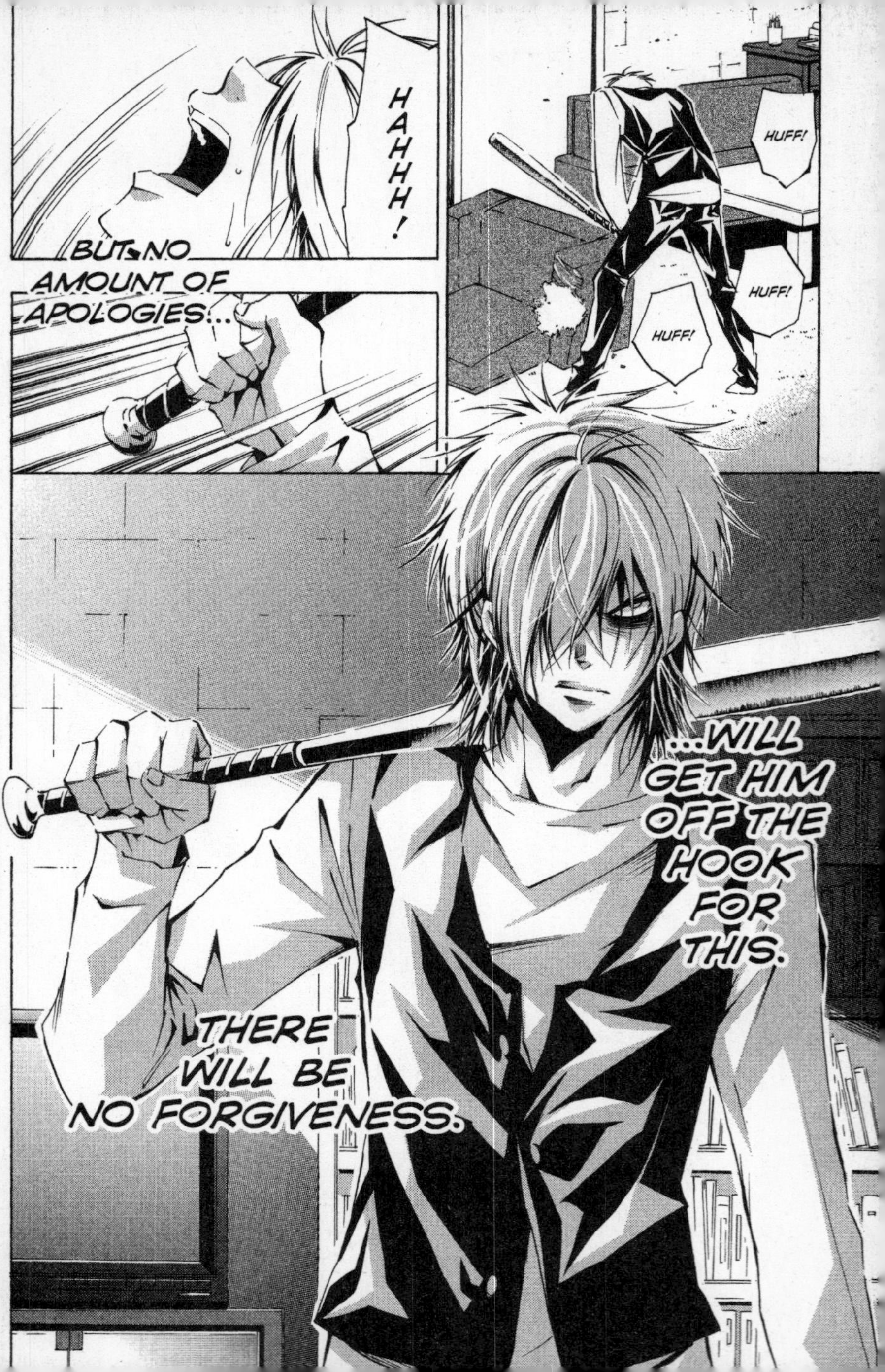
HUFF!
HUFF!
HUFF!
HAHHH!
BUT NO AMOUNT OF APOLOGIES...
...WILL GET HIM OFF THE HOOK FOR THIS.
THERE WILL BE NO FORGIVENESS.

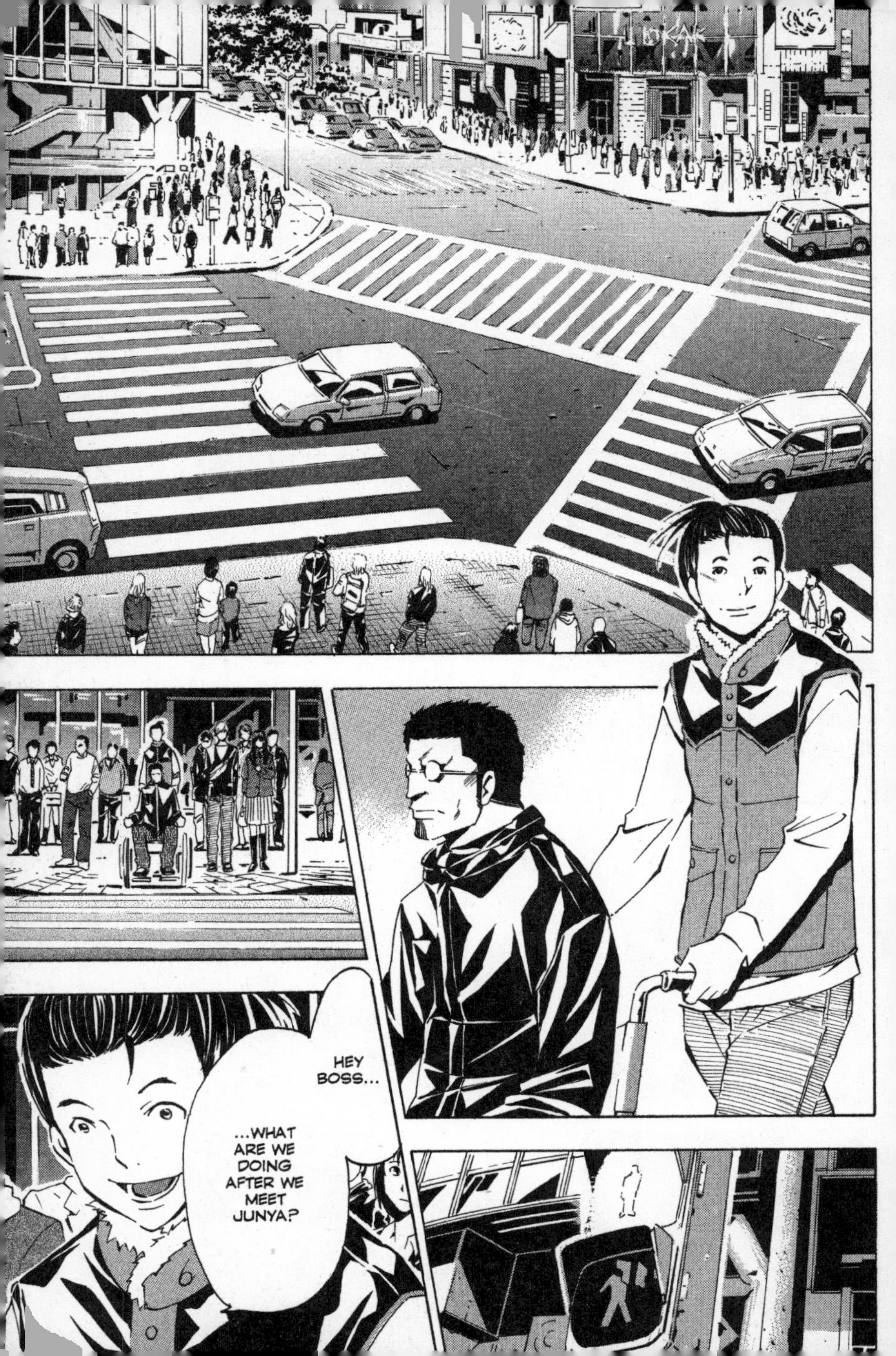
HEY BOSS...
...WHAT ARE WE DOING AFTER WE MEET JUNYA?

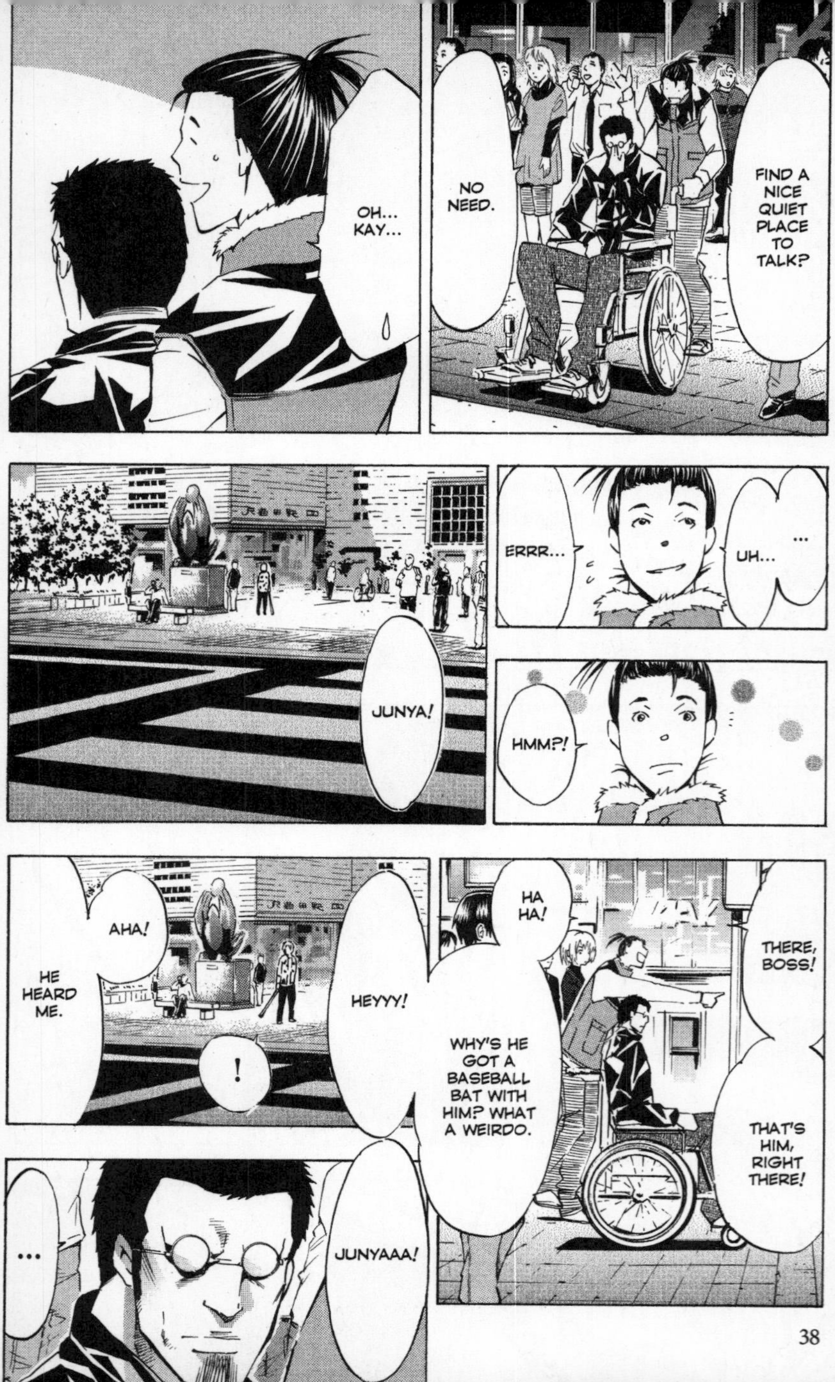
FIND A NICE QUIET PLACE TO TALK?
NO NEED.
OH... KAY...
...
UH...
ERRR...
HMM?!
JUNYA!
THERE, BOSS!
HA HA!
THAT'S HIM, RIGHT THERE!
WHY'S HE GOT A BASEBALL BAT WITH HIM? WHAT A WEIRDO.
HEYYY!
AHA!
HE HEARD ME.
!
JUNYAAA!
...

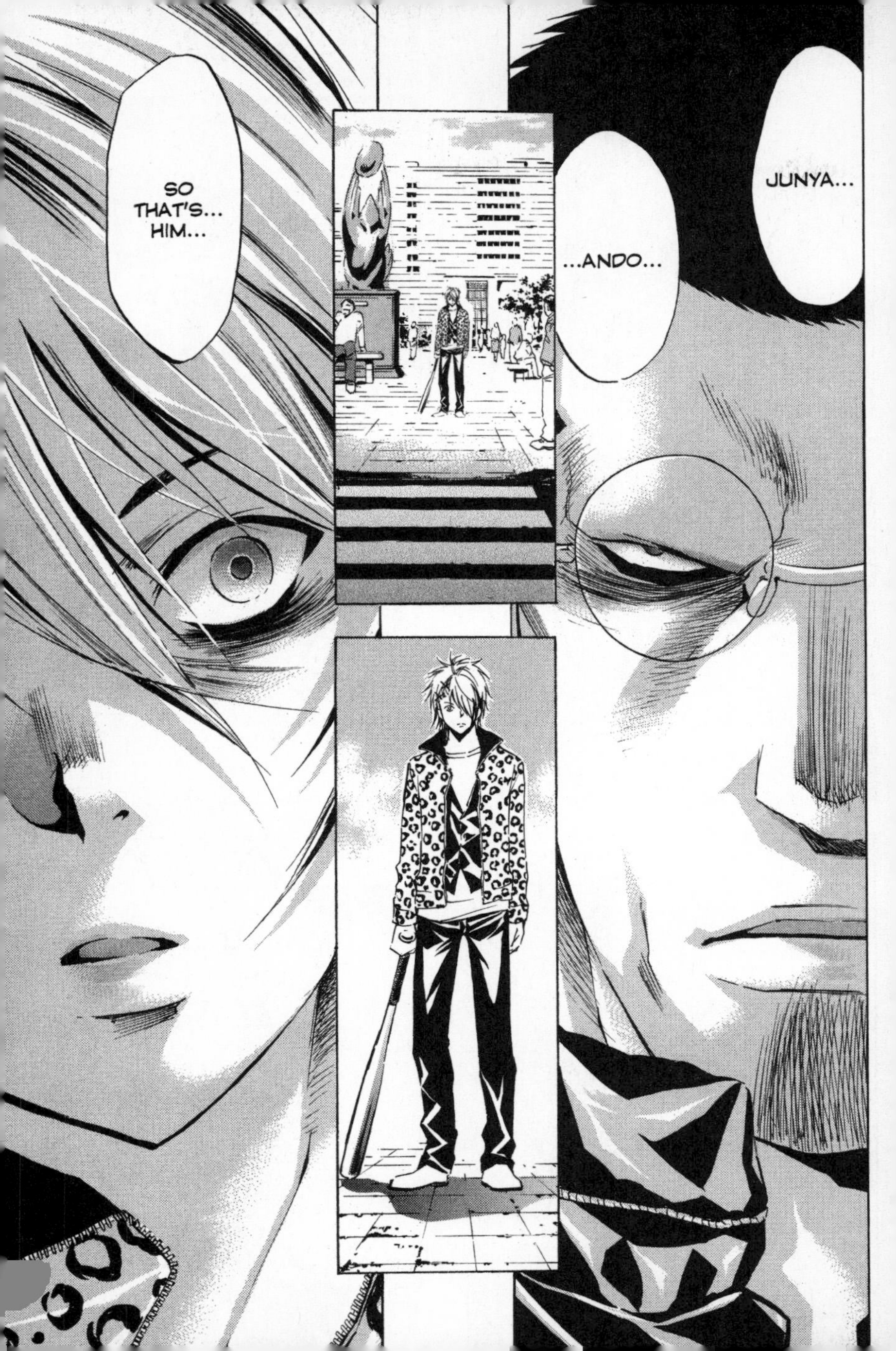
JUNYA...
...ANDO...
SO THAT'S... HIM...

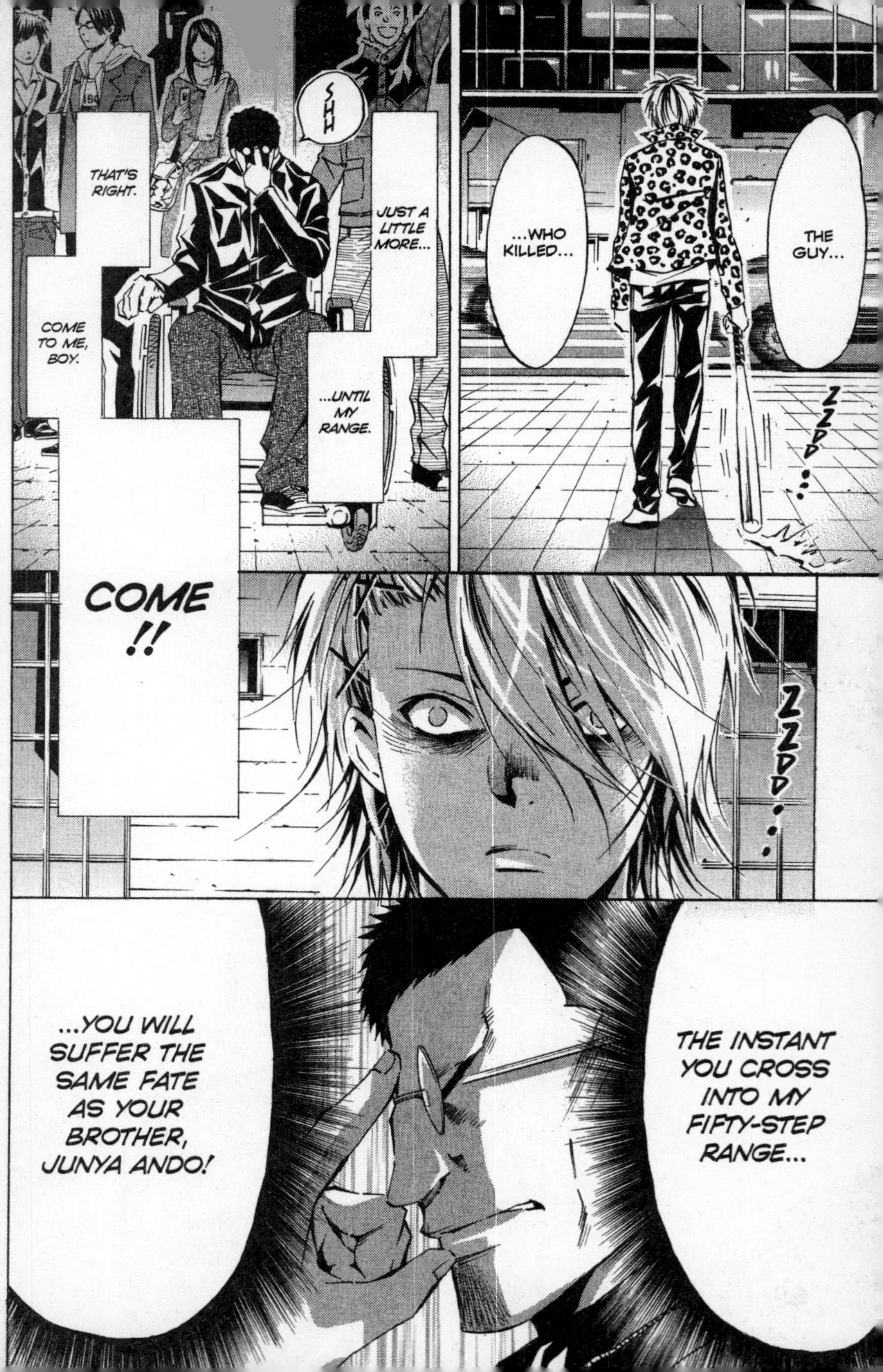
THE GUY...
...WHO KILLED...
ZZDD...
SHH
JUST A LITTLE MORE...
...UNTIL MY RANGE.
THAT'S RIGHT.
COME TO ME, BOY.
COME!!
ZZDD...
THE INSTANT YOU CROSS INTO MY FIFTY-STEP RANGE...
...YOU WILL SUFFER THE SAME FATE AS YOUR BROTHER, JUNYA ANDO!

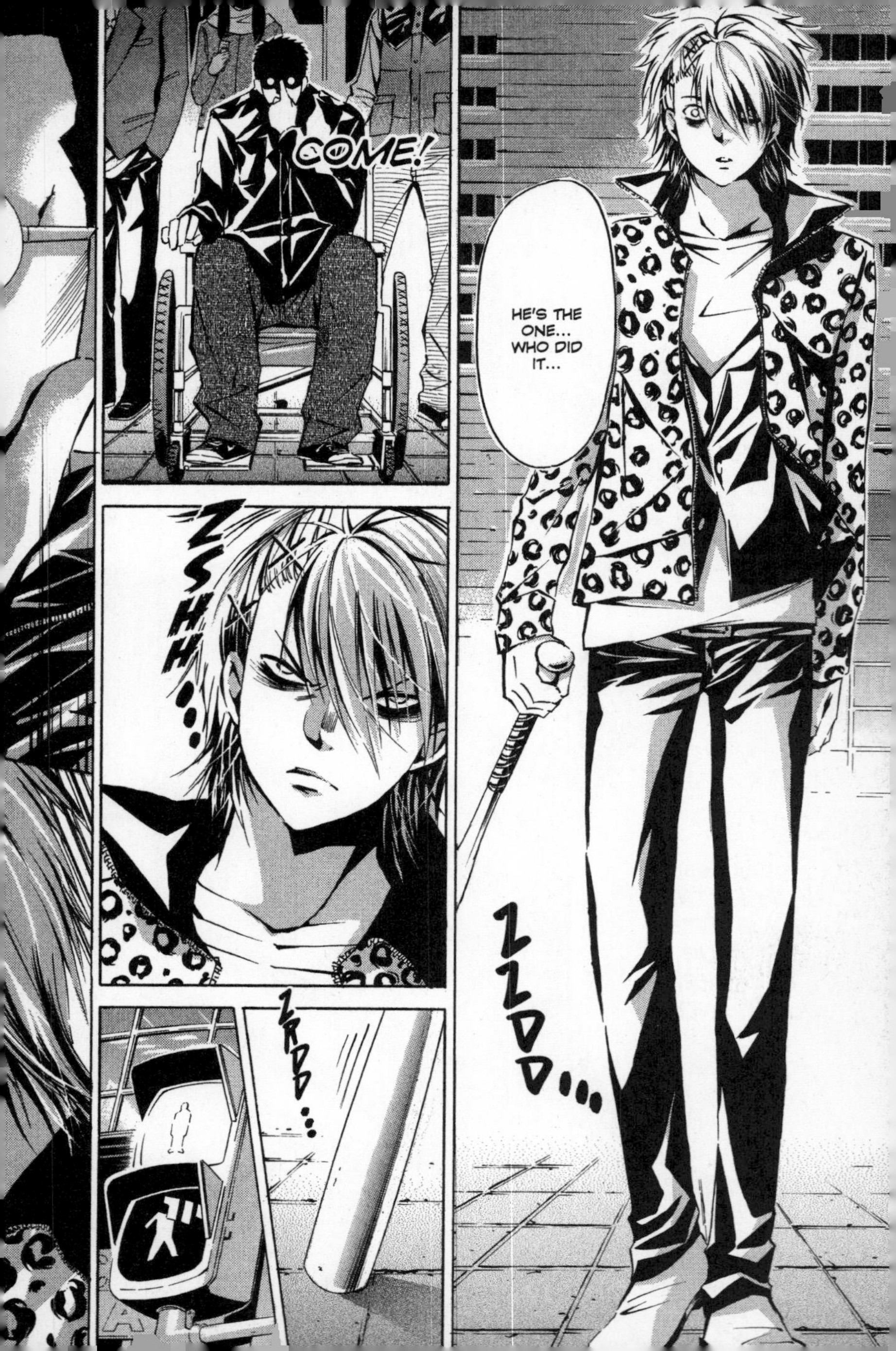
HE'S THE ONE... WHO DID IT...
ZZDD...
COME!
ZSHH...
ZRDD...

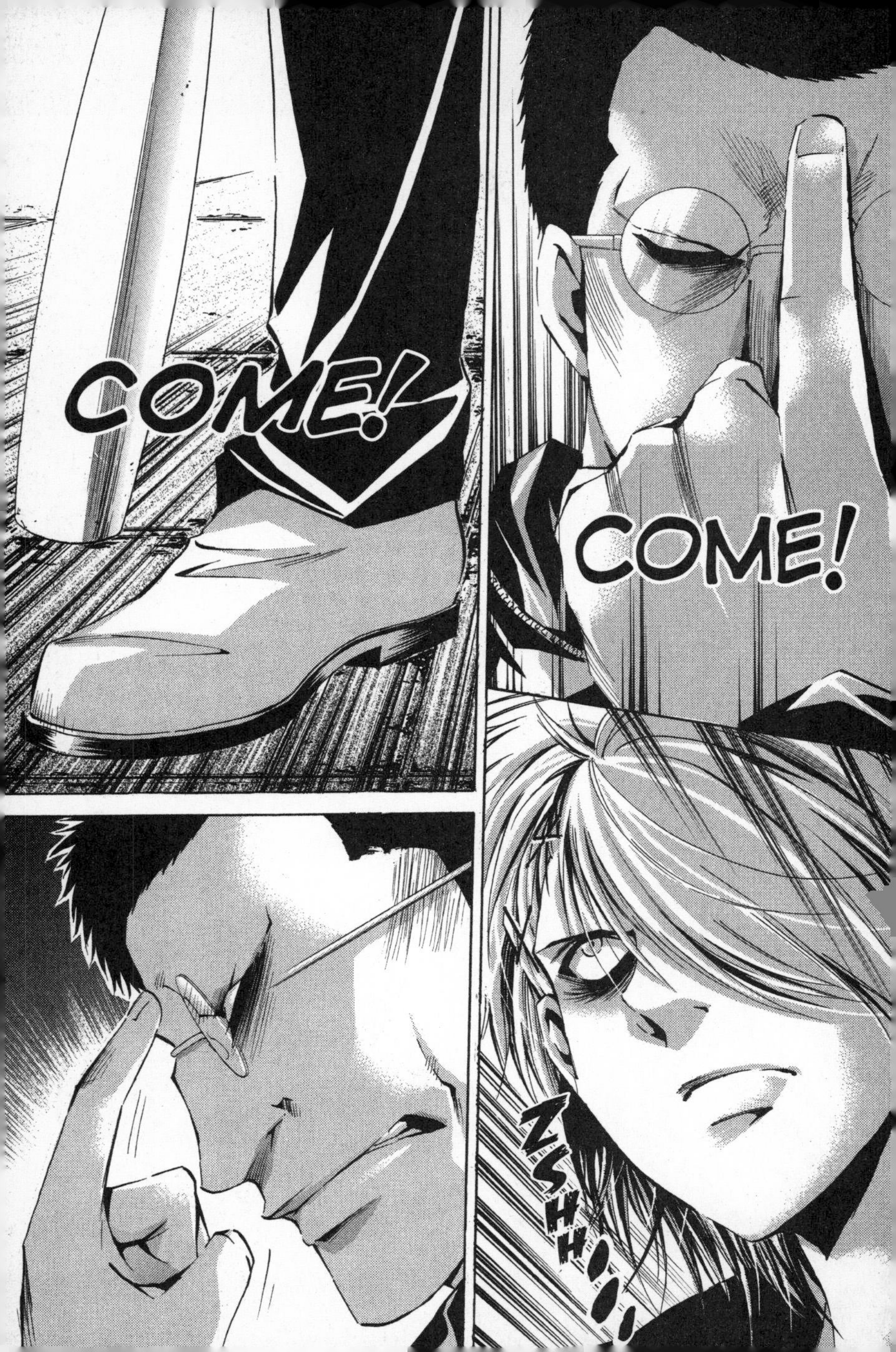
COME!
COME!
ZSHH...

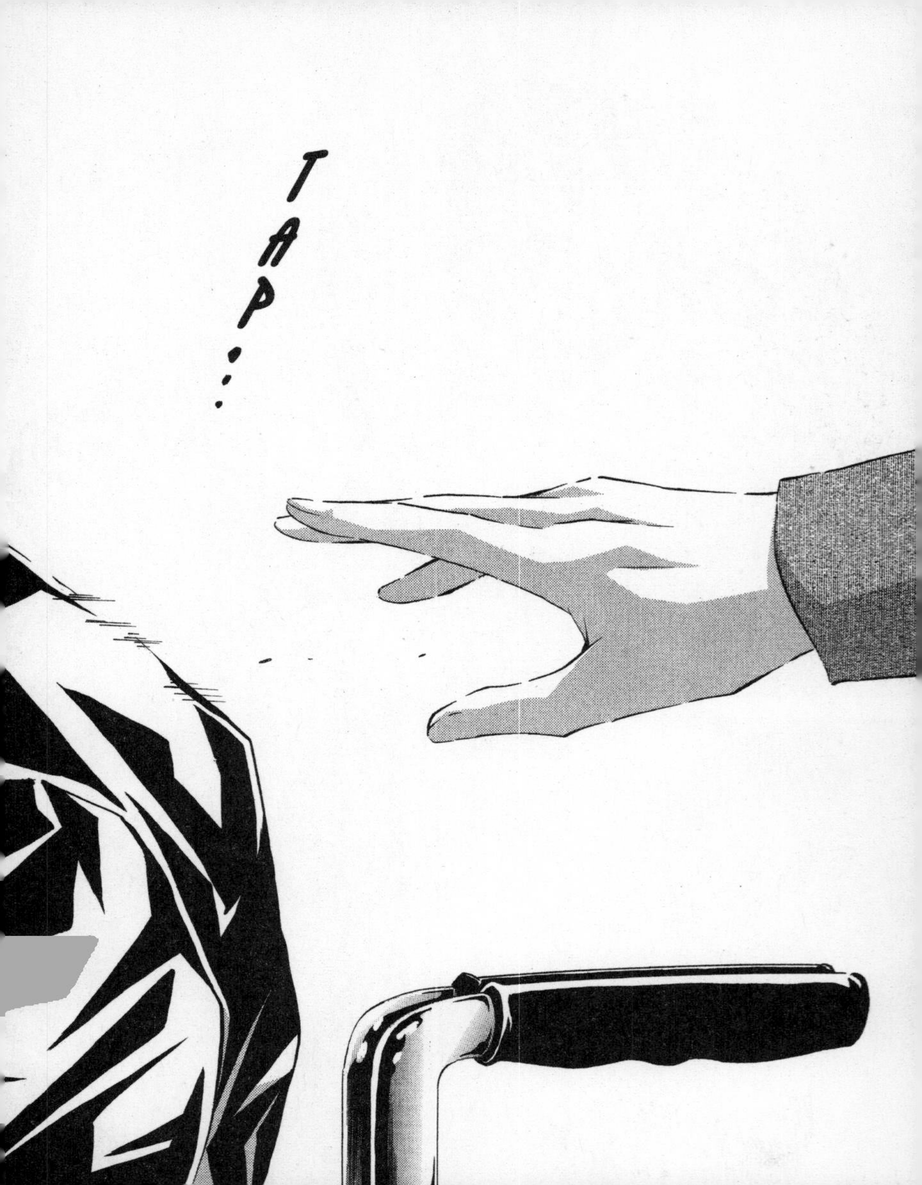
TAP...

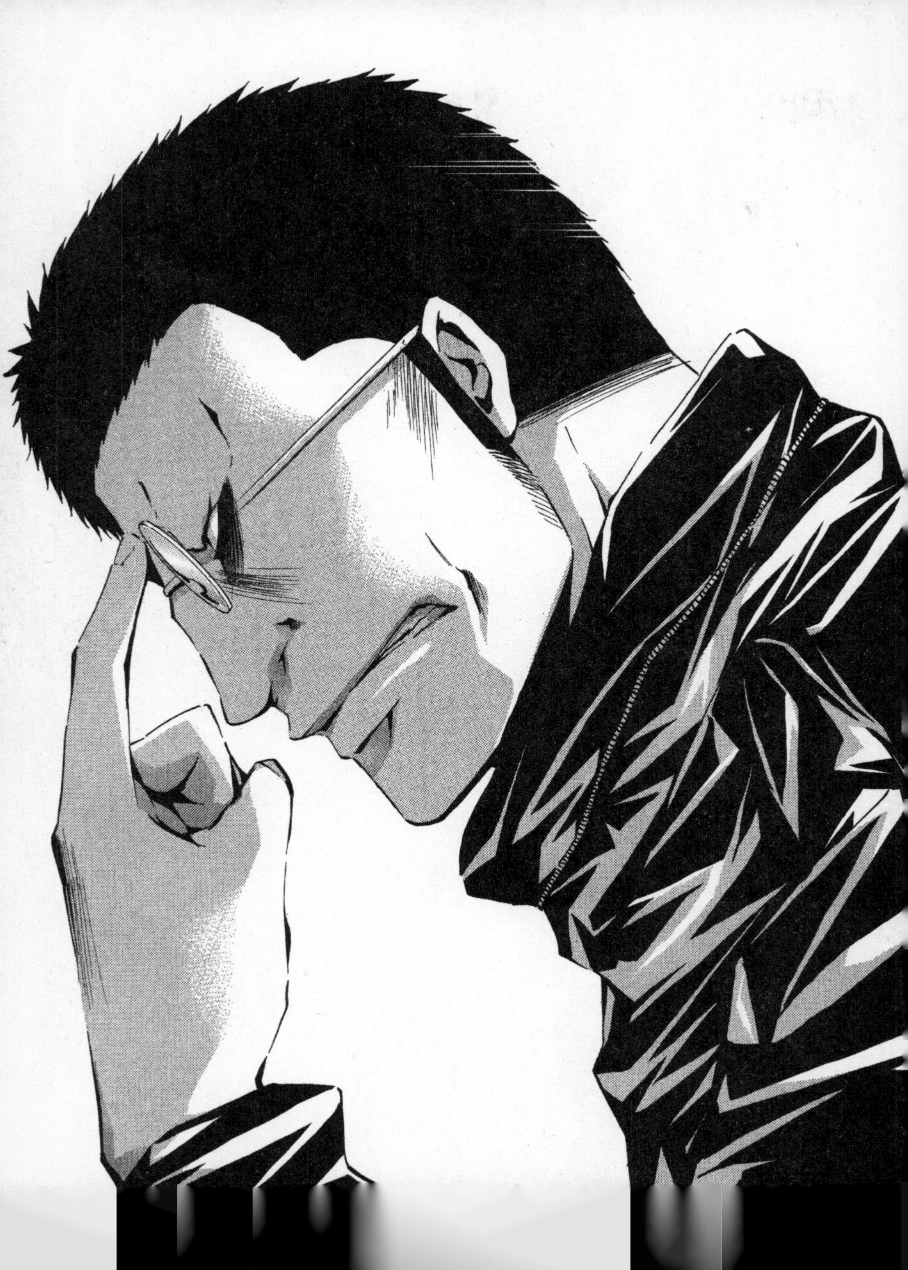

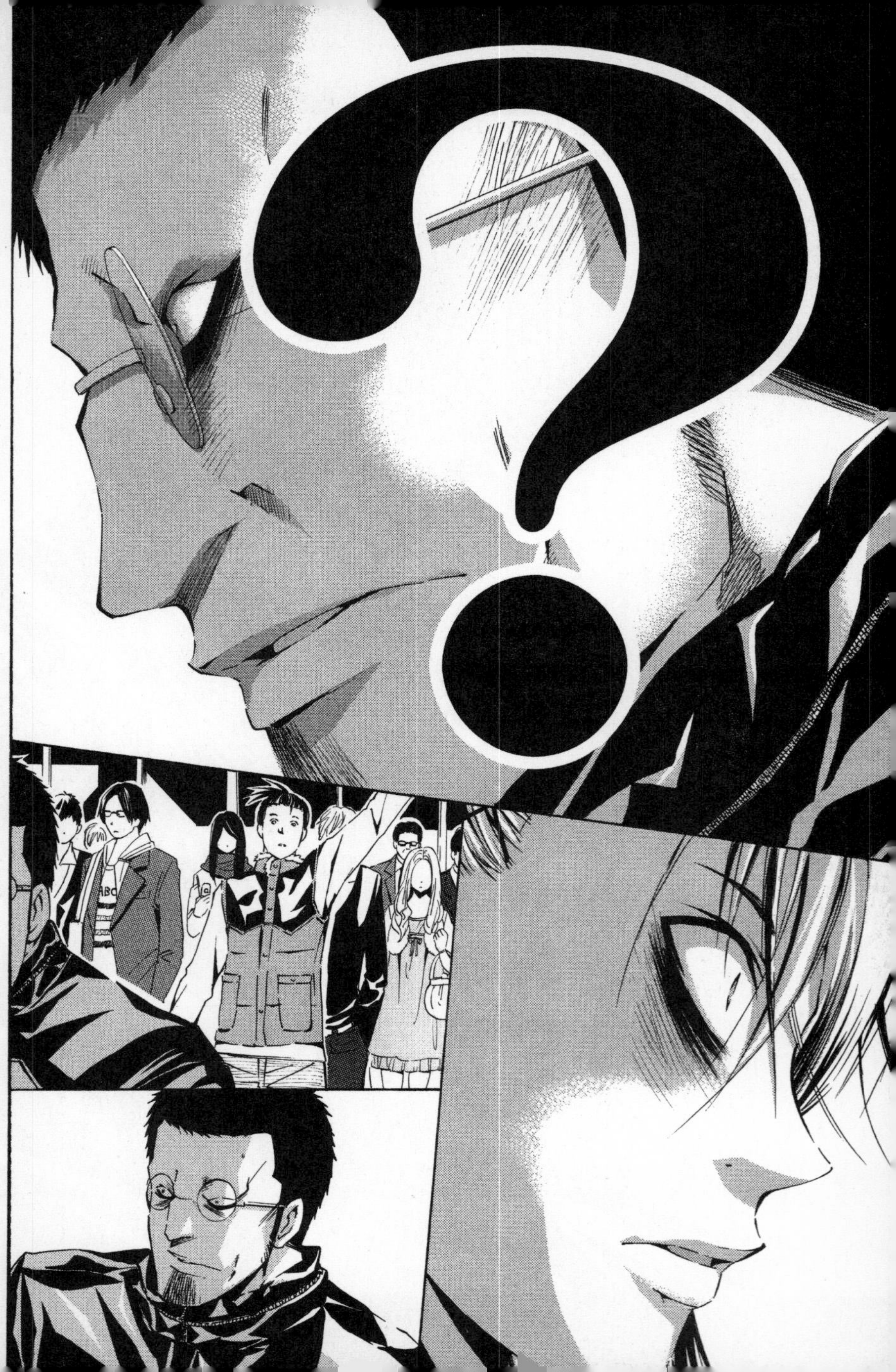

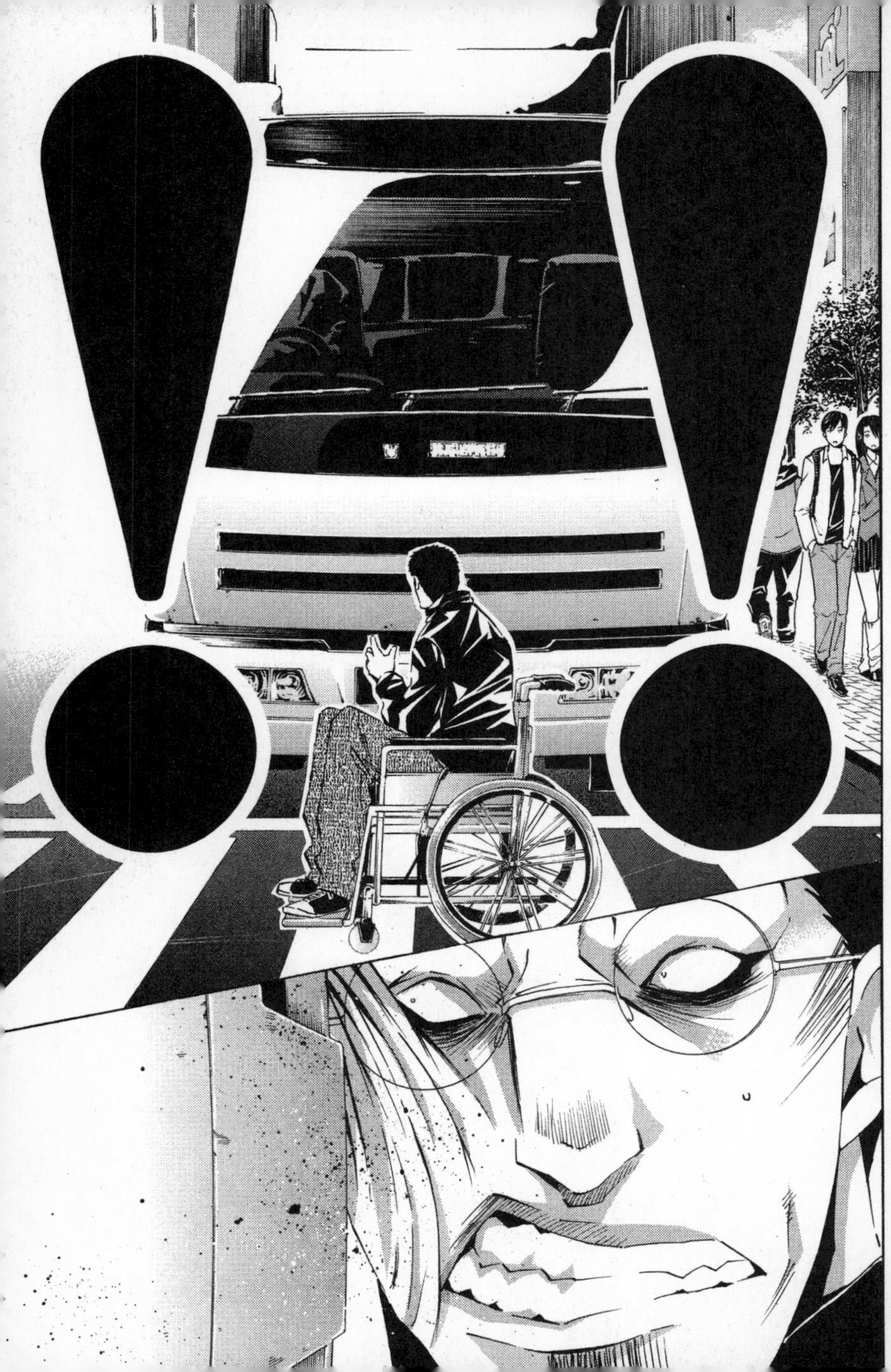

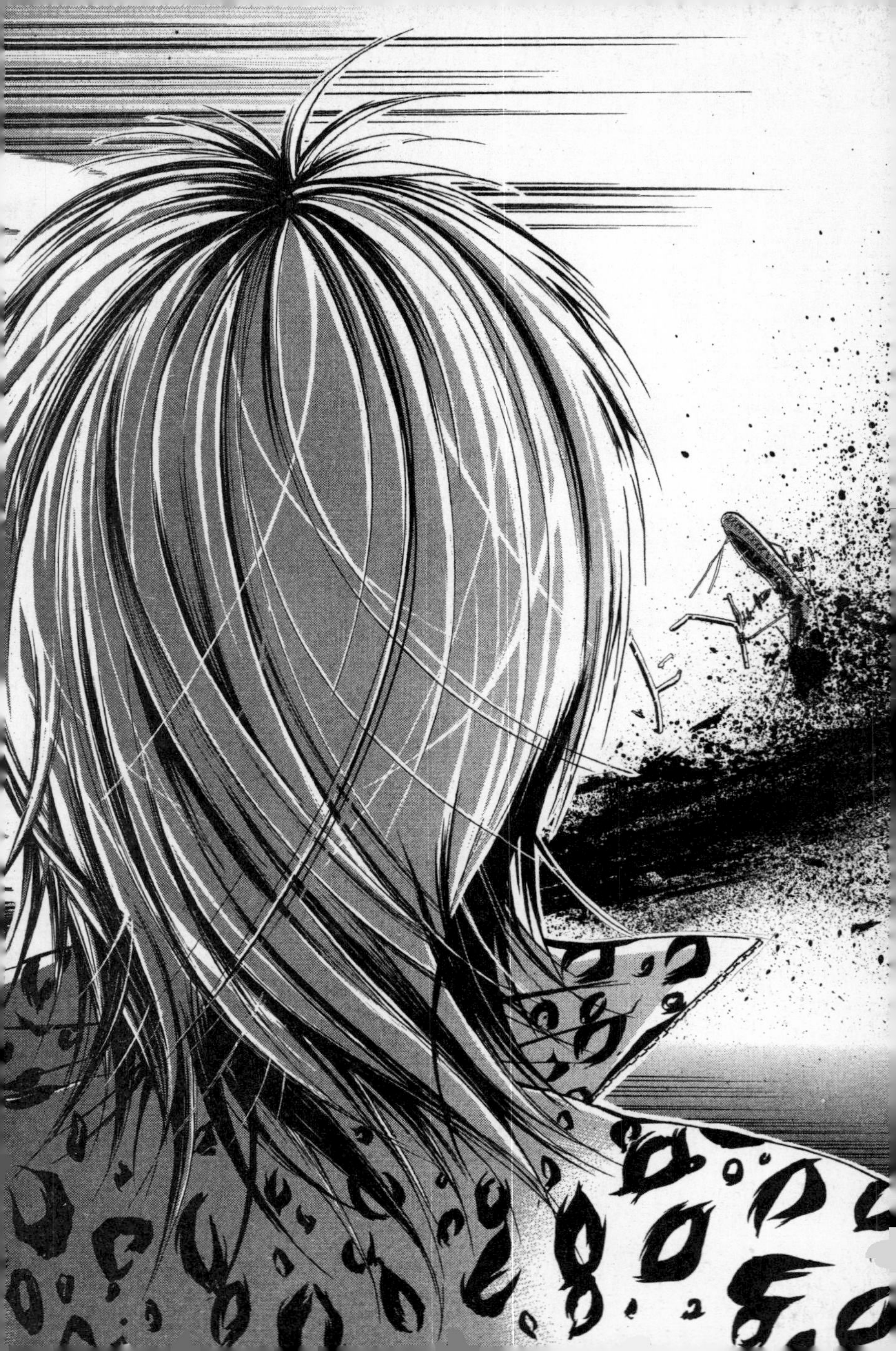

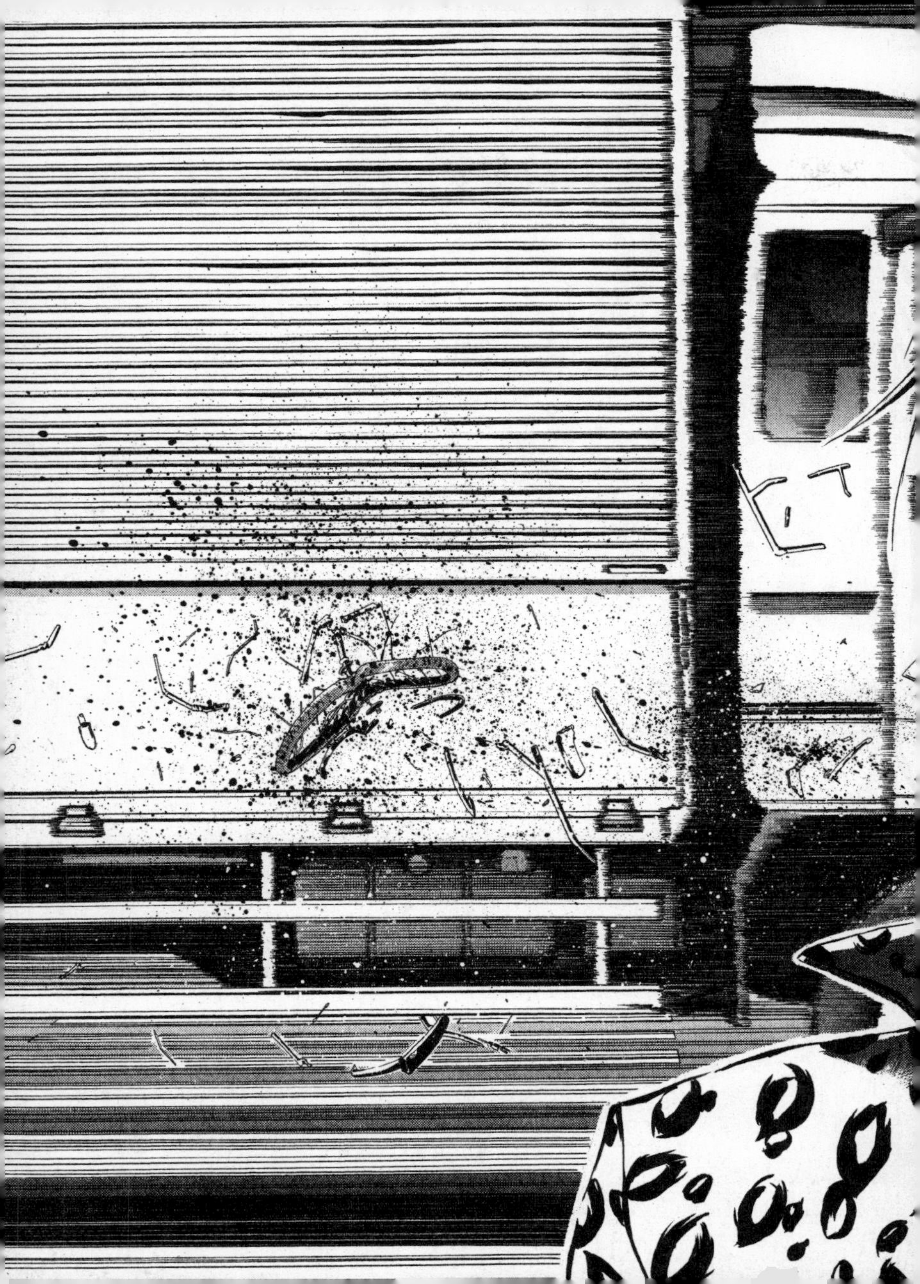

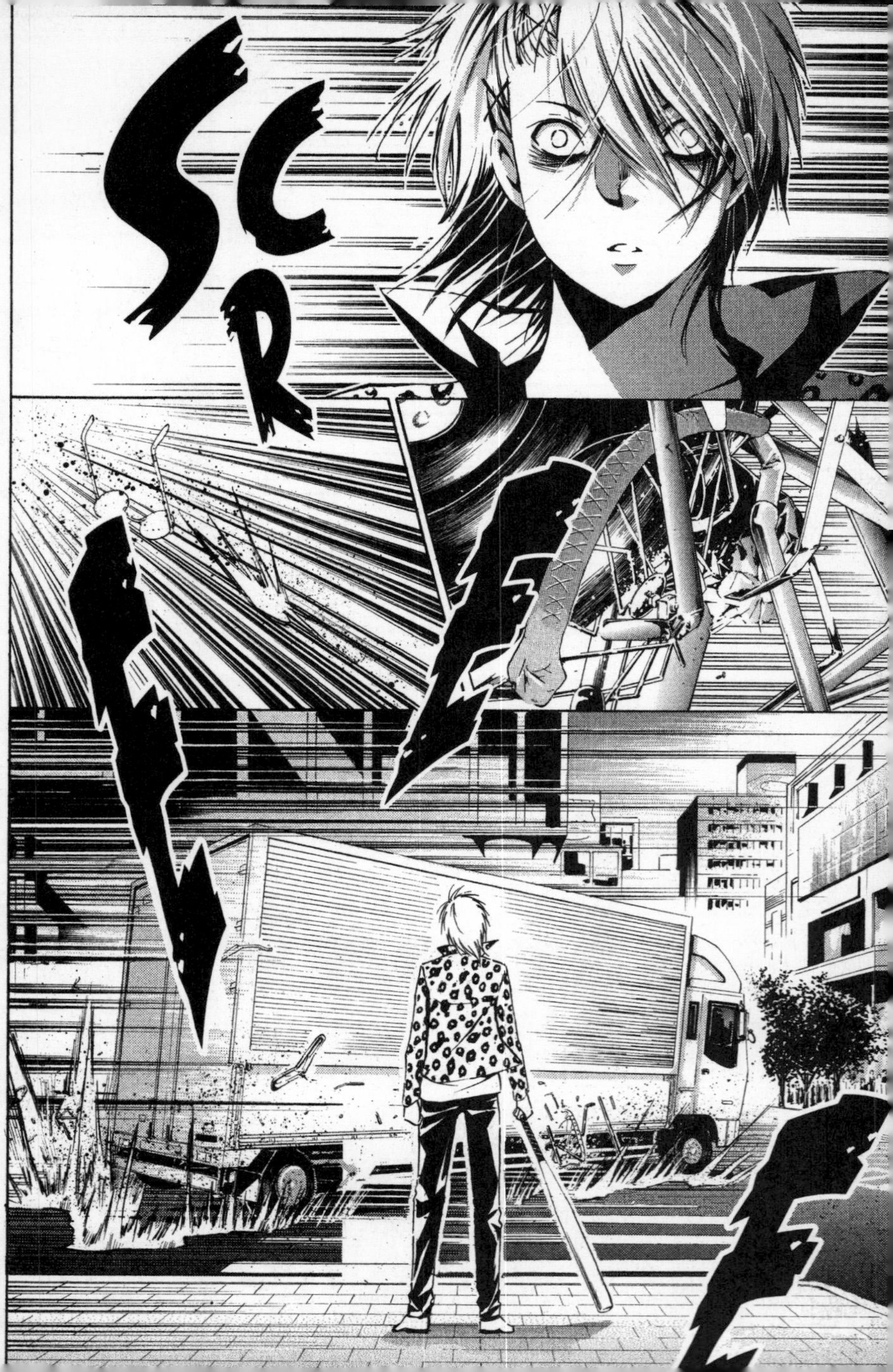
SCR

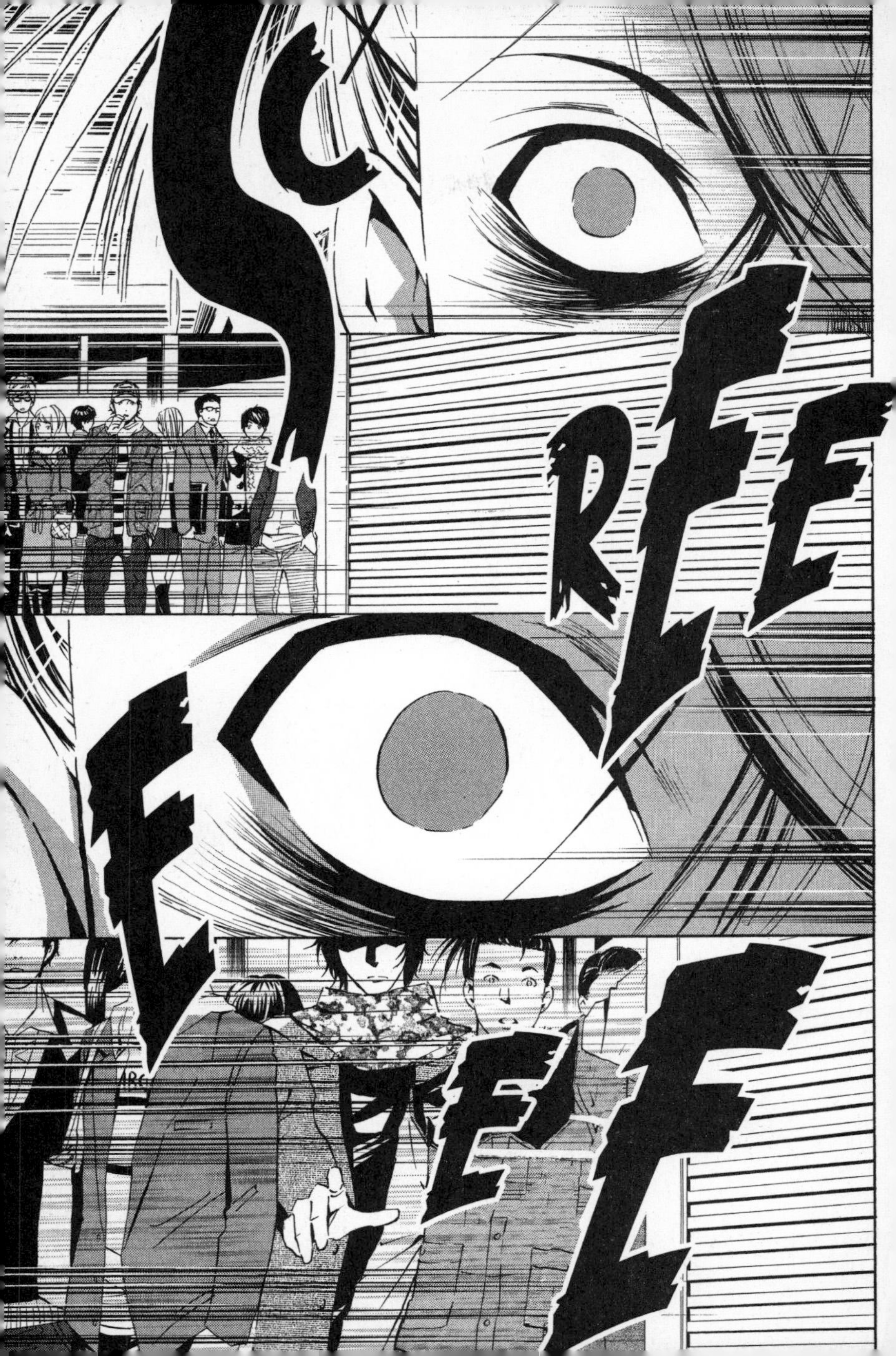

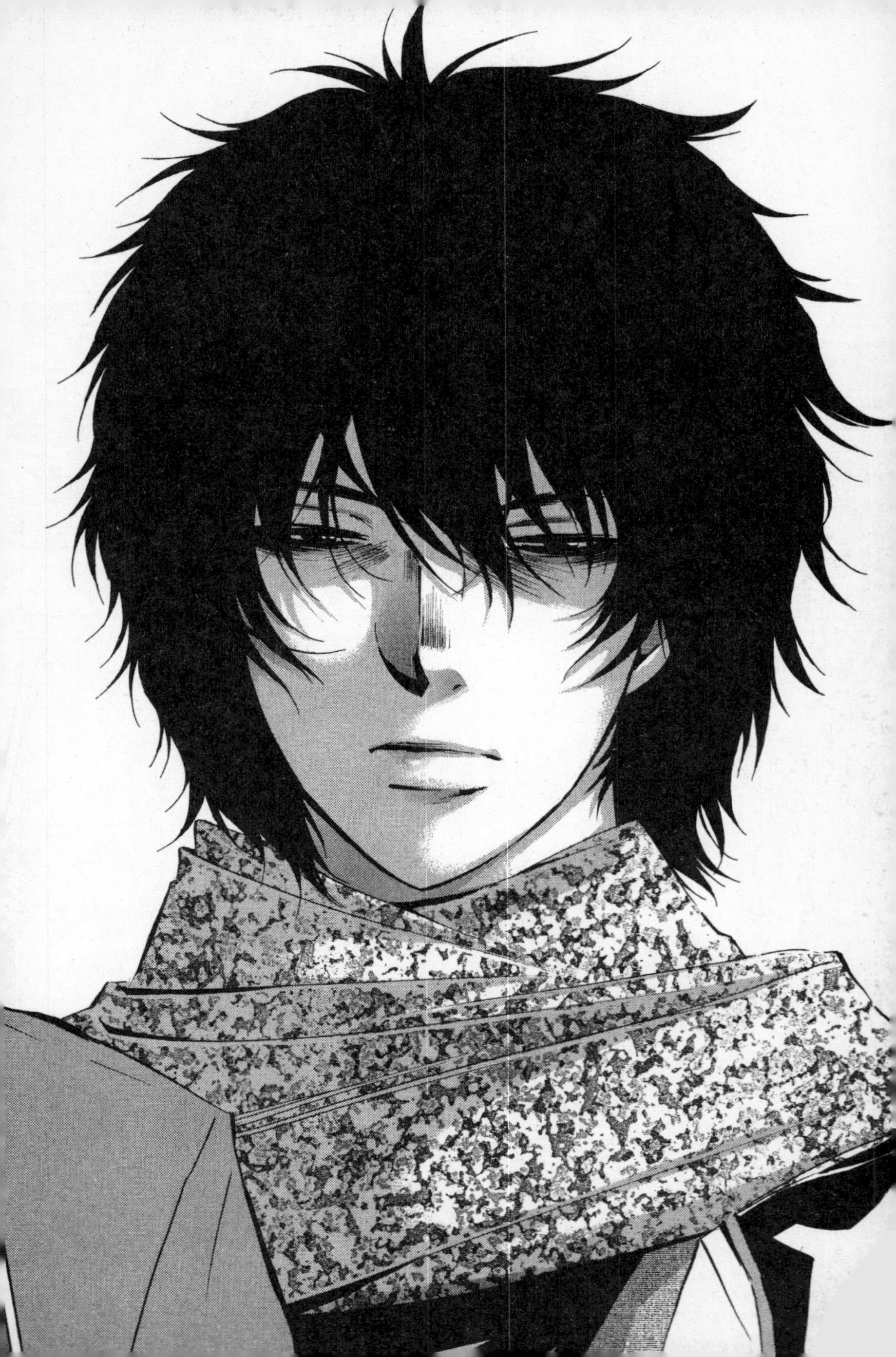

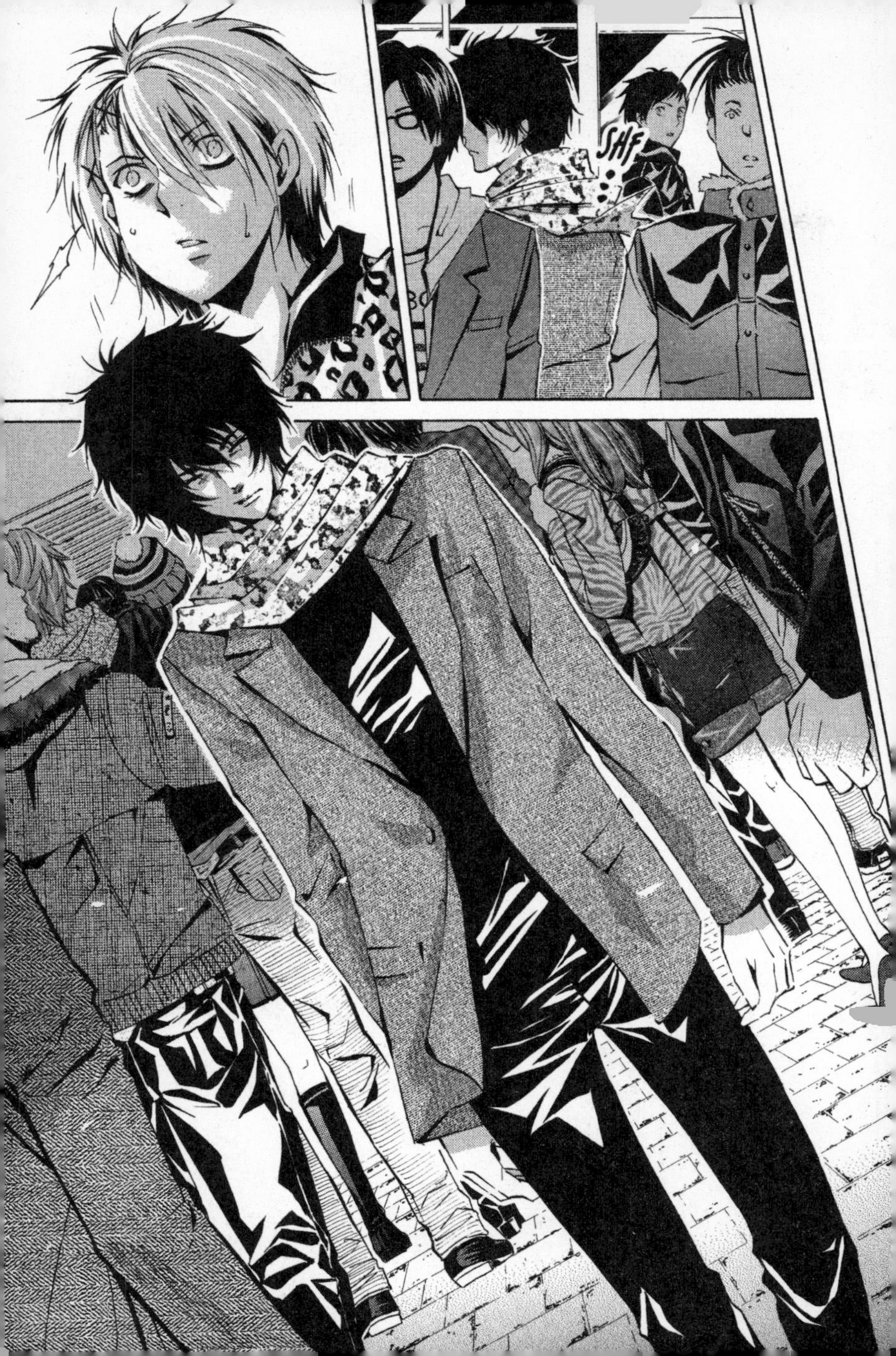
SHF

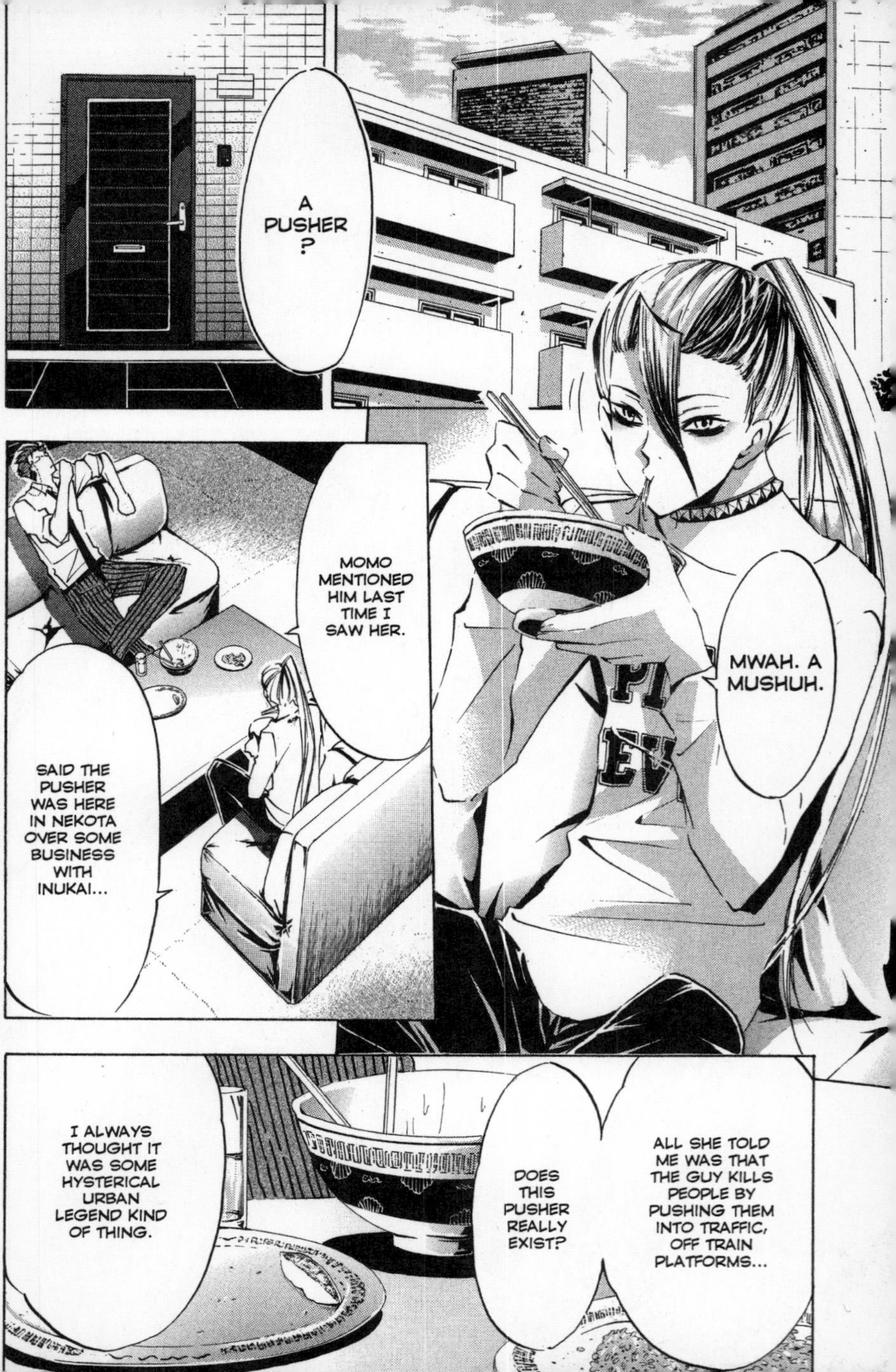
A PUSHER?
MWAH. A MUSHUH.
MOMO MENTIONED HIM LAST TIME I SAW HER.
SAID THE PUSHER WAS HERE IN NEKOTA OVER SOME BUSINESS WITH INUKAI...
ALL SHE TOLD ME WAS THAT THE GUY KILLS PEOPLE BY PUSHING THEM INTO TRAFFIC, OFF TRAIN PLATFORMS...
DOES THIS PUSHER REALLY EXIST?
I ALWAYS THOUGHT IT WAS SOME HYSTERICAL URBAN LEGEND KIND OF THING.

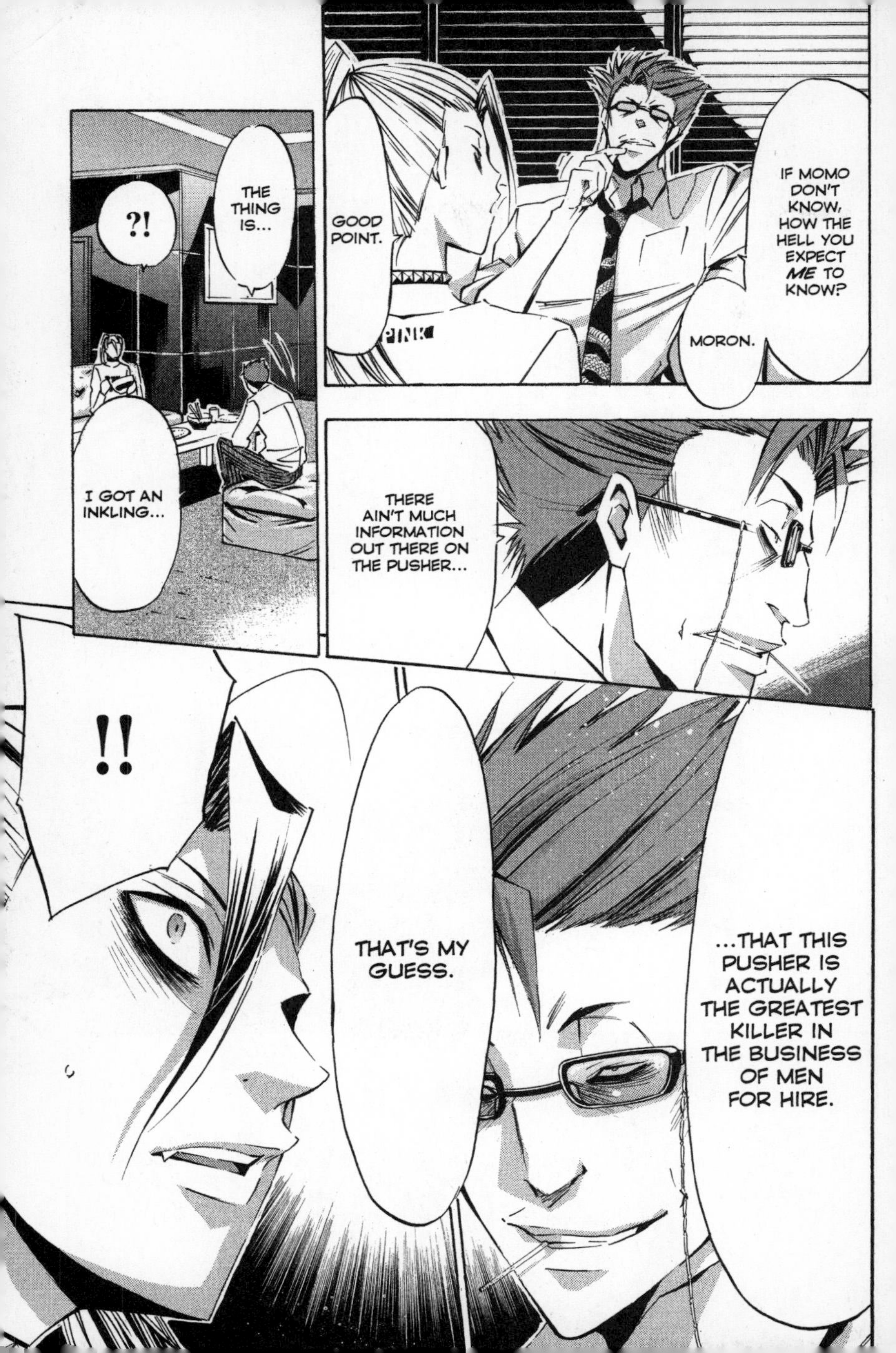
IF MOMO DON'T KNOW, HOW THE HELL YOU EXPECT *ME* TO KNOW?
MORON.
GOOD POINT.
PINK
THERE AIN'T MUCH INFORMATION OUT THERE ON THE PUSHER...
THE THING IS...
?!
I GOT AN INKLING...
...THAT THIS PUSHER IS ACTUALLY THE GREATEST KILLER IN THE BUSINESS OF MEN FOR HIRE.
THAT'S MY GUESS.
!!

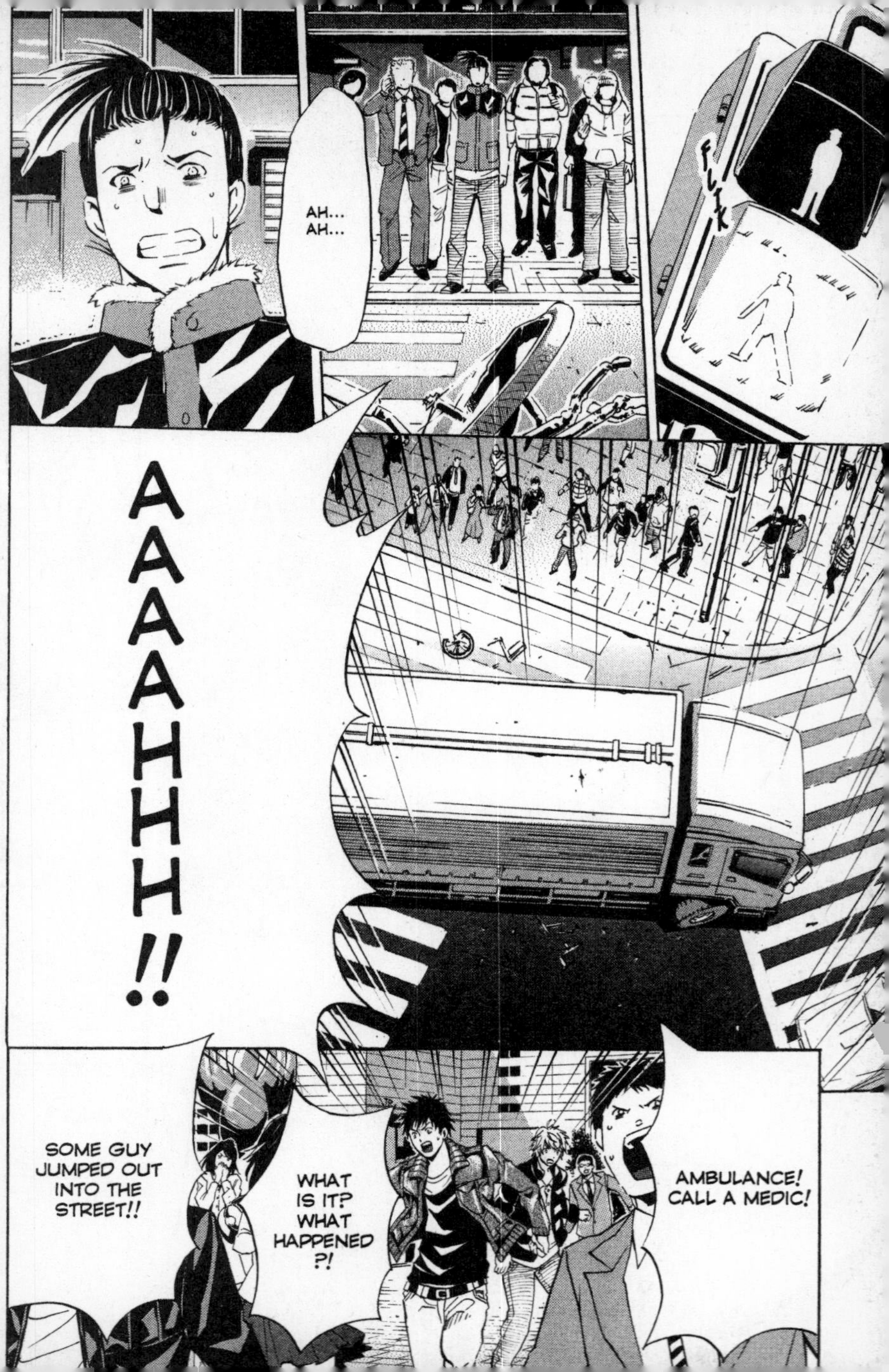
AH... AH...
AAAAHHH!!
AMBULANCE! CALL A MEDIC!
WHAT IS IT? WHAT HAPPENED?!
SOME GUY JUMPED OUT INTO THE STREET!!

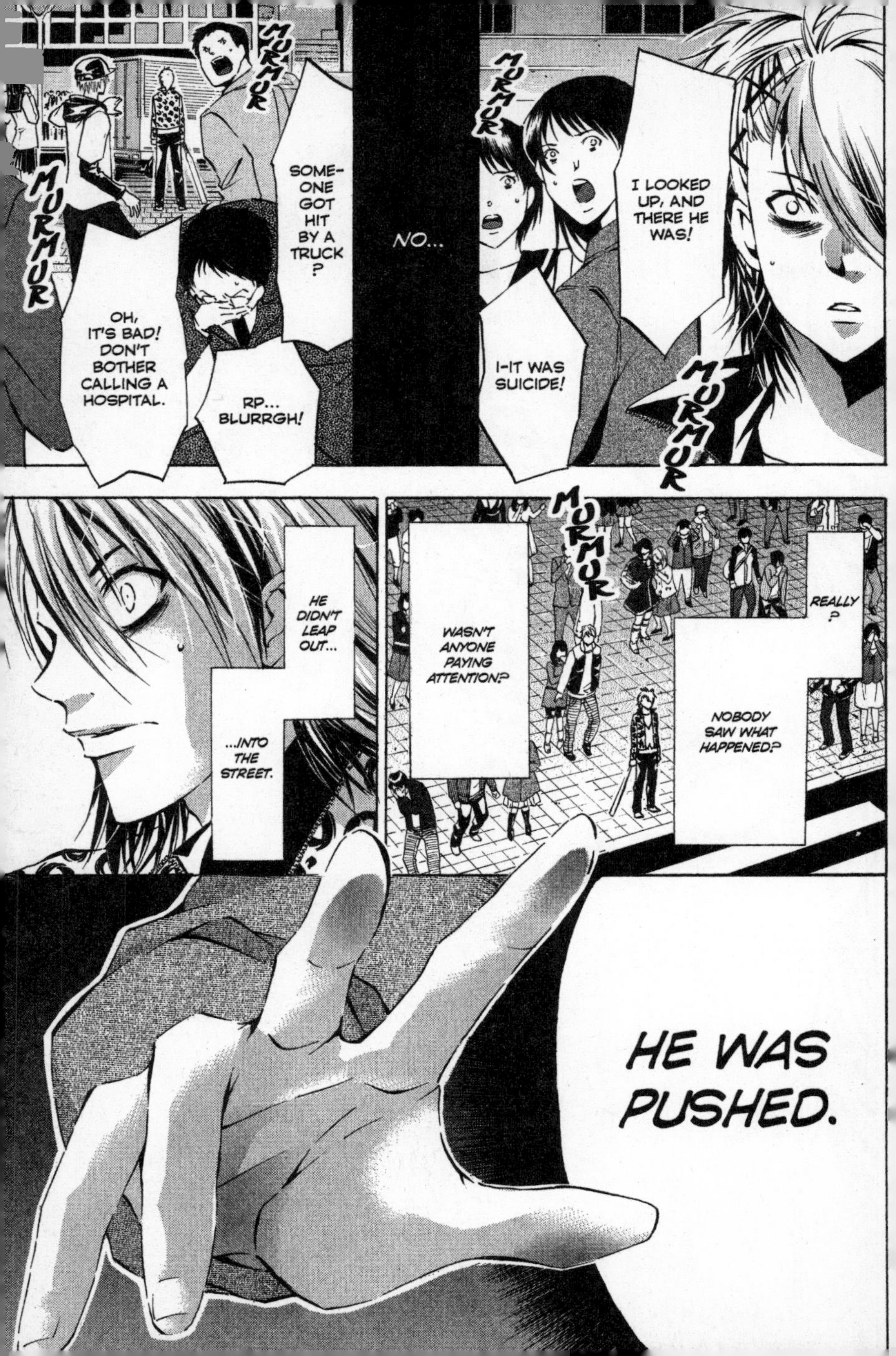
I LOOKED UP, AND THERE HE WAS!
MURMUR
I-IT WAS SUICIDE!
MURMUR
NO...
SOME-ONE GOT HIT BY A TRUCK?
MURMUR
OH, IT'S BAD! DON'T BOTHER CALLING A HOSPITAL.
RP... BLURRGH!
MURMUR
REALLY?
NOBODY SAW WHAT HAPPENED?
WASN'T ANYONE PAYING ATTENTION?
MURMUR
HE DIDN'T LEAP OUT...
...INTO THE STREET.
HE WAS PUSHED.

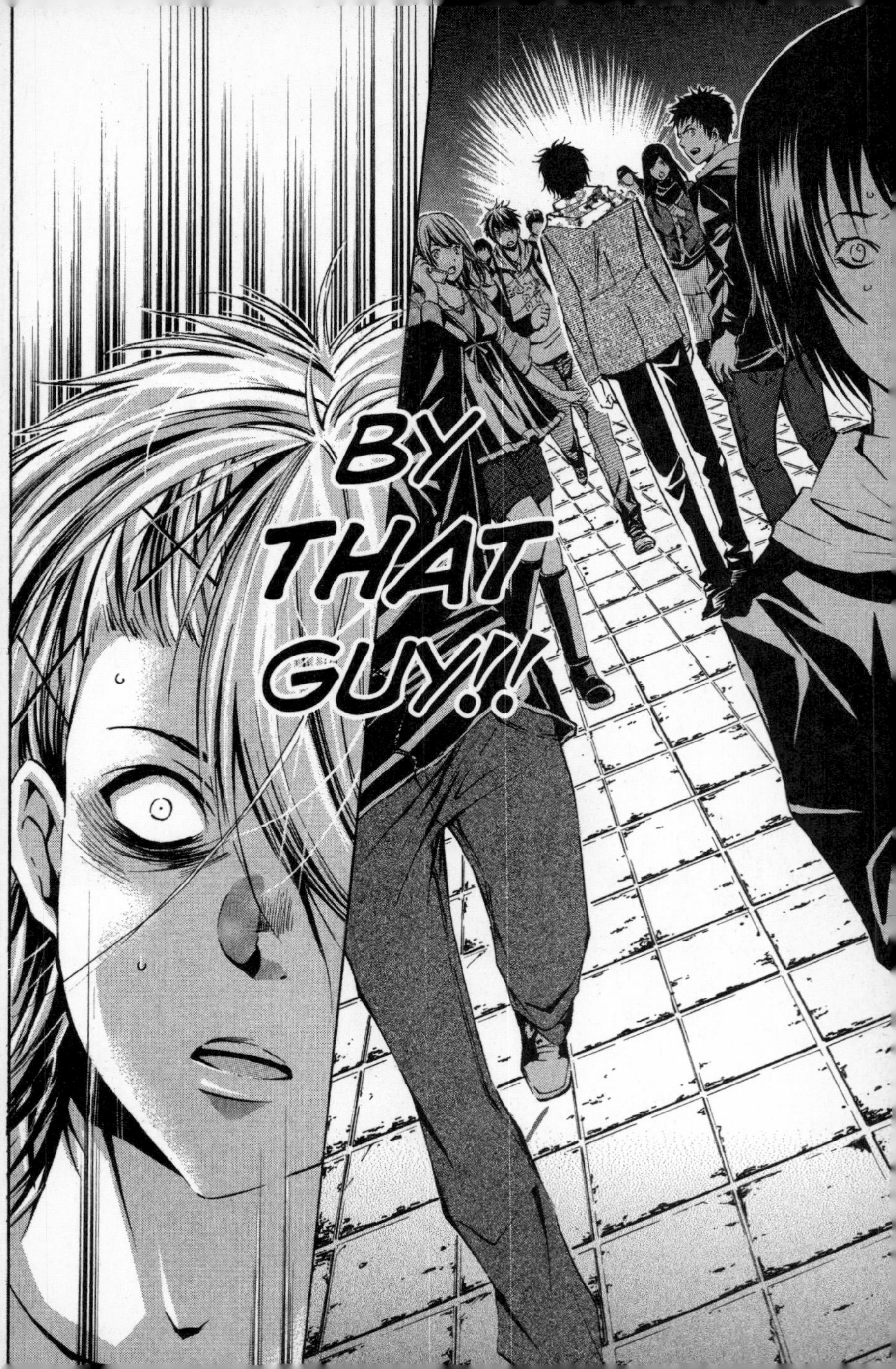
BY THAT GUY!!

Chapter 71 Right Or Left?!

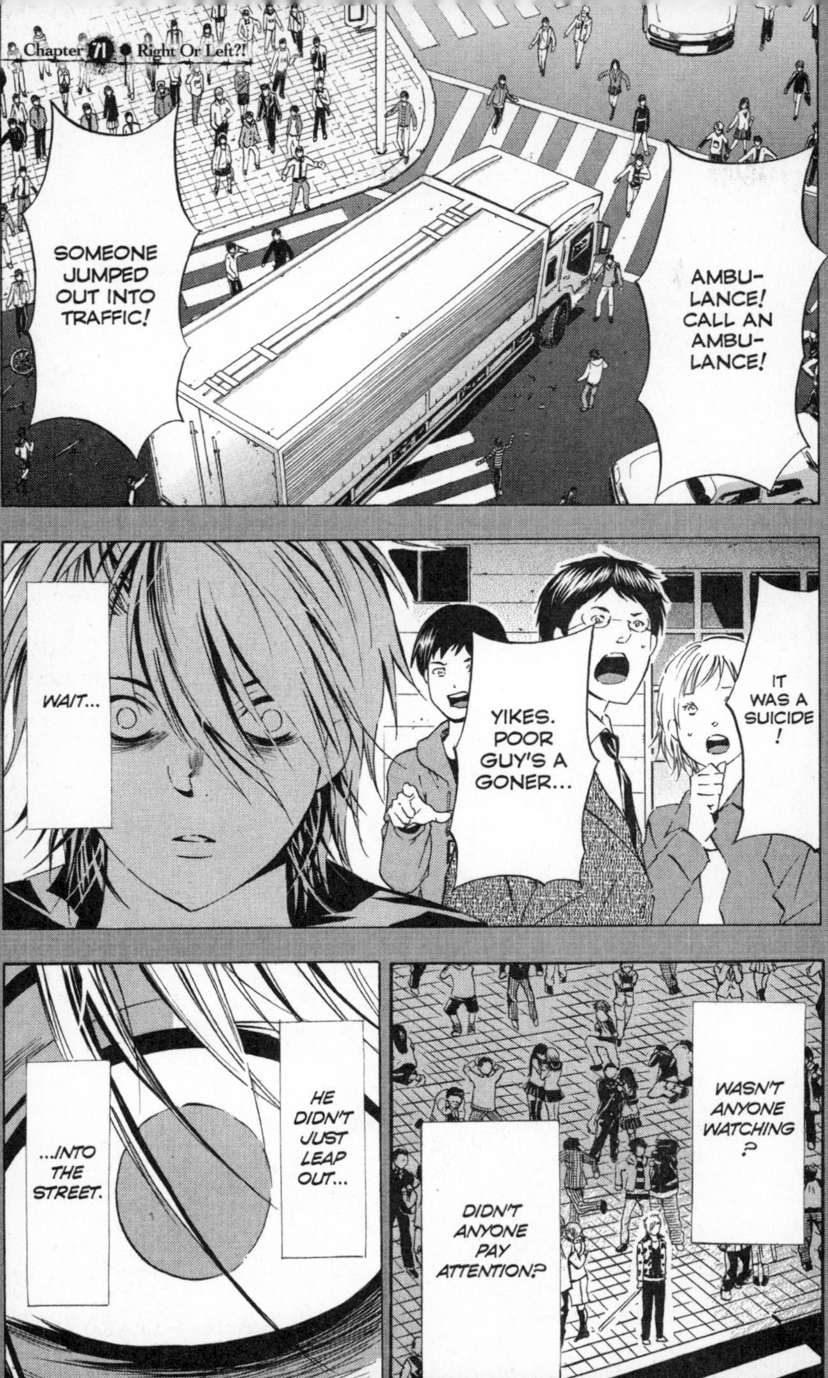
AMBULANCE! CALL AN AMBULANCE!
SOMEONE JUMPED OUT INTO TRAFFIC!
IT WAS A SUICIDE!
YIKES. POOR GUY'S A GONER...
WAIT...
WASN'T ANYONE WATCHING?
DIDN'T ANYONE PAY ATTENTION?
HE DIDN'T JUST LEAP OUT...
...INTO THE STREET.

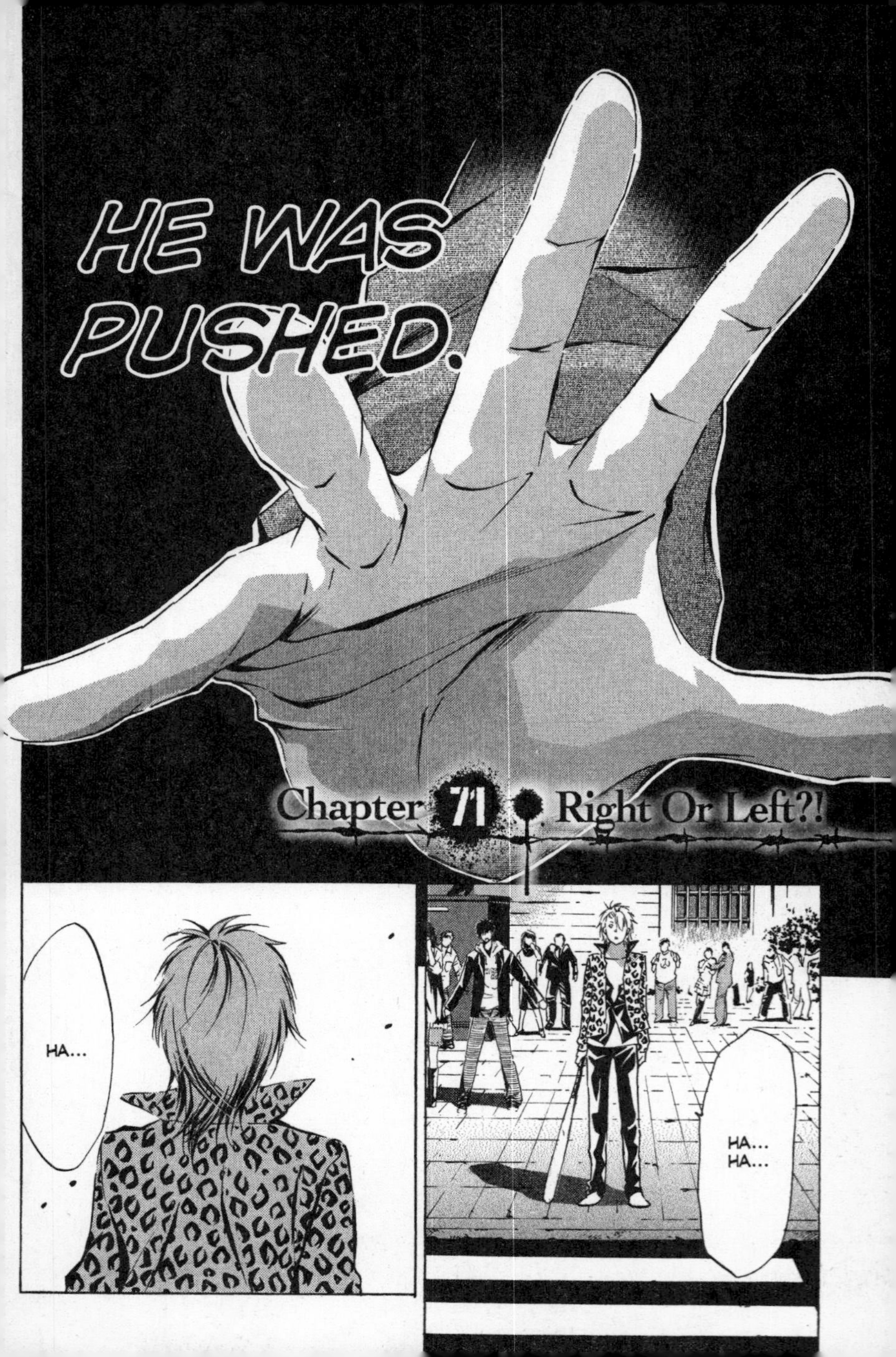
HE WAS PUSHED.
Chapter 71 Right Or Left?!
HA... HA...
HA...

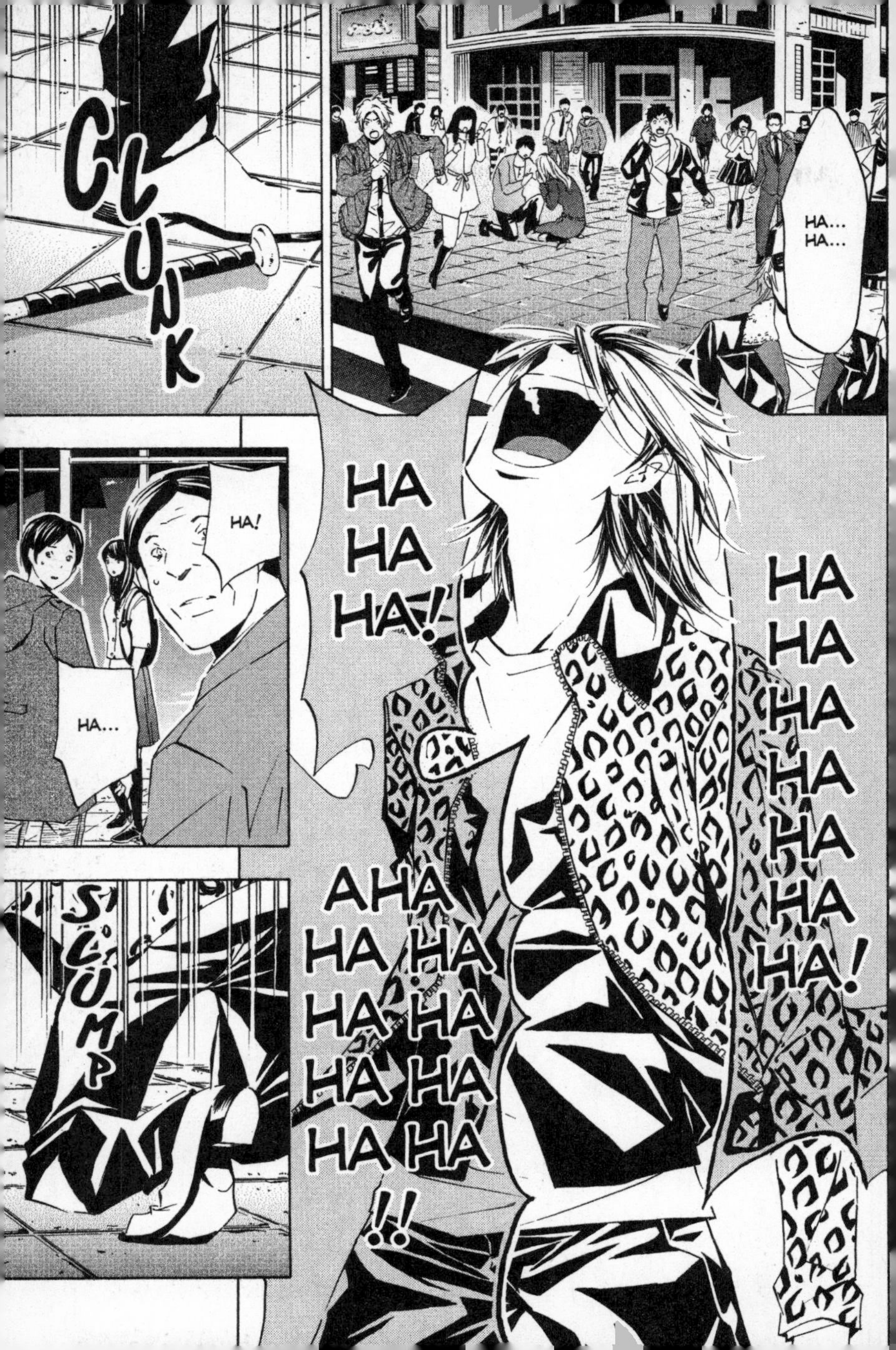

HA... HA...
CLUNK
HA HA HA HA HA HA HA HA!
HA HA HA!
AHA HA HA HA HA HA HA HA HA HA HA!!
HA!
HA...
SLUMP

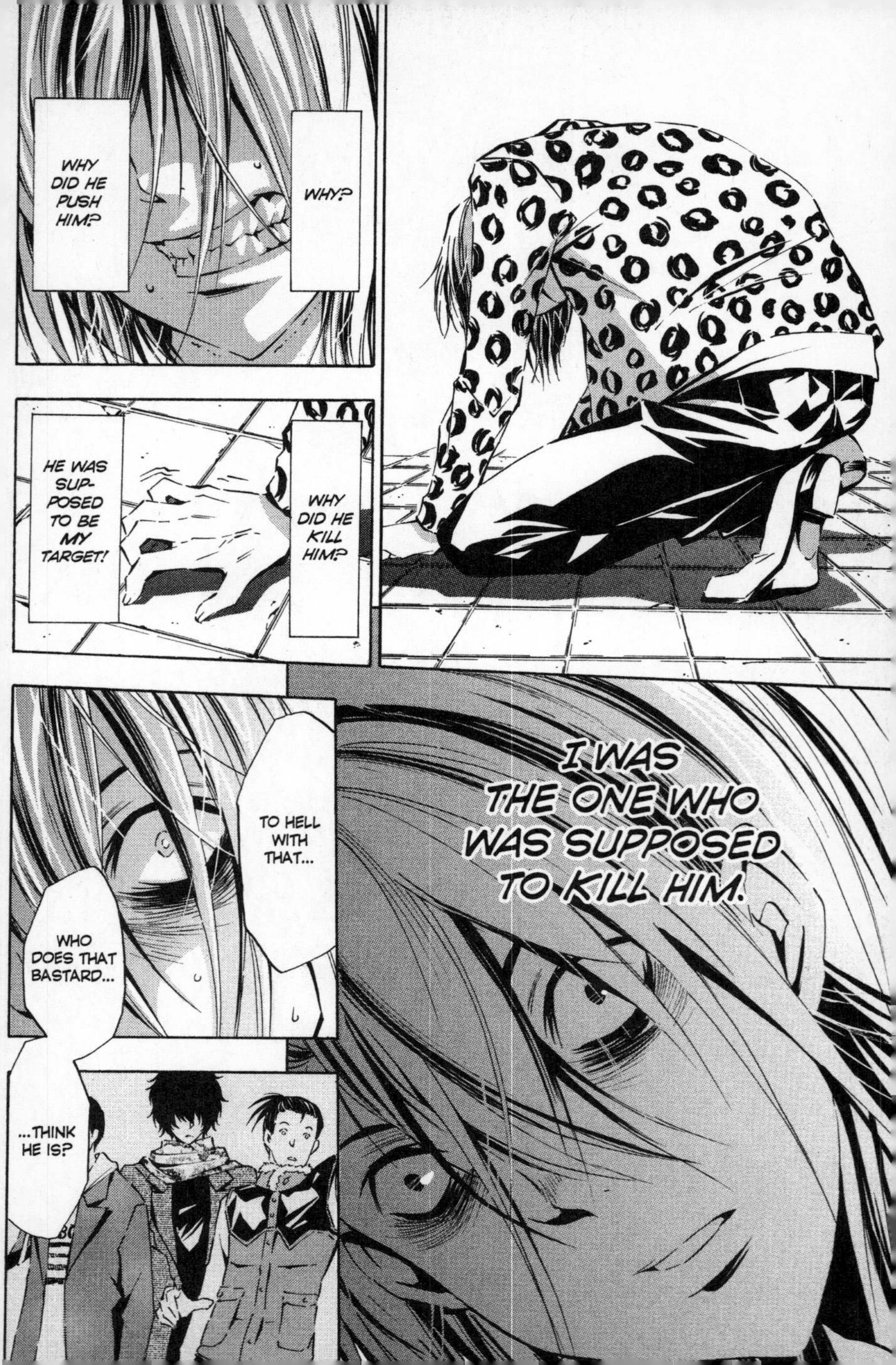
WHY?
WHY DID HE PUSH HIM?
WHY DID HE KILL HIM?
HE WAS SUP-POSED TO BE MY TARGET!
I WAS THE ONE WHO WAS SUPPOSED TO KILL HIM.
TO HELL WITH THAT...
WHO DOES THAT BASTARD...
...THINK HE IS?

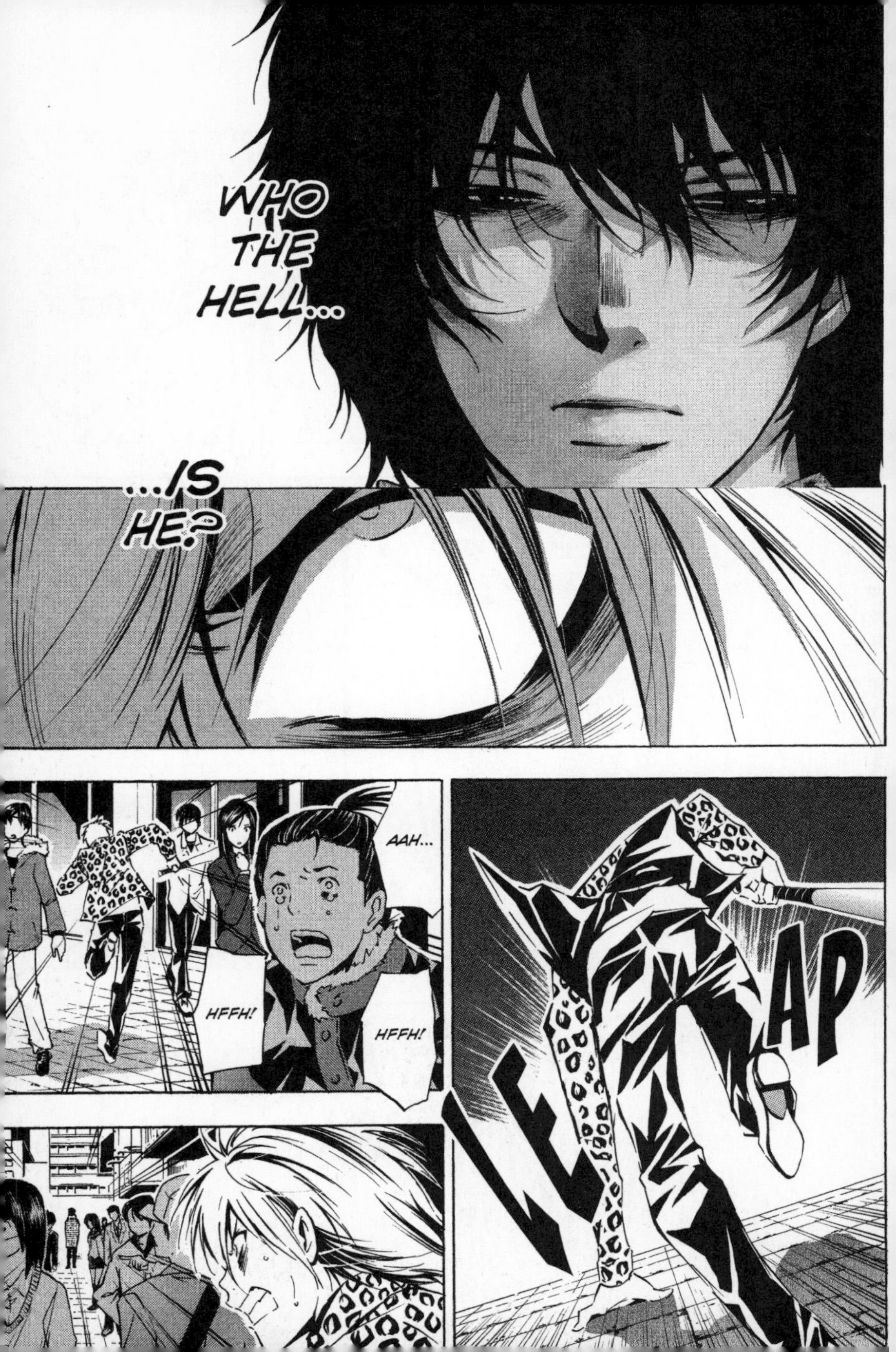
WHO THE HELL...
...IS HE?
AAH...
HFFH!
HFFH!

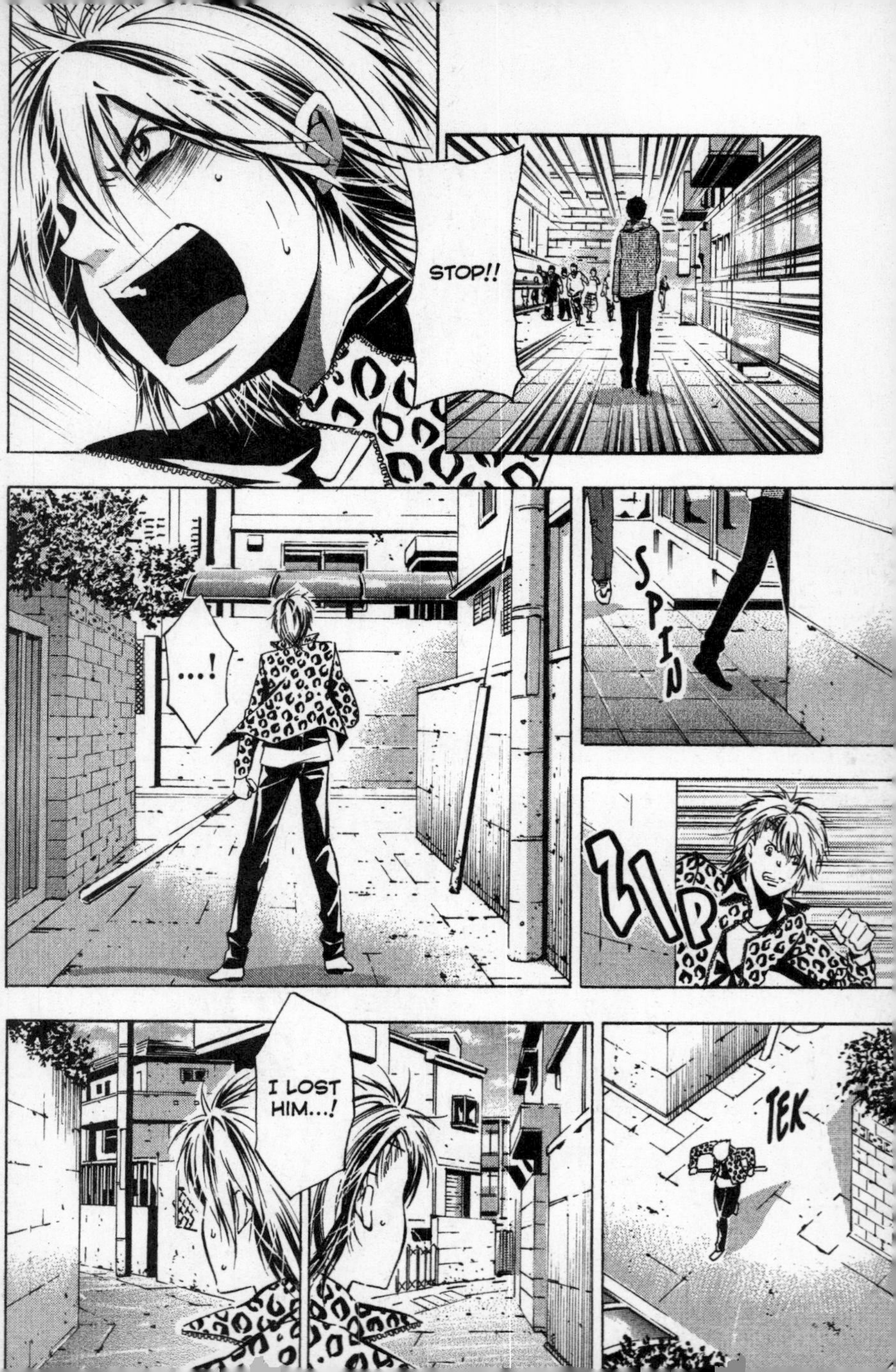
STOP!!
SPIN
ZIP
...!
TEK
I LOST HIM...!

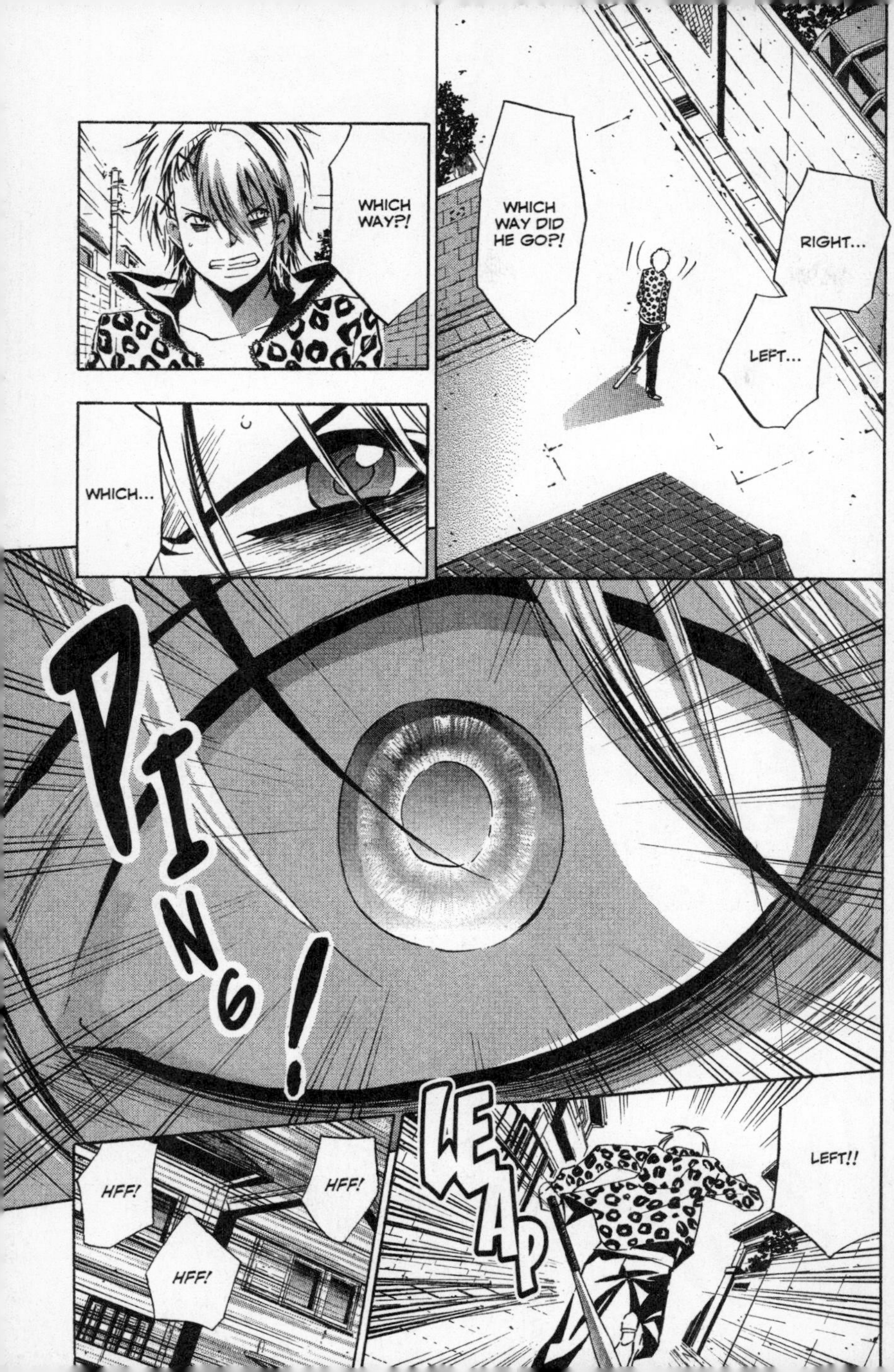
WHICH WAY DID HE GO?!
RIGHT...
LEFT...
WHICH WAY?!
WHICH...
PING!
LEFT!!
LEAP
HFF!
HFF!
HFF!

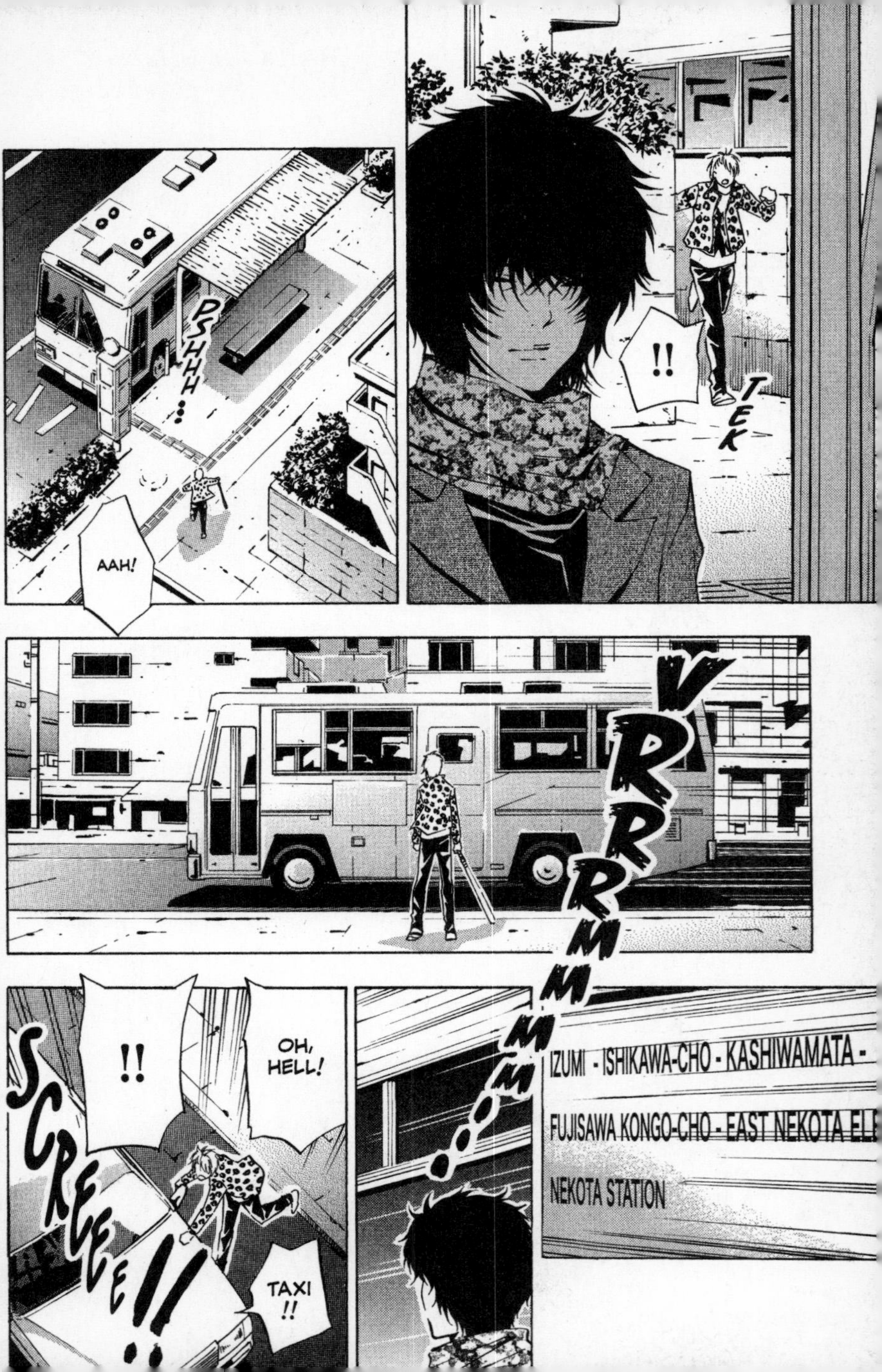
!!
TEK
PSHHH..
AAH!
VRRRMMMMMM...
IZUMI - ISHIKAWA-CHO - KASHIWAMATA -
FUJISAWA KONGO-CHO - EAST NEKOTA EL
NEKOTA STATION
OH, HELL!
!!
SCREEE!!
TAXI !!

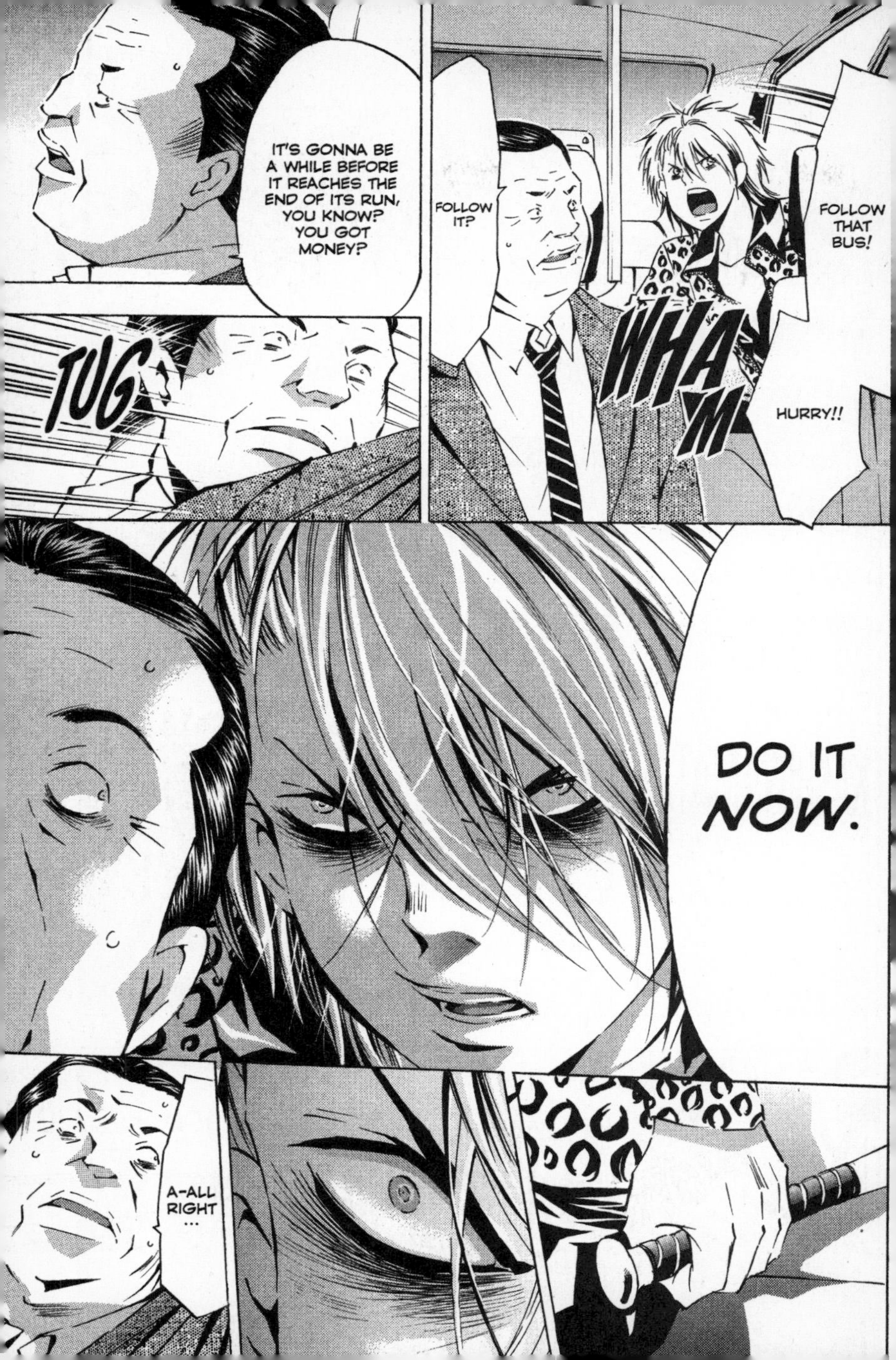
FOLLOW THAT BUS!
FOLLOW IT?
WHAM
HURRY!!
IT'S GONNA BE A WHILE BEFORE IT REACHES THE END OF ITS RUN, YOU KNOW? YOU GOT MONEY?
TUG
DO IT NOW.
A-ALL RIGHT ...

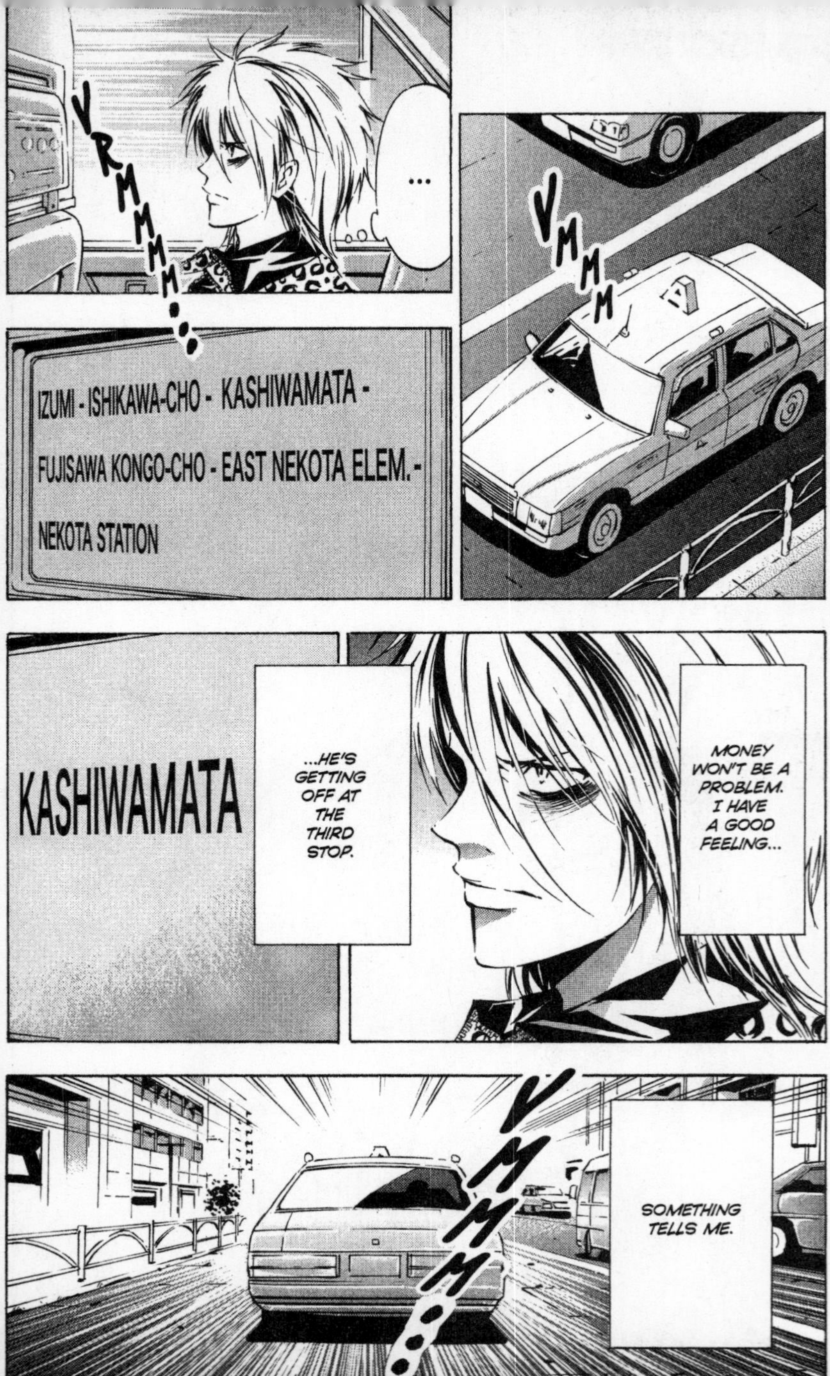
VMMM
VRMMMM...
...
IZUMI - ISHIKAWA-CHO - KASHIWAMATA -
FUJISAWA KONGO-CHO - EAST NEKOTA ELEM. -
NEKOTA STATION
MONEY WON'T BE A PROBLEM. I HAVE A GOOD FEELING...
...HE'S GETTING OFF AT THE THIRD STOP.
KASHIWAMATA
SOMETHING TELLS ME.
VMMMM...

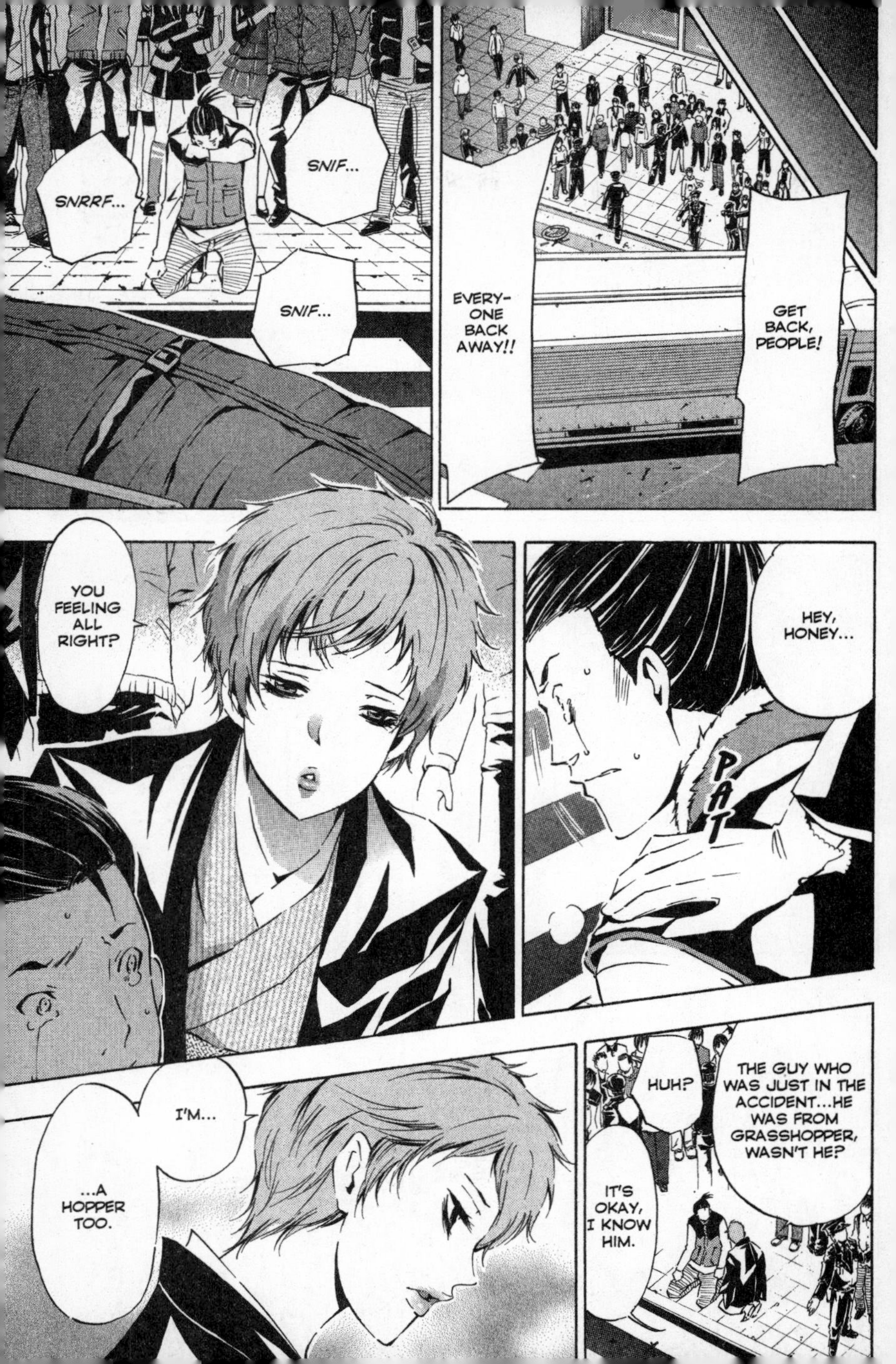
GET BACK, PEOPLE!
EVERY-ONE BACK AWAY!!
SNIF...
SNRRF...
SNIF...
HEY, HONEY...
PAT
YOU FEELING ALL RIGHT?
THE GUY WHO WAS JUST IN THE ACCIDENT...HE WAS FROM GRASSHOPPER, WASN'T HE?
HUH?
IT'S OKAY, I KNOW HIM.
I'M...
...A HOPPER TOO.

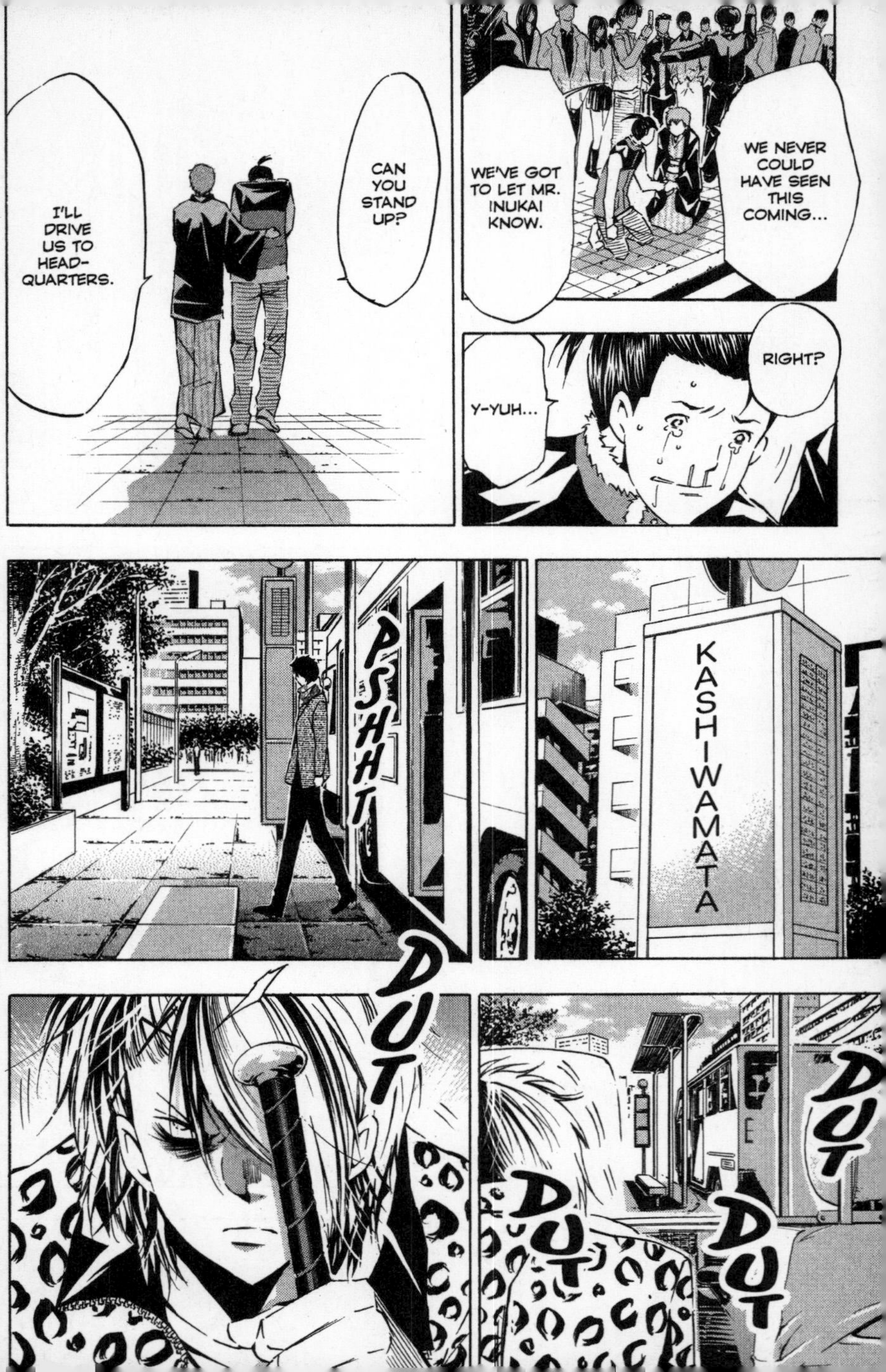
WE NEVER COULD HAVE SEEN THIS COMING...
WE'VE GOT TO LET MR. INUKAI KNOW.
RIGHT?
Y-YUH...
CAN YOU STAND UP?
I'LL DRIVE US TO HEAD-QUARTERS.
KASHIWAMATA
PSHHHT
DUT
DUT
DUT
DUT
DUT

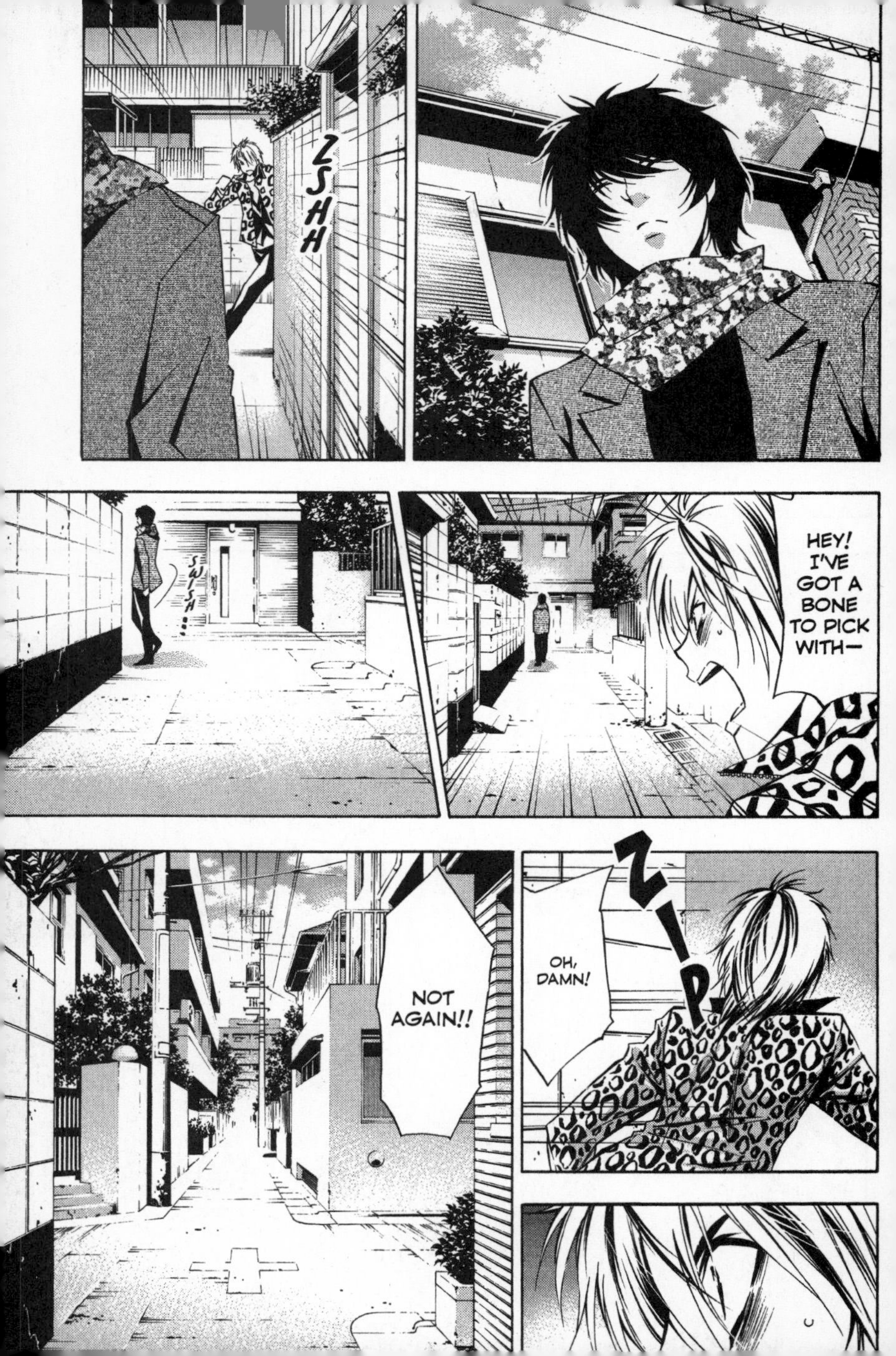
ZSHH
HEY! I'VE GOT A BONE TO PICK WITH—
SWISH...
ZIP
OH, DAMN!
NOT AGAIN!!

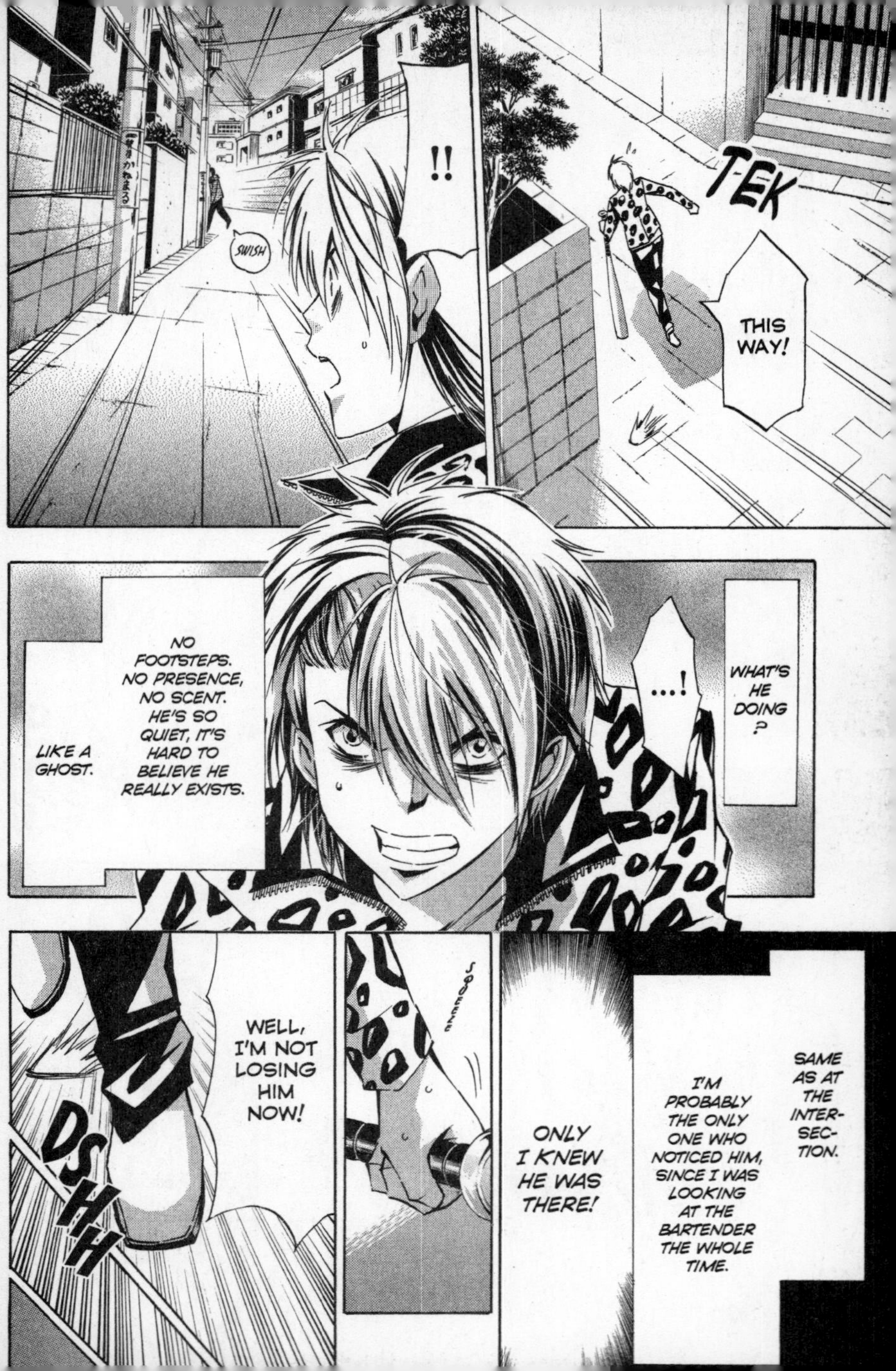
T-EK
THIS WAY!
!!
SWISH
WHAT'S HE DOING?
...!
NO FOOTSTEPS. NO PRESENCE, NO SCENT. HE'S SO QUIET, IT'S HARD TO BELIEVE HE REALLY EXISTS.
LIKE A GHOST.
SAME AS AT THE INTER-SEC-TION.
I'M PROBABLY THE ONLY ONE WHO NOTICED HIM, SINCE I WAS LOOKING AT THE BARTENDER THE WHOLE TIME.
ONLY I KNEW HE WAS THERE!
SQUEEEZE
WELL, I'M NOT LOSING HIM NOW!
DSHH

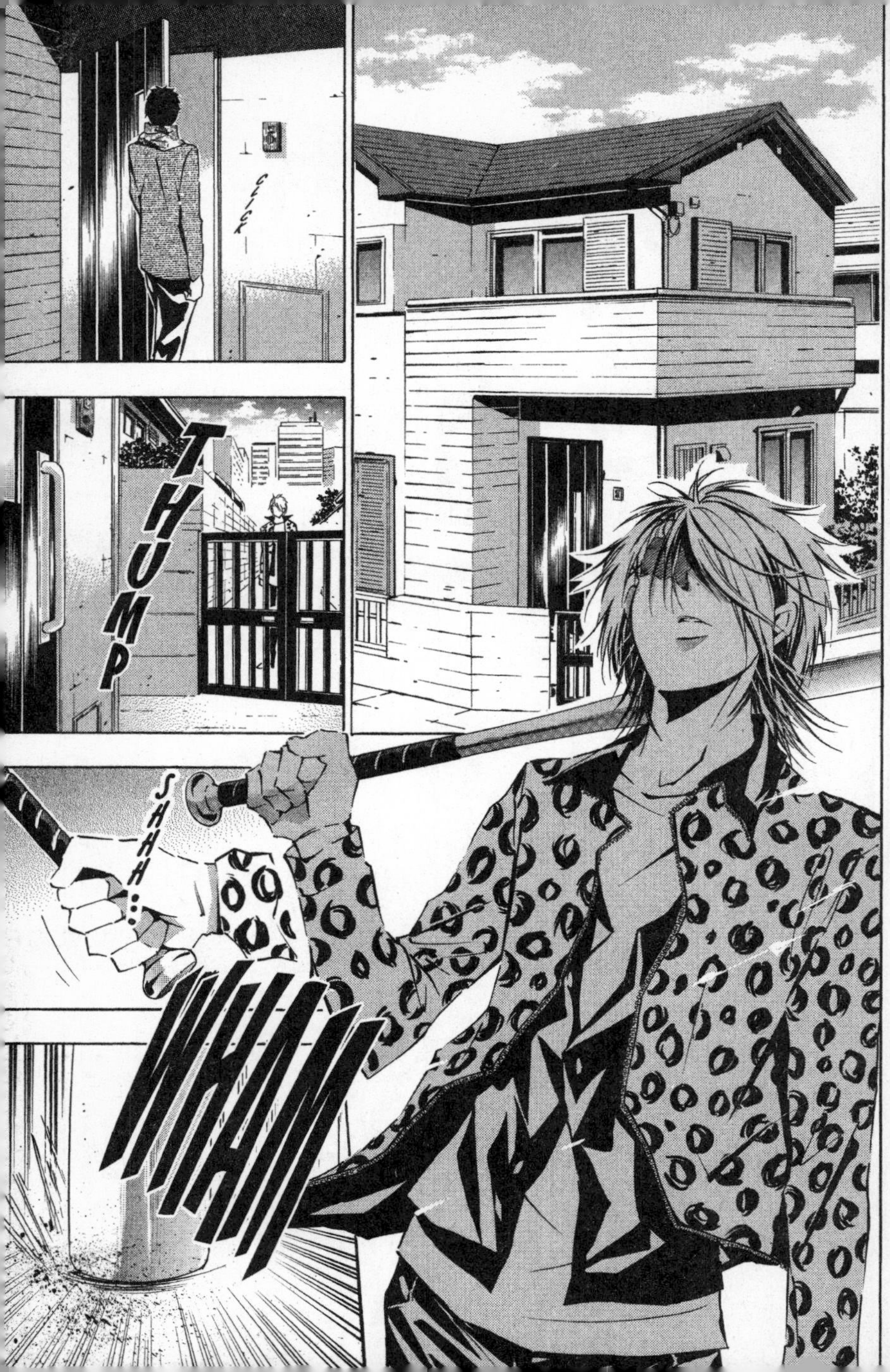
CLICK
THUMP
SHHHH...
WHAM

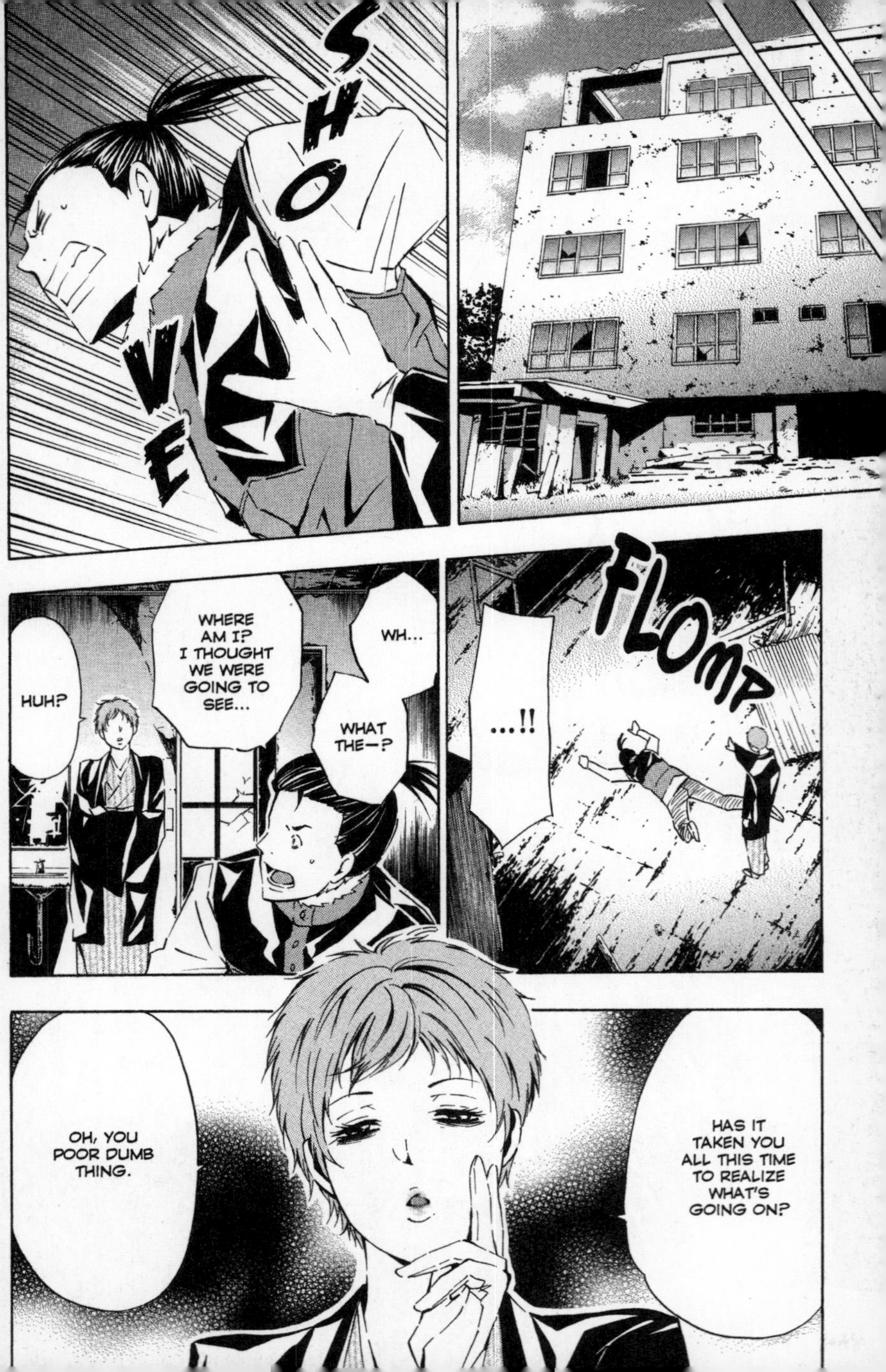
SHOVE
FLOMP
...!!
WH...
WHAT THE—?
WHERE AM I? I THOUGHT WE WERE GOING TO SEE...
HUH?
HAS IT TAKEN YOU ALL THIS TIME TO REALIZE WHAT'S GOING ON?
OH, YOU POOR DUMB THING.

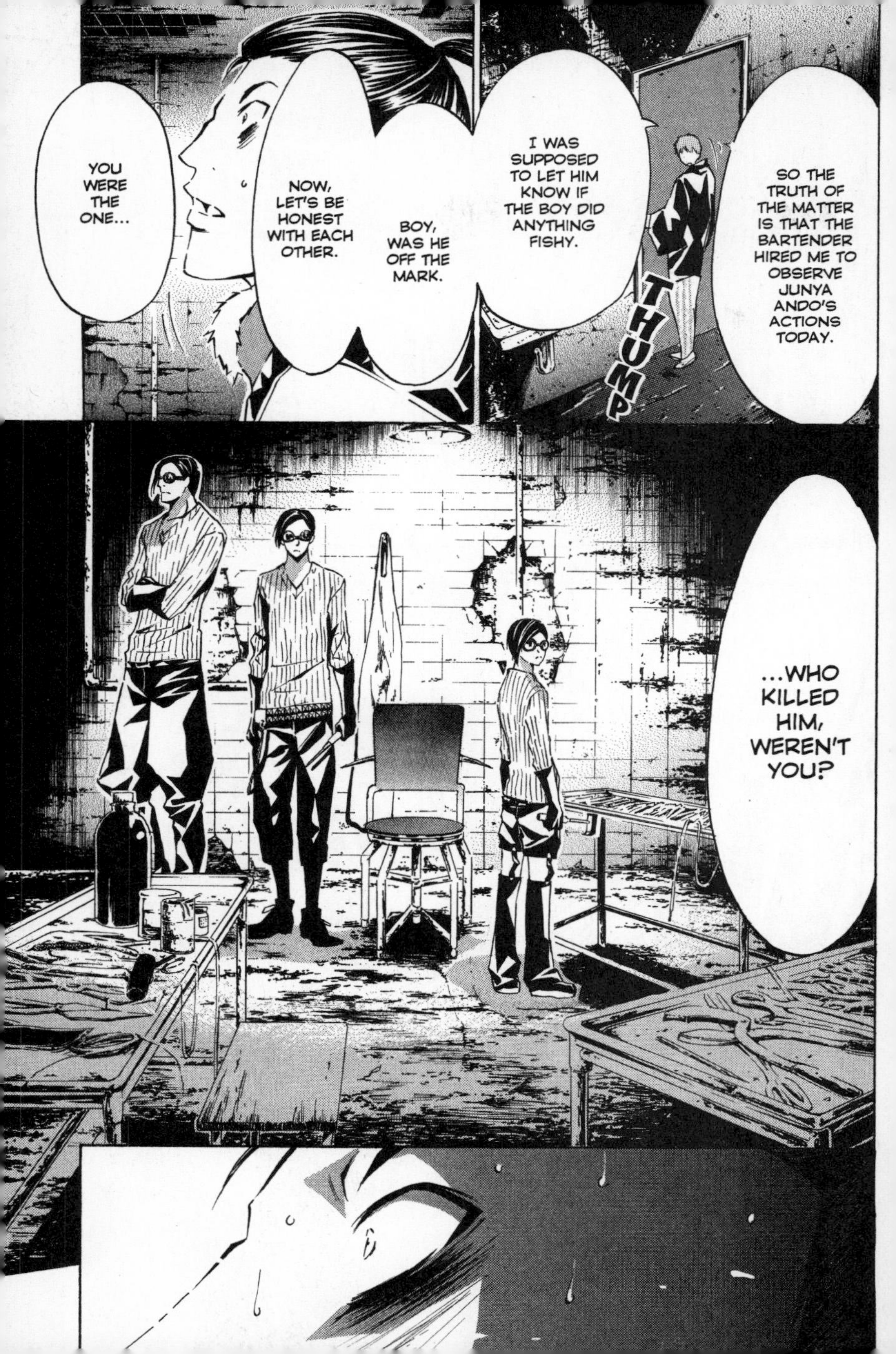
SO THE TRUTH OF THE MATTER IS THAT THE BARTENDER HIRED ME TO OBSERVE JUNYA ANDO'S ACTIONS TODAY.
THUMP
I WAS SUPPOSED TO LET HIM KNOW IF THE BOY DID ANYTHING FISHY.
BOY, WAS HE OFF THE MARK.
NOW, LET'S BE HONEST WITH EACH OTHER.
YOU WERE THE ONE...
...WHO KILLED HIM, WEREN'T YOU?

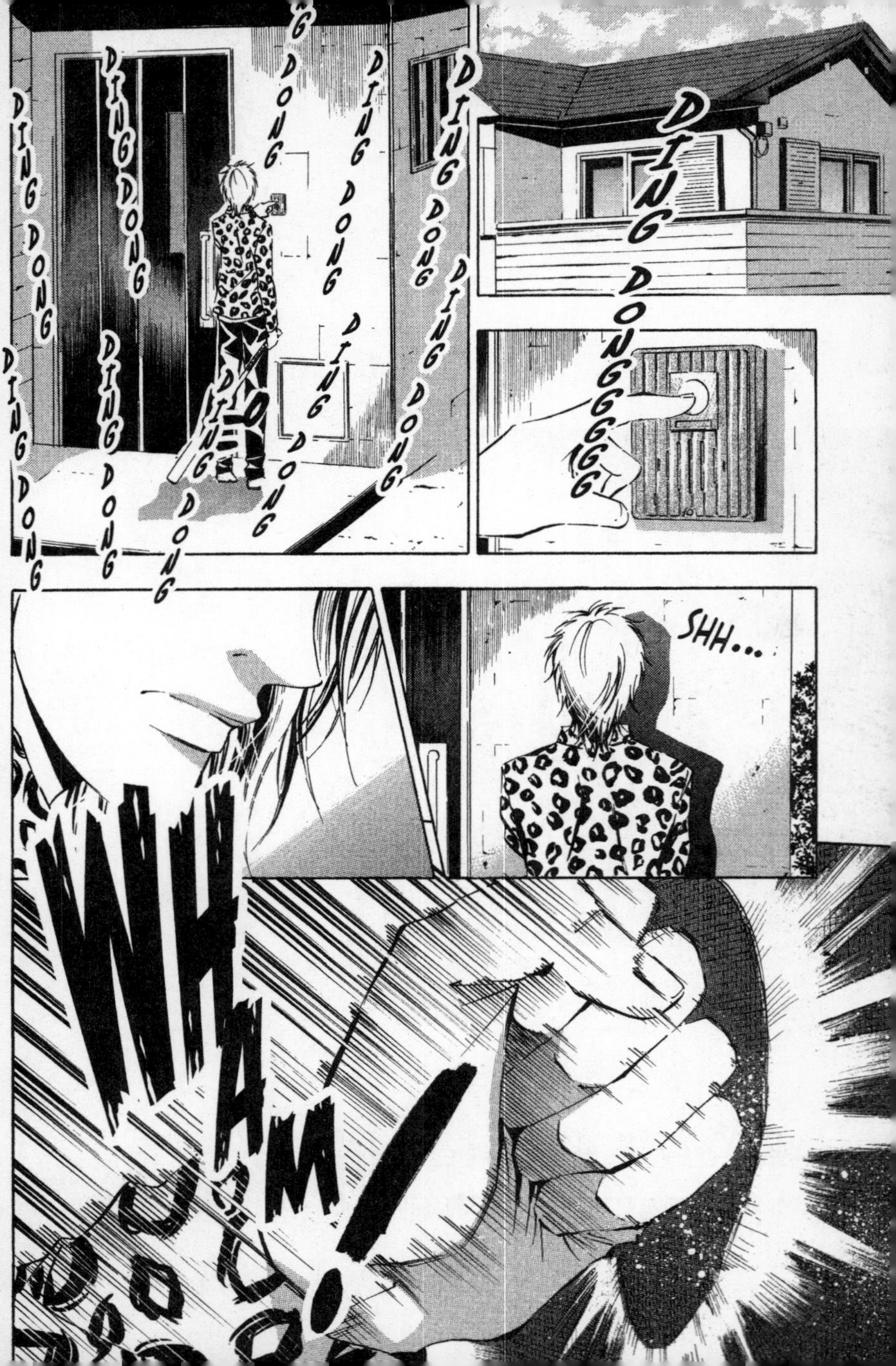
DING DONGGGGGGGG
DING DONG
DING DONG
DING DONG
DING DONG
DING DONG
DING DONG
DING DONG
DING DONG
DING DONG
DING DONG
SHH...
WHAM!

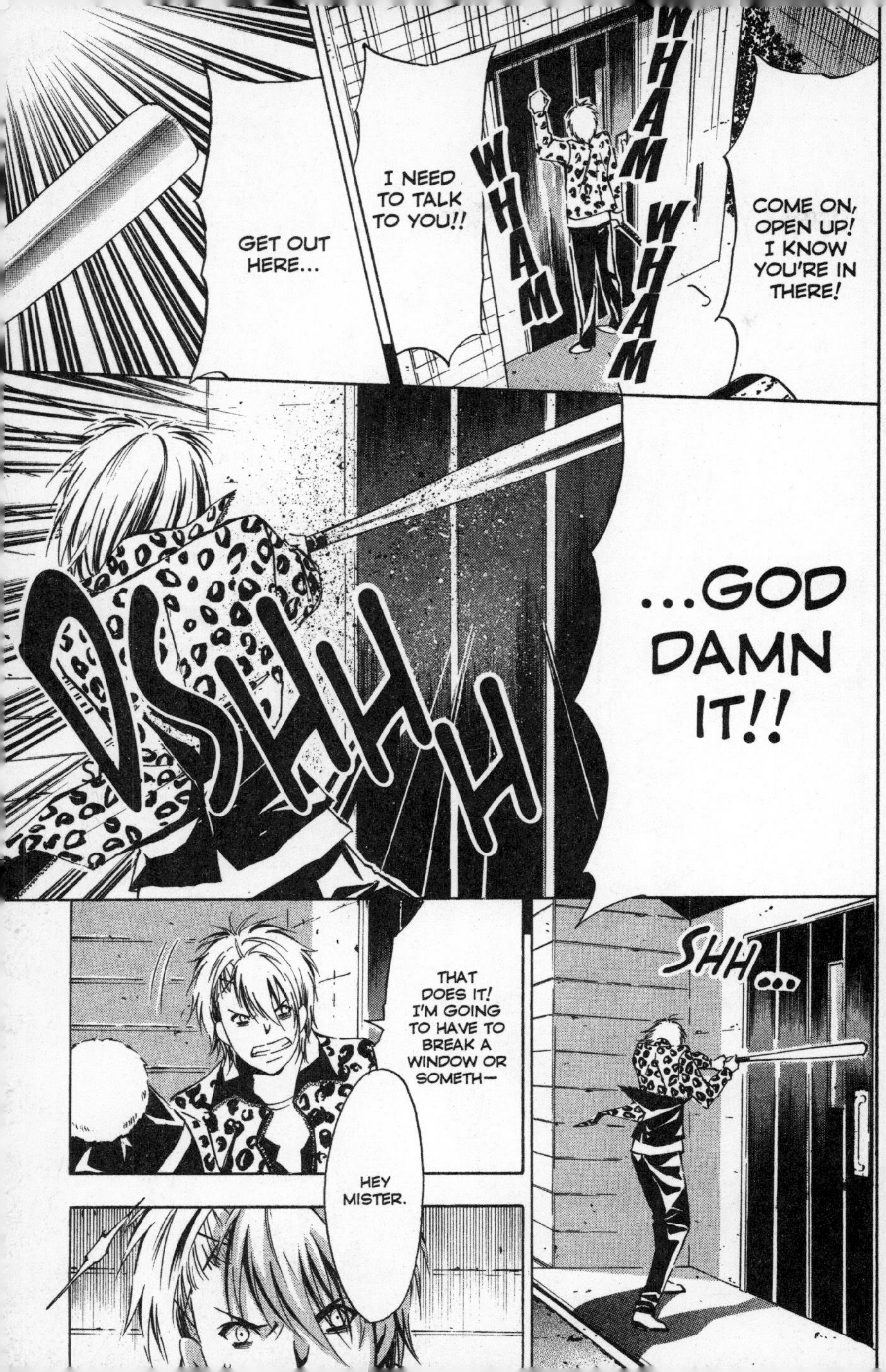
COME ON, OPEN UP! I KNOW YOU'RE IN THERE!
WHAM WHAM
WHAM
I NEED TO TALK TO YOU!!
GET OUT HERE...
...GOD DAMN IT!!
DSHHH
SHH...
THAT DOES IT! I'M GOING TO HAVE TO BREAK A WINDOW OR SOMETH—
HEY MISTER.

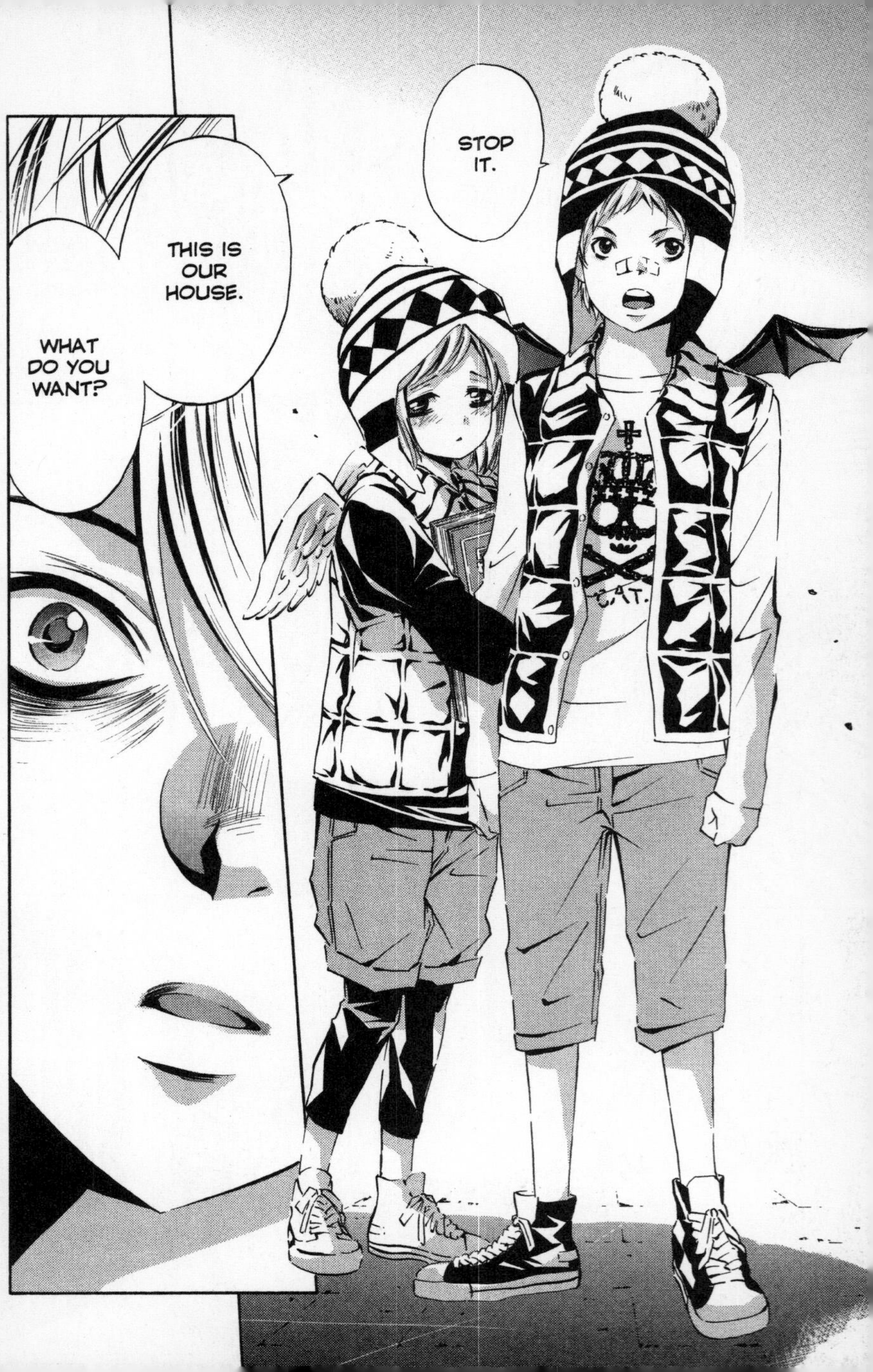
STOP IT.
THIS IS OUR HOUSE.
WHAT DO YOU WANT?

Chapter 72 • Murmurs

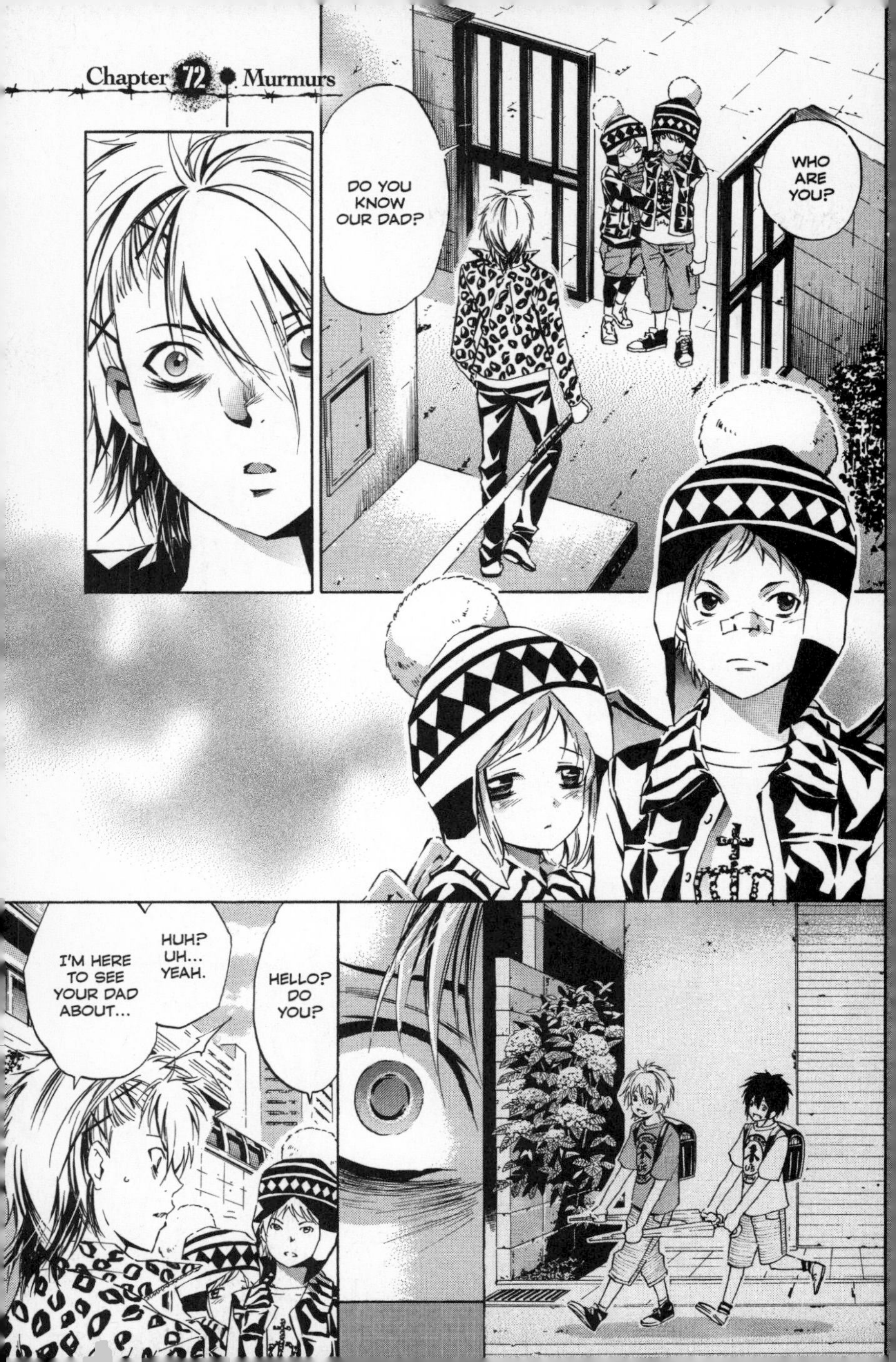
WHO ARE YOU?
DO YOU KNOW OUR DAD?
HELLO? DO YOU?
HUH? UH... YEAH.
I'M HERE TO SEE YOUR DAD ABOUT...

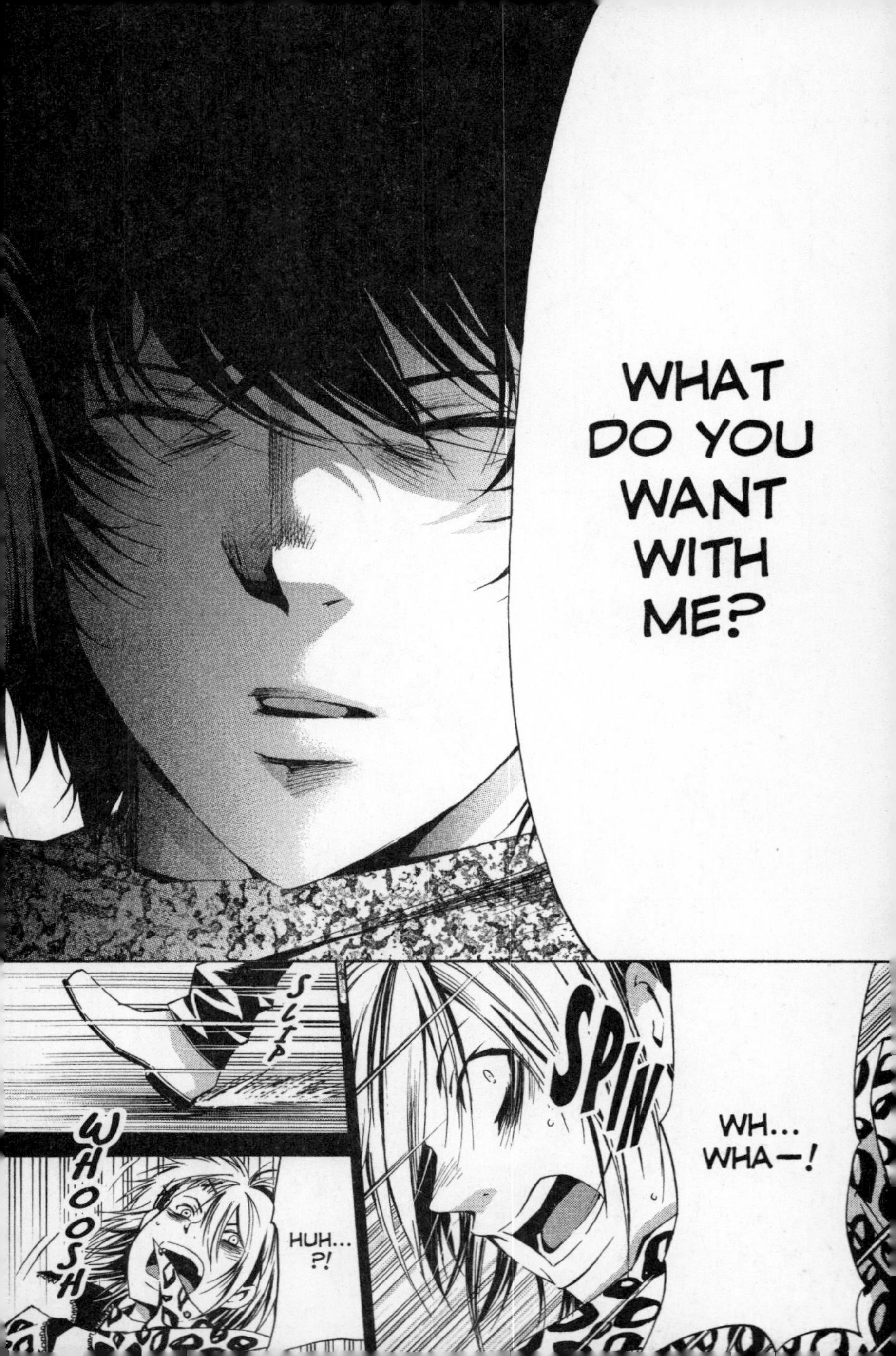
WHAT DO YOU WANT WITH ME?
SPIN
WH... WHA—!
SLIP
WHOOSH
HUH... ?!

Chapter 72 Murmurs

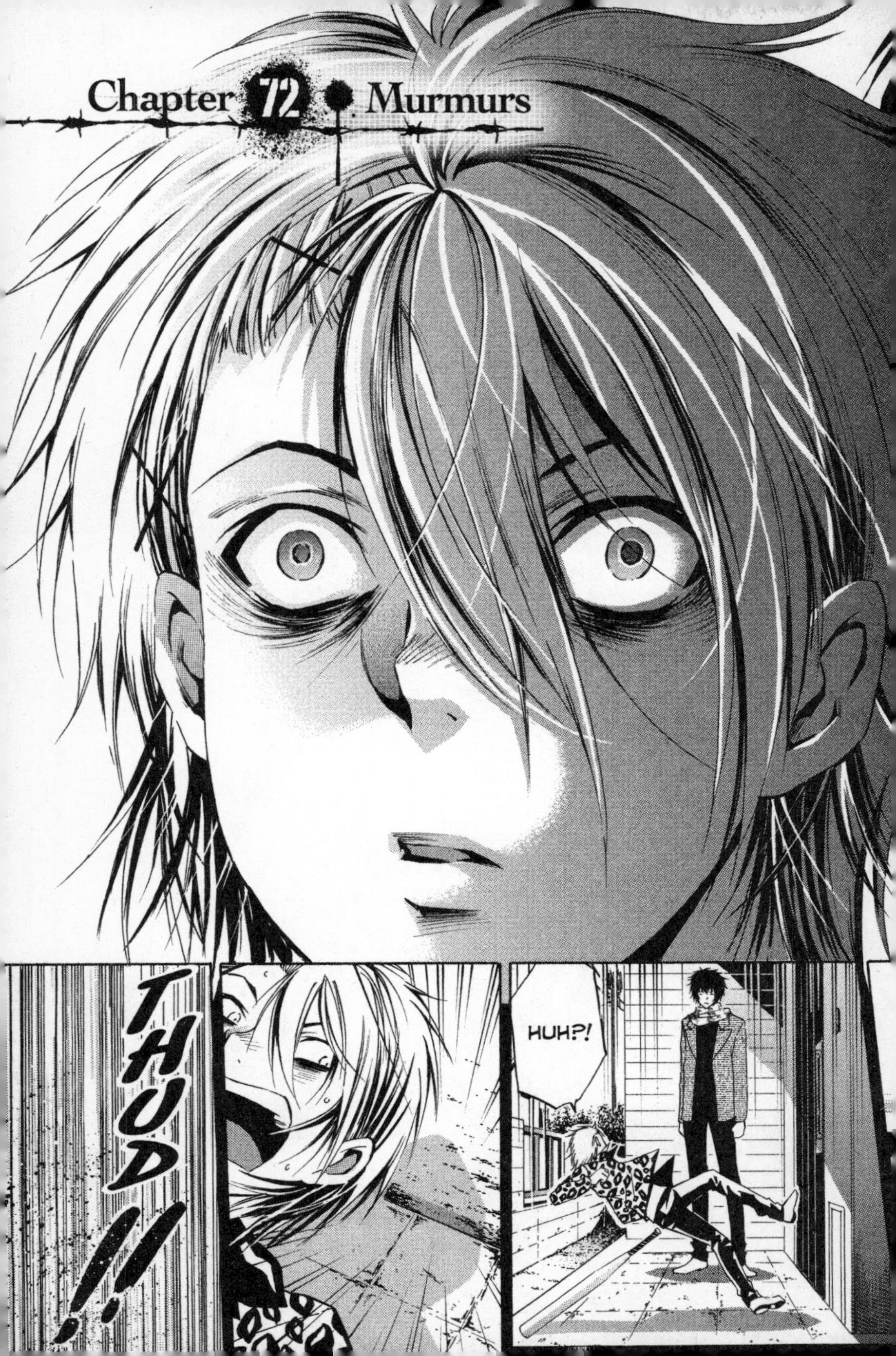
HUH?!
THUD!!

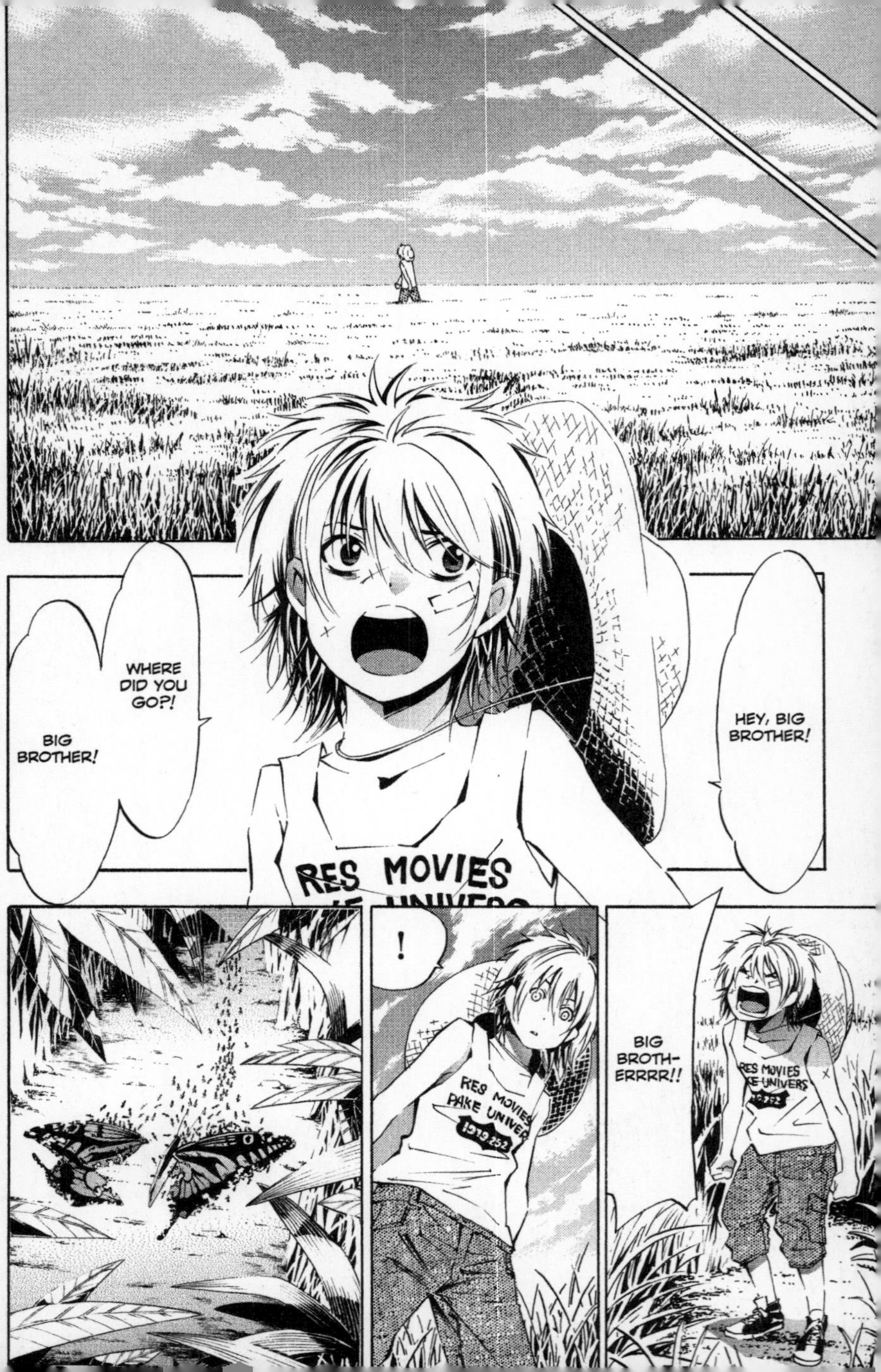
HEY, BIG BROTHER!
WHERE DID YOU GO?!
BIG BROTHER!
BIG BROTH-ERRRR!!
!

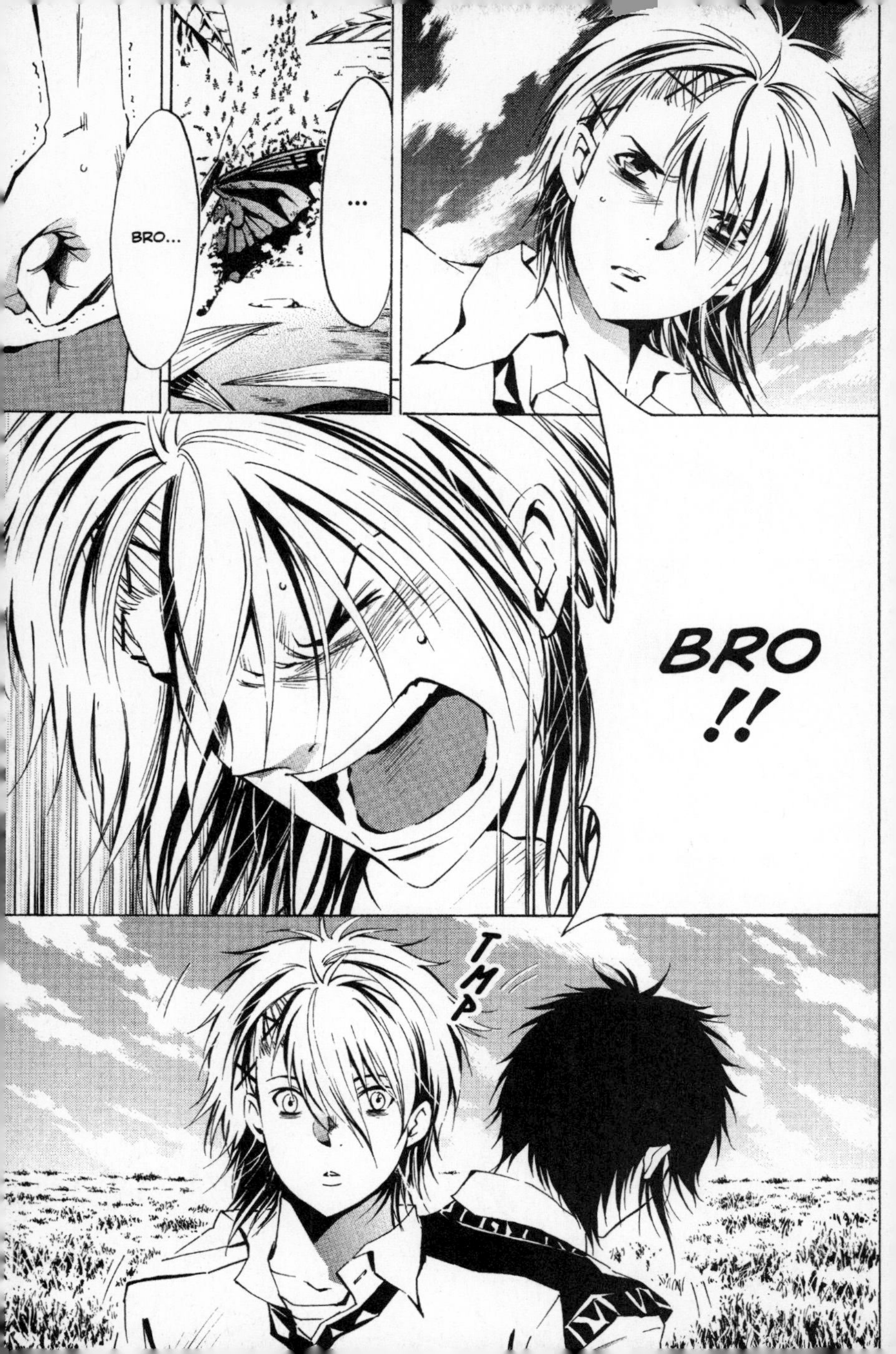
...
BRO...
BRO !!
TMP

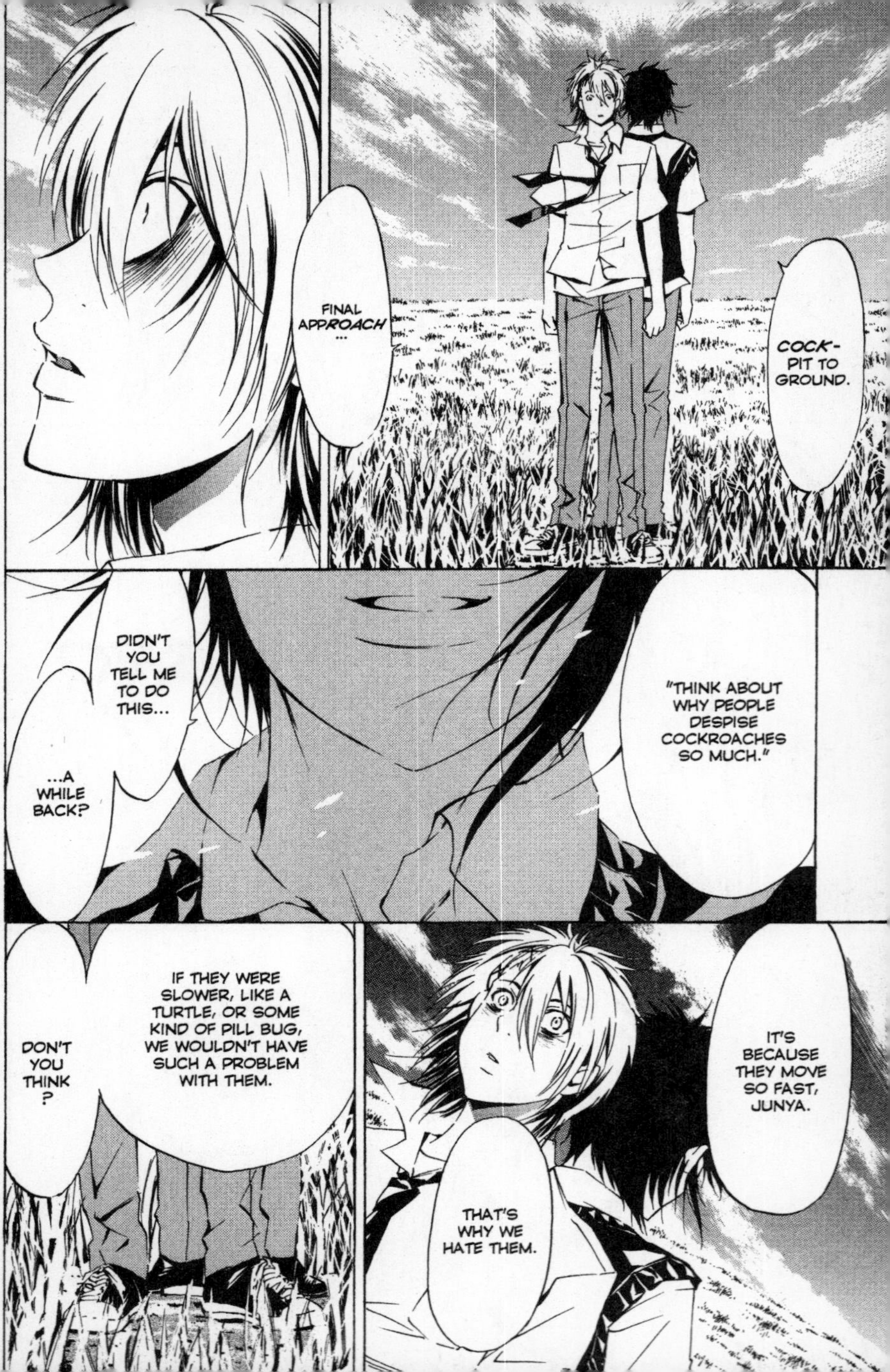
COCK-PIT TO GROUND.
FINAL APPROACH...
"THINK ABOUT WHY PEOPLE DESPISE COCKROACHES SO MUCH."
DIDN'T YOU TELL ME TO DO THIS...
...A WHILE BACK?
IT'S BECAUSE THEY MOVE SO FAST, JUNYA.
THAT'S WHY WE HATE THEM.
IF THEY WERE SLOWER, LIKE A TURTLE, OR SOME KIND OF PILL BUG, WE WOULDN'T HAVE SUCH A PROBLEM WITH THEM.
DON'T YOU THINK?

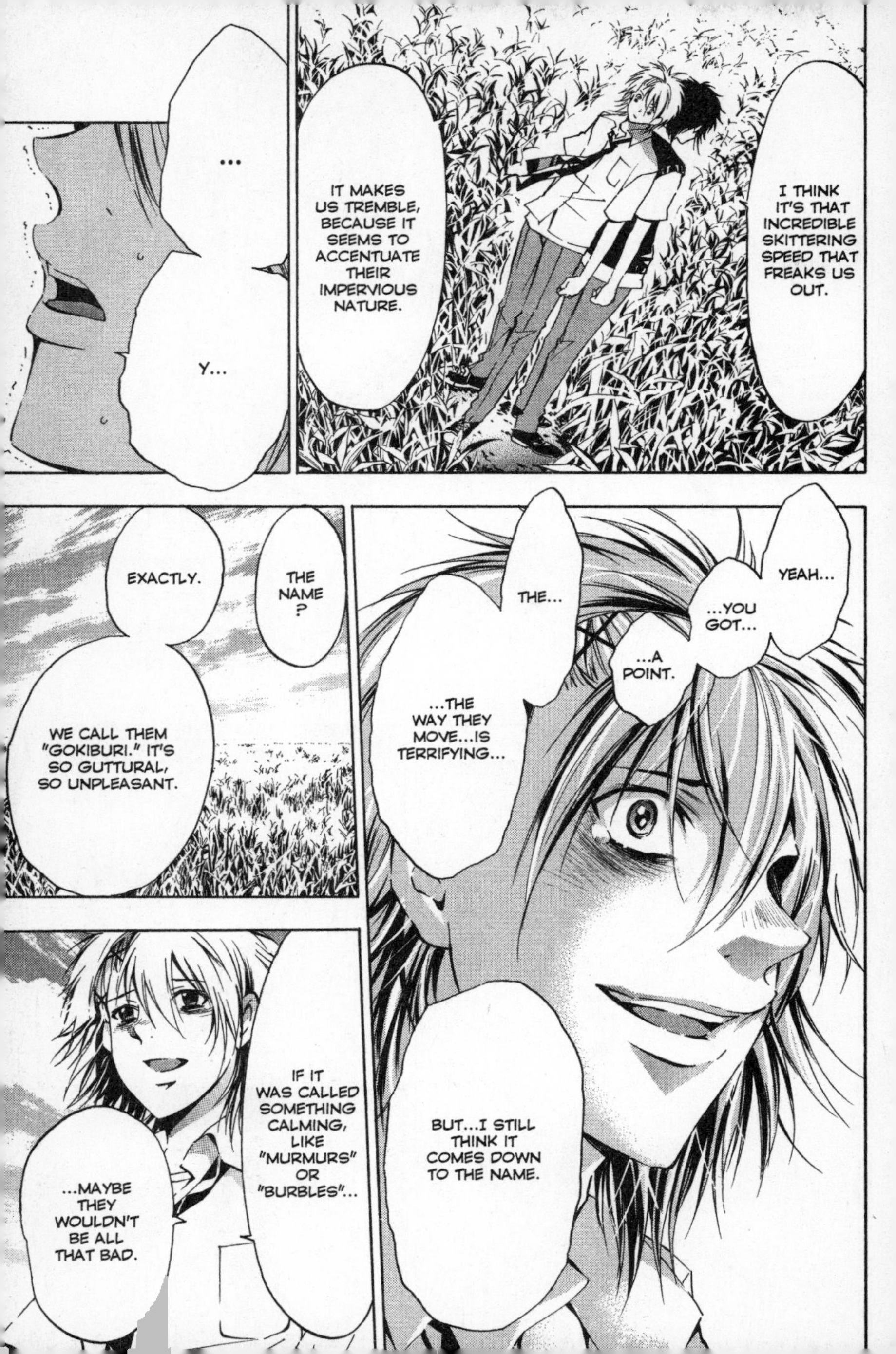
I THINK IT'S THAT INCREDIBLE SKITTERING SPEED THAT FREAKS US OUT.
IT MAKES US TREMBLE, BECAUSE IT SEEMS TO ACCENTUATE THEIR IMPERVIOUS NATURE.
...
Y...
YEAH...
...YOU GOT...
...A POINT.
THE...
...THE WAY THEY MOVE...IS TERRIFYING...
BUT...I STILL THINK IT COMES DOWN TO THE NAME.
THE NAME?
EXACTLY.
WE CALL THEM "GOKIBURI." IT'S SO GUTTURAL, SO UNPLEASANT.
IF IT WAS CALLED SOMETHING CALMING, LIKE "MURMURS" OR "BURBLES"...
...MAYBE THEY WOULDN'T BE ALL THAT BAD.

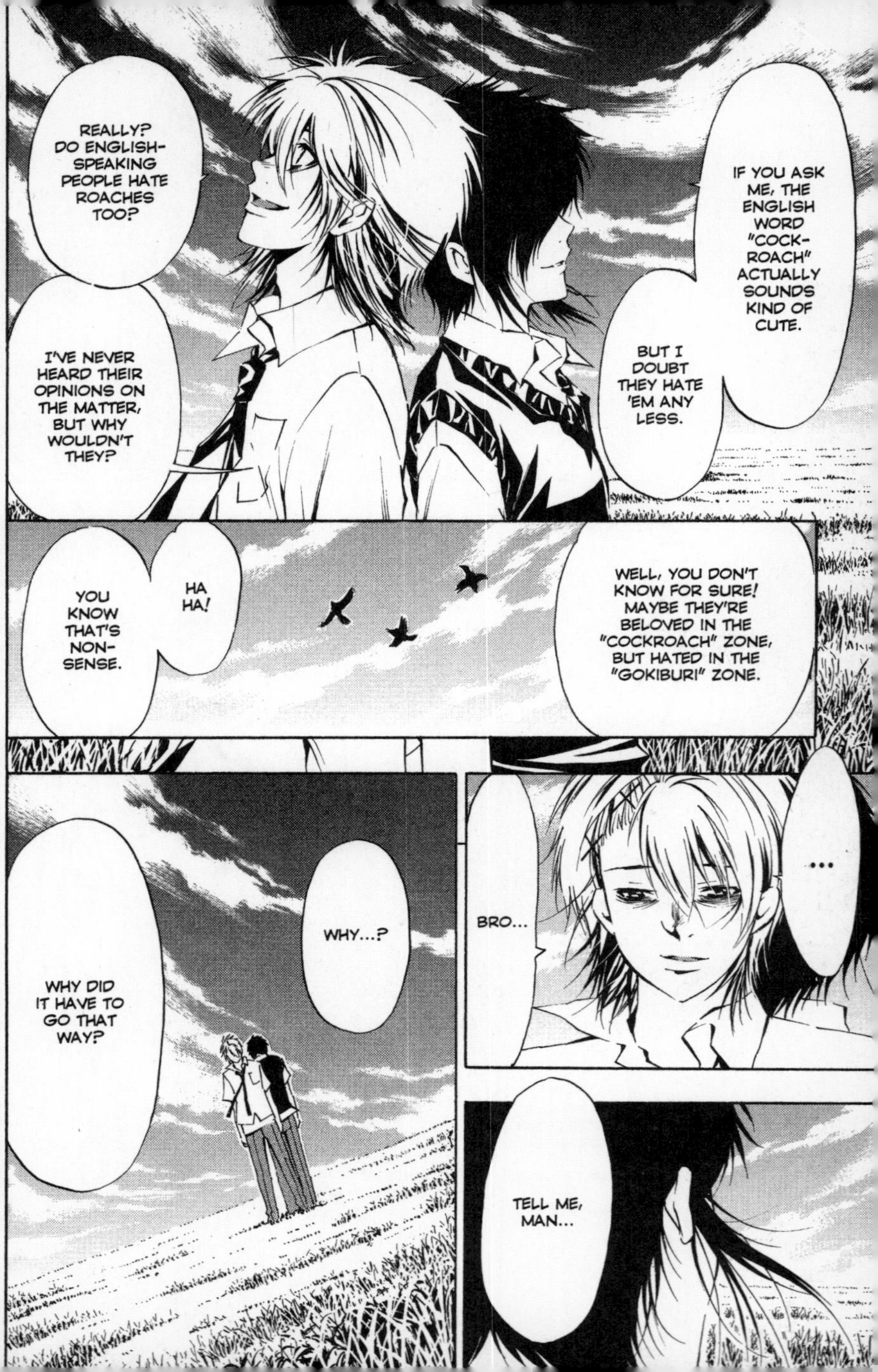
IF YOU ASK ME, THE ENGLISH WORD "COCK-ROACH" ACTUALLY SOUNDS KIND OF CUTE.
BUT I DOUBT THEY HATE 'EM ANY LESS.
REALLY? DO ENGLISH-SPEAKING PEOPLE HATE ROACHES TOO?
I'VE NEVER HEARD THEIR OPINIONS ON THE MATTER, BUT WHY WOULDN'T THEY?
WELL, YOU DON'T KNOW FOR SURE! MAYBE THEY'RE BELOVED IN THE "COCKROACH" ZONE, BUT HATED IN THE "GOKIBURI" ZONE.
HA HA!
YOU KNOW THAT'S NON-SENSE.
...
BRO...
TELL ME, MAN...
WHY...?
WHY DID IT HAVE TO GO THAT WAY?

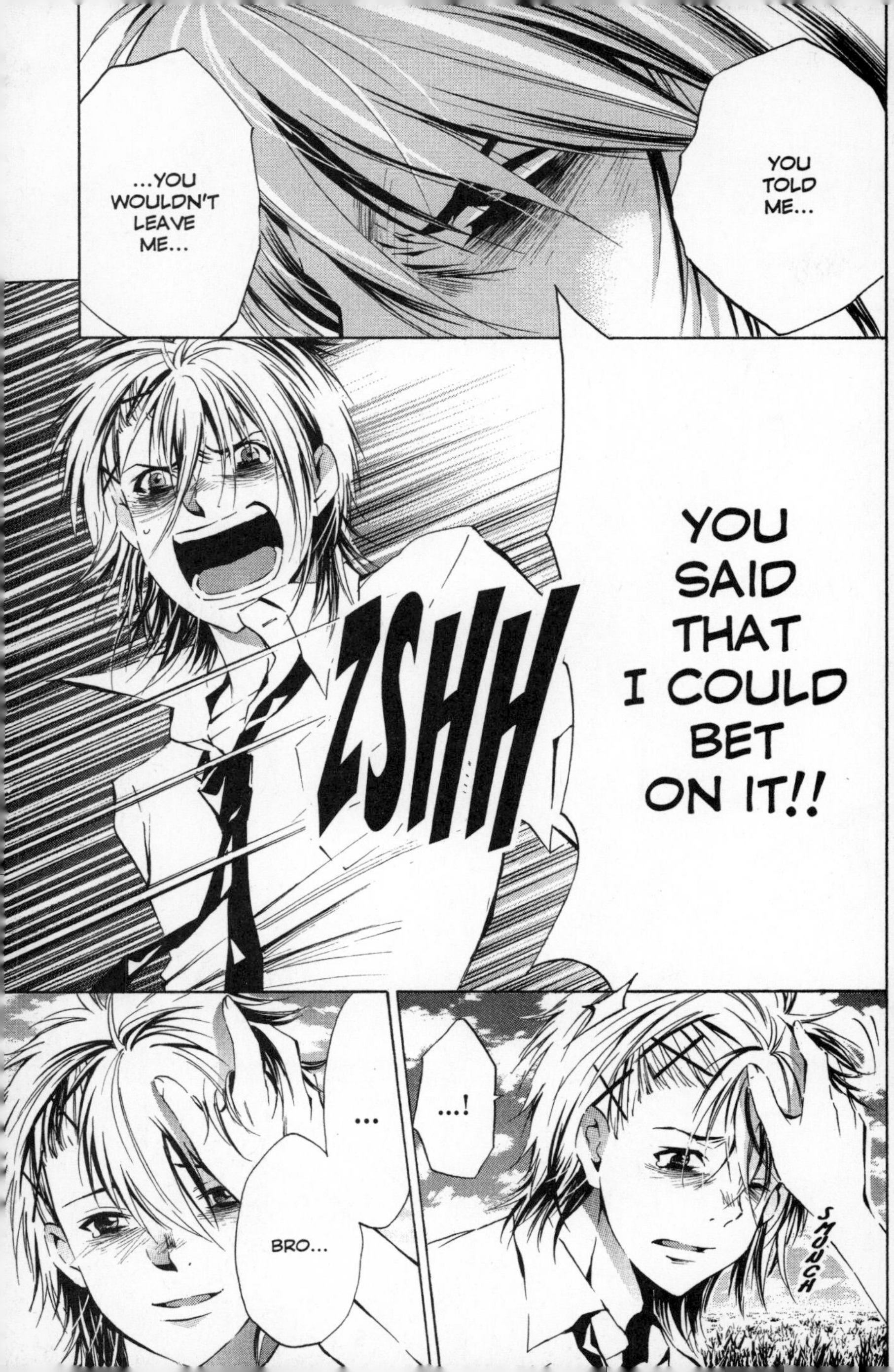
YOU TOLD ME...
...YOU WOULDN'T LEAVE ME...
YOU SAID THAT I COULD BET ON IT!!
ZSHH
...!
SMOUCH
...
BRO...

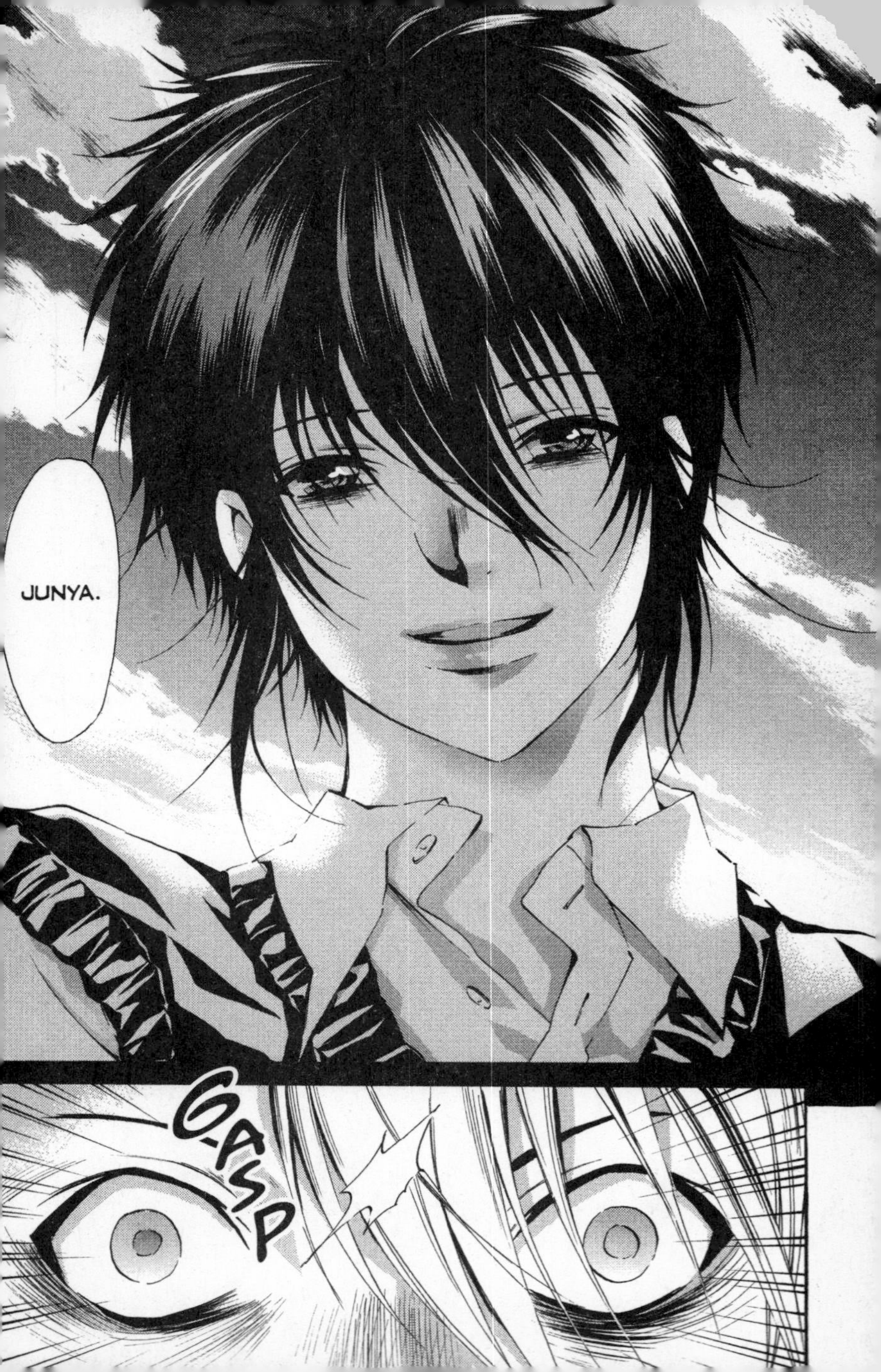
JUNYA.
GASP

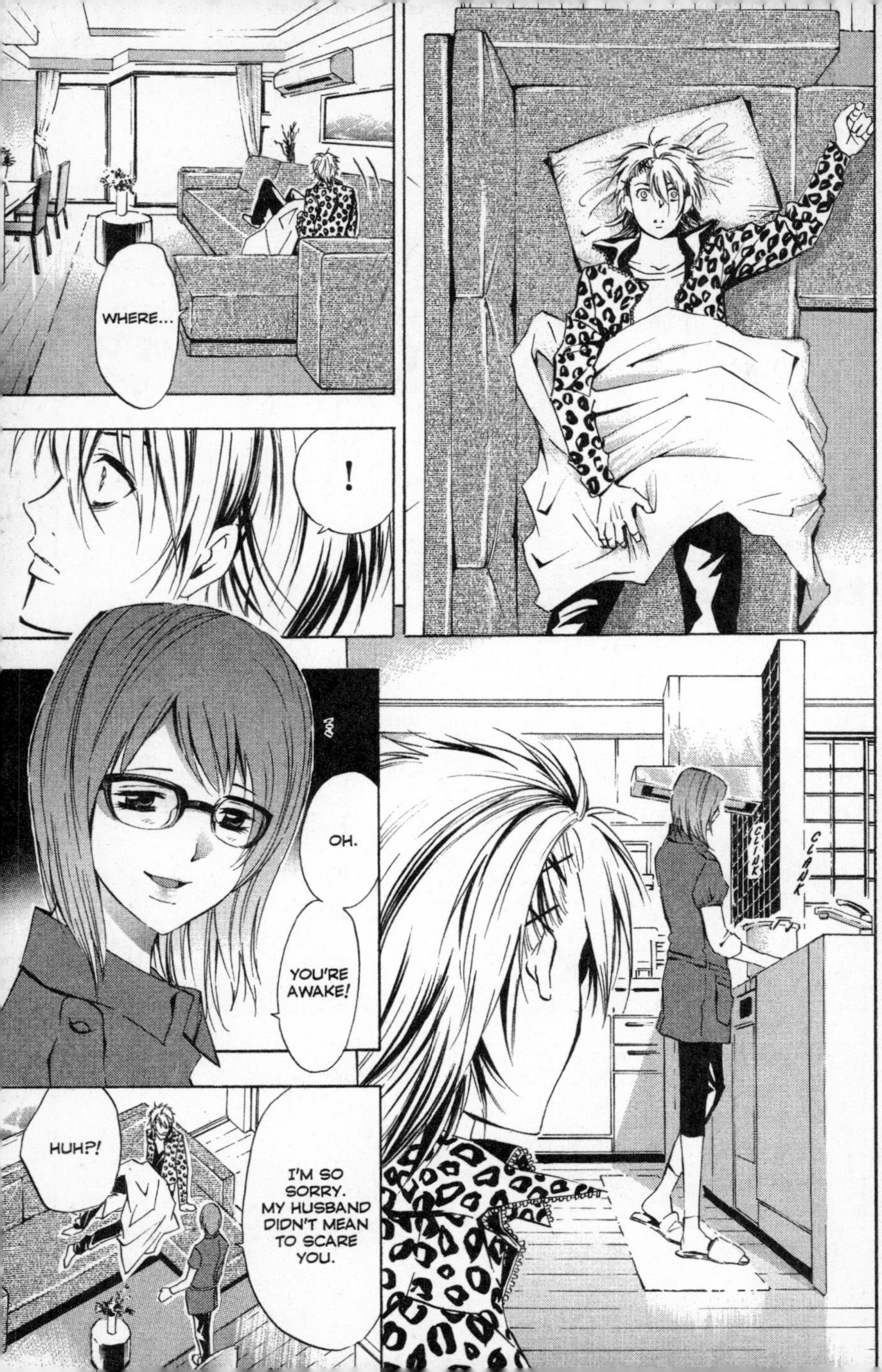
WHERE...
!
CLANK
CLINK
OH.
YOU'RE AWAKE!
I'M SO SORRY. MY HUSBAND DIDN'T MEAN TO SCARE YOU.
HUH?!

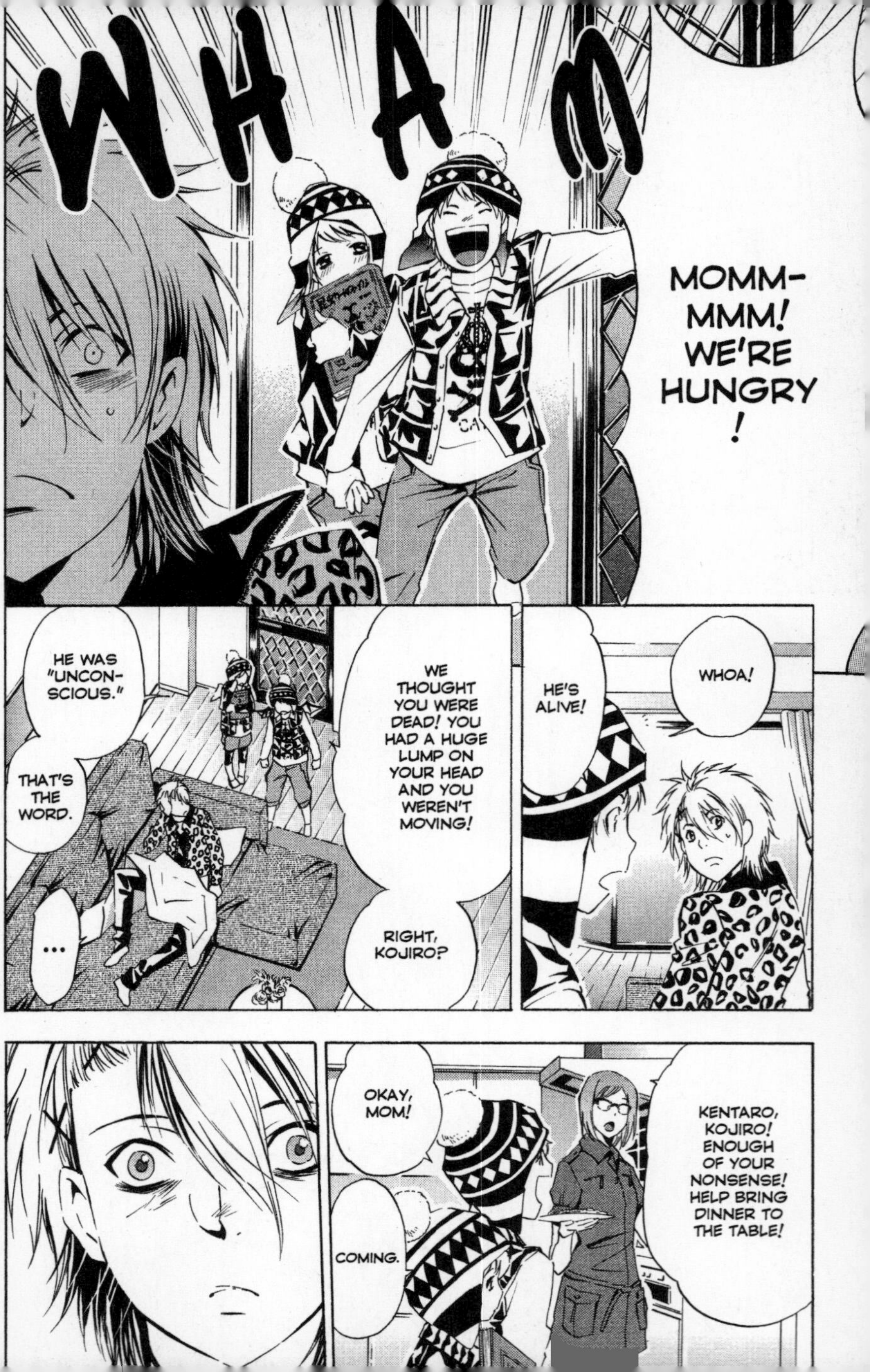
WHAM
MOMM-MMM! WE'RE HUNGRY!
WHOA!
HE'S ALIVE!
WE THOUGHT YOU WERE DEAD! YOU HAD A HUGE LUMP ON YOUR HEAD AND YOU WEREN'T MOVING!
RIGHT, KOJIRO?
HE WAS "UNCONSCIOUS."
THAT'S THE WORD.
...
KENTARO, KOJIRO! ENOUGH OF YOUR NONSENSE! HELP BRING DINNER TO THE TABLE!
OKAY, MOM!
COMING.

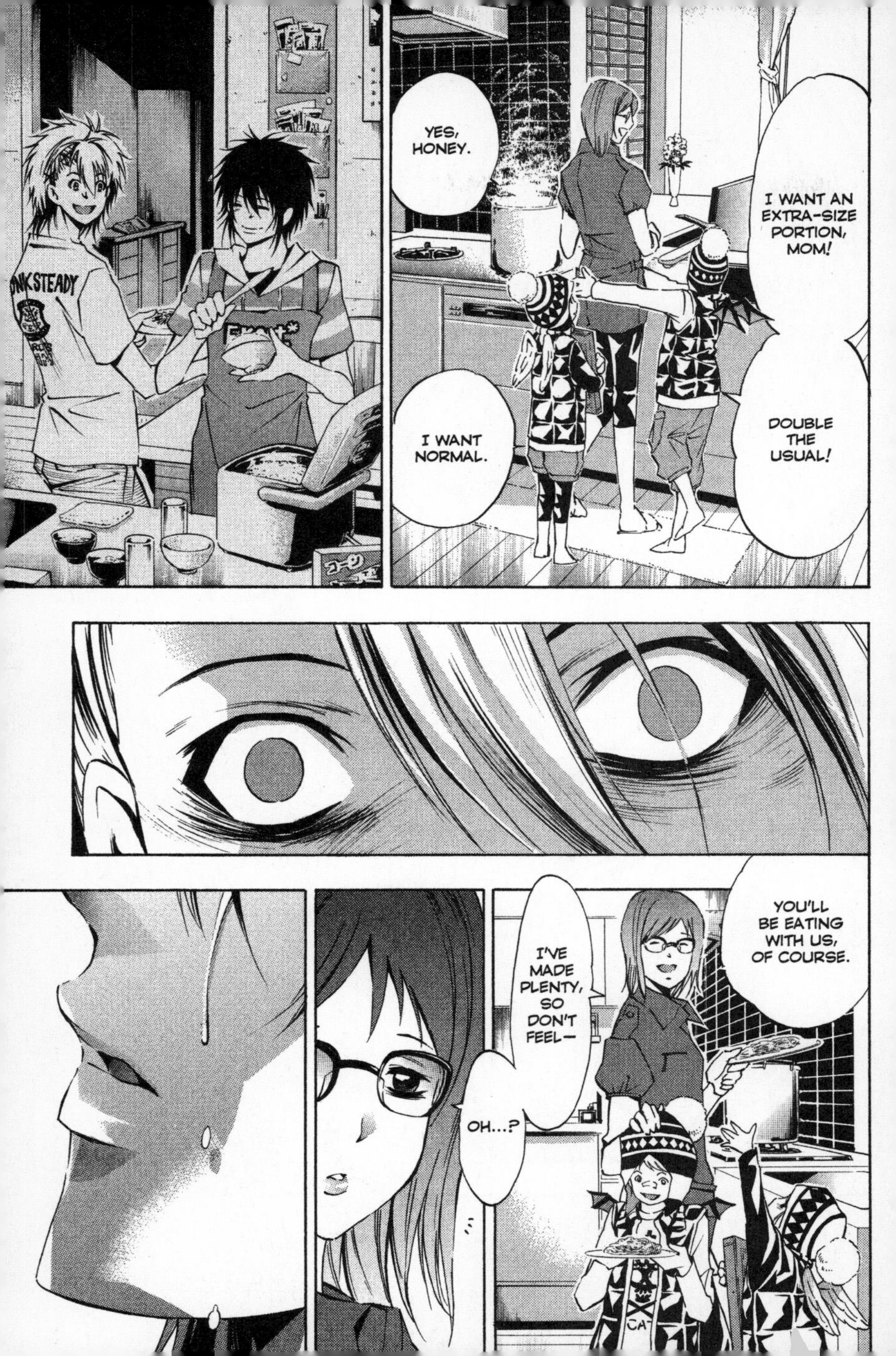
I WANT AN EXTRA-SIZE PORTION, MOM!
YES, HONEY.
DOUBLE THE USUAL!
I WANT NORMAL.
YOU'LL BE EATING WITH US, OF COURSE.
I'VE MADE PLENTY, SO DON'T FEEL—
OH...?

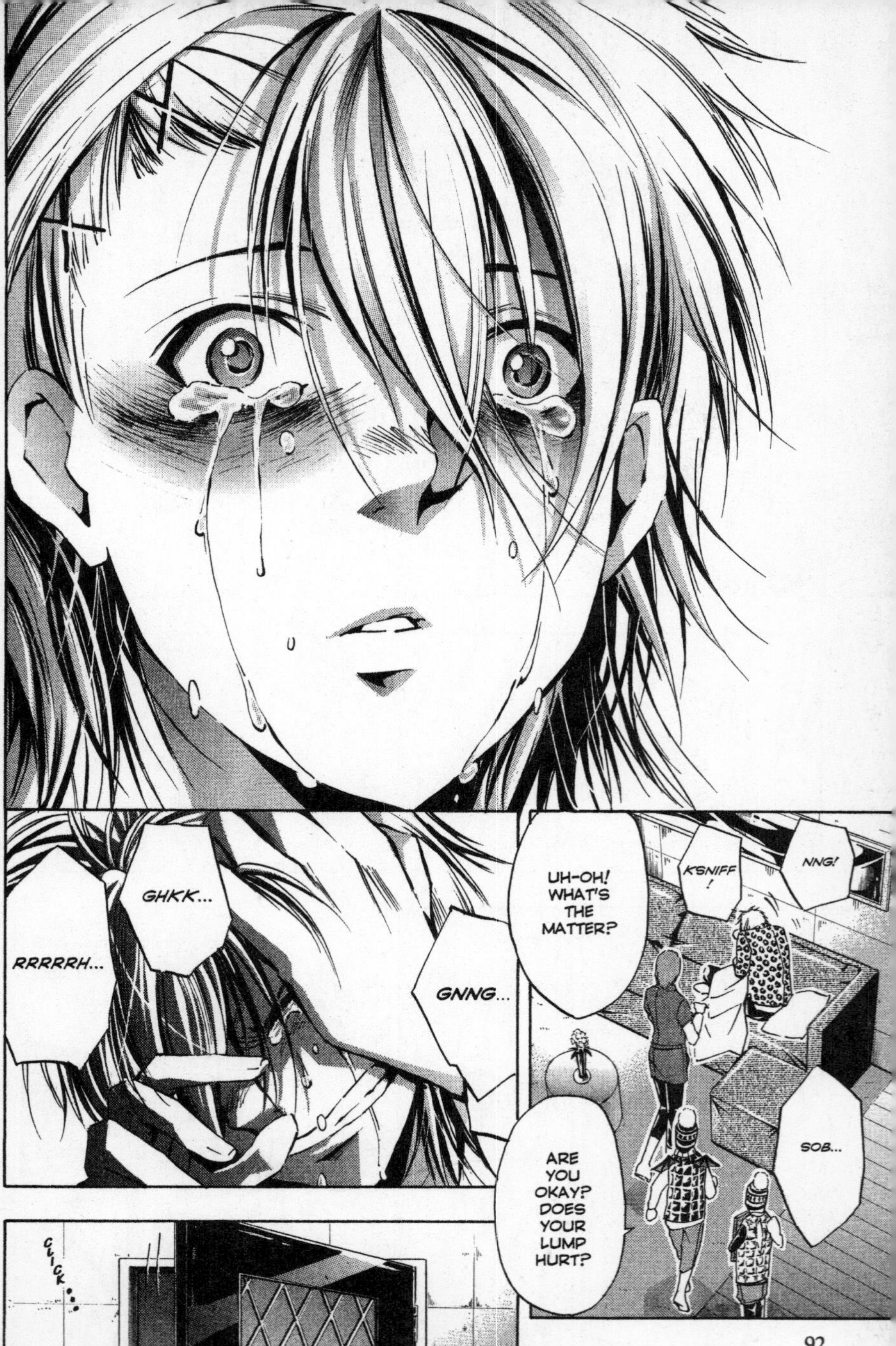
NNG!
K'SNIFF!
UH-OH! WHAT'S THE MATTER?
SOB...
ARE YOU OKAY? DOES YOUR LUMP HURT?
GNNG...
GHKK...
RRRRRH...
CLICK

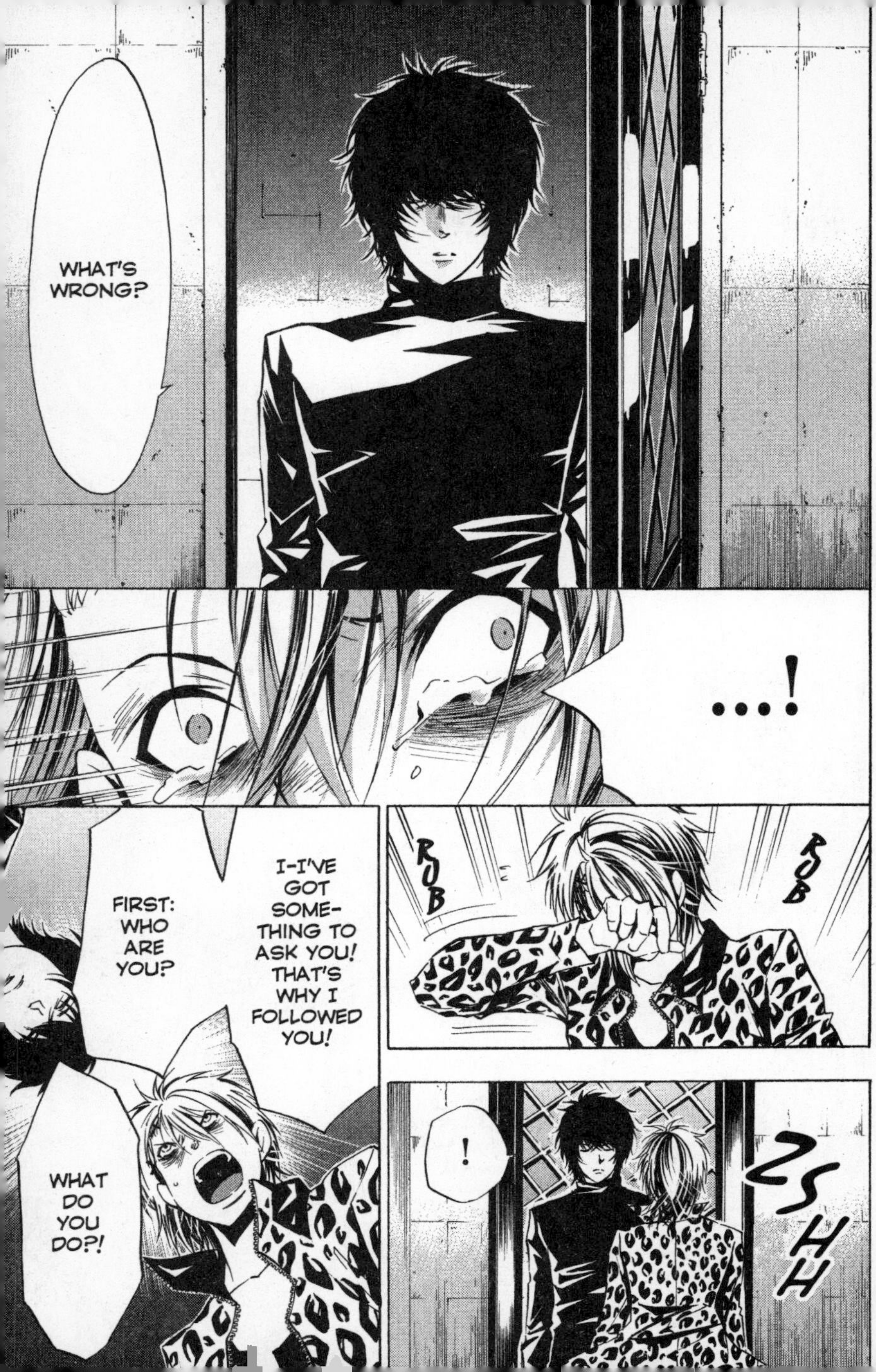
WHAT'S WRONG?
...!
RUB
RUB
!
ZSHH
I-I'VE GOT SOMETHING TO ASK YOU! THAT'S WHY I FOLLOWED YOU!
FIRST: WHO ARE YOU?
WHAT DO YOU DO?!

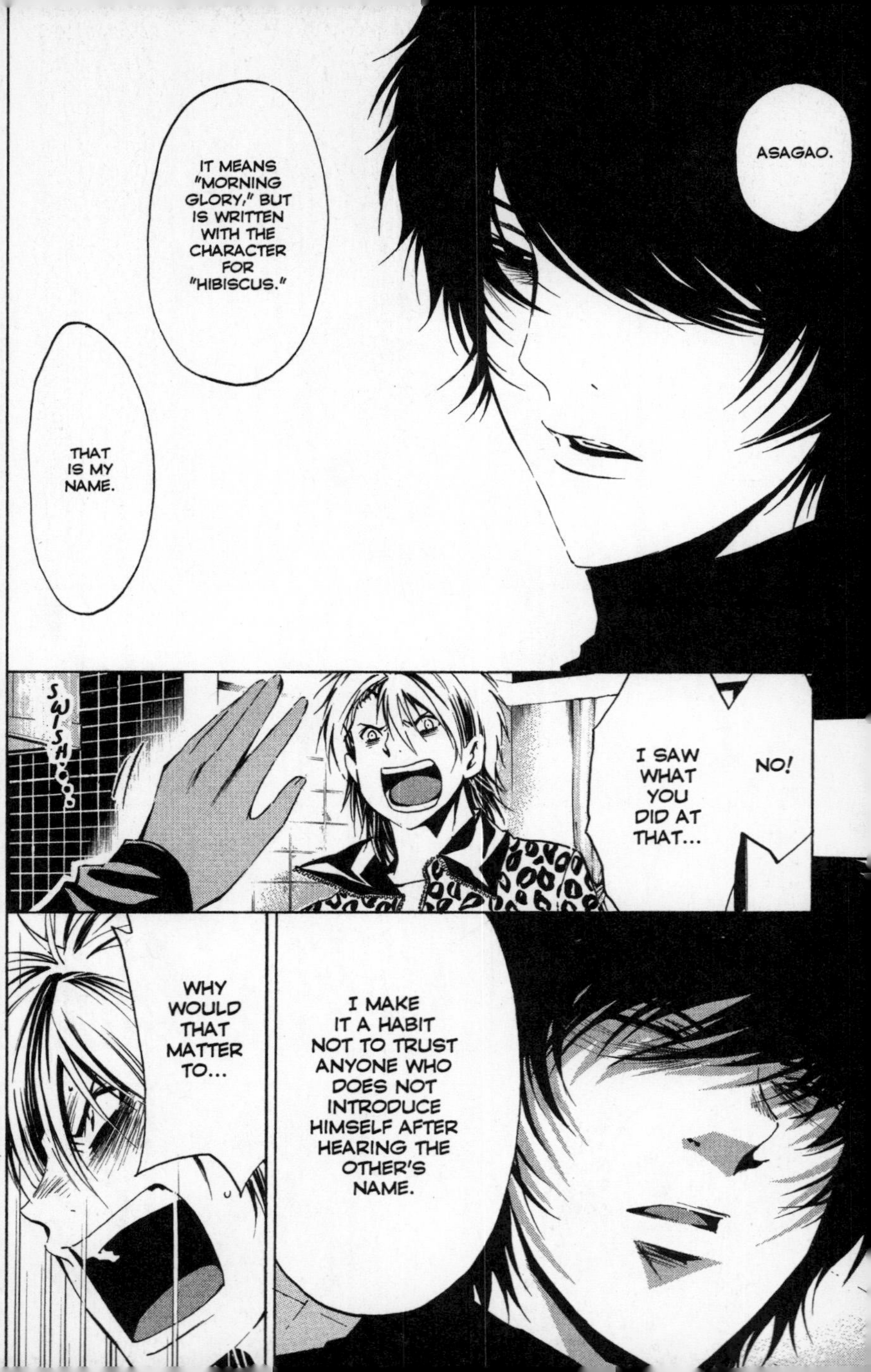
ASAGAO.
IT MEANS "MORNING GLORY," BUT IS WRITTEN WITH THE CHARACTER FOR "HIBISCUS."
THAT IS MY NAME.
NO!
I SAW WHAT YOU DID AT THAT...
SWISHOO
I MAKE IT A HABIT NOT TO TRUST ANYONE WHO DOES NOT INTRODUCE HIMSELF AFTER HEARING THE OTHER'S NAME.
WHY WOULD THAT MATTER TO...

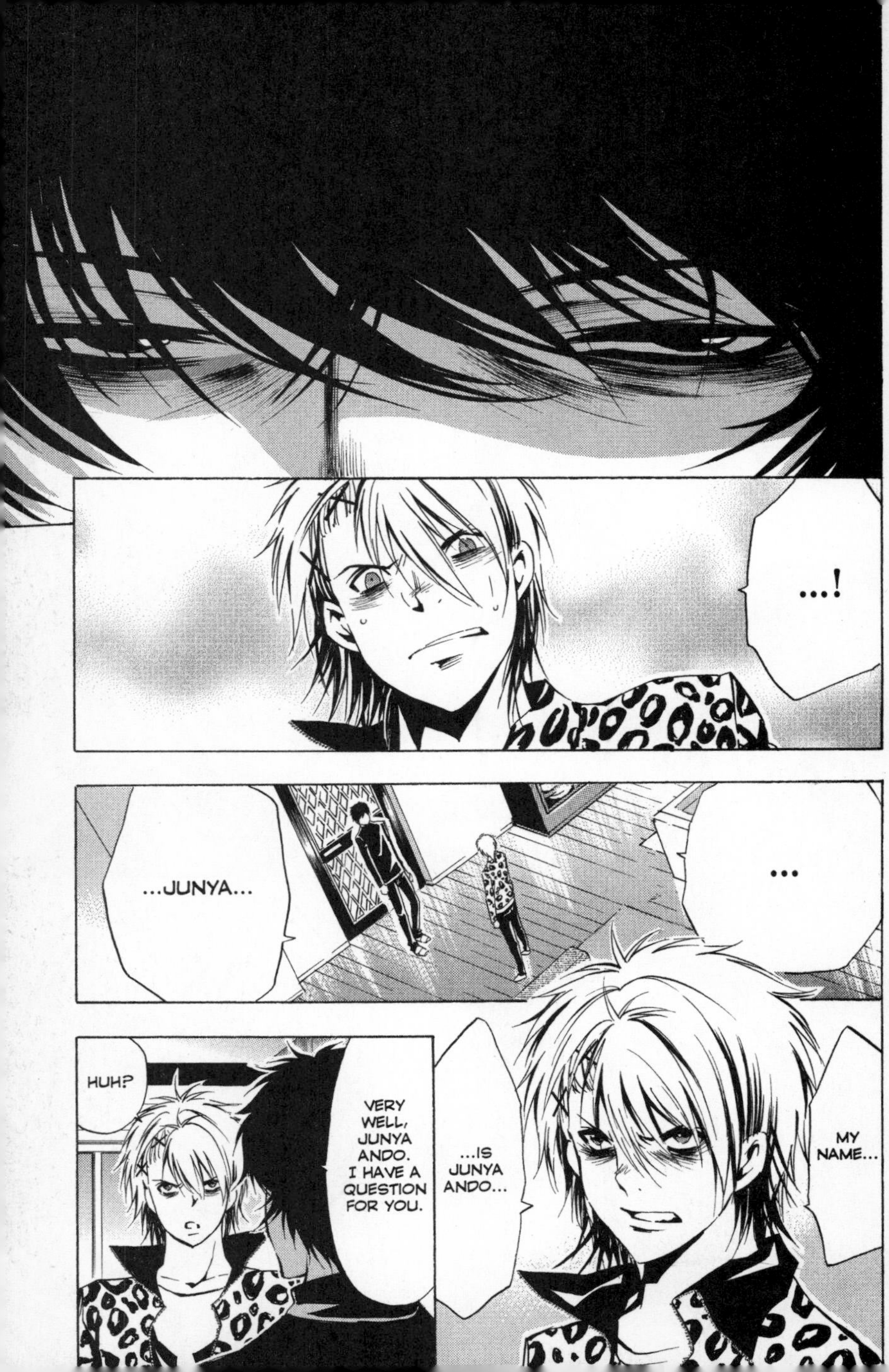
...!
...
...JUNYA...
MY NAME...
...IS JUNYA ANDO...
VERY WELL, JUNYA ANDO. I HAVE A QUESTION FOR YOU.
HUH?

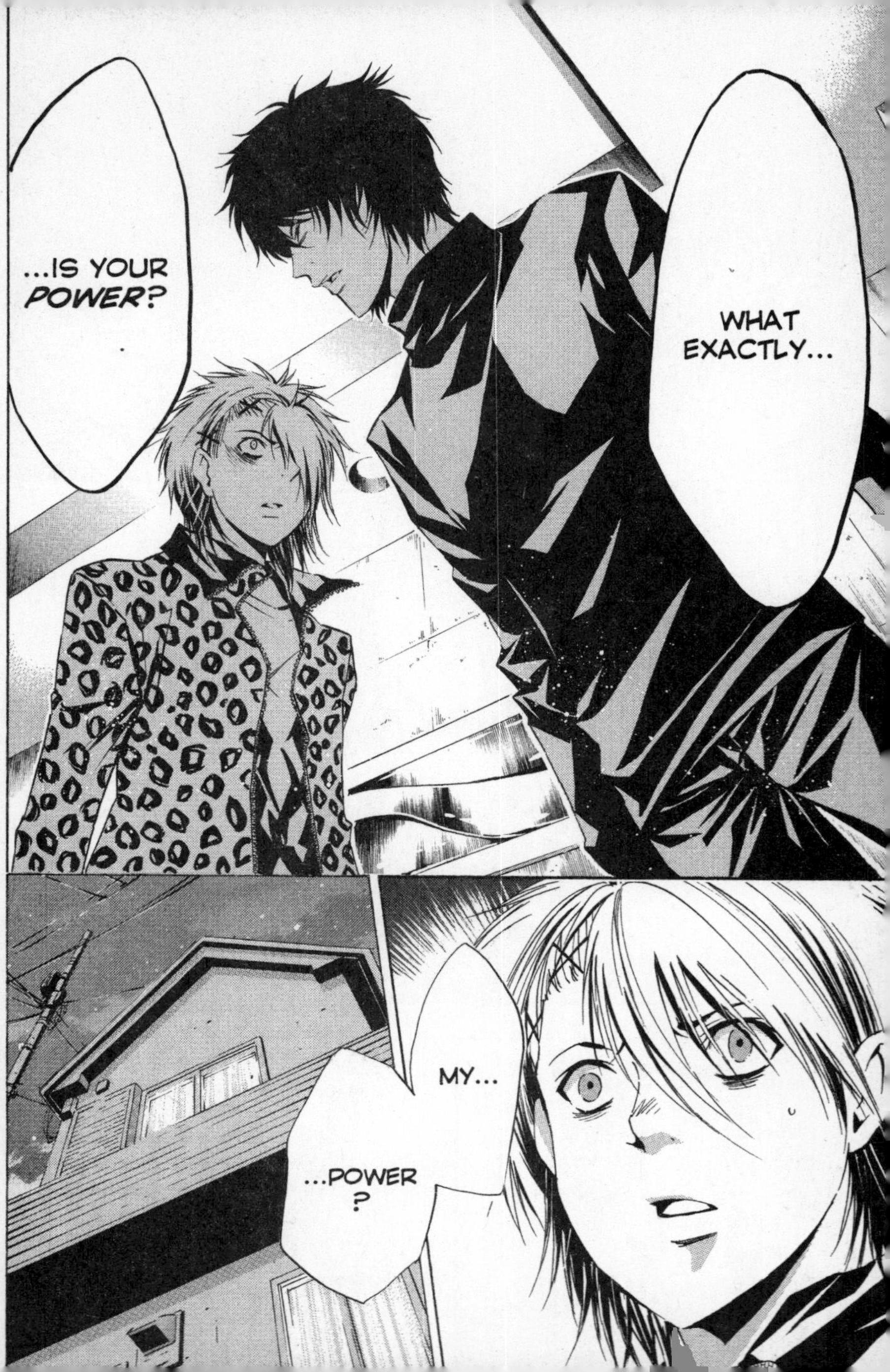
WHAT EXACTLY...
...IS YOUR *POWER*?
MY...
...POWER ?

Chapter 73 Claretta

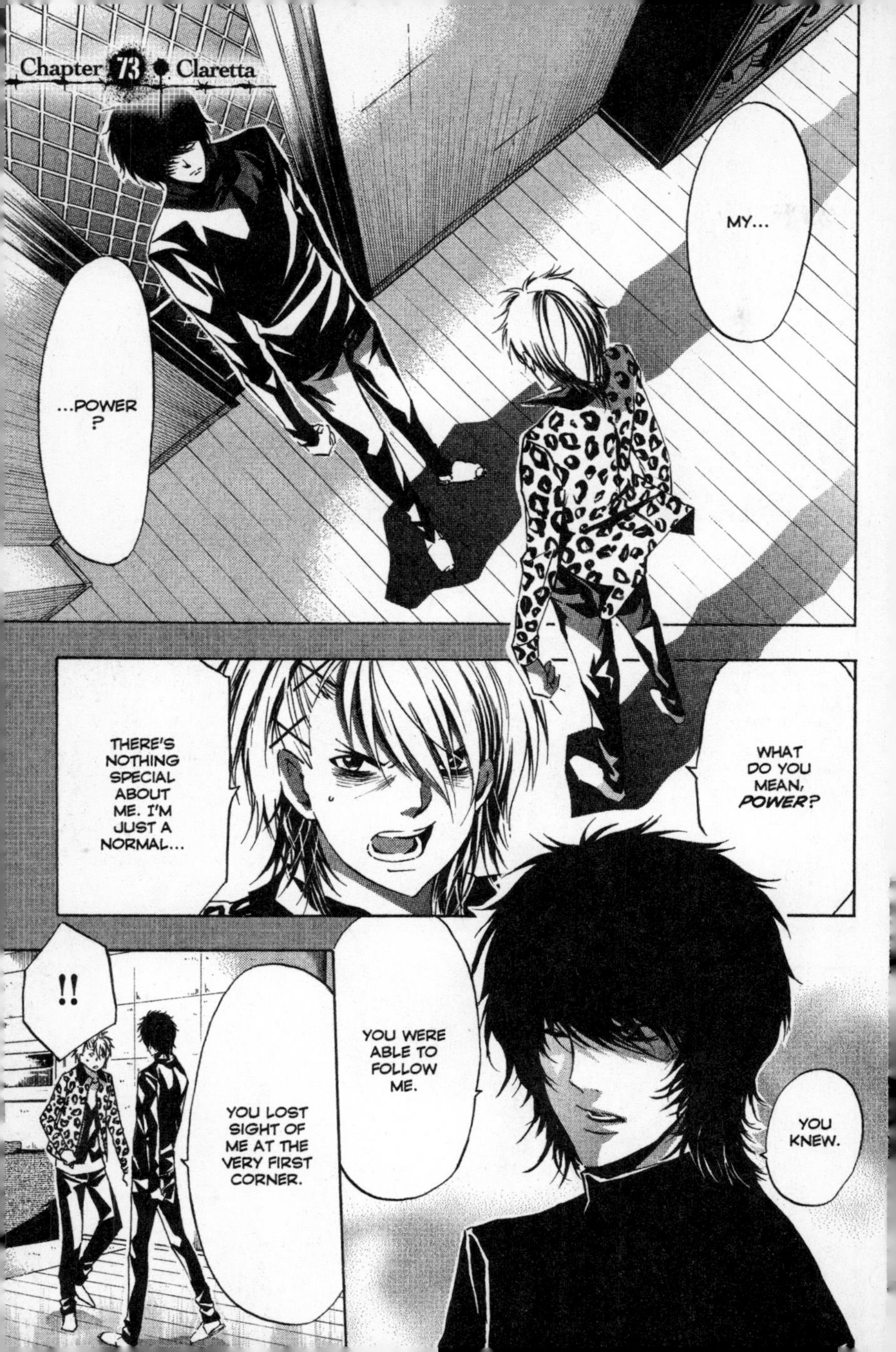
MY...
...POWER?
WHAT DO YOU MEAN, *POWER*?
THERE'S NOTHING SPECIAL ABOUT ME. I'M JUST A NORMAL...
YOU KNEW.
YOU WERE ABLE TO FOLLOW ME.
YOU LOST SIGHT OF ME AT THE VERY FIRST CORNER.
!!

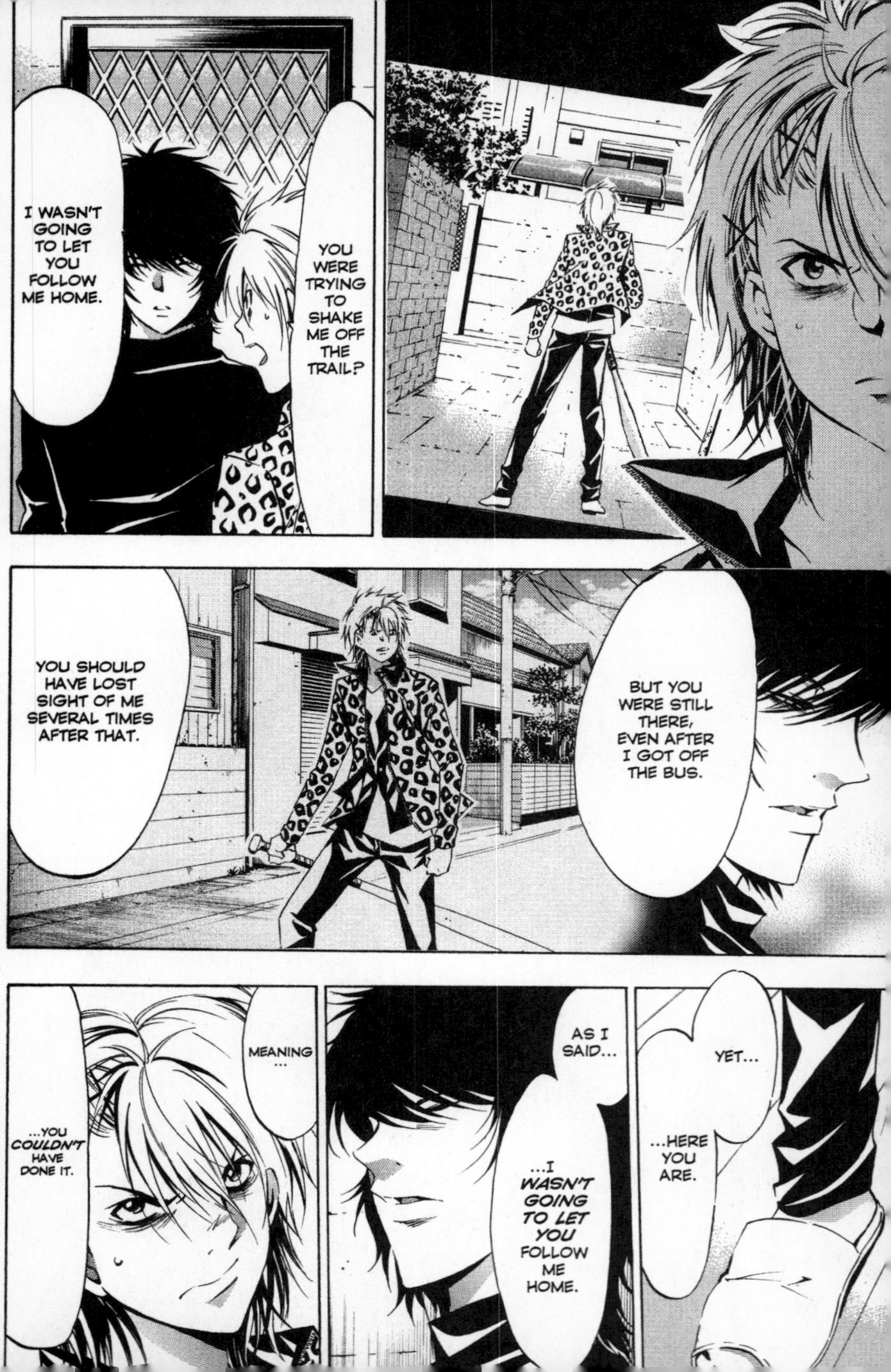
YOU WERE TRYING TO SHAKE ME OFF THE TRAIL?
I WASN'T GOING TO LET YOU FOLLOW ME HOME.
BUT YOU WERE STILL THERE, EVEN AFTER I GOT OFF THE BUS.
YOU SHOULD HAVE LOST SIGHT OF ME SEVERAL TIMES AFTER THAT.
YET...
...HERE YOU ARE.
AS I SAID...
...I *WASN'T GOING TO LET YOU* FOLLOW ME HOME.
MEANING...
...YOU *COULDN'T* HAVE DONE IT.

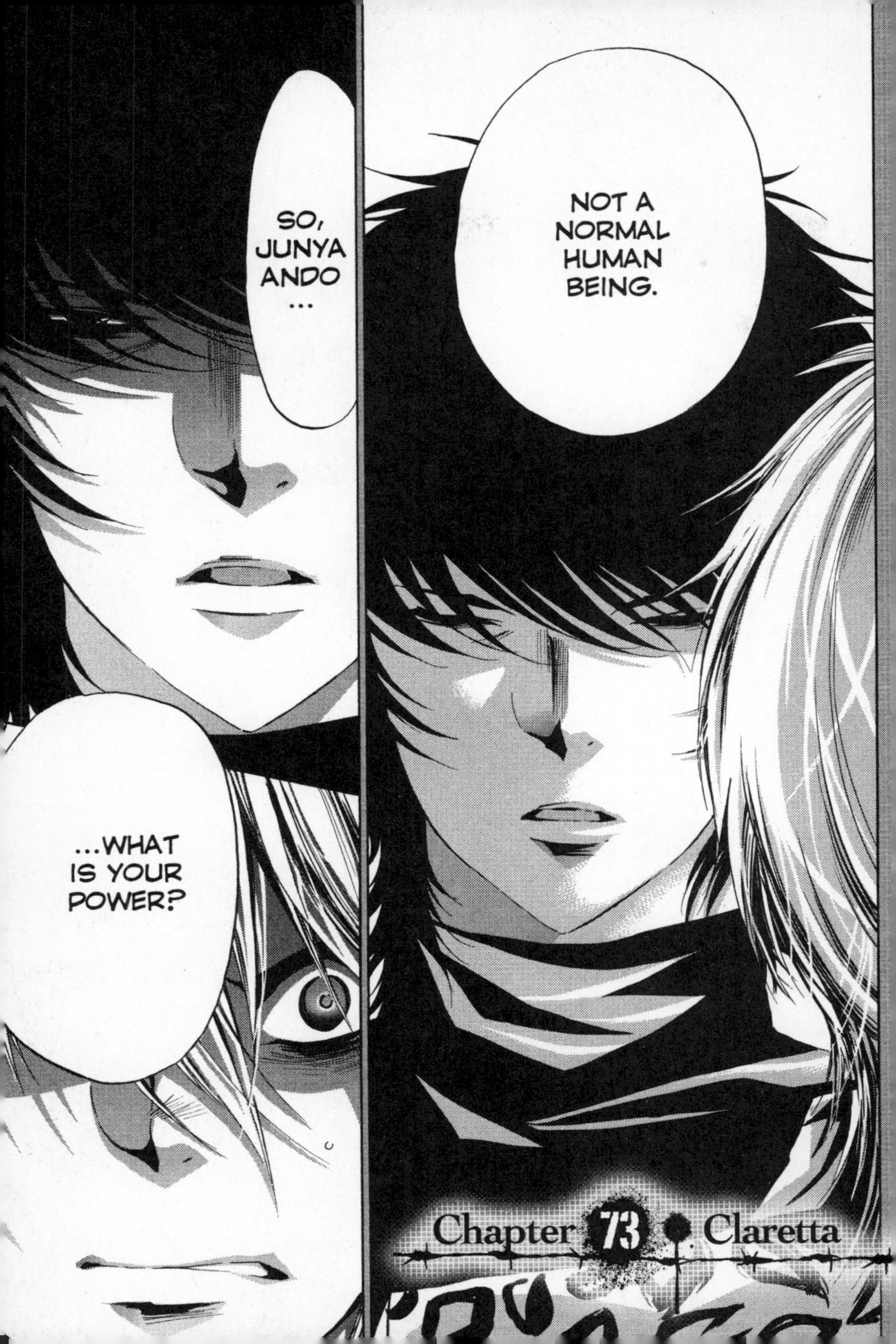
NOT A NORMAL HUMAN BEING.
Chapter 73 Claretta
SO, JUNYA ANDO ...
...WHAT IS YOUR POWER?

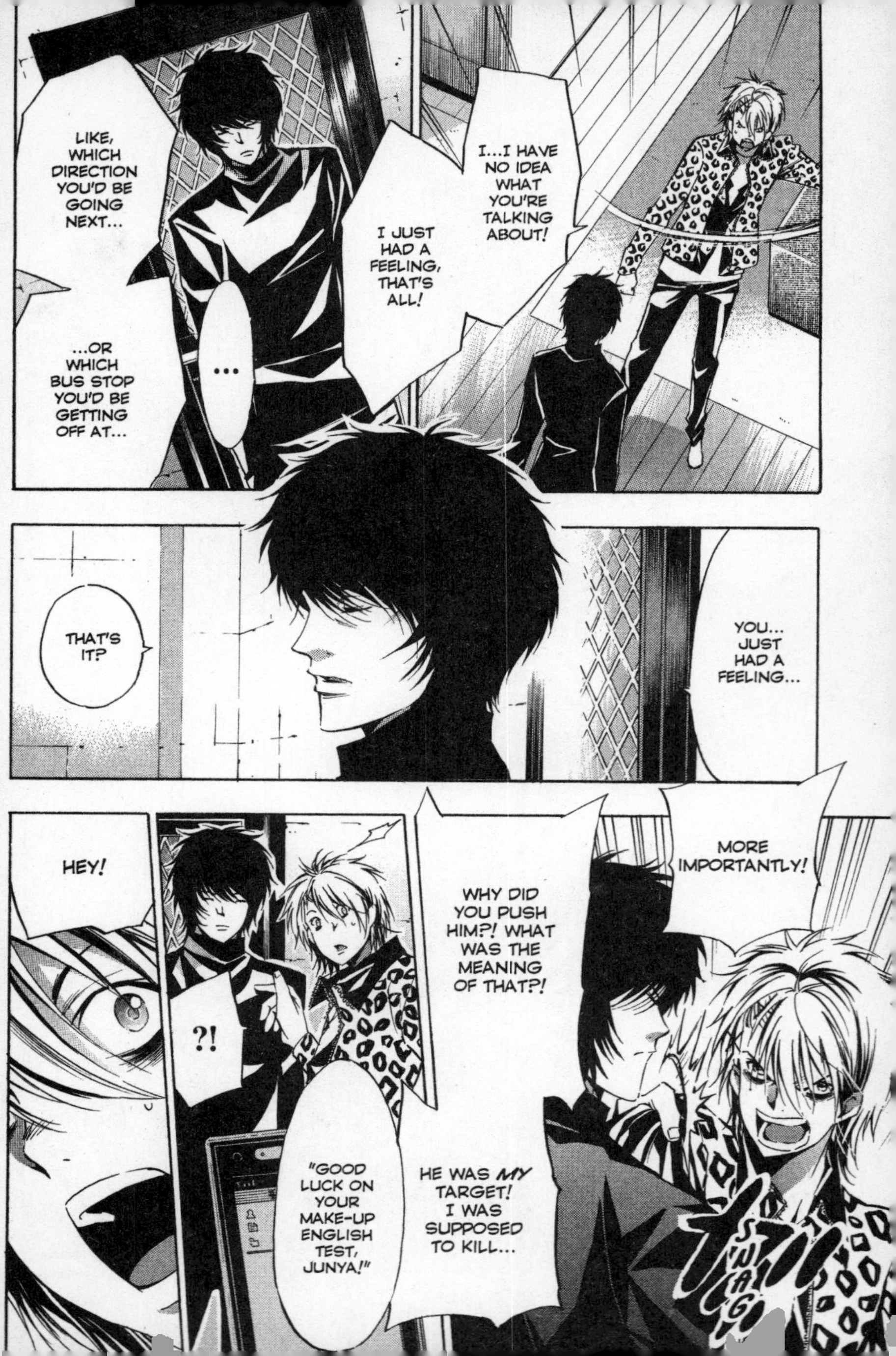
I...I HAVE NO IDEA WHAT YOU'RE TALKING ABOUT!
I JUST HAD A FEELING, THAT'S ALL!
LIKE, WHICH DIRECTION YOU'D BE GOING NEXT...
...OR WHICH BUS STOP YOU'D BE GETTING OFF AT...
...
YOU... JUST HAD A FEELING...
THAT'S IT?
MORE IMPORTANTLY!
WHY DID YOU PUSH HIM?! WHAT WAS THE MEANING OF THAT?!
HE WAS *MY* TARGET! I WAS SUPPOSED TO KILL...
SWAG
?!
"GOOD LUCK ON YOUR MAKE-UP ENGLISH TEST, JUNYA!"
HEY!

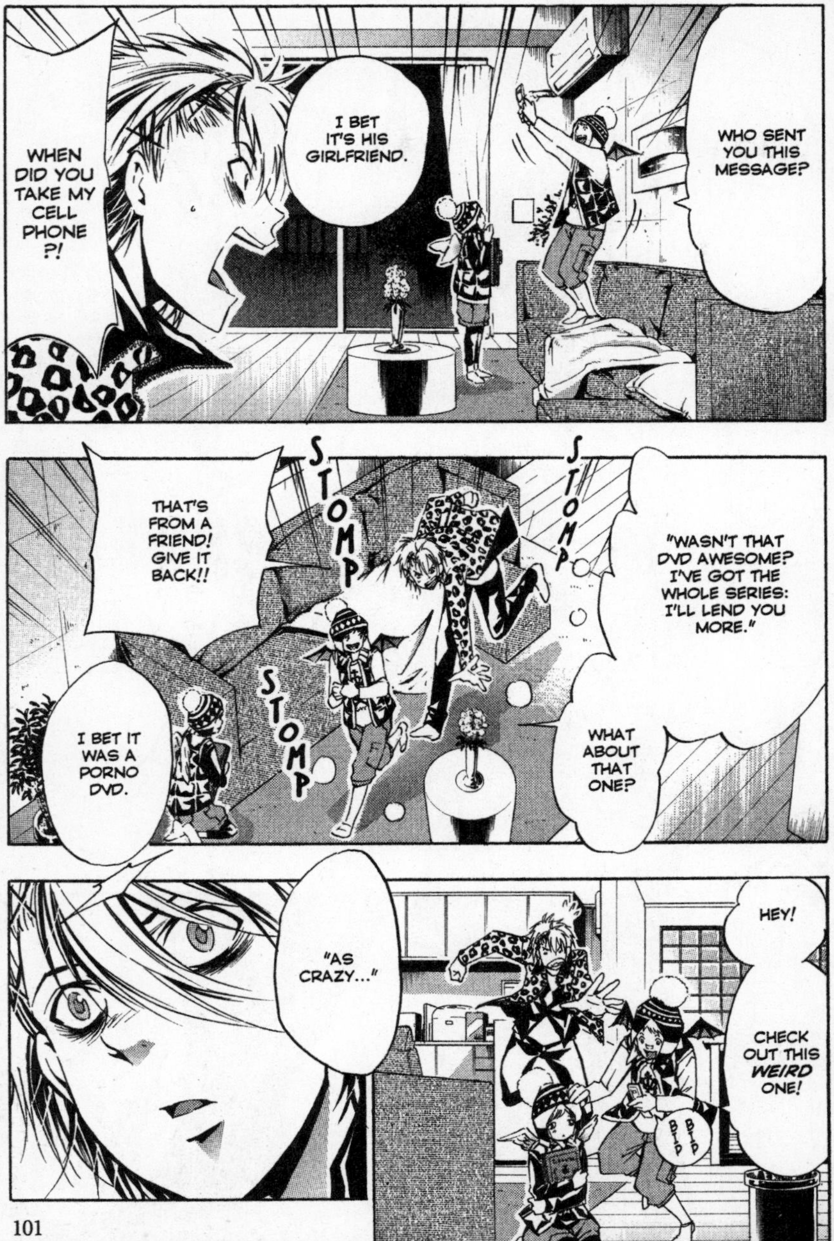
WHO SENT YOU THIS MESSAGE?
I BET IT'S HIS GIRLFRIEND.
WHEN DID YOU TAKE MY CELL PHONE ?!
"WASN'T THAT DVD AWESOME? I'VE GOT THE WHOLE SERIES: I'LL LEND YOU MORE."
STOMP
WHAT ABOUT THAT ONE?
STOMP
THAT'S FROM A FRIEND! GIVE IT BACK!!
STOMP
STOMP
I BET IT WAS A PORNO DVD.
HEY!
CHECK OUT THIS *WEIRD* ONE!
BIP BIP
"AS CRAZY..."

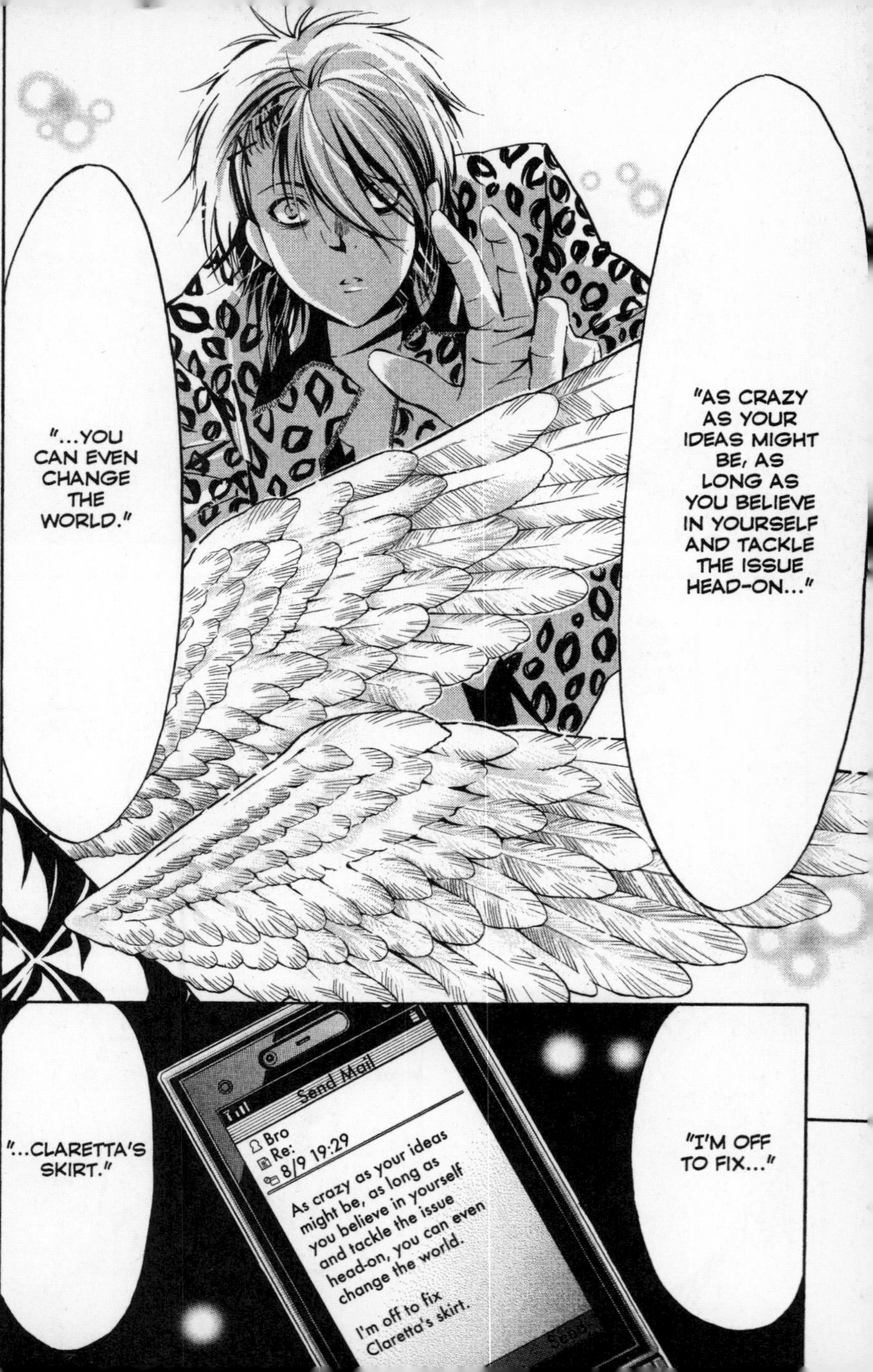
"AS CRAZY AS YOUR IDEAS MIGHT BE, AS LONG AS YOU BELIEVE IN YOURSELF AND TACKLE THE ISSUE HEAD-ON..."
"...YOU CAN EVEN CHANGE THE WORLD."
"I'M OFF TO FIX..."
Send Mail
Bro
Re:
8/9 19:29
As crazy as your ideas might be, as long as you believe in yourself and tackle the issue head-on, you can even change the world.
I'm off to fix Claretta's skirt.
"...CLARETTA'S SKIRT."

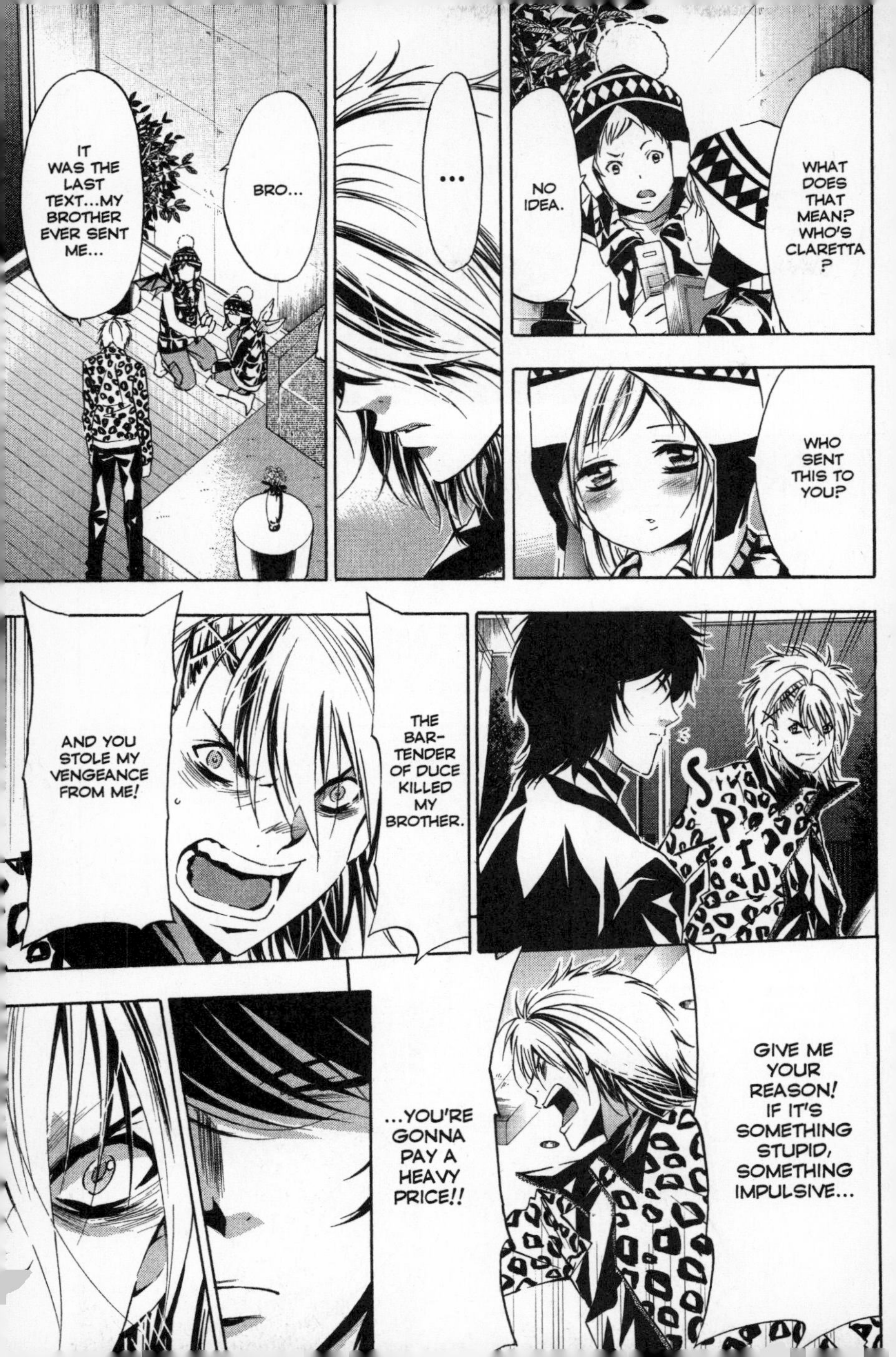
WHAT DOES THAT MEAN? WHO'S CLARETTA?
NO IDEA.
WHO SENT THIS TO YOU?
...
BRO...
IT WAS THE LAST TEXT...MY BROTHER EVER SENT ME...
THE BAR-TENDER OF DUCE KILLED MY BROTHER.
AND YOU STOLE MY VENGEANCE FROM ME!
GIVE ME YOUR REASON! IF IT'S SOMETHING STUPID, SOMETHING IMPULSIVE...
...YOU'RE GONNA PAY A HEAVY PRICE!!

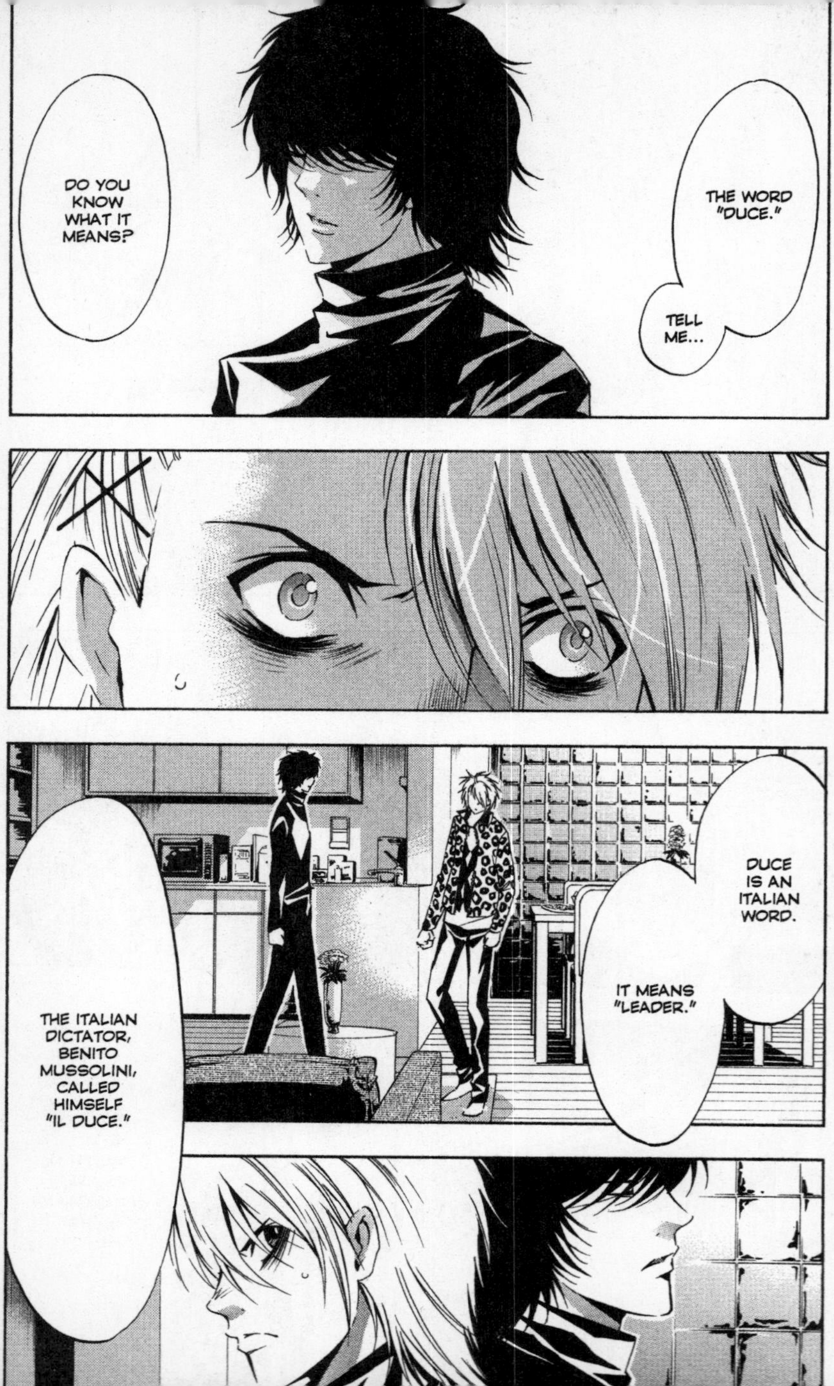
THE WORD "DUCE."
TELL ME...
DO YOU KNOW WHAT IT MEANS?
DUCE IS AN ITALIAN WORD.
IT MEANS "LEADER."
THE ITALIAN DICTATOR, BENITO MUSSOLINI, CALLED HIMSELF "IL DUCE."

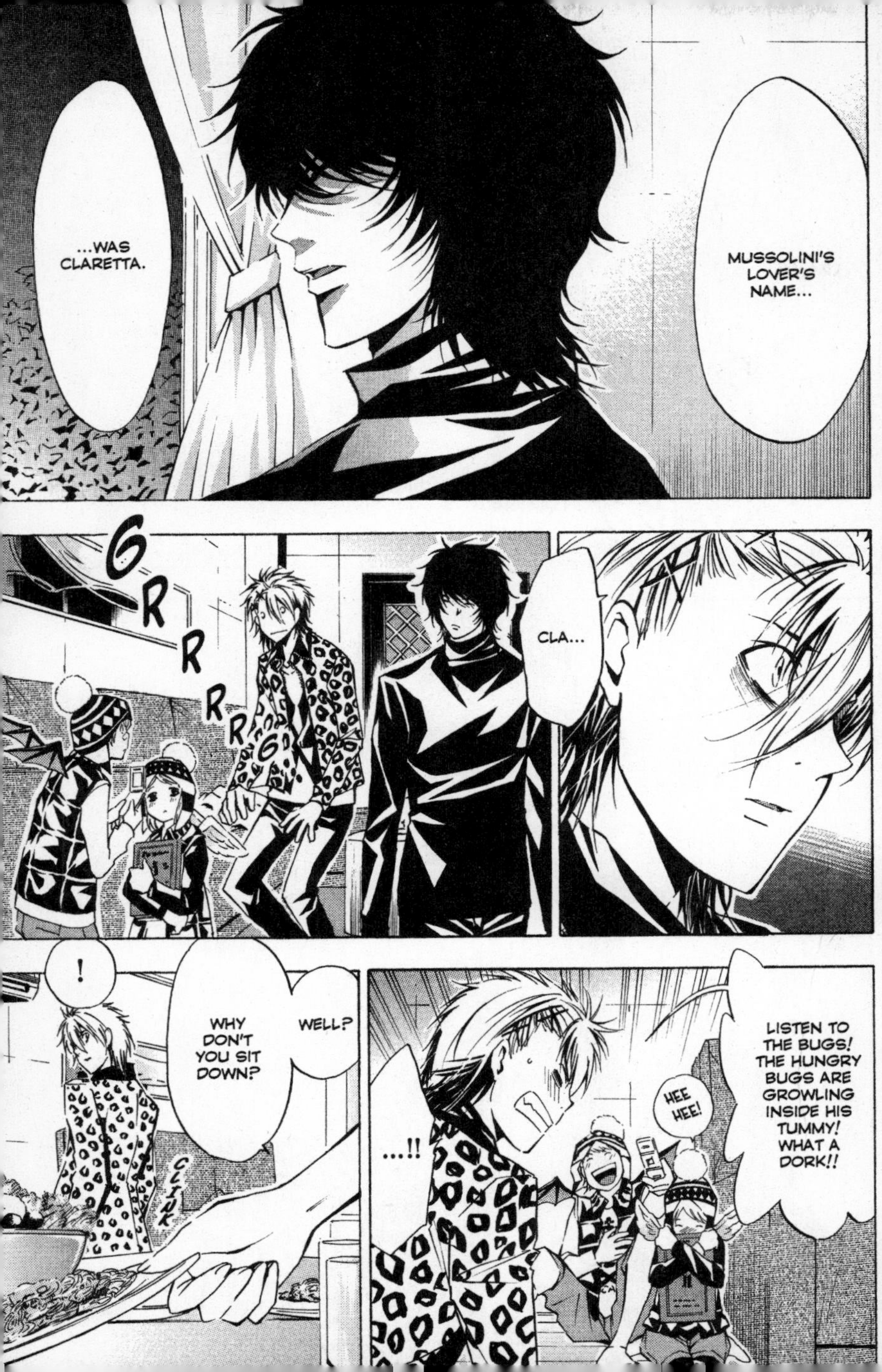

MUSSOLINI'S LOVER'S NAME...
...WAS CLARETTA.
CLA...
GRRRRG
LISTEN TO THE BUGS! THE HUNGRY BUGS ARE GROWLING INSIDE HIS TUMMY! WHAT A DORK!!
HEE HEE!
...!!
!
WELL?
WHY DON'T YOU SIT DOWN?
CLINK

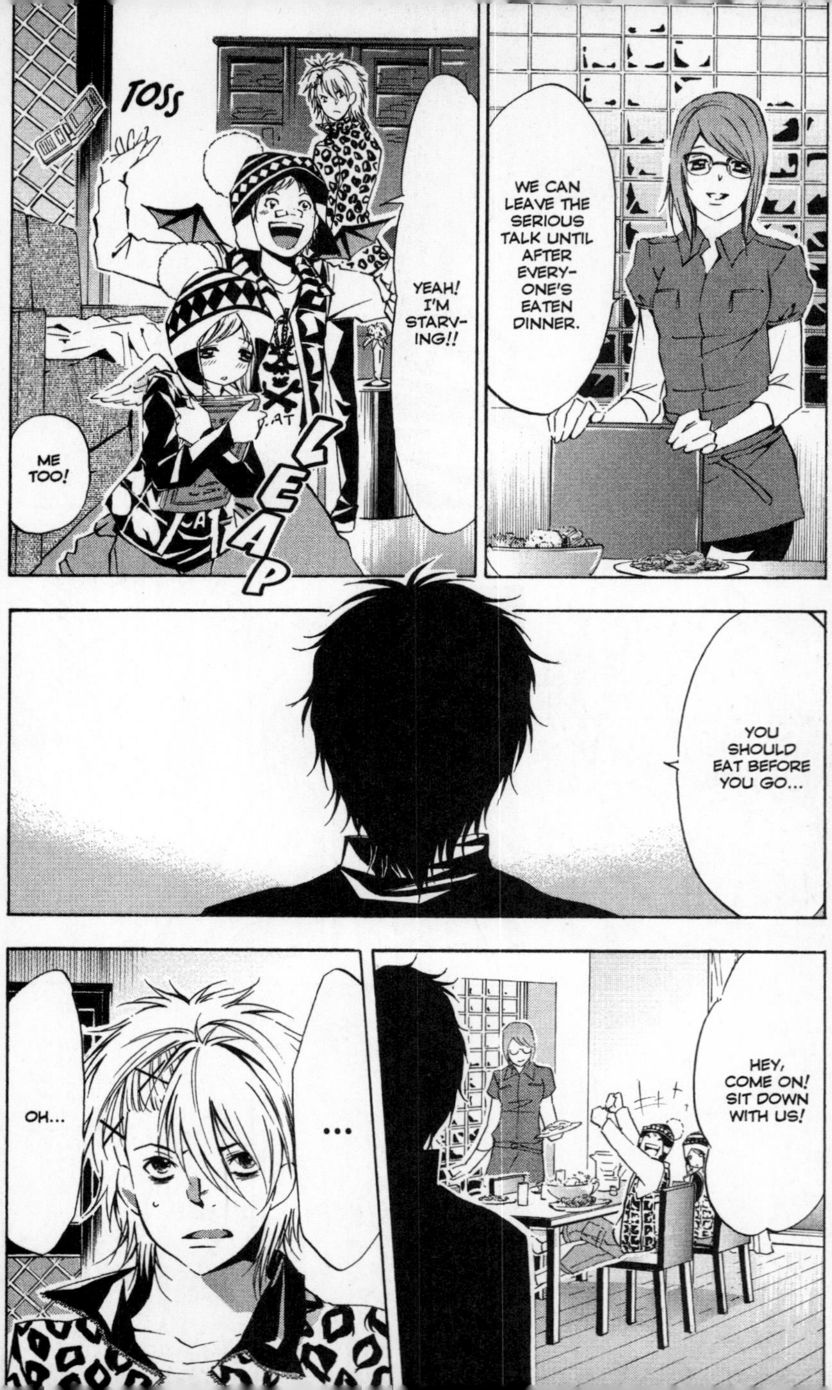
WE CAN LEAVE THE SERIOUS TALK UNTIL AFTER EVERYONE'S EATEN DINNER.
YEAH! I'M STARVING!!
TOSS
LEAP
ME TOO!
YOU SHOULD EAT BEFORE YOU GO...
HEY, COME ON! SIT DOWN WITH US!
...
OH...

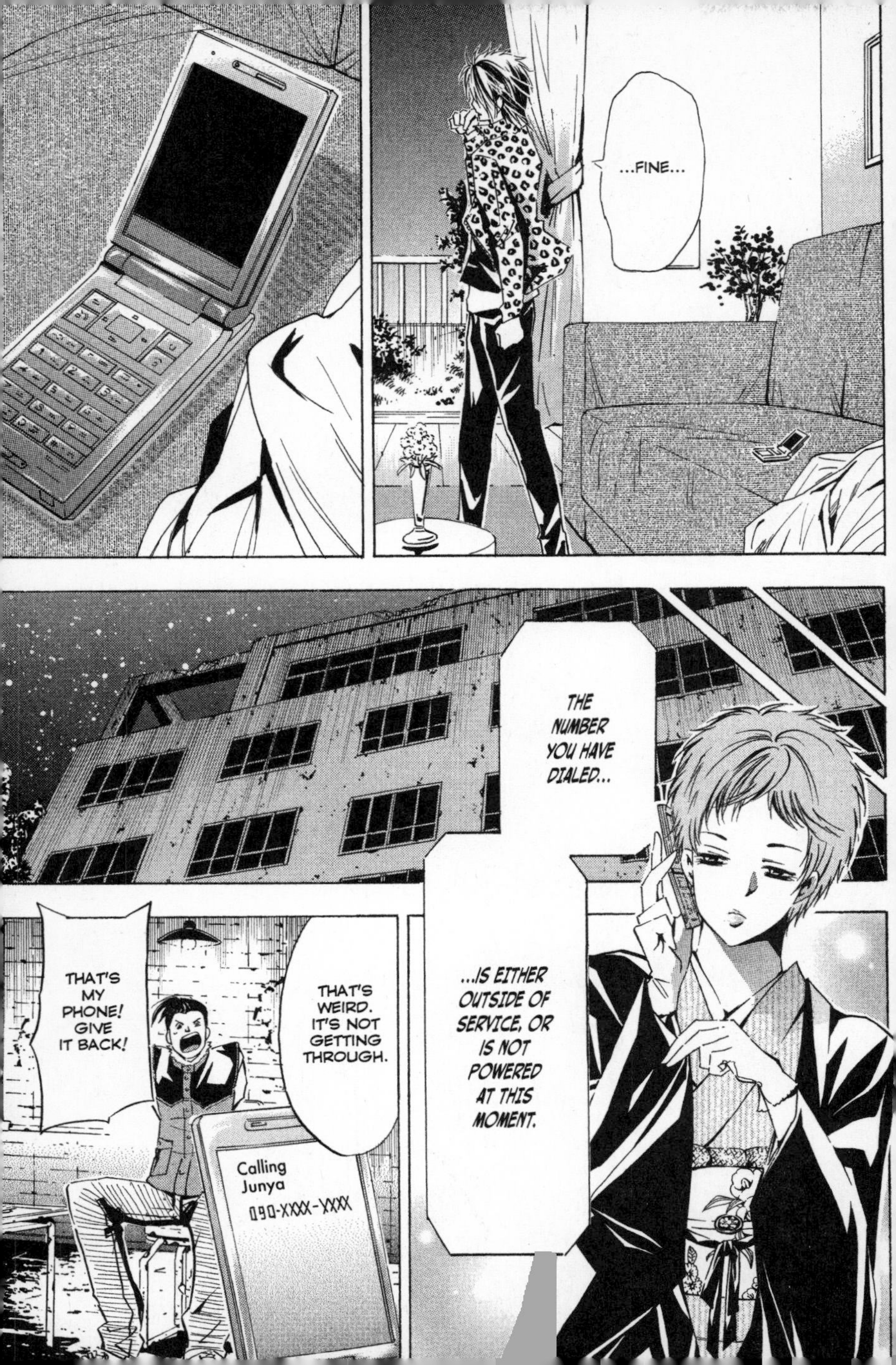
...FINE...
THE NUMBER YOU HAVE DIALED...
...IS EITHER OUTSIDE OF SERVICE, OR IS NOT POWERED AT THIS MOMENT.
THAT'S WEIRD. IT'S NOT GETTING THROUGH.
THAT'S MY PHONE! GIVE IT BACK!
Calling Junya
090-XXXX-XXXX

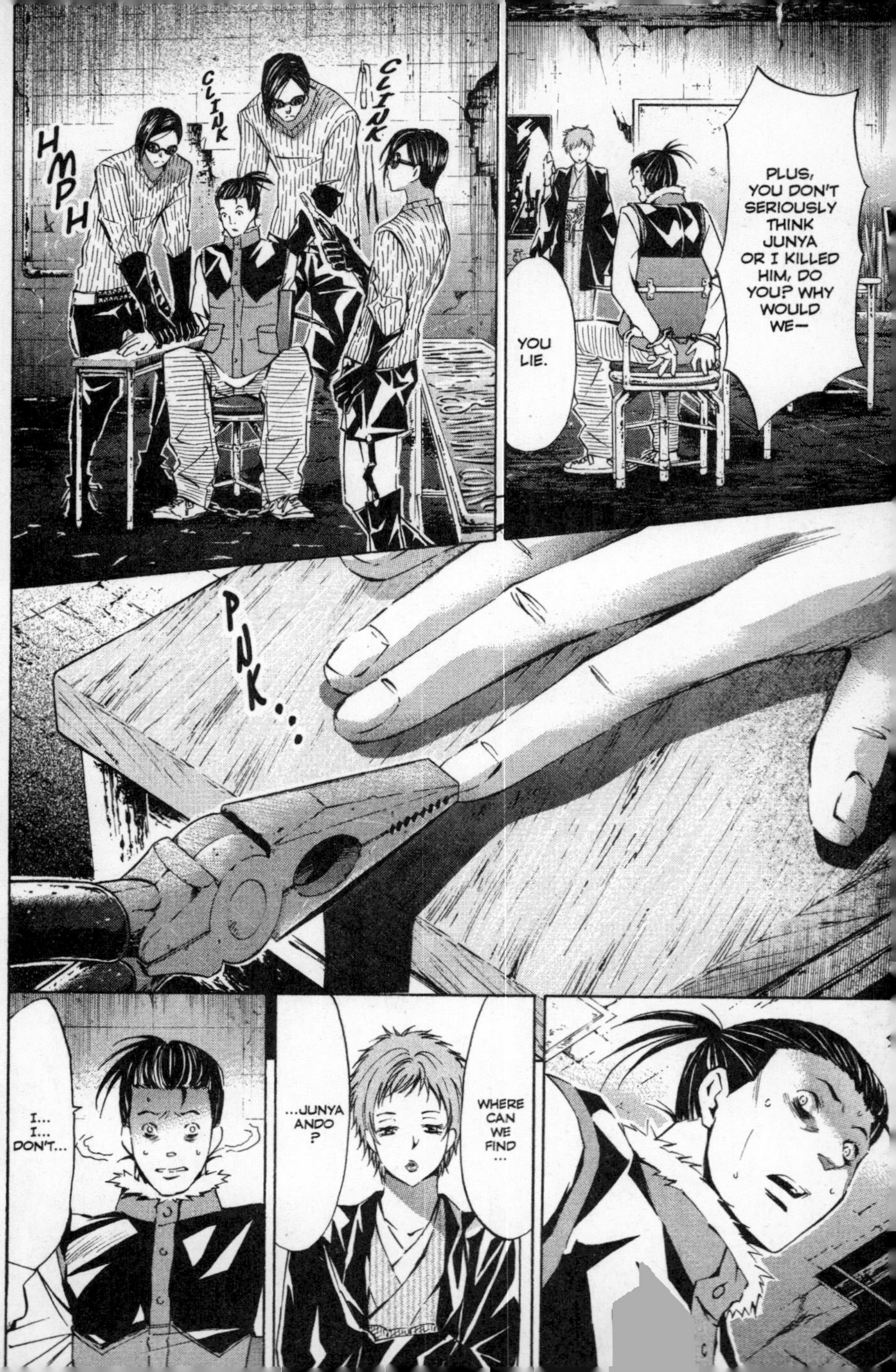
PLUS, YOU DON'T SERIOUSLY THINK JUNYA OR I KILLED HIM, DO YOU? WHY WOULD WE—
YOU LIE.
CLINK
CLINK
HMPH
PNK...
WHERE CAN WE FIND ...
...JUNYA ANDO ?
I... I... DON'T...

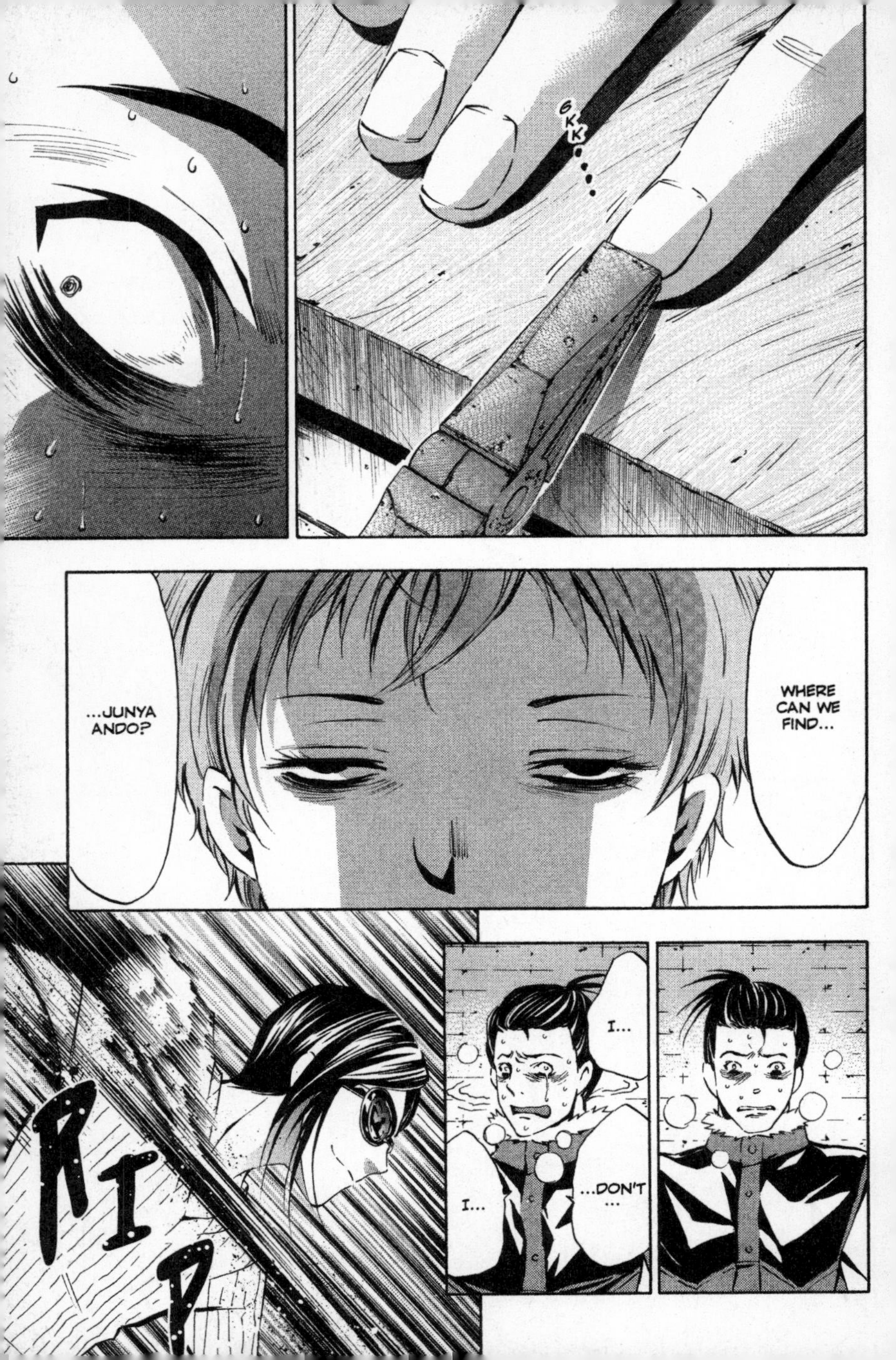

GKK...
WHERE CAN WE FIND...
...JUNYA ANDO?
I...
...DON'T ...
I...
RIP

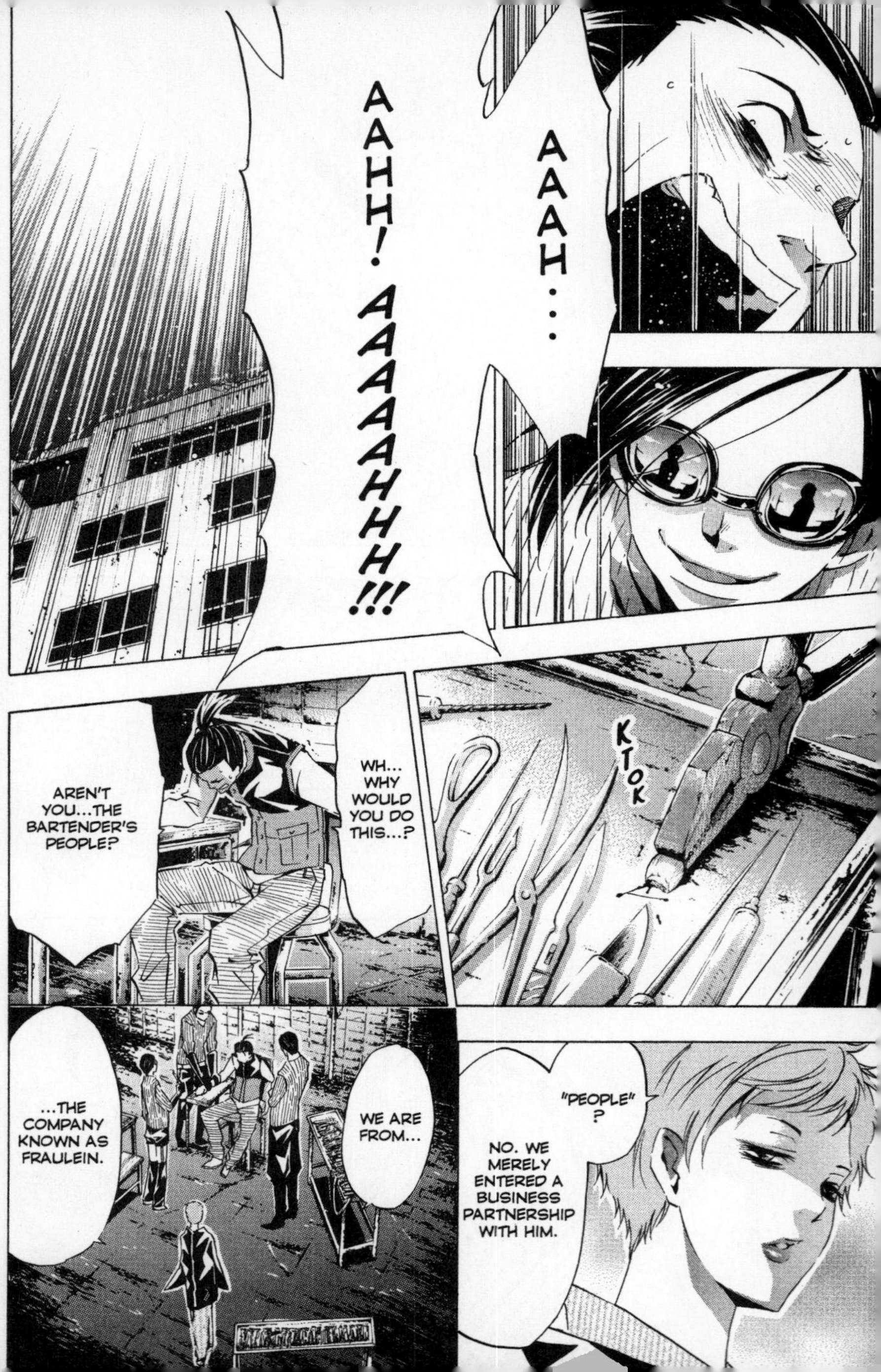
AAAAH...
AAHH! AAAAAHHH!!!
KTOK
WH... WHY WOULD YOU DO THIS...?
AREN'T YOU...THE BARTENDER'S PEOPLE?
"PEOPLE"?
NO. WE MERELY ENTERED A BUSINESS PARTNERSHIP WITH HIM.
WE ARE FROM...
...THE COMPANY KNOWN AS FRAULEIN.

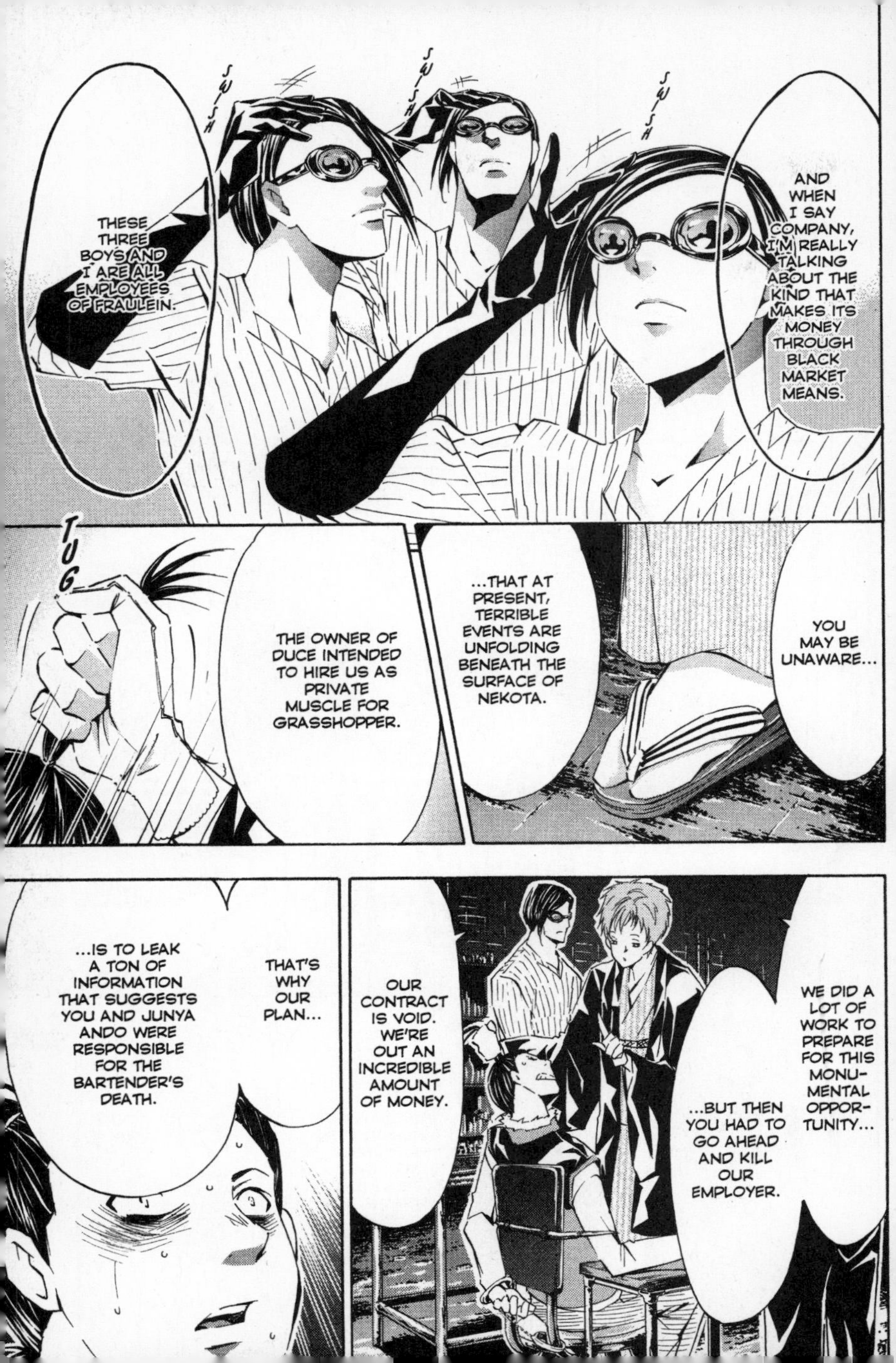
SWISH
SWISH
SWISH
AND WHEN I SAY COMPANY, I'M REALLY TALKING ABOUT THE KIND THAT MAKES ITS MONEY THROUGH BLACK MARKET MEANS.
THESE THREE BOYS AND I ARE ALL EMPLOYEES OF FRAULEIN.
YOU MAY BE UNAWARE...
...THAT AT PRESENT, TERRIBLE EVENTS ARE UNFOLDING BENEATH THE SURFACE OF NEKOTA.
THE OWNER OF DUCE INTENDED TO HIRE US AS PRIVATE MUSCLE FOR GRASSHOPPER.
TUG
WE DID A LOT OF WORK TO PREPARE FOR THIS MONU-MENTAL OPPOR-TUNITY...
...BUT THEN YOU HAD TO GO AHEAD AND KILL OUR EMPLOYER.
OUR CONTRACT IS VOID. WE'RE OUT AN INCREDIBLE AMOUNT OF MONEY.
THAT'S WHY OUR PLAN...
...IS TO LEAK A TON OF INFORMATION THAT SUGGESTS YOU AND JUNYA ANDO WERE RESPONSIBLE FOR THE BARTENDER'S DEATH.

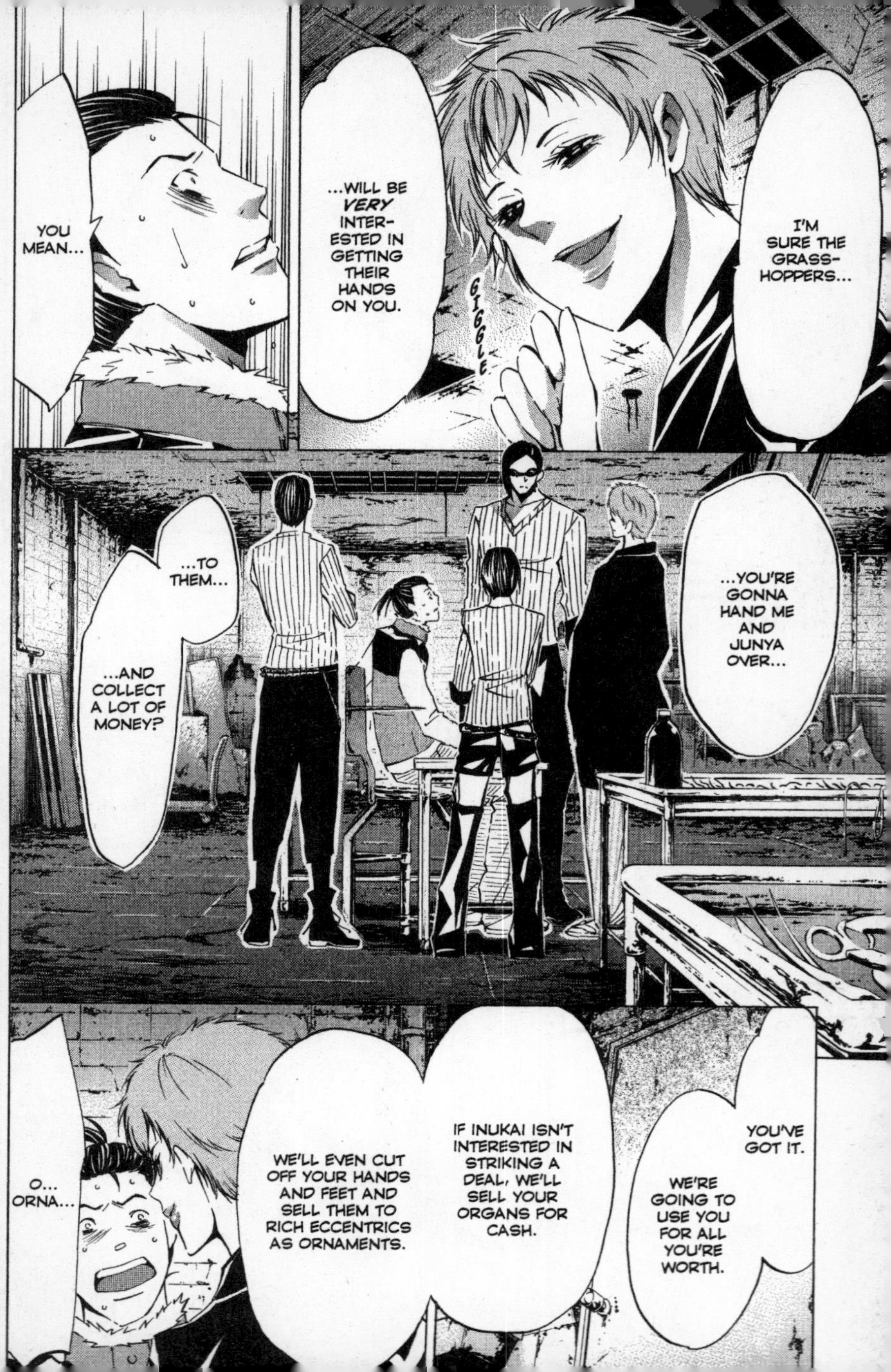

I'M SURE THE GRASS-HOPPERS...
...WILL BE VERY INTER-ESTED IN GETTING THEIR HANDS ON YOU.
GIGGLE
YOU MEAN...
...YOU'RE GONNA HAND ME AND JUNYA OVER...
...TO THEM...
...AND COLLECT A LOT OF MONEY?
YOU'VE GOT IT.
WE'RE GOING TO USE YOU FOR ALL YOU'RE WORTH.
IF INUKAI ISN'T INTERESTED IN STRIKING A DEAL, WE'LL SELL YOUR ORGANS FOR CASH.
WE'LL EVEN CUT OFF YOUR HANDS AND FEET AND SELL THEM TO RICH ECCENTRICS AS ORNAMENTS.
O... ORNA...

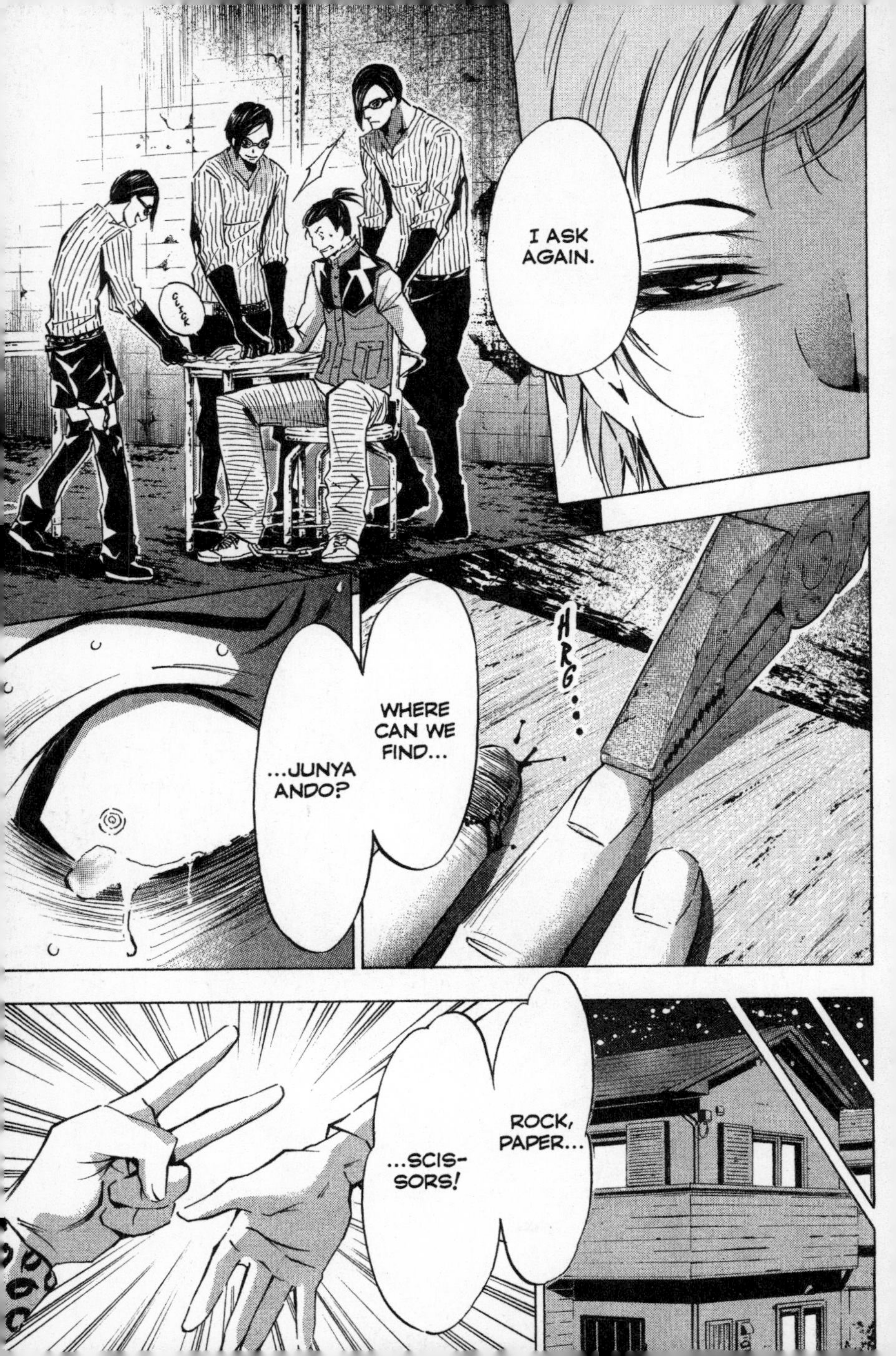
I ASK AGAIN.
CLICK
HRG...
WHERE CAN WE FIND...
...JUNYA ANDO?
ROCK, PAPER...
...SCIS-SORS!

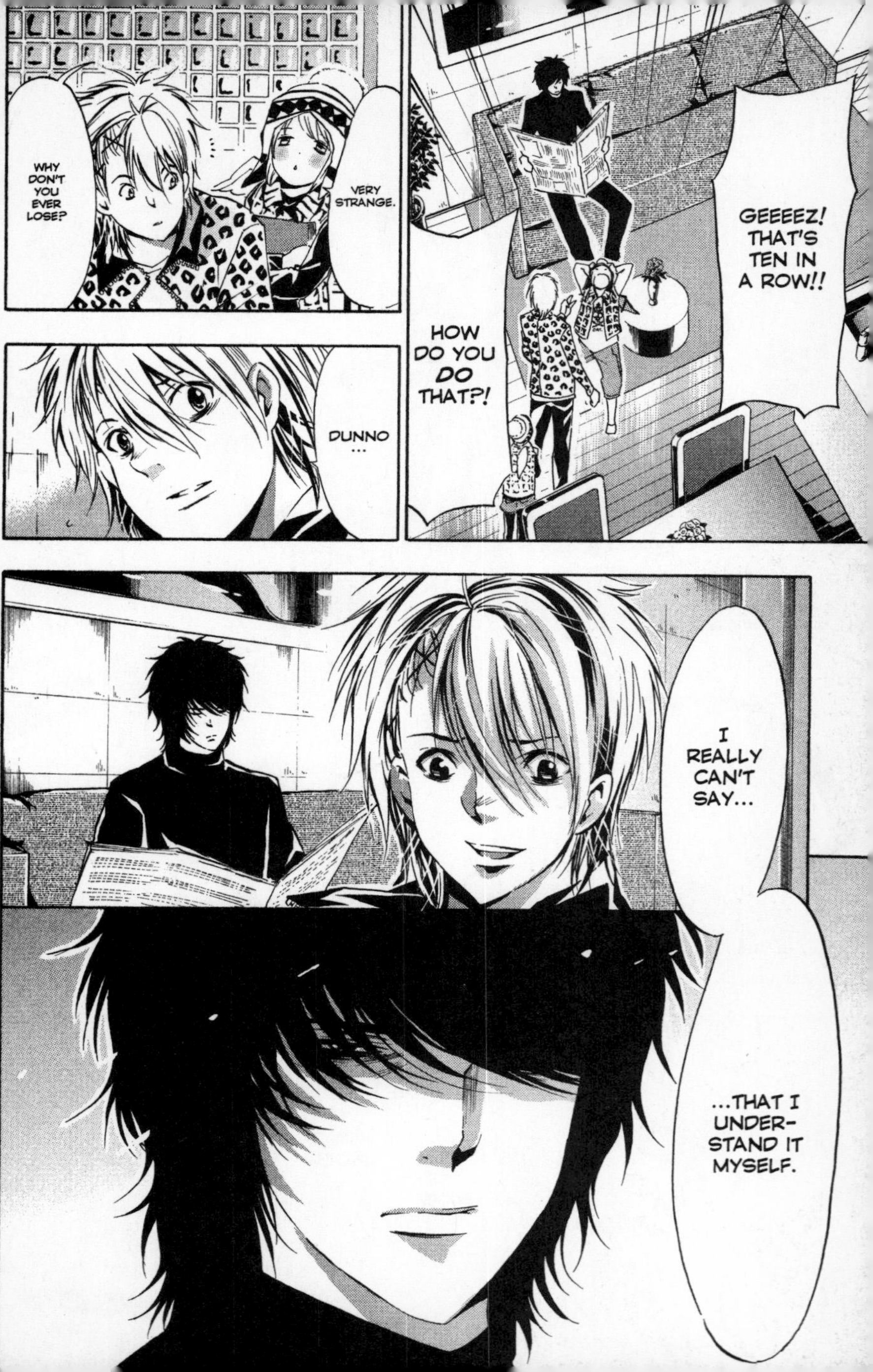
GEEEEZ! THAT'S TEN IN A ROW!!
HOW DO YOU DO THAT?!
VERY STRANGE.
WHY DON'T YOU EVER LOSE?
DUNNO ...
I REALLY CAN'T SAY...
...THAT I UNDER-STAND IT MYSELF.

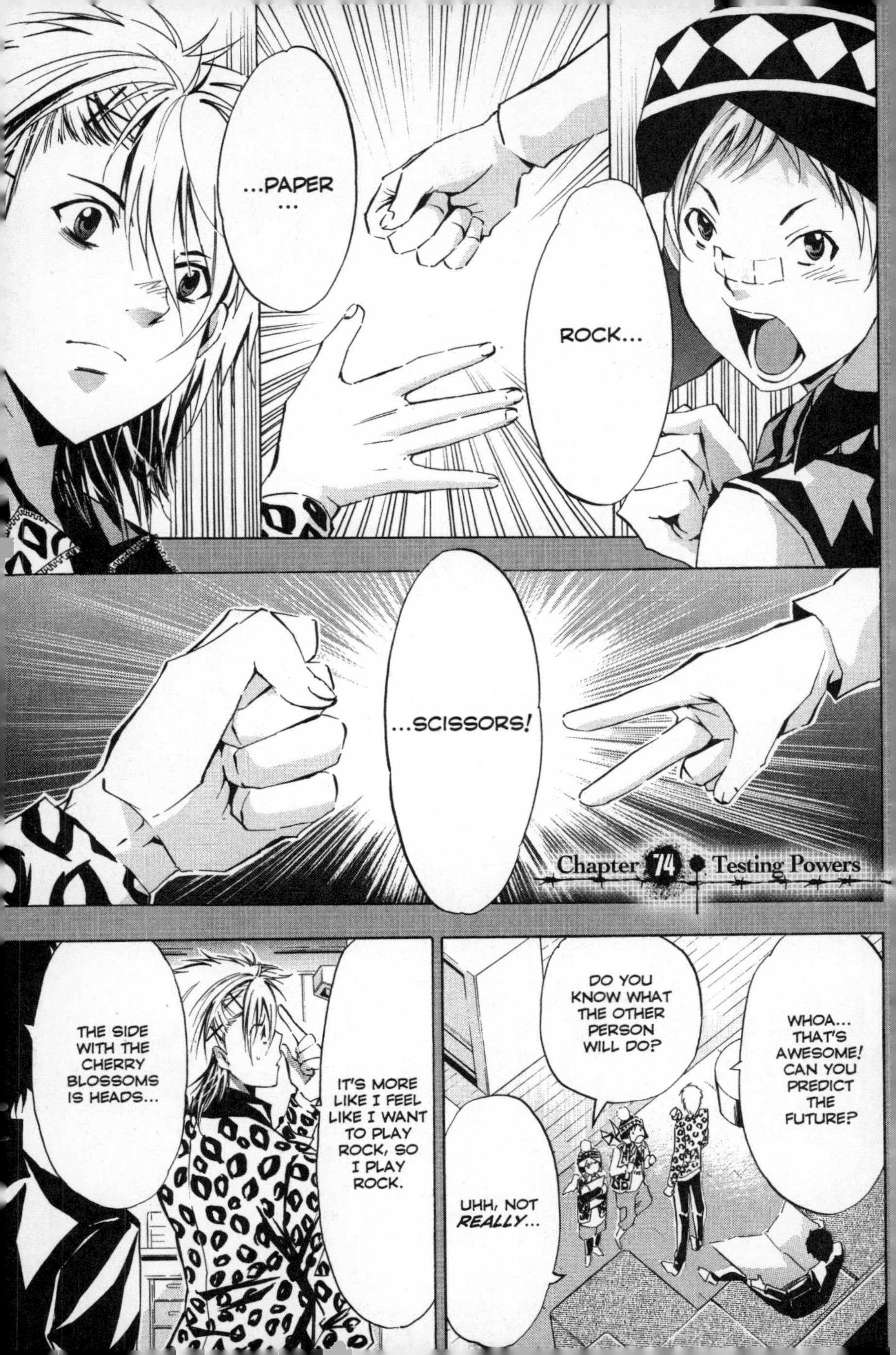
ROCK...
...PAPER ...
...SCISSORS!
Chapter 74 Testing Powers
WHOA... THAT'S AWESOME! CAN YOU PREDICT THE FUTURE?
DO YOU KNOW WHAT THE OTHER PERSON WILL DO?
UHH, NOT REALLY...
IT'S MORE LIKE I FEEL LIKE I WANT TO PLAY ROCK, SO I PLAY ROCK.
THE SIDE WITH THE CHERRY BLOSSOMS IS HEADS...

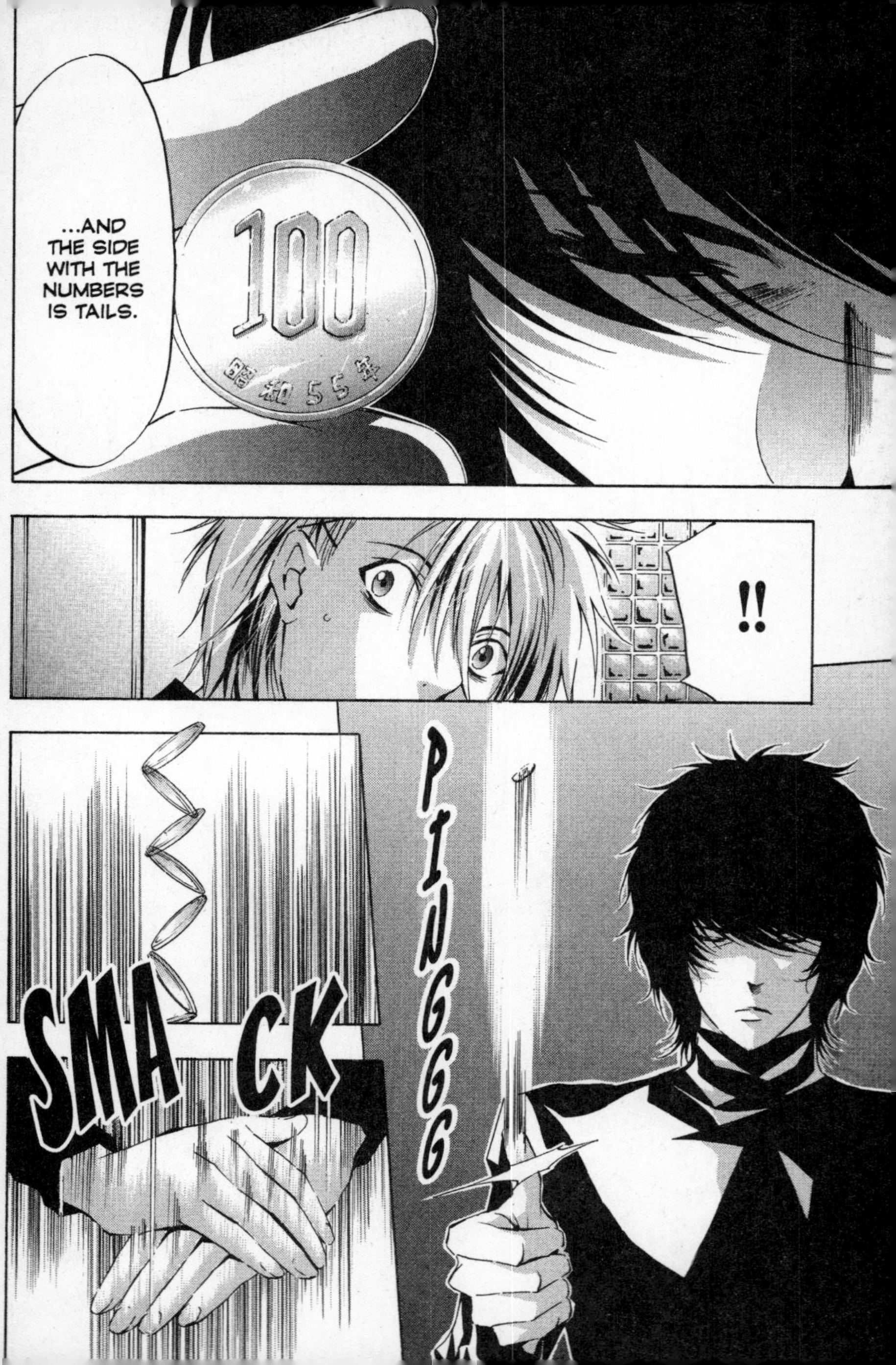
...AND THE SIDE WITH THE NUMBERS IS TAILS.
100
昭和55年
!!
PINGGG
SMACK

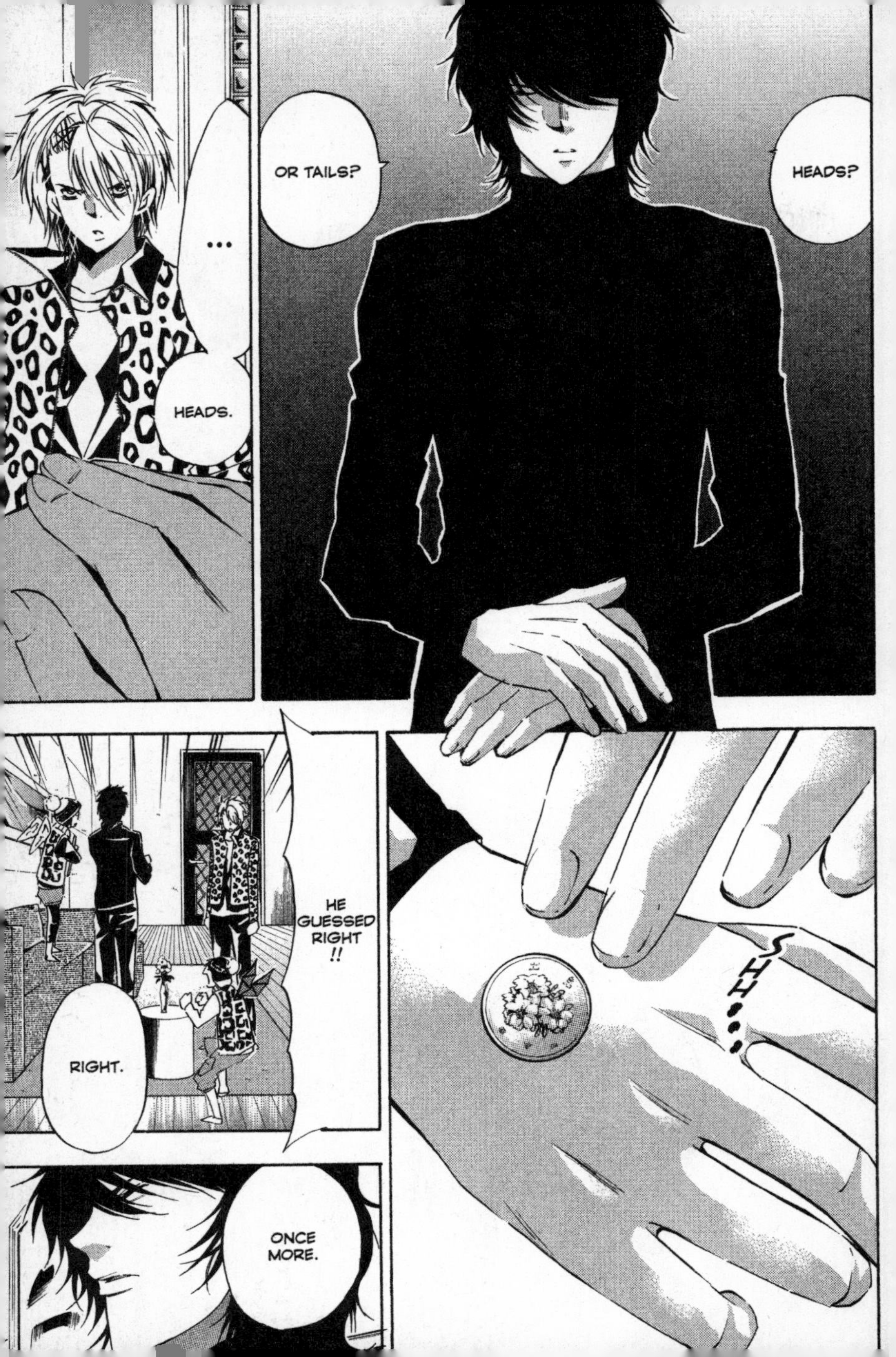
HEADS?
OR TAILS?
...
HEADS.
SHH...
HE GUESSED RIGHT !!
RIGHT.
ONCE MORE.

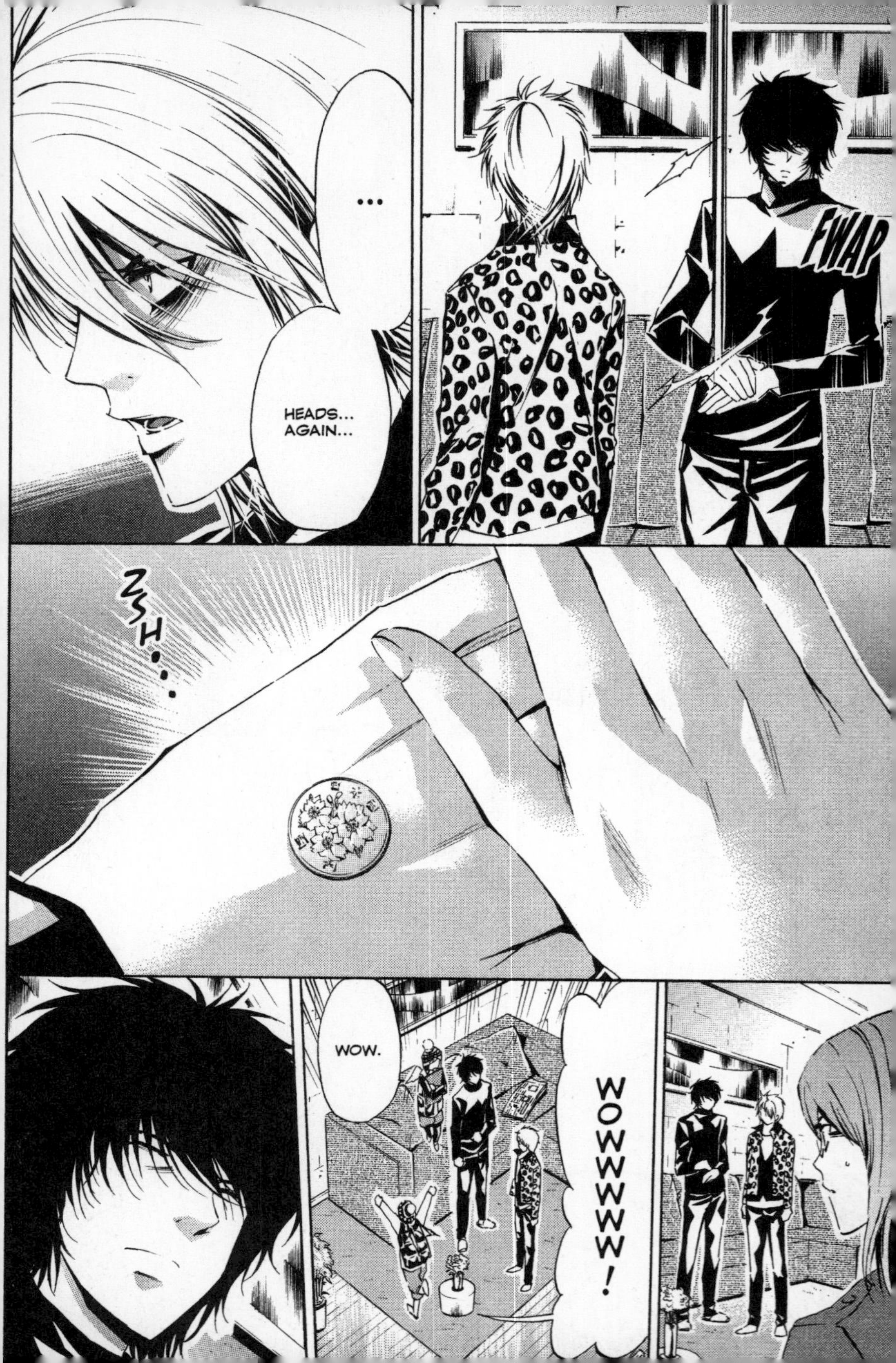
FWAP
...
HEADS... AGAIN...
ZSH...
WOWWWWW!
WOW.

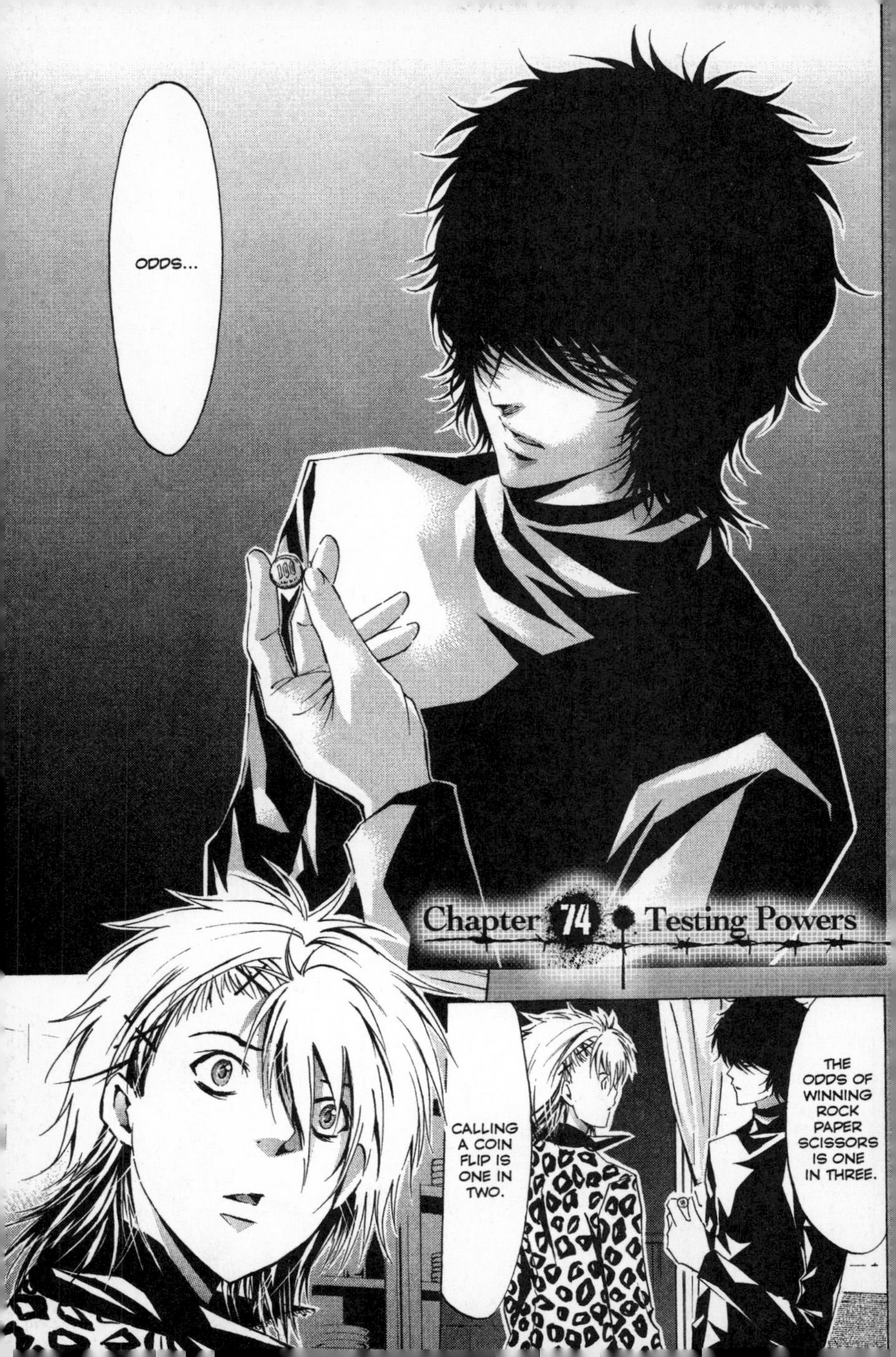
ODDS...
Chapter 74 Testing Powers
THE ODDS OF WINNING ROCK PAPER SCISSORS IS ONE IN THREE.
CALLING A COIN FLIP IS ONE IN TWO.

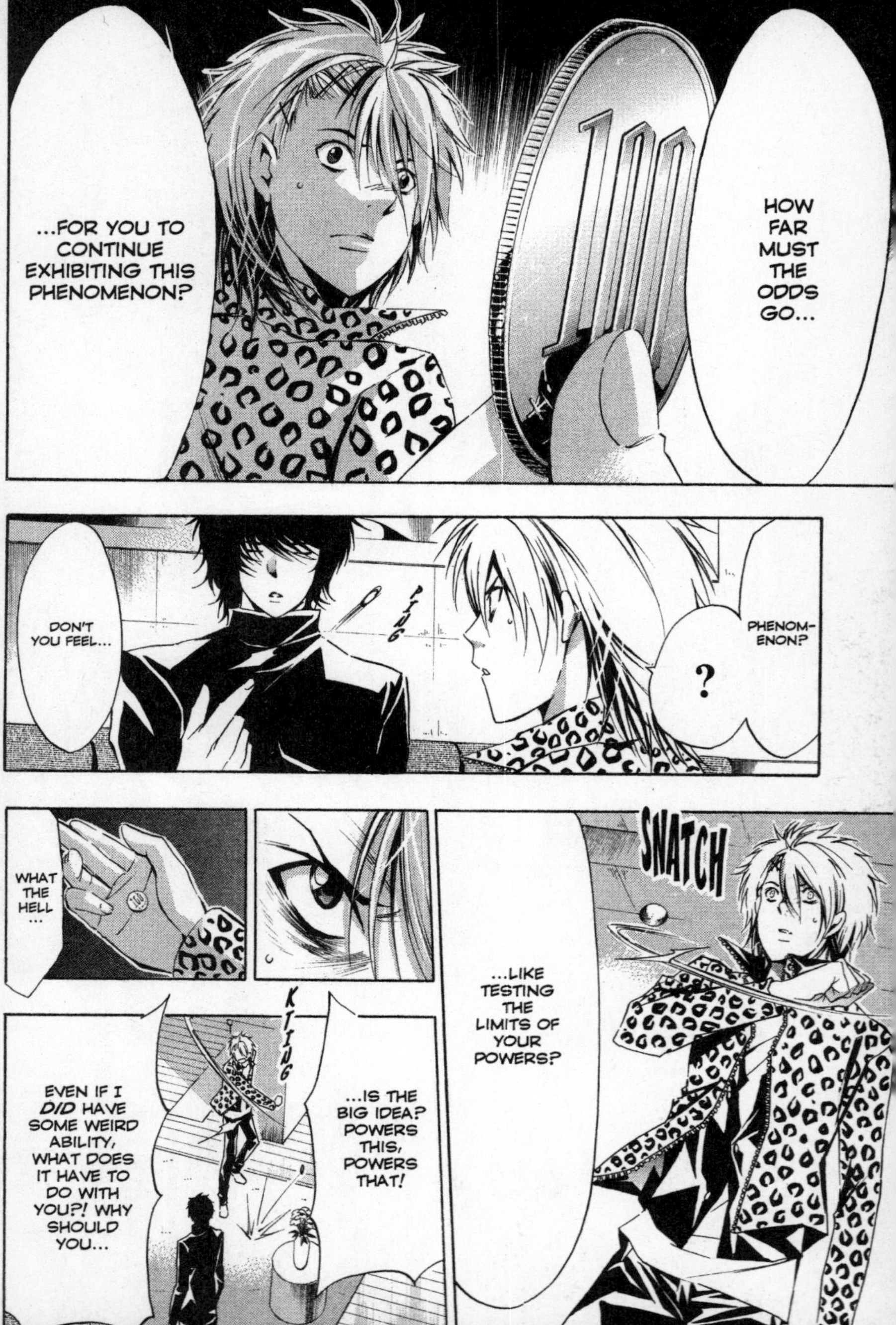
HOW FAR MUST THE ODDS GO...
...FOR YOU TO CONTINUE EXHIBITING THIS PHENOMENON?
PHENOM-ENON?
?
PING
DON'T YOU FEEL...
SNATCH
...LIKE TESTING THE LIMITS OF YOUR POWERS?
WHAT THE HELL...
KTING
...IS THE BIG IDEA? POWERS THIS, POWERS THAT!
EVEN IF I *DID* HAVE SOME WEIRD ABILITY, WHAT DOES IT HAVE TO DO WITH YOU?! WHY SHOULD YOU...

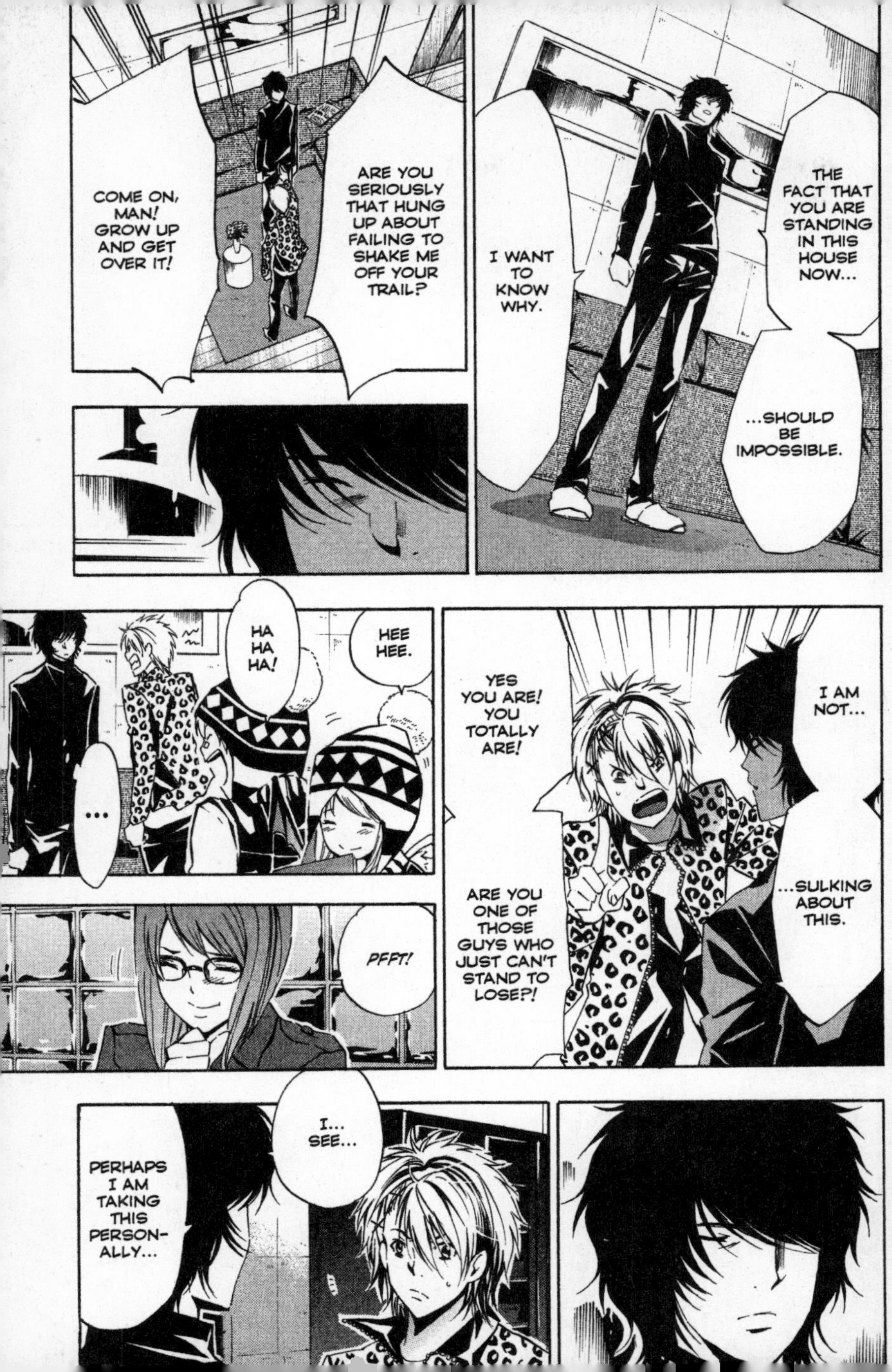
THE FACT THAT YOU ARE STANDING IN THIS HOUSE NOW...
...SHOULD BE IMPOSSIBLE.
I WANT TO KNOW WHY.
ARE YOU SERIOUSLY THAT HUNG UP ABOUT FAILING TO SHAKE ME OFF YOUR TRAIL?
COME ON, MAN! GROW UP AND GET OVER IT!
I AM NOT...
...SULKING ABOUT THIS.
YES YOU ARE! YOU TOTALLY ARE!
ARE YOU ONE OF THOSE GUYS WHO JUST CAN'T STAND TO LOSE?!
HEE HEE.
HA HA HA!
...
PFFT!
I... SEE...
PERHAPS I AM TAKING THIS PERSON-ALLY...

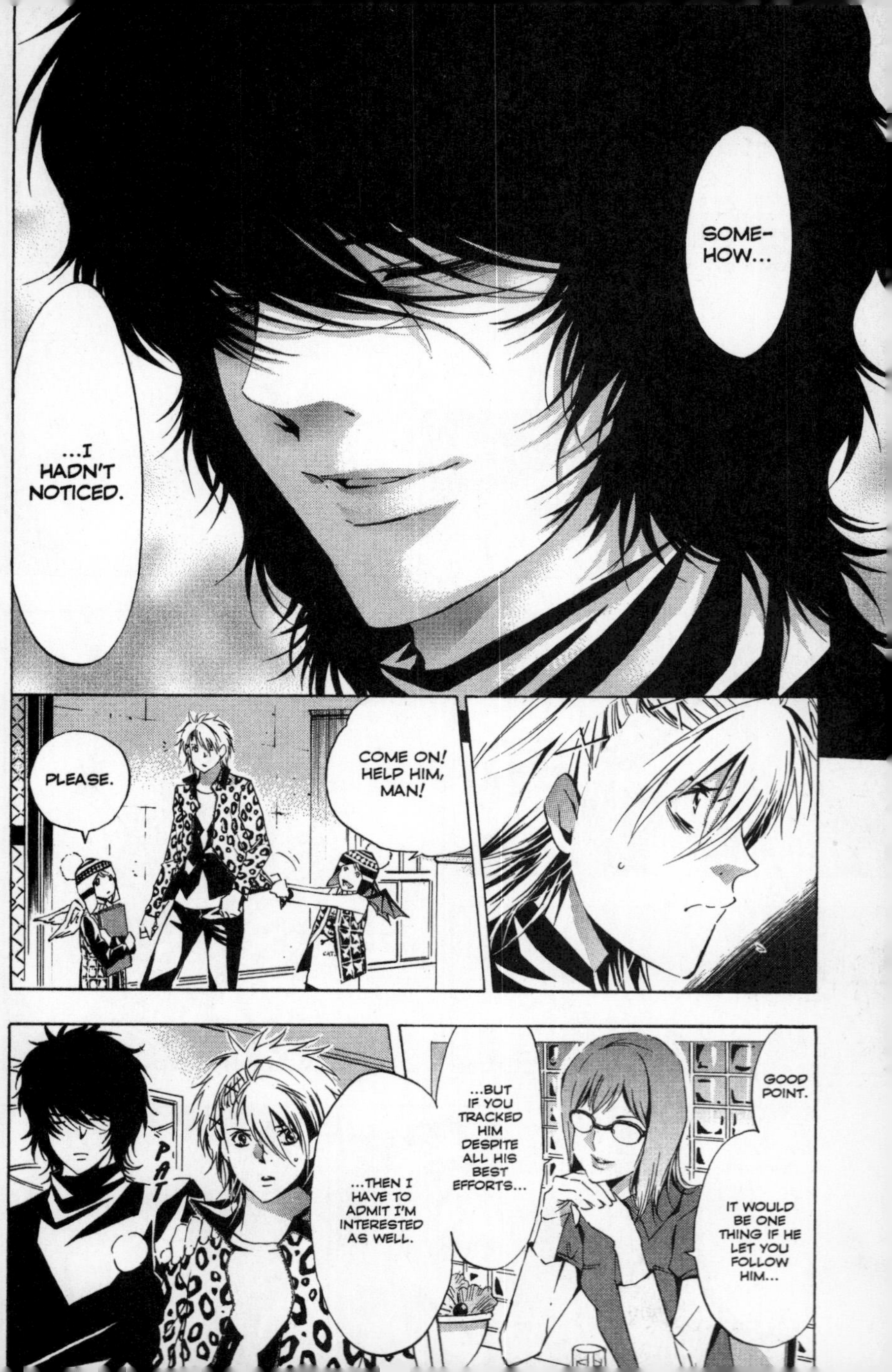
SOME-HOW...
...I HADN'T NOTICED.
COME ON! HELP HIM, MAN!
PLEASE.
GOOD POINT.
IT WOULD BE ONE THING IF HE LET YOU FOLLOW HIM...
...BUT IF YOU TRACKED HIM DESPITE ALL HIS BEST EFFORTS...
...THEN I HAVE TO ADMIT I'M INTERESTED AS WELL.
PAT

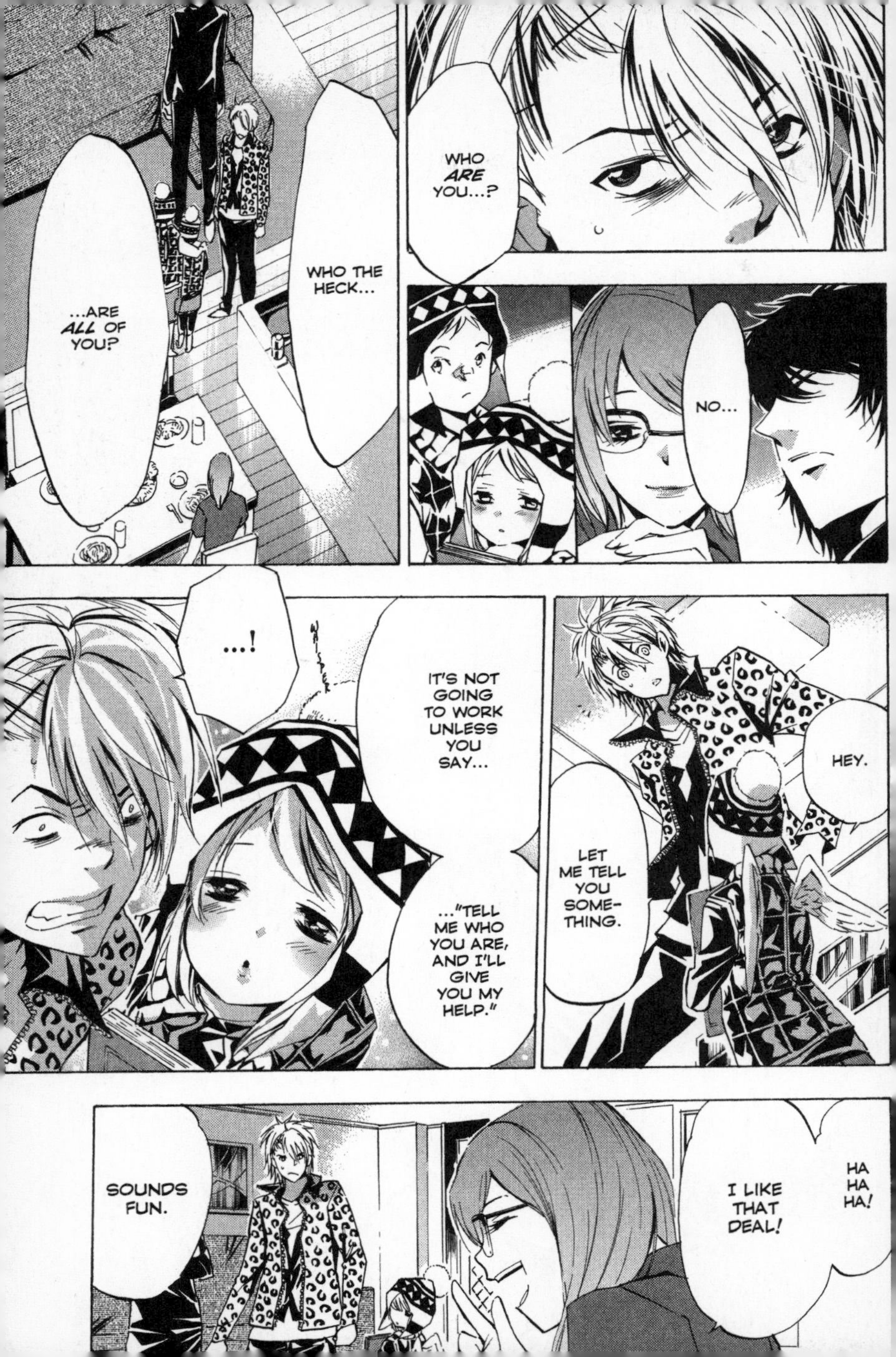
WHO *ARE* YOU...?
NO...
WHO THE HECK...
...ARE *ALL* OF YOU?
HEY.
LET ME TELL YOU SOME-THING.
IT'S NOT GOING TO WORK UNLESS YOU SAY...
..."TELL ME WHO YOU ARE, AND I'LL GIVE YOU MY HELP."
...!
HA HA HA!
I LIKE THAT DEAL!
SOUNDS FUN.

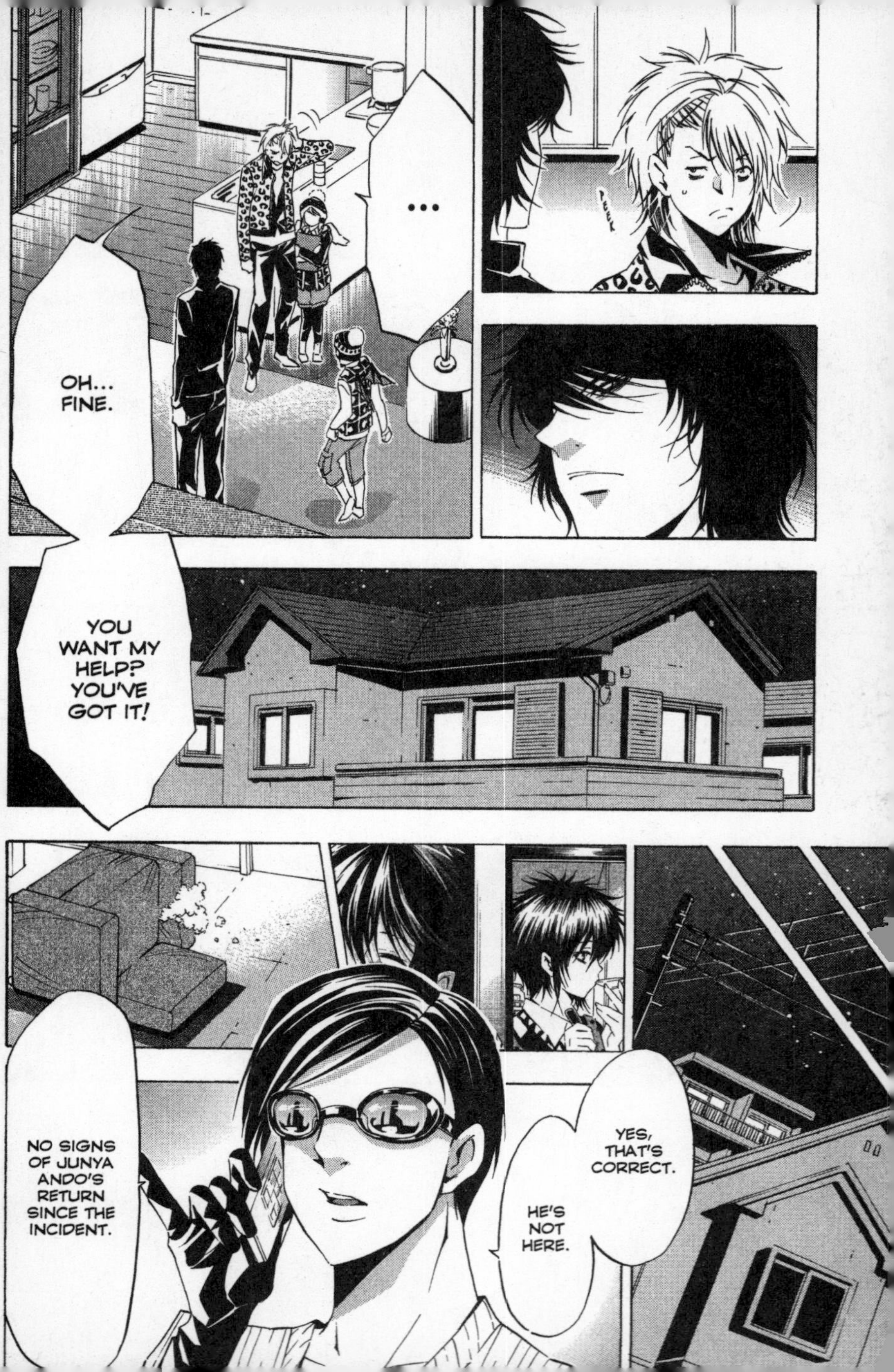
PEEK
...
OH... FINE.
YOU WANT MY HELP? YOU'VE GOT IT!
YES, THAT'S CORRECT.
HE'S NOT HERE.
NO SIGNS OF JUNYA ANDO'S RETURN SINCE THE INCIDENT.

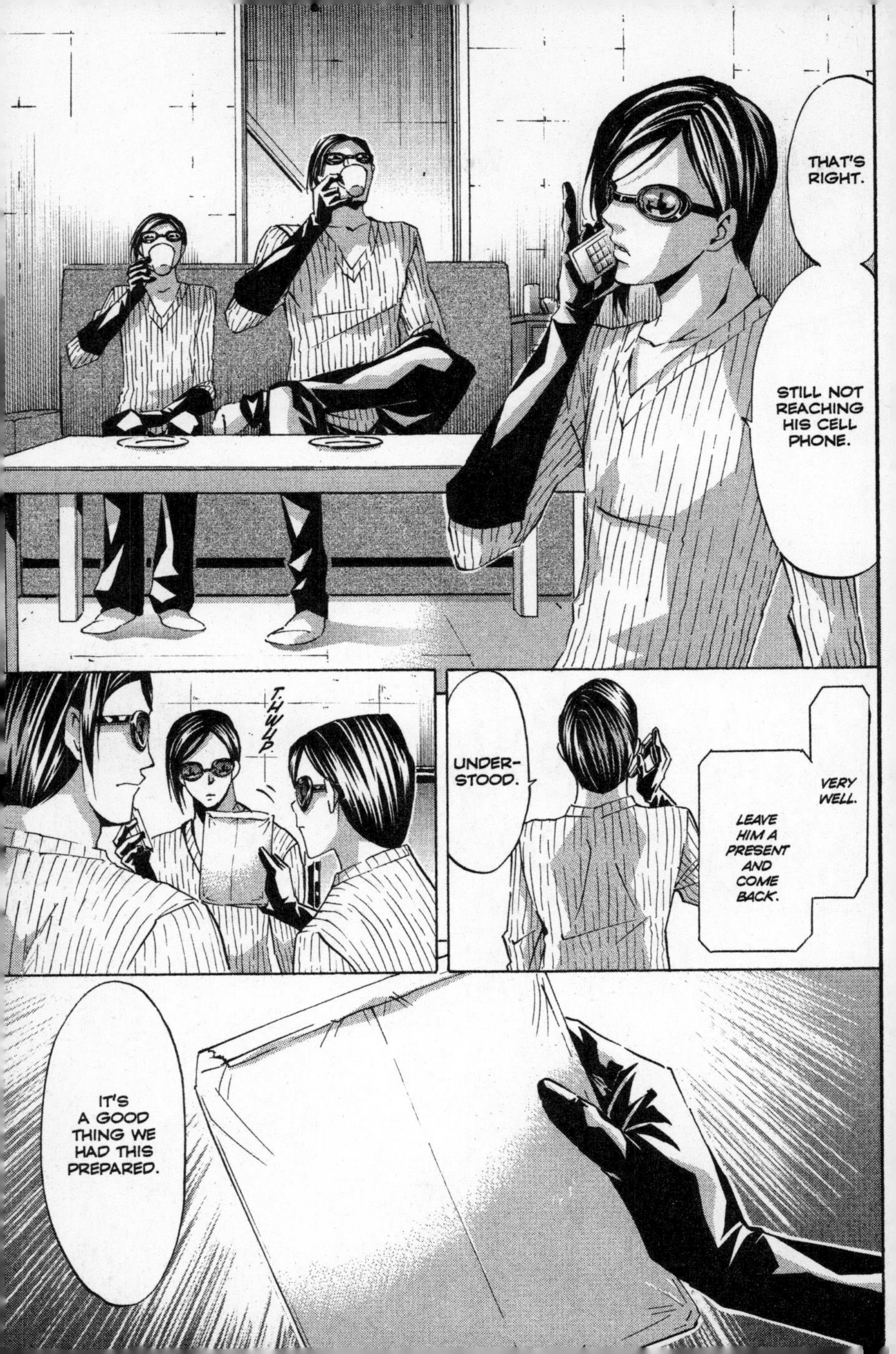

THAT'S RIGHT.
STILL NOT REACHING HIS CELL PHONE.
VERY WELL.
LEAVE HIM A PRESENT AND COME BACK.
UNDER-STOOD.
T.HWUP.
IT'S A GOOD THING WE HAD THIS PREPARED.

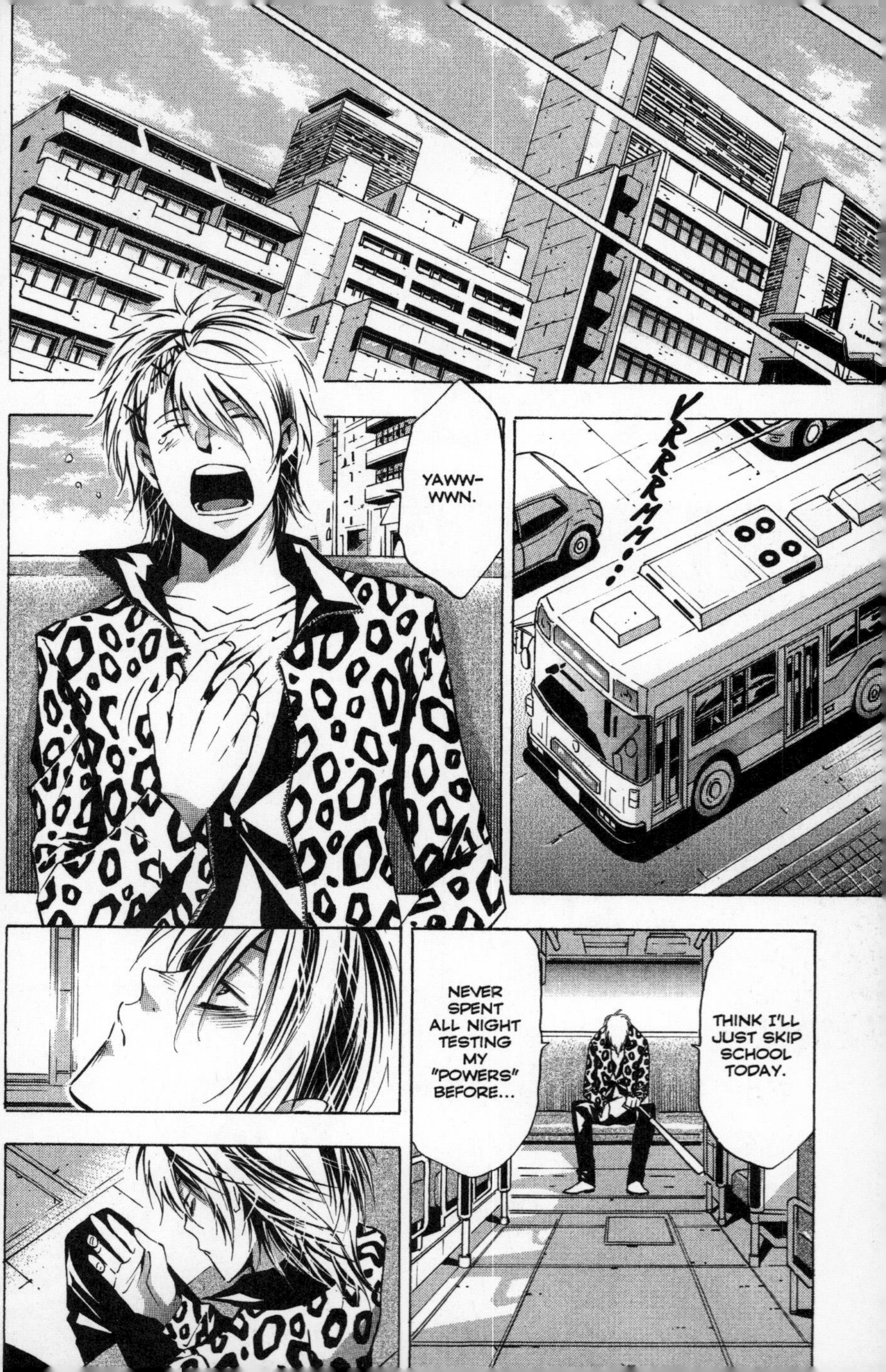
VRRRMM...
YAWW-WWN.
THINK I'LL JUST SKIP SCHOOL TODAY.
NEVER SPENT ALL NIGHT TESTING MY "POWERS" BEFORE...

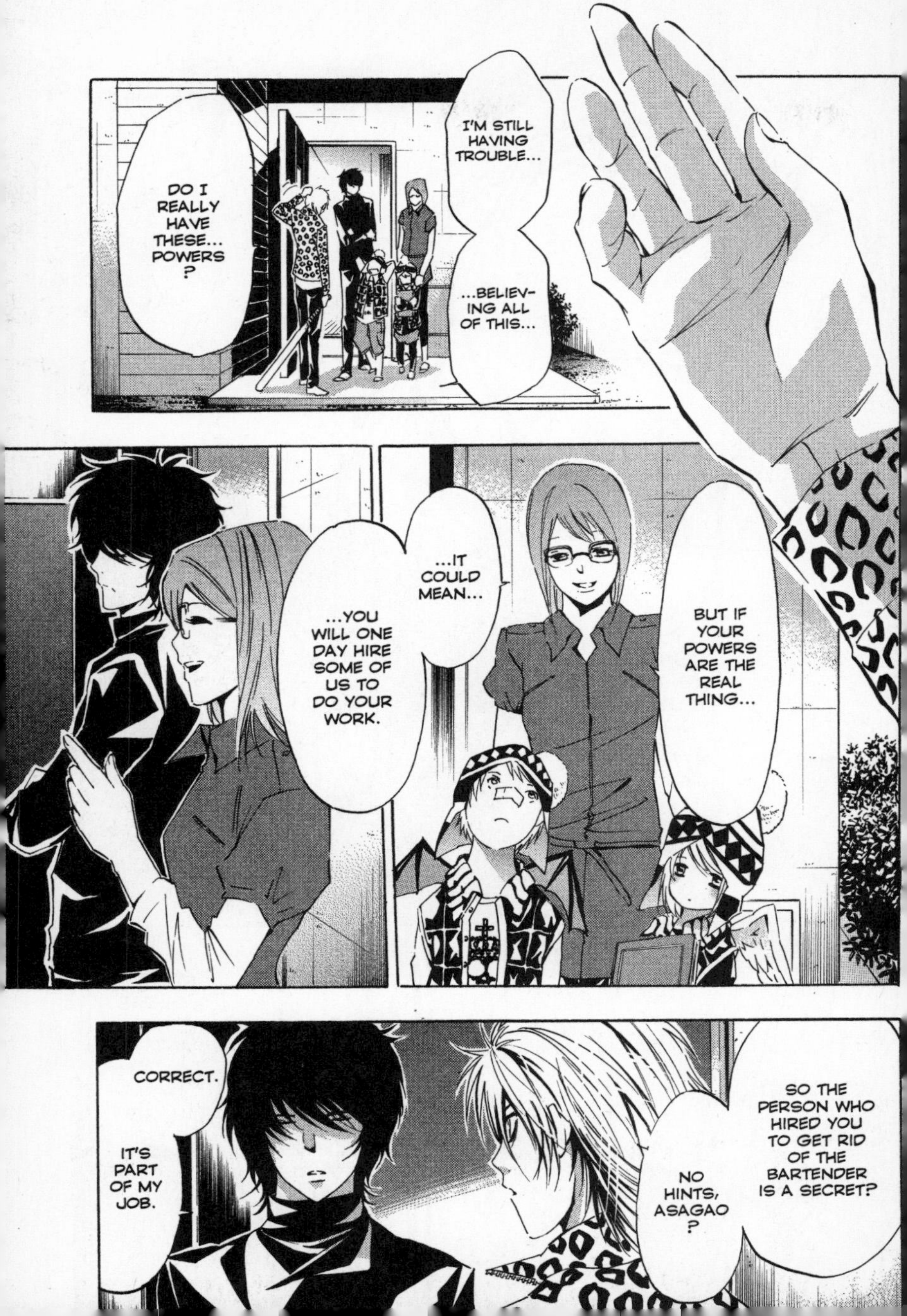
I'M STILL HAVING TROUBLE...
...BELIEVING ALL OF THIS...
DO I REALLY HAVE THESE... POWERS?
BUT IF YOUR POWERS ARE THE REAL THING...
...IT COULD MEAN...
...YOU WILL ONE DAY HIRE SOME OF US TO DO YOUR WORK.
SO THE PERSON WHO HIRED YOU TO GET RID OF THE BARTENDER IS A SECRET?
NO HINTS, ASAGAO?
CORRECT.
IT'S PART OF MY JOB.

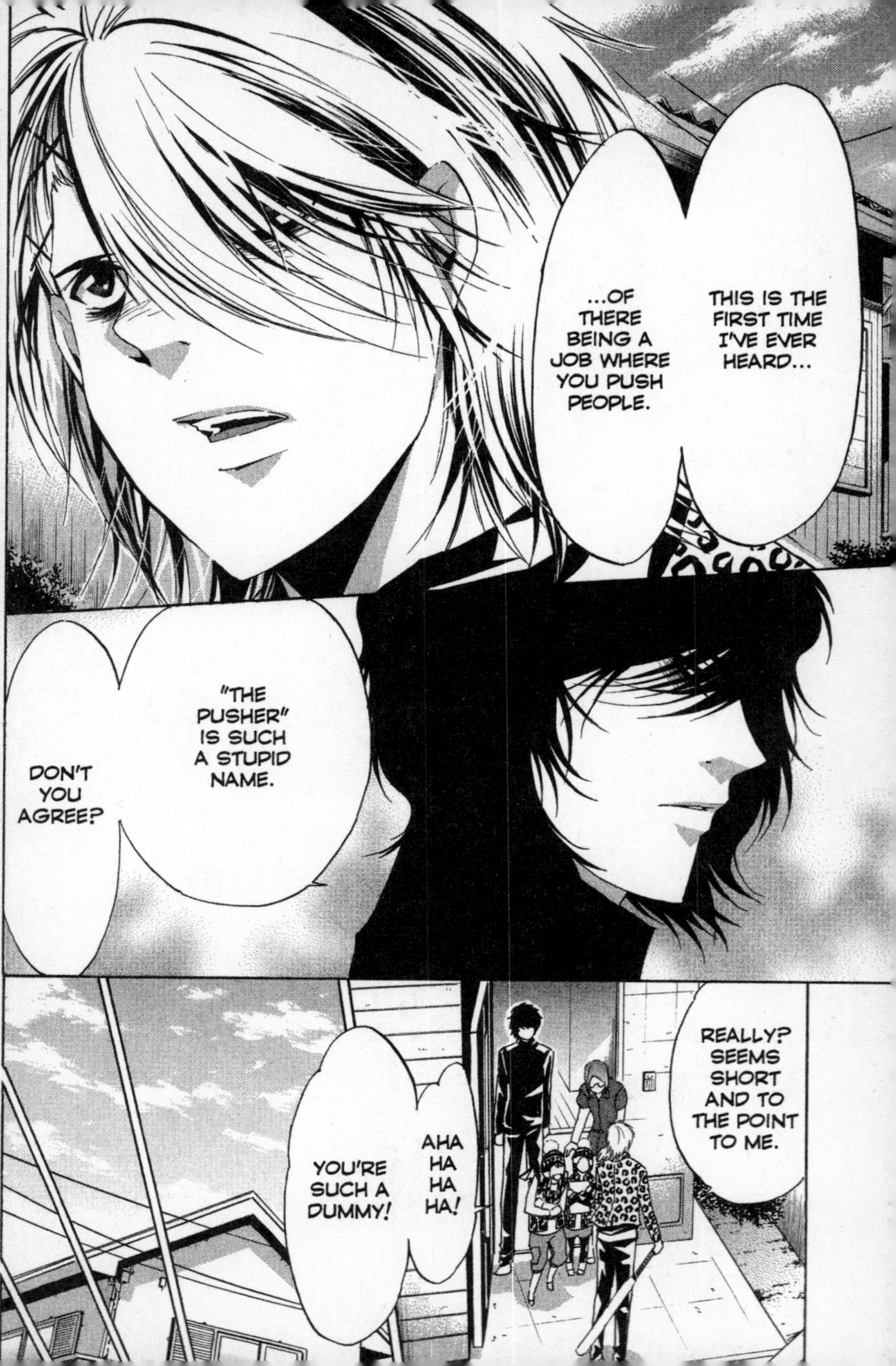
THIS IS THE FIRST TIME I'VE EVER HEARD...
...OF THERE BEING A JOB WHERE YOU PUSH PEOPLE.
"THE PUSHER" IS SUCH A STUPID NAME.
DON'T YOU AGREE?
REALLY? SEEMS SHORT AND TO THE POINT TO ME.
AHA HA HA HA!
YOU'RE SUCH A DUMMY!

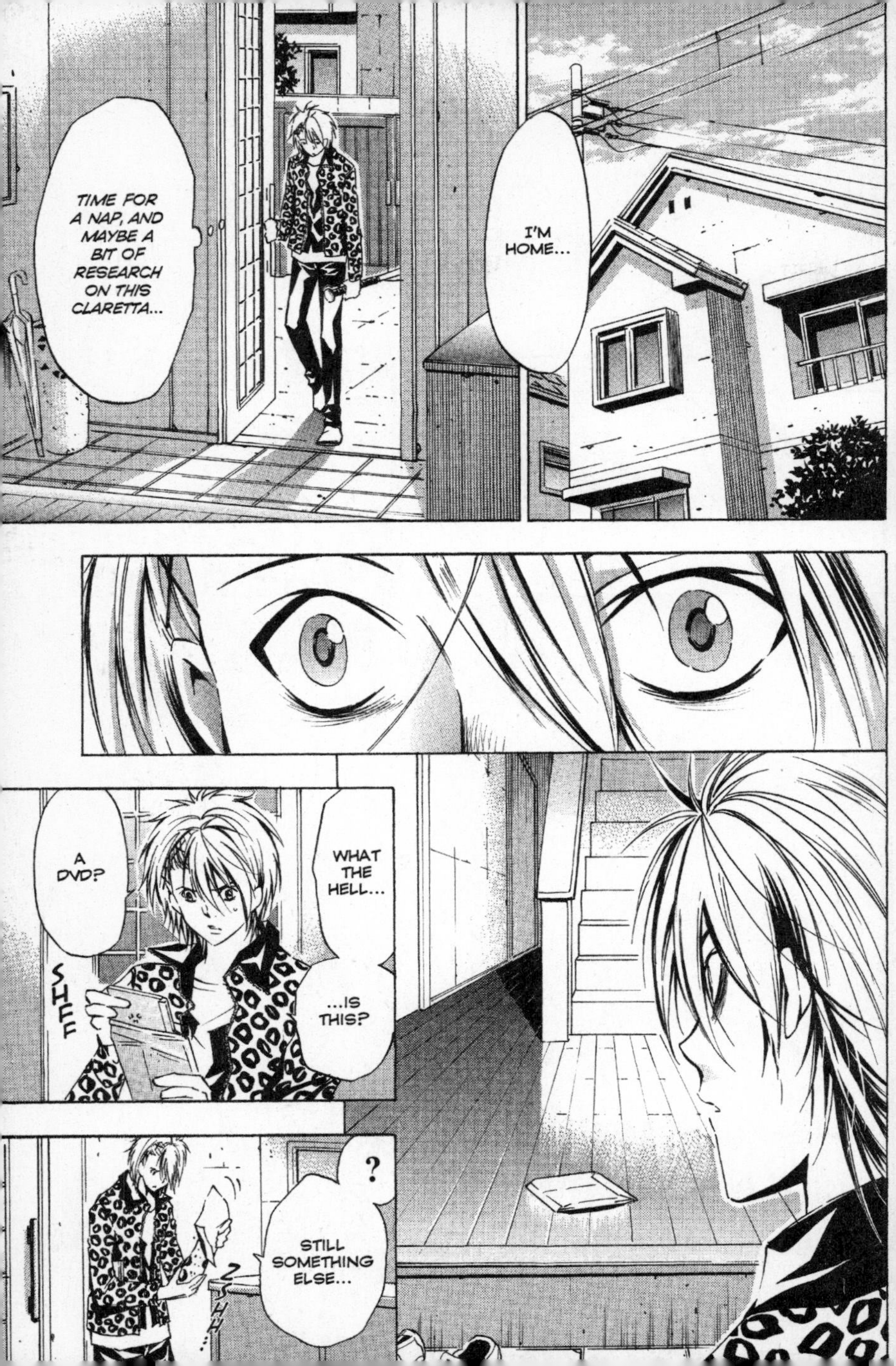
I'M HOME...
TIME FOR A NAP, AND MAYBE A BIT OF RESEARCH ON THIS CLARETTA...
WHAT THE HELL...
...IS THIS?
A DVD?
SHEFF
?
STILL SOMETHING ELSE...
ZSHH

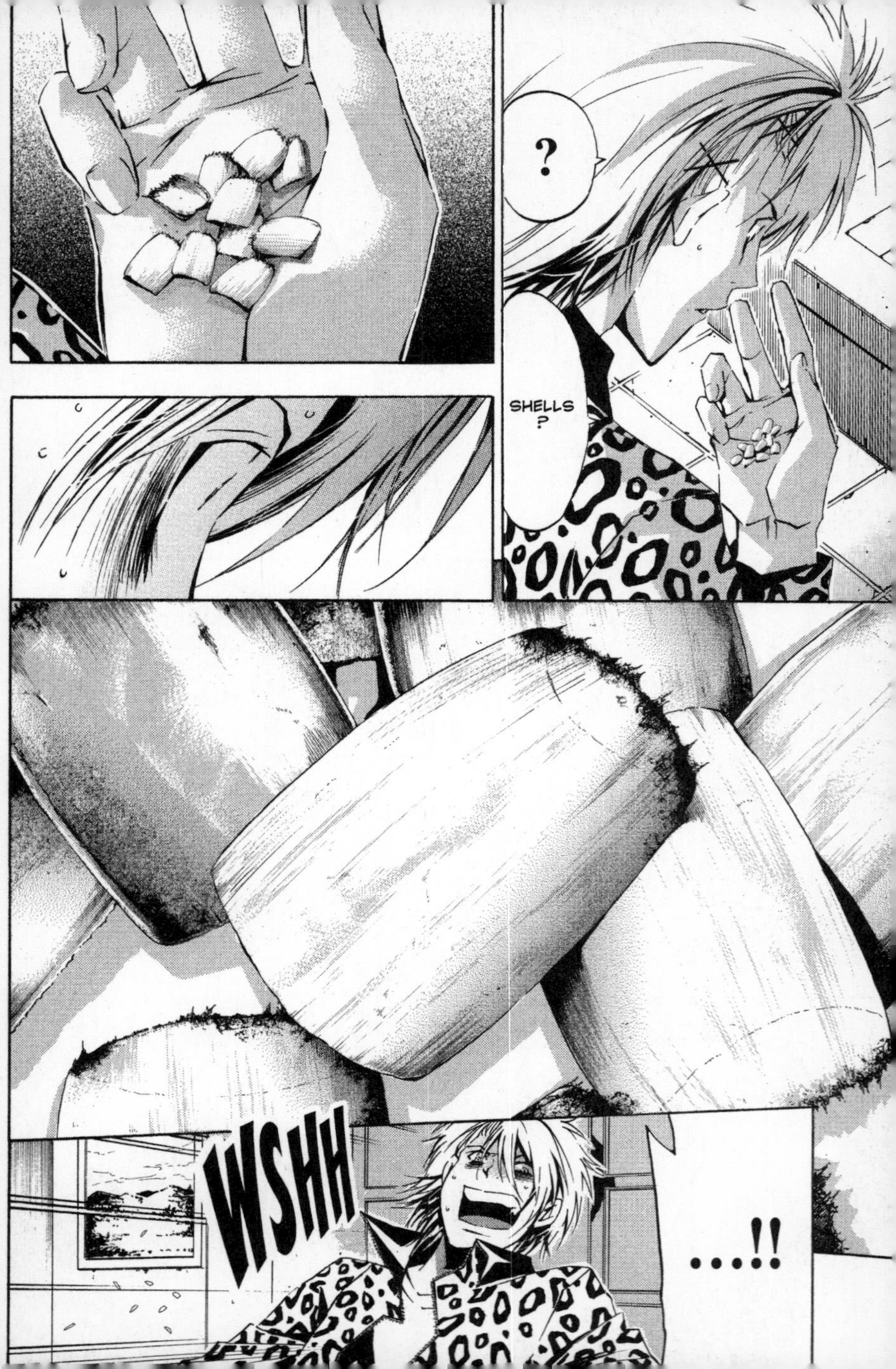
?
SHELLS ?
....!!
WSHH

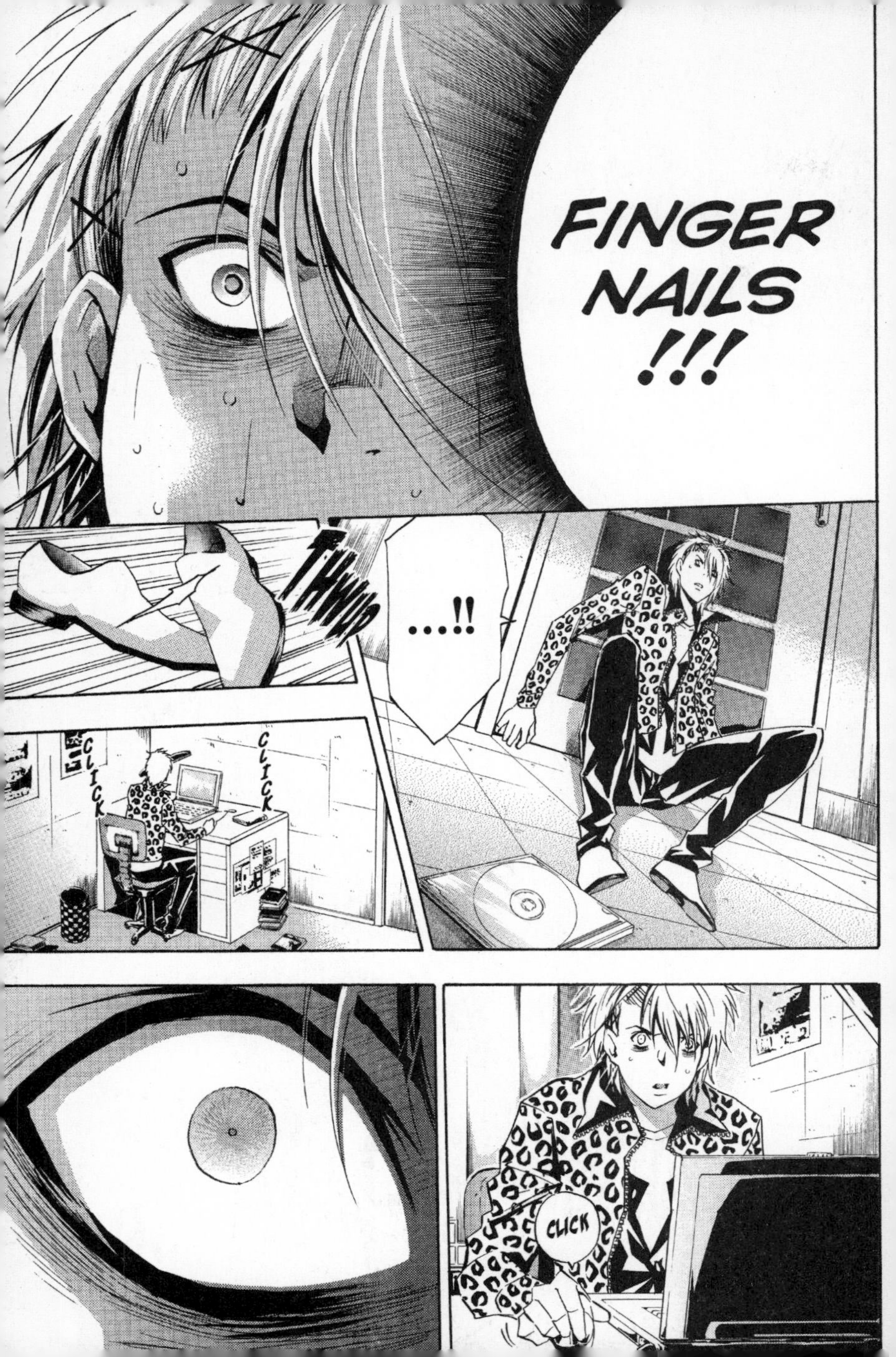
FINGER NAILS !!!
...!!
THWUD
CLICK
CLICK
CLICK

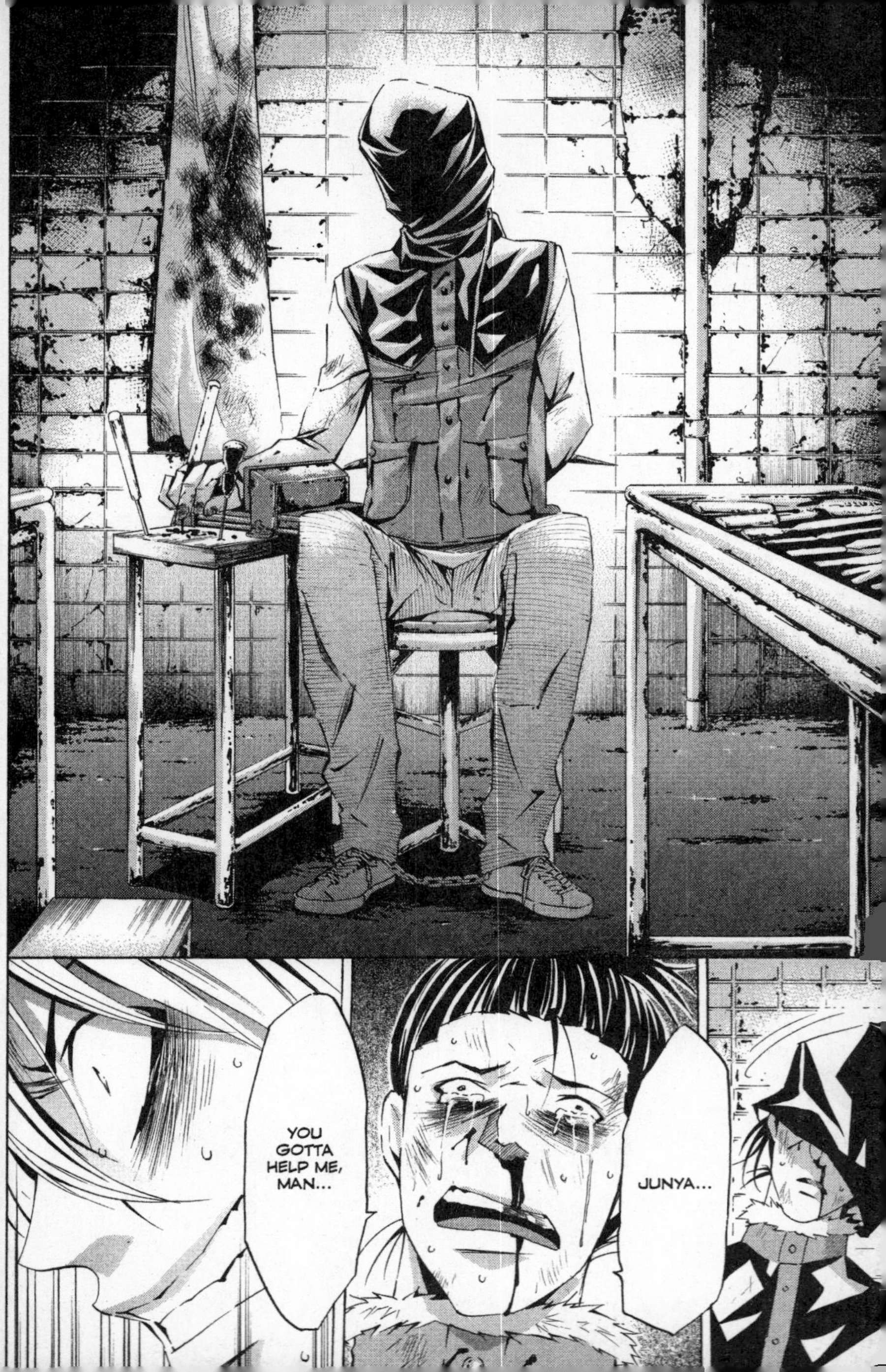
JUNYA...
YOU GOTTA HELP ME, MAN...

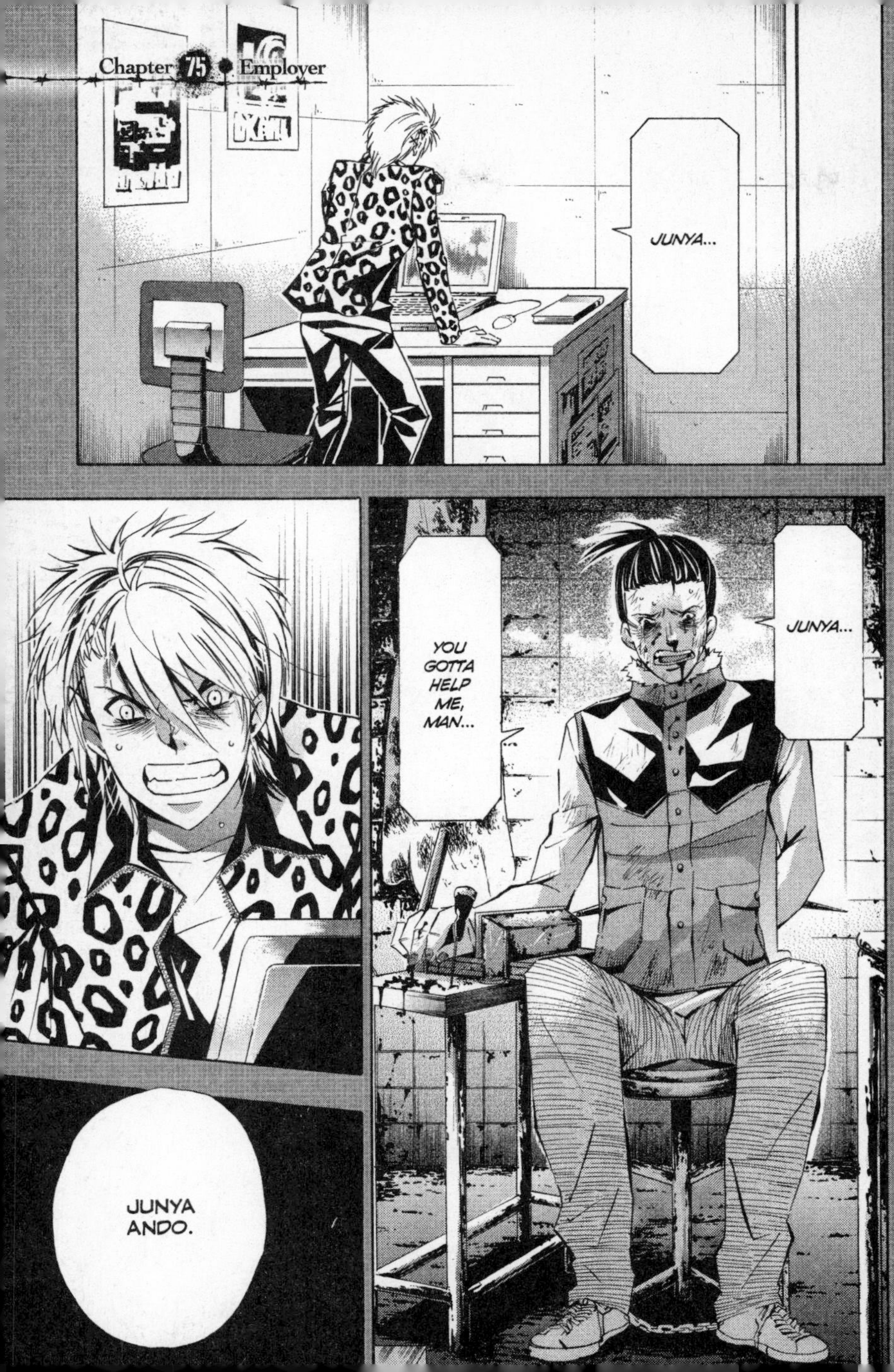
Chapter 75 Employer
JUNYA...
JUNYA...
YOU GOTTA HELP ME, MAN...
JUNYA ANDO.

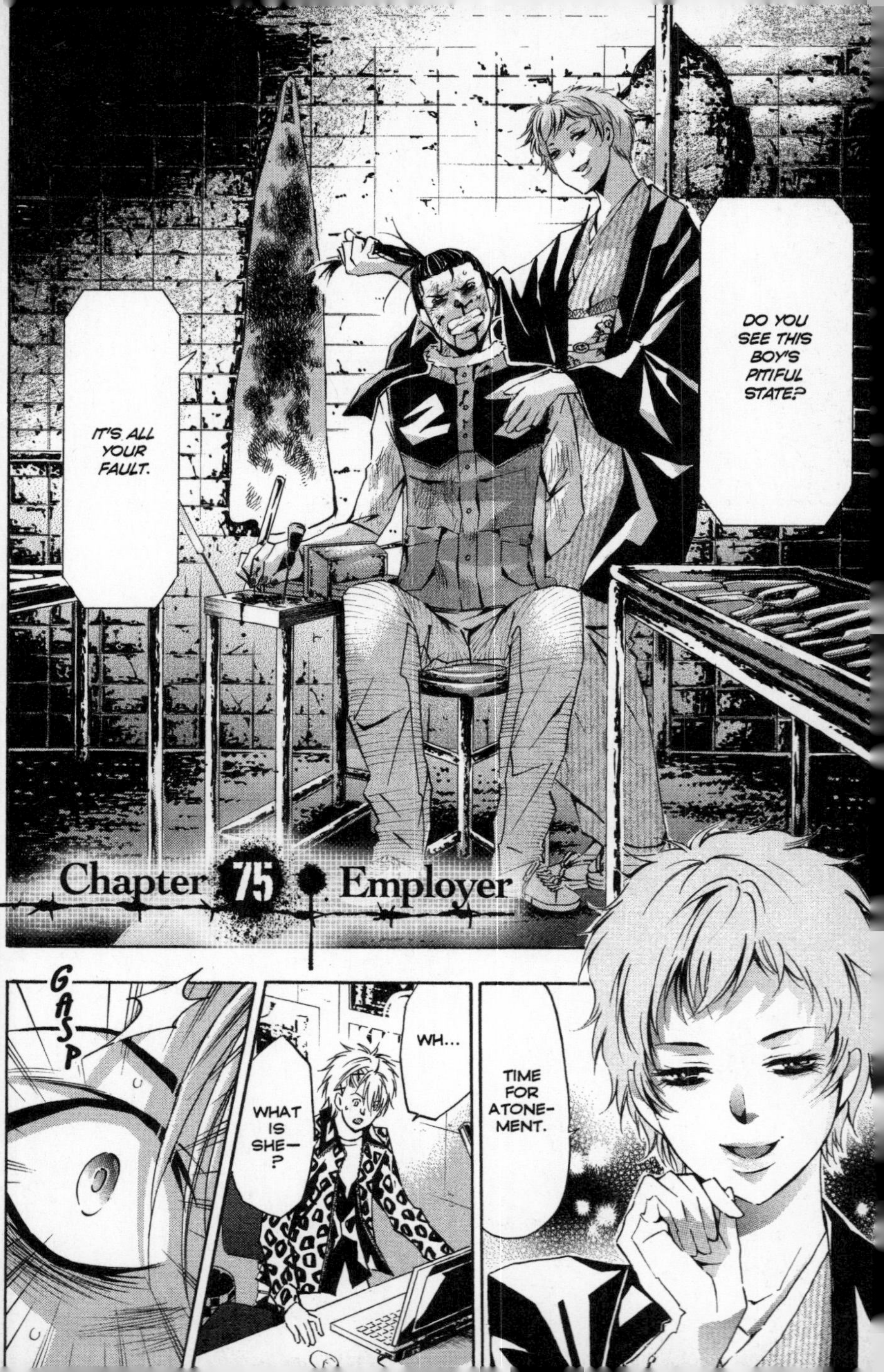
DO YOU SEE THIS BOY'S PITIFUL STATE?
IT'S ALL YOUR FAULT.
Chapter 75 Employer
TIME FOR ATONEMENT.
WH...
WHAT IS SHE—?
GASP

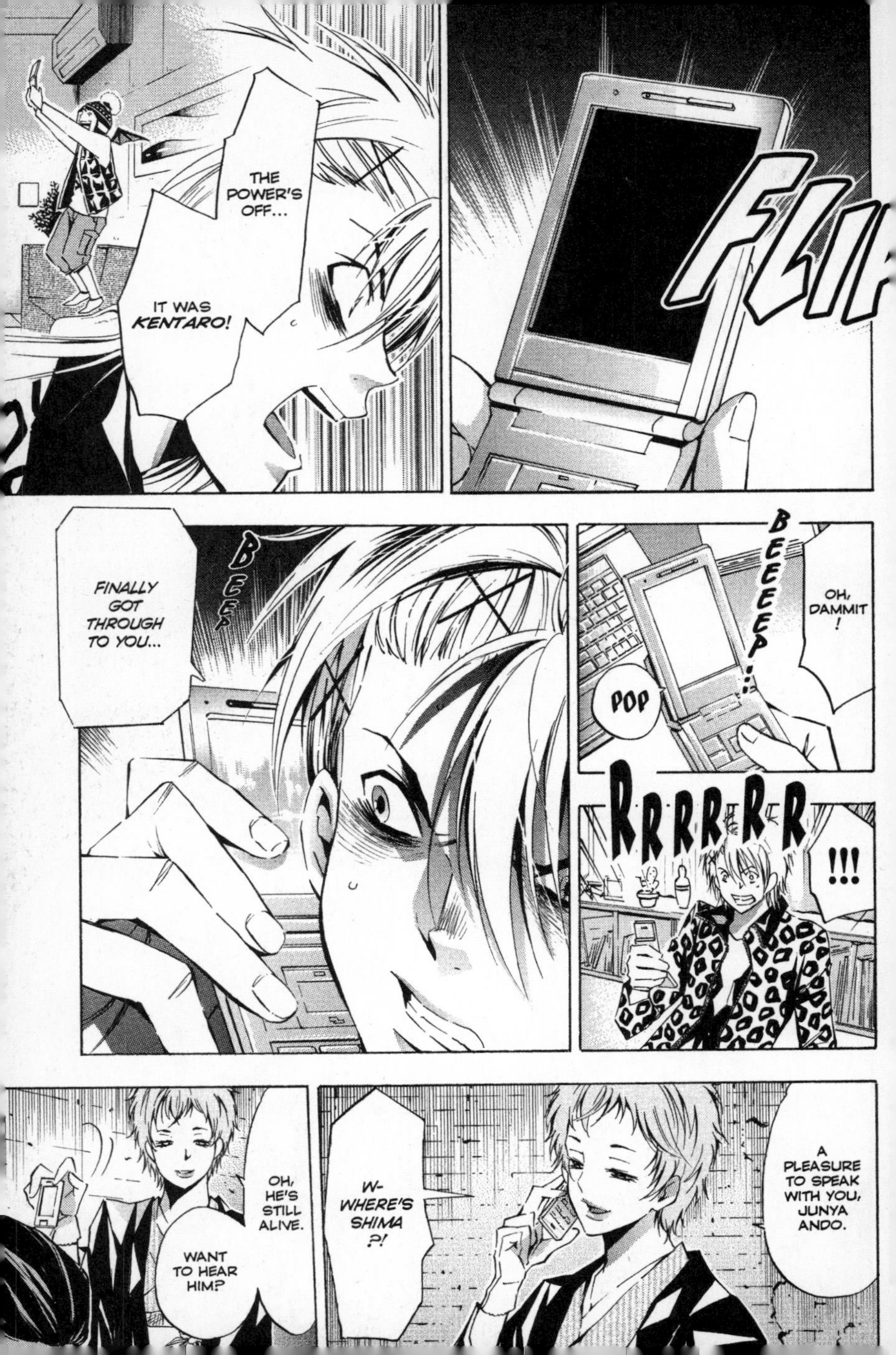
FLIP
THE POWER'S OFF...
IT WAS KENTARO!
OH, DAMMIT!
BEEEEEP...
POP
RRRRRR
!!!
FINALLY GOT THROUGH TO YOU...
BEEP
A PLEASURE TO SPEAK WITH YOU, JUNYA ANDO.
W-WHERE'S SHIMA?!
OH, HE'S STILL ALIVE.
WANT TO HEAR HIM?

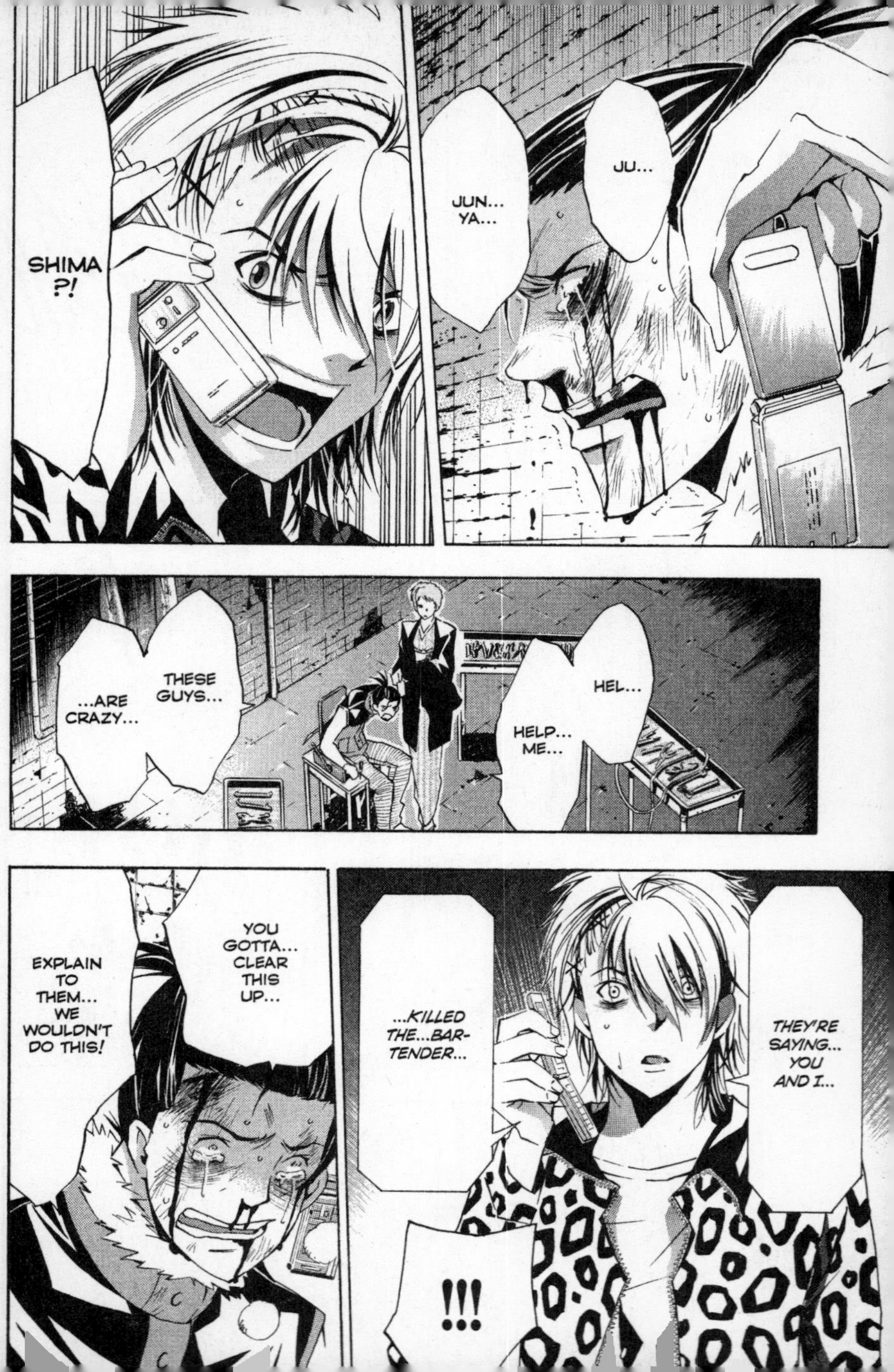

JU...
JUN... YA...
SHIMA ?!
HEL... HELP... ME...
THESE GUYS... ...ARE CRAZY...
THEY'RE SAYING... YOU AND I...
...KILLED THE...BAR-TENDER...
!!!
YOU GOTTA... CLEAR THIS UP...
EXPLAIN TO THEM... WE WOULDN'T DO THIS!

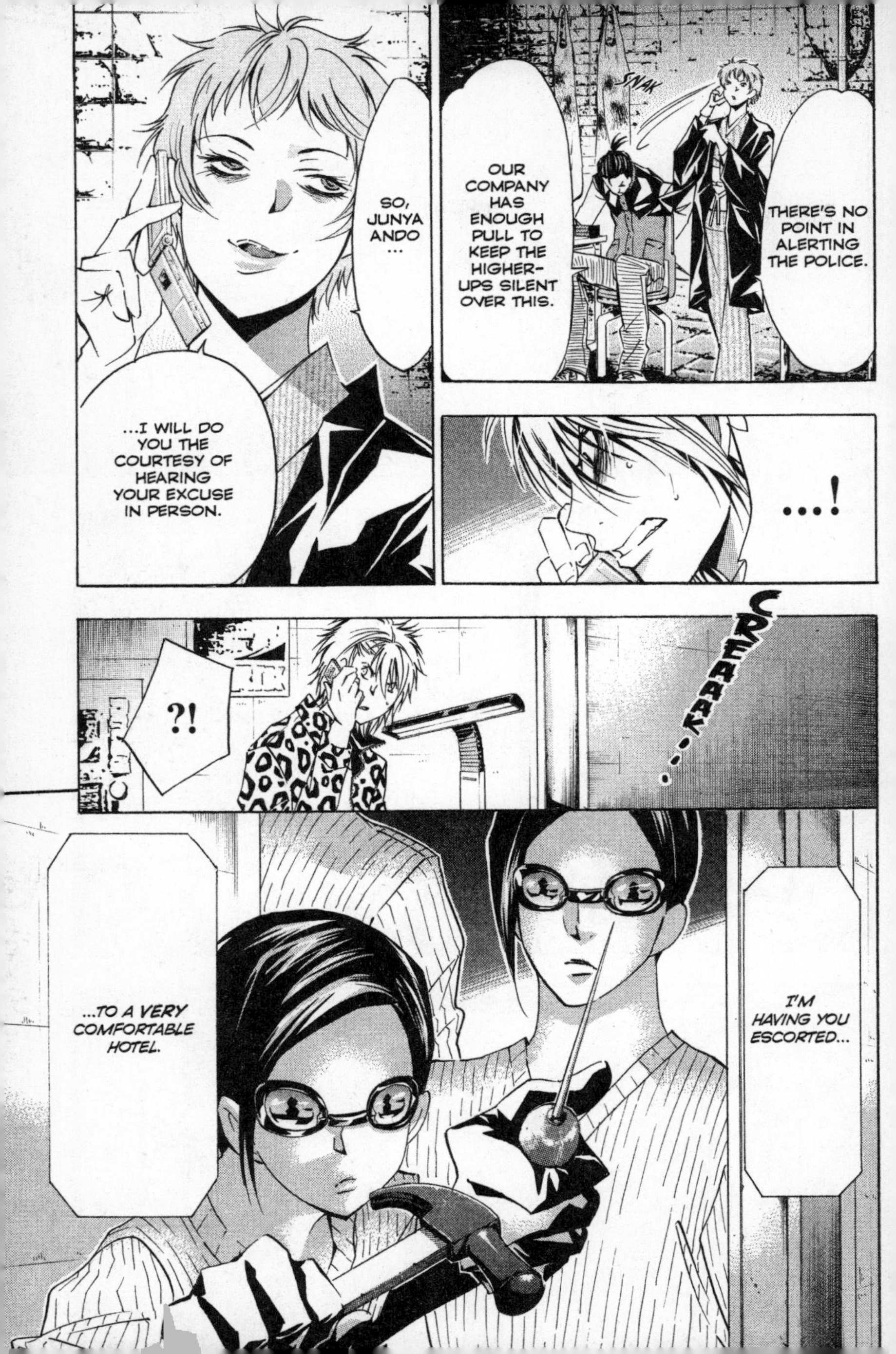
THERE'S NO POINT IN ALERTING THE POLICE.
SNAK
OUR COMPANY HAS ENOUGH PULL TO KEEP THE HIGHER-UPS SILENT OVER THIS.
...!
SO, JUNYA ANDO ...
...I WILL DO YOU THE COURTESY OF HEARING YOUR EXCUSE IN PERSON.
CREAAAK...
?!
I'M HAVING YOU ESCORTED...
...TO A *VERY* COMFORTABLE HOTEL.

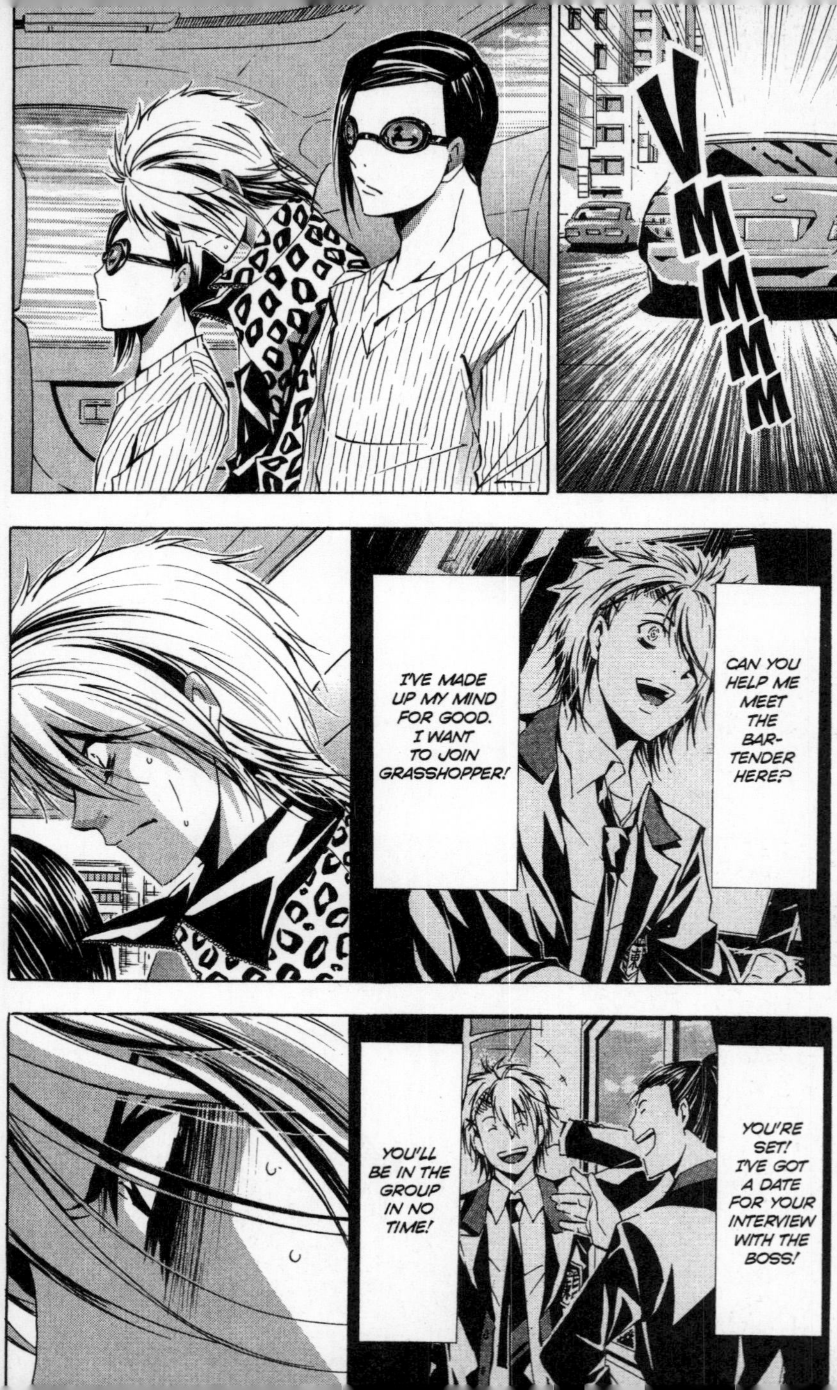
VMMMMM
CAN YOU HELP ME MEET THE BAR-TENDER HERE?
I'VE MADE UP MY MIND FOR GOOD. I WANT TO JOIN GRASSHOPPER!
YOU'RE SET! I'VE GOT A DATE FOR YOUR INTERVIEW WITH THE BOSS!
YOU'LL BE IN THE GROUP IN NO TIME!

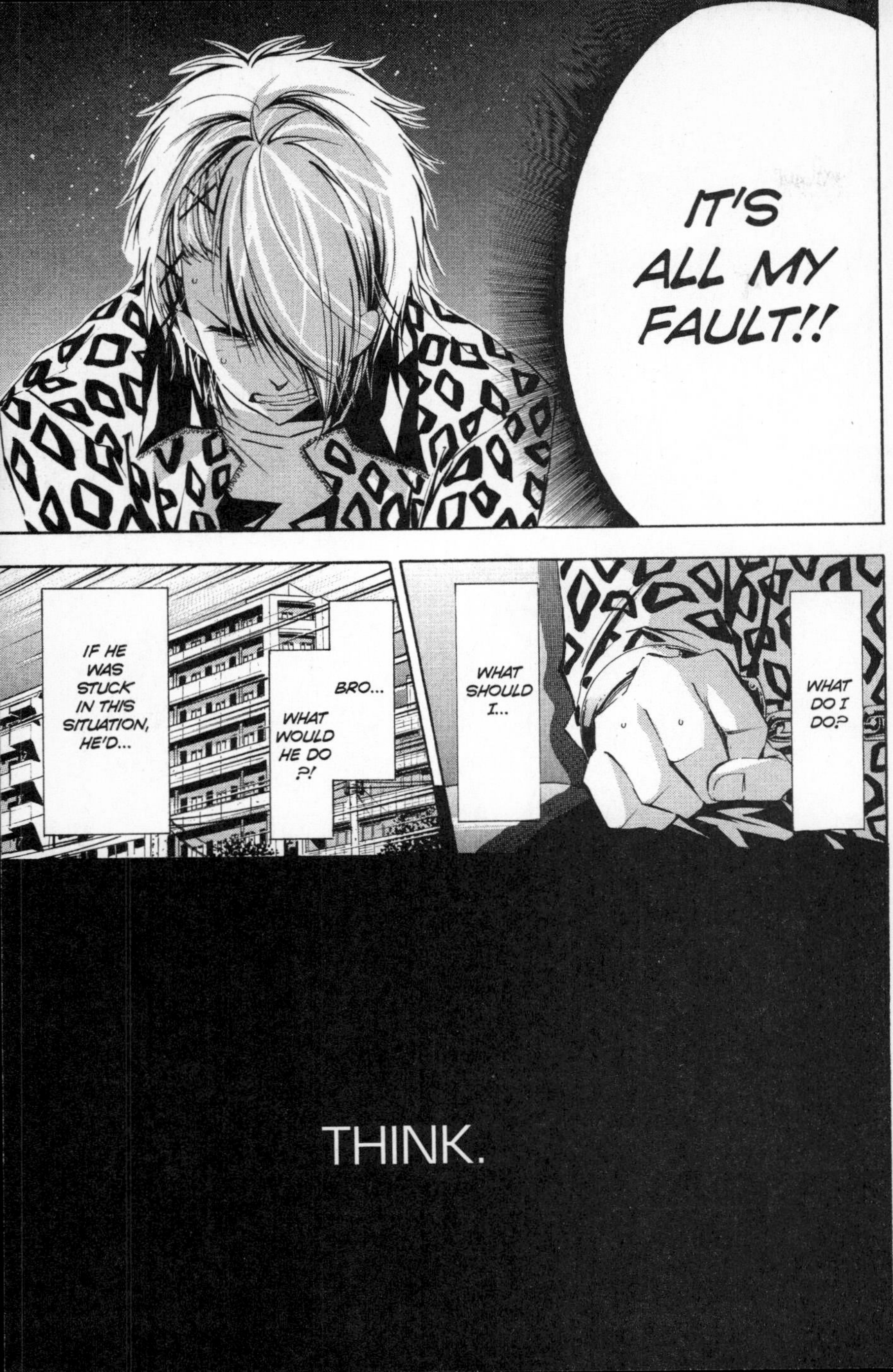
IT'S ALL MY FAULT!!
WHAT DO I DO?
WHAT SHOULD I...
BRO...
WHAT WOULD HE DO ?!
IF HE WAS STUCK IN THIS SITUATION, HE'D...
THINK.

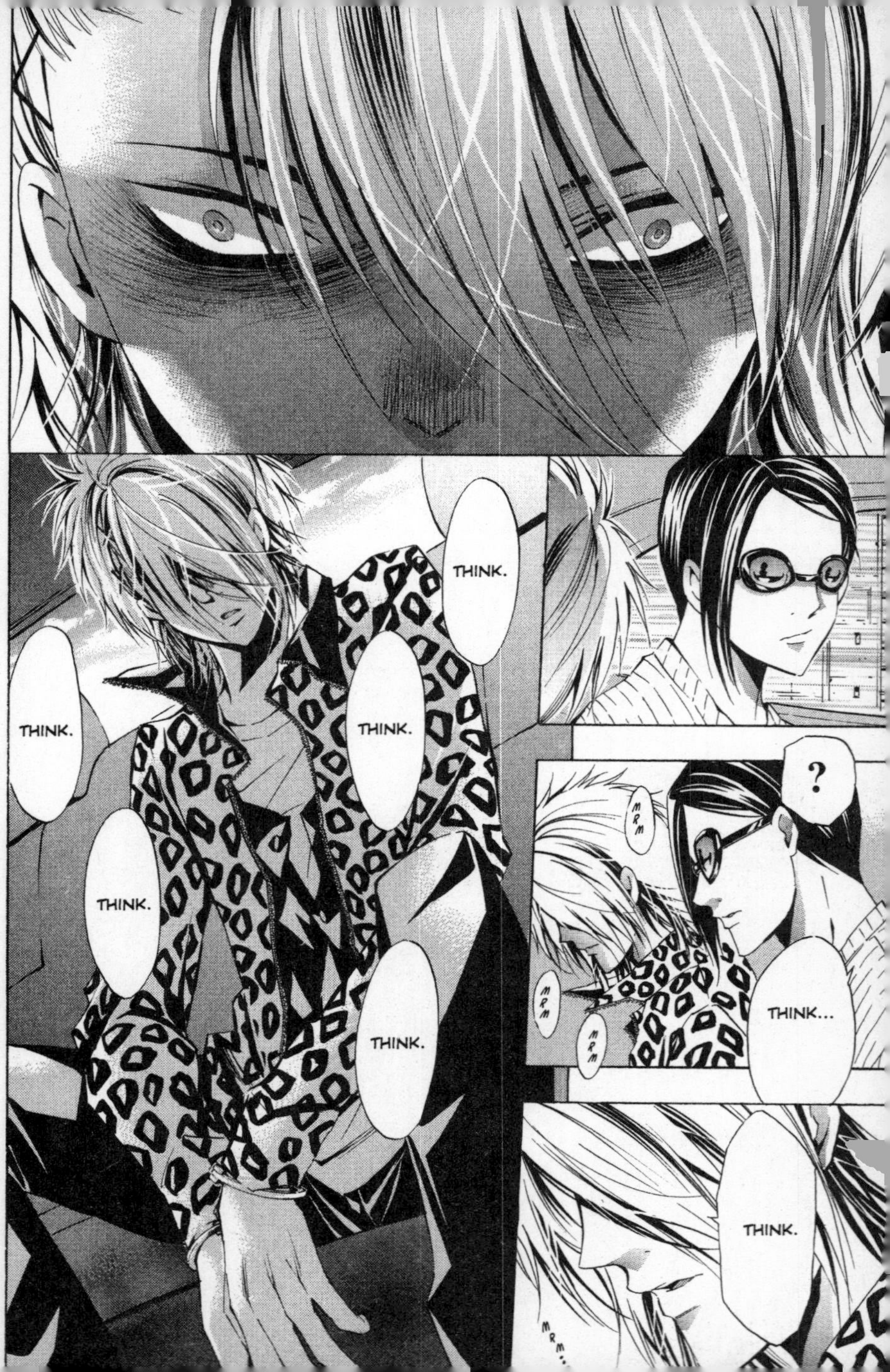
?
MRM
THINK...
MRM
MRM
THINK.
MRM..
THINK.
THINK.
THINK.
THINK.
THINK.

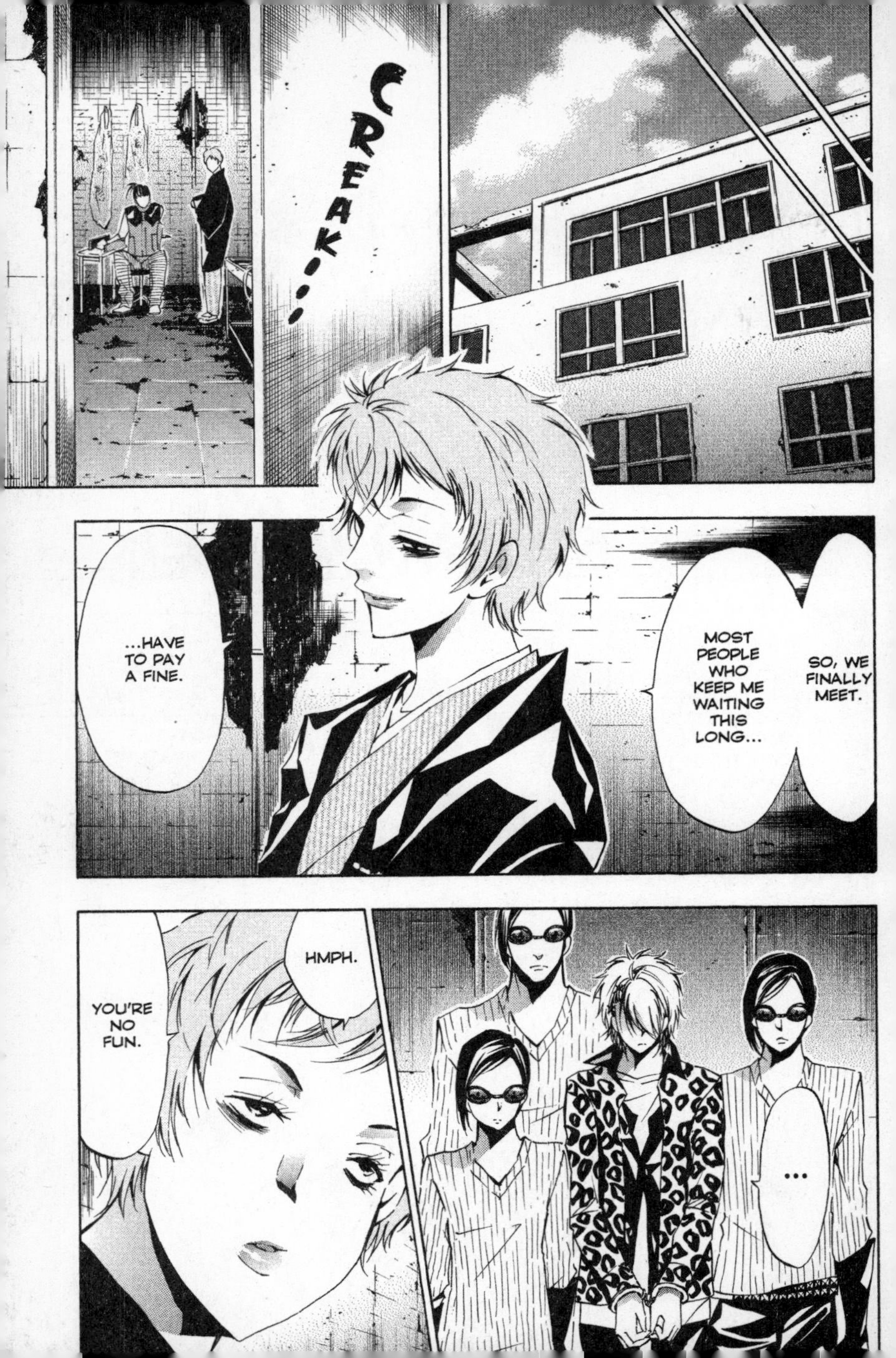
CREAK...
SO, WE FINALLY MEET.
MOST PEOPLE WHO KEEP ME WAITING THIS LONG...
...HAVE TO PAY A FINE.
...
HMPH.
YOU'RE NO FUN.

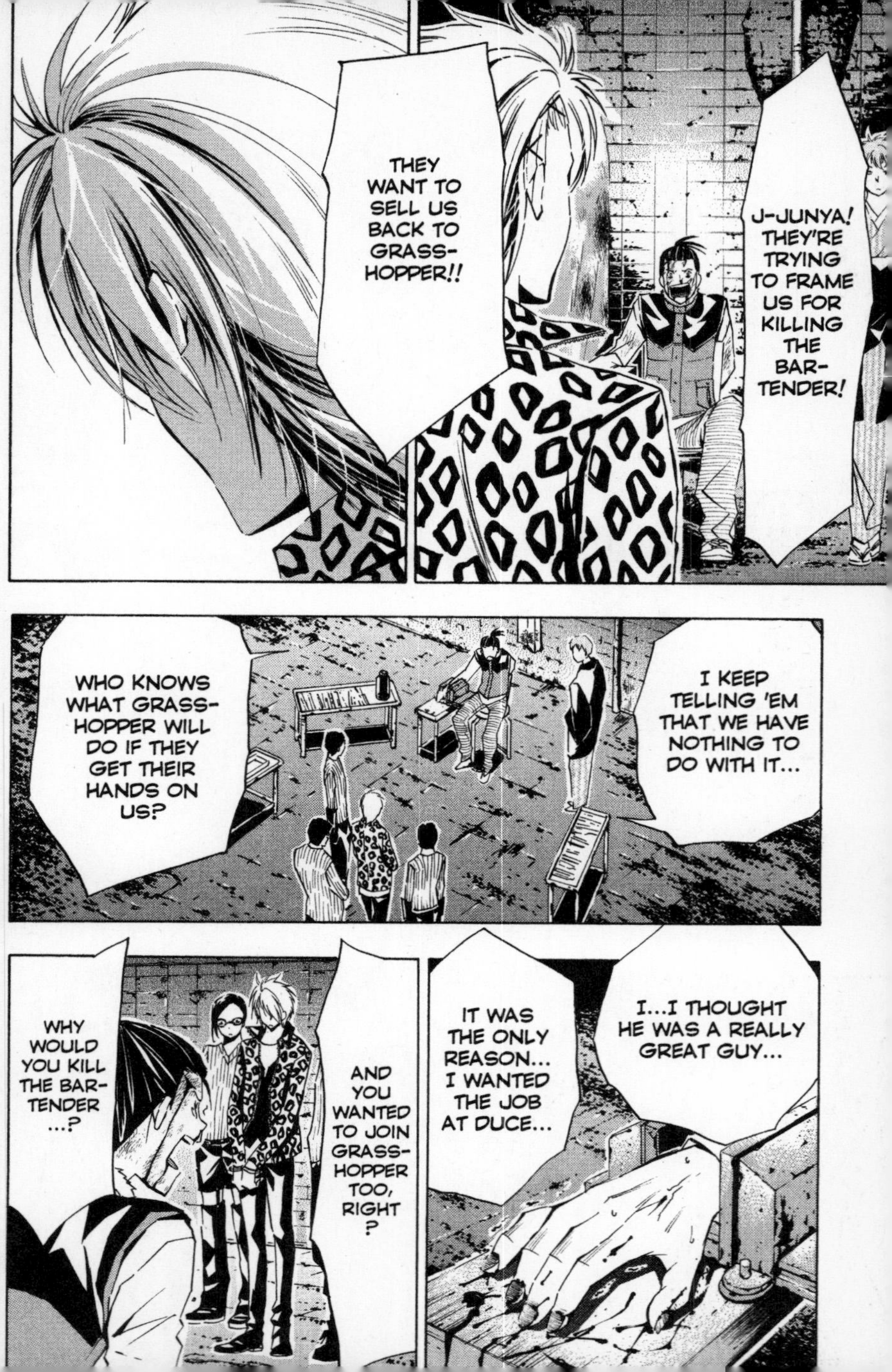
J-JUNYA! THEY'RE TRYING TO FRAME US FOR KILLING THE BAR-TENDER!
THEY WANT TO SELL US BACK TO GRASS-HOPPER!!
I KEEP TELLING 'EM THAT WE HAVE NOTHING TO DO WITH IT...
WHO KNOWS WHAT GRASS-HOPPER WILL DO IF THEY GET THEIR HANDS ON US?
I...I THOUGHT HE WAS A REALLY GREAT GUY...
IT WAS THE ONLY REASON... I WANTED THE JOB AT DUCE...
AND YOU WANTED TO JOIN GRASS-HOPPER TOO, RIGHT?
WHY WOULD YOU KILL THE BAR-TENDER...?

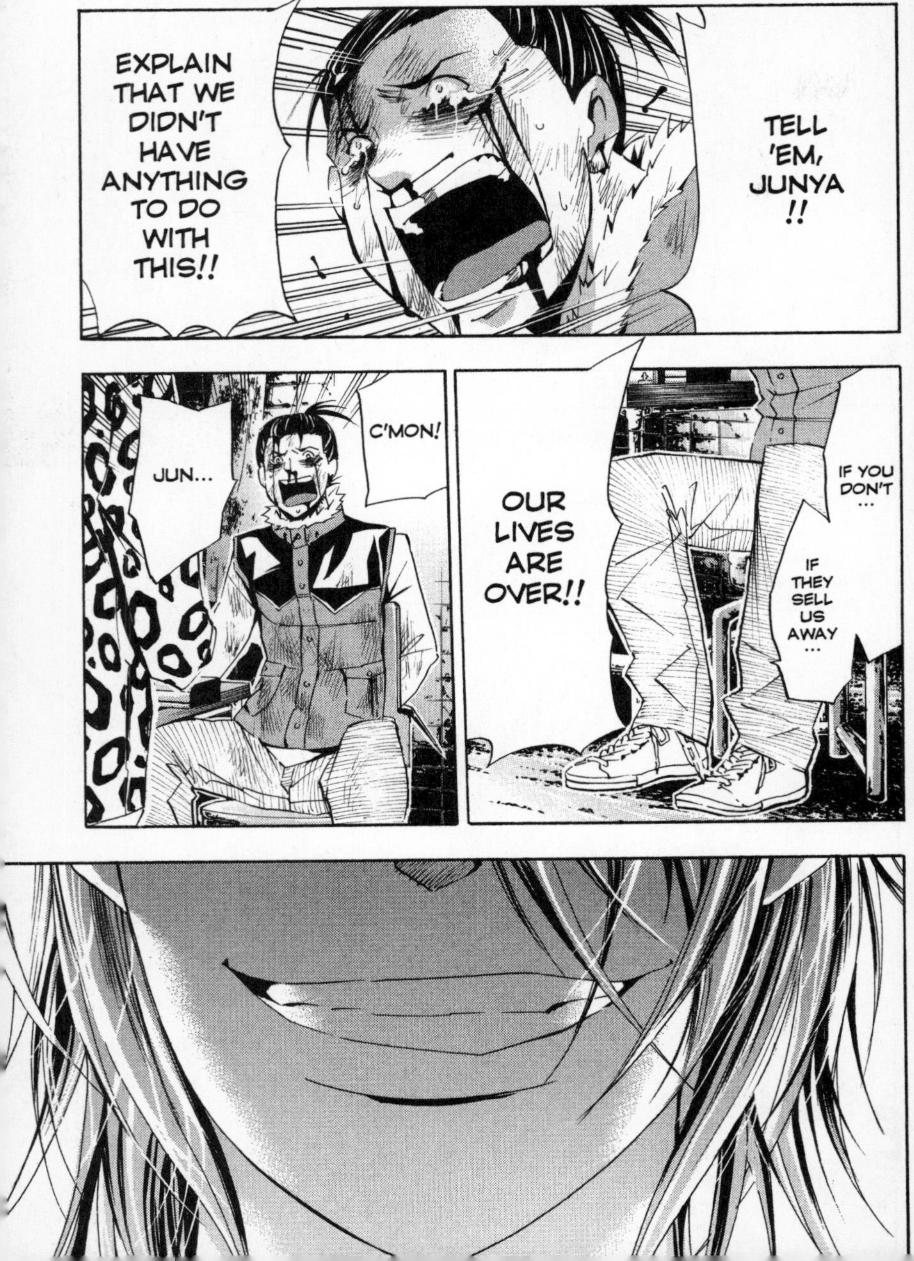
TELL 'EM, JUNYA!!
EXPLAIN THAT WE DIDN'T HAVE ANYTHING TO DO WITH THIS!!
IF YOU DON'T...
IF THEY SELL US AWAY...
OUR LIVES ARE OVER!!
C'MON!
JUN...

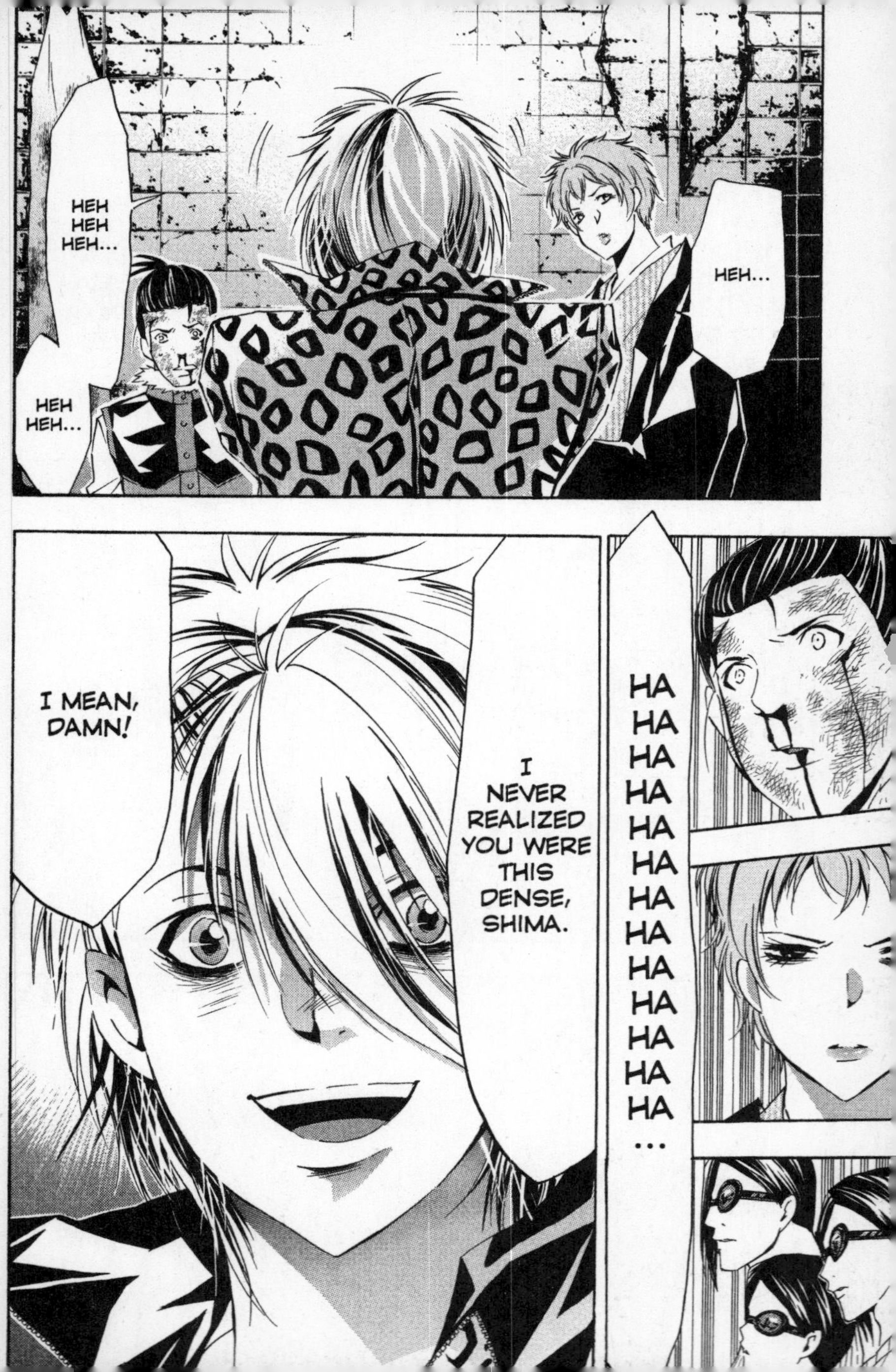
HEH...
HEH HEH HEH...
HEH HEH...
HA HA HA HA HA HA HA HA HA HA HA HA HA HA ...
I NEVER REALIZED YOU WERE THIS DENSE, SHIMA.
I MEAN, DAMN!

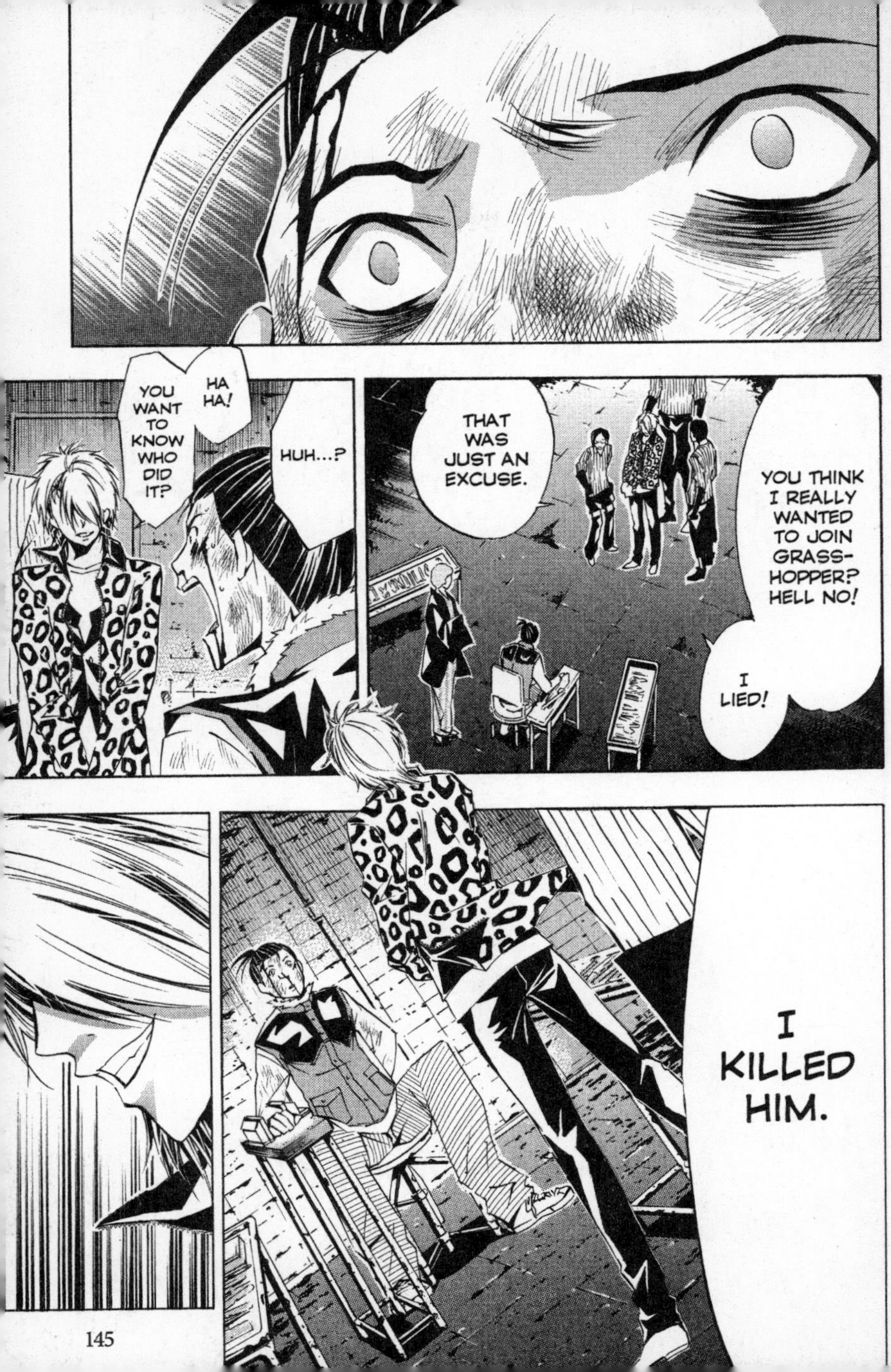
YOU THINK I REALLY WANTED TO JOIN GRASS-HOPPER? HELL NO!
I LIED!
THAT WAS JUST AN EXCUSE.
HUH...?
HA HA!
YOU WANT TO KNOW WHO DID IT?
I KILLED HIM.

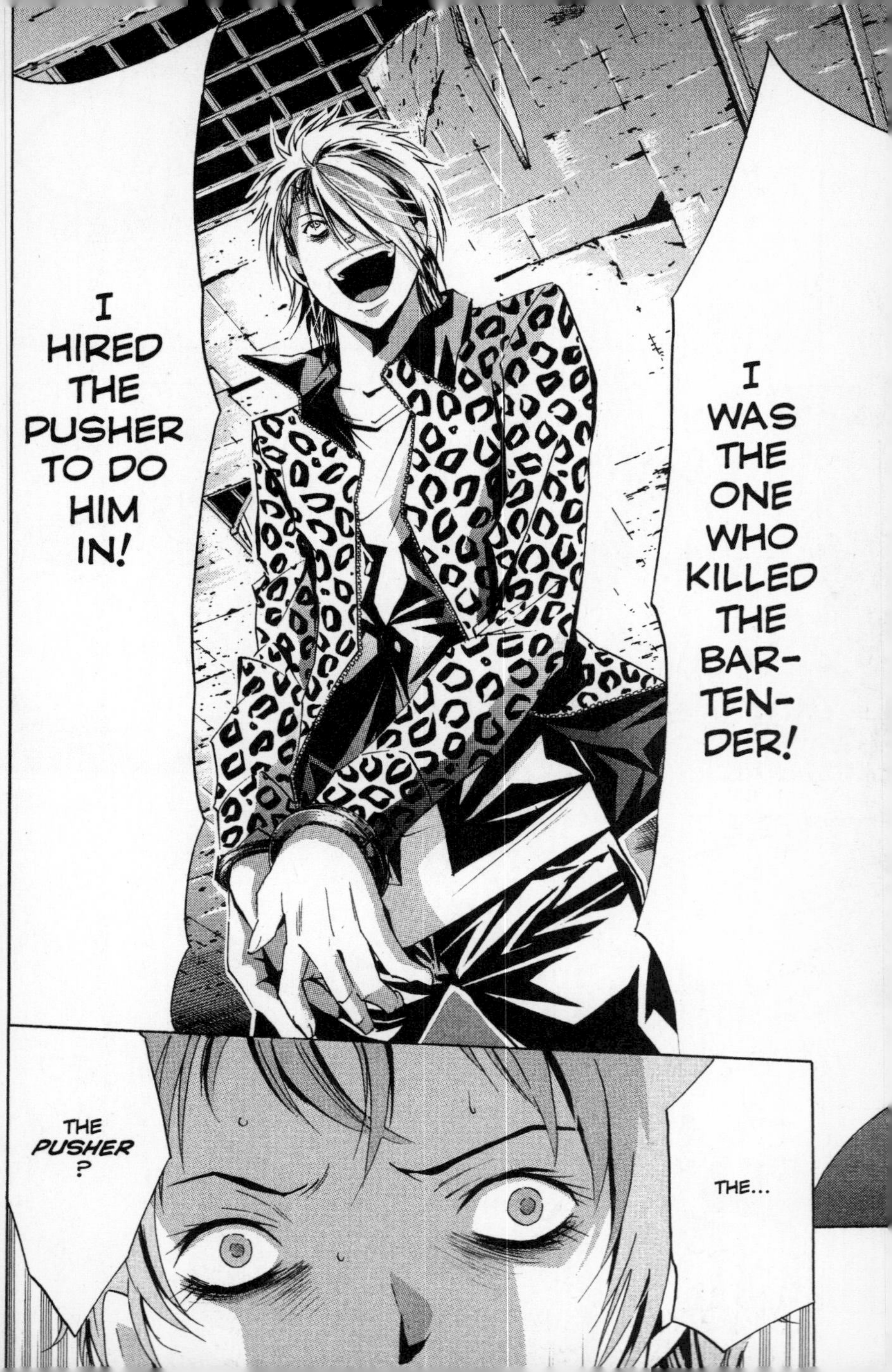
I WAS THE ONE WHO KILLED THE BAR-TENDER!
I HIRED THE PUSHER TO DO HIM IN!
THE...
THE *PUSHER*?

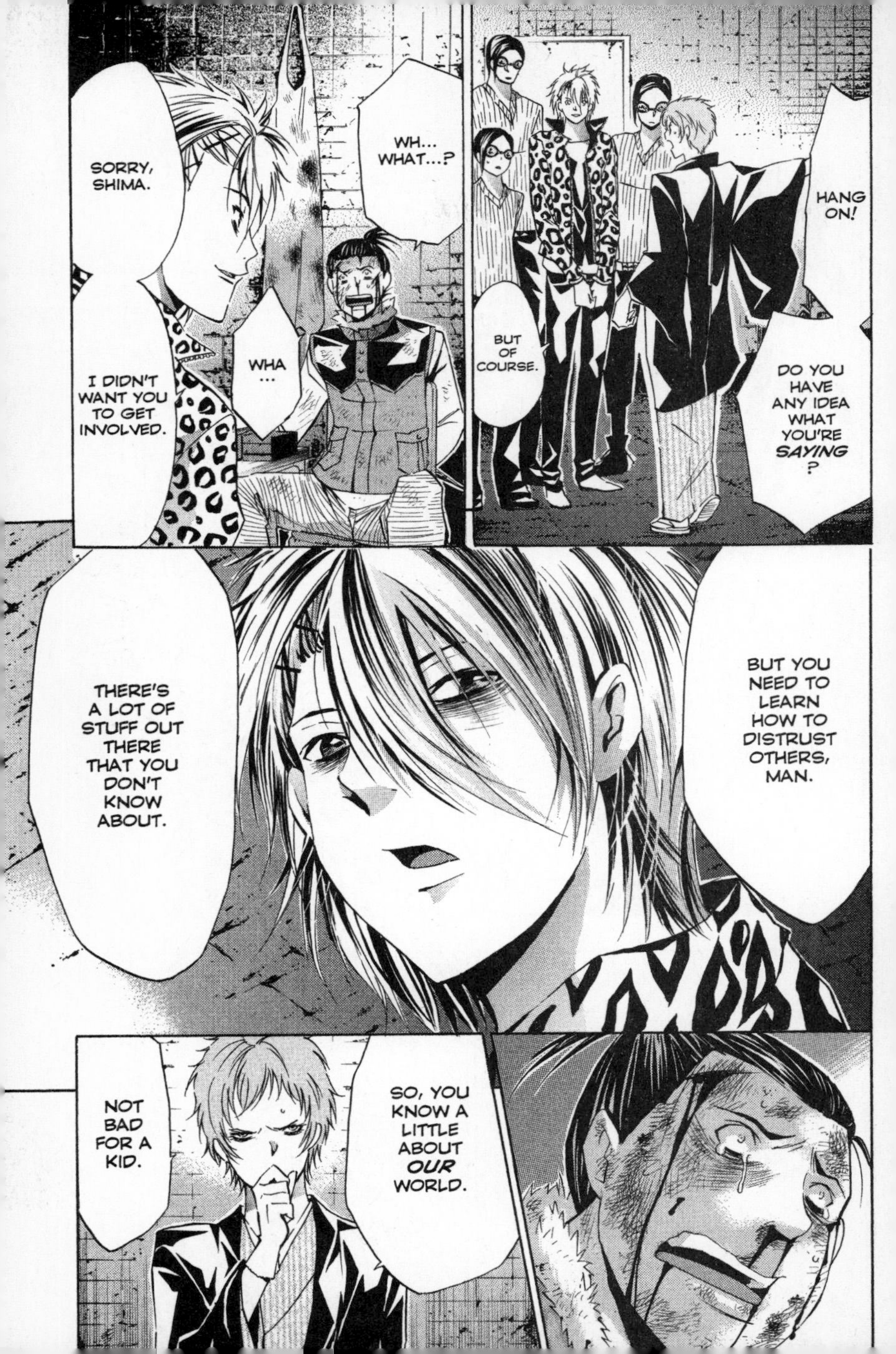
HANG ON!
DO YOU HAVE ANY IDEA WHAT YOU'RE *SAYING*?
BUT OF COURSE.
WH... WHAT...?
SORRY, SHIMA.
WHA ...
I DIDN'T WANT YOU TO GET INVOLVED.
BUT YOU NEED TO LEARN HOW TO DISTRUST OTHERS, MAN.
THERE'S A LOT OF STUFF OUT THERE THAT YOU DON'T KNOW ABOUT.
SO, YOU KNOW A LITTLE ABOUT *OUR* WORLD.
NOT BAD FOR A KID.

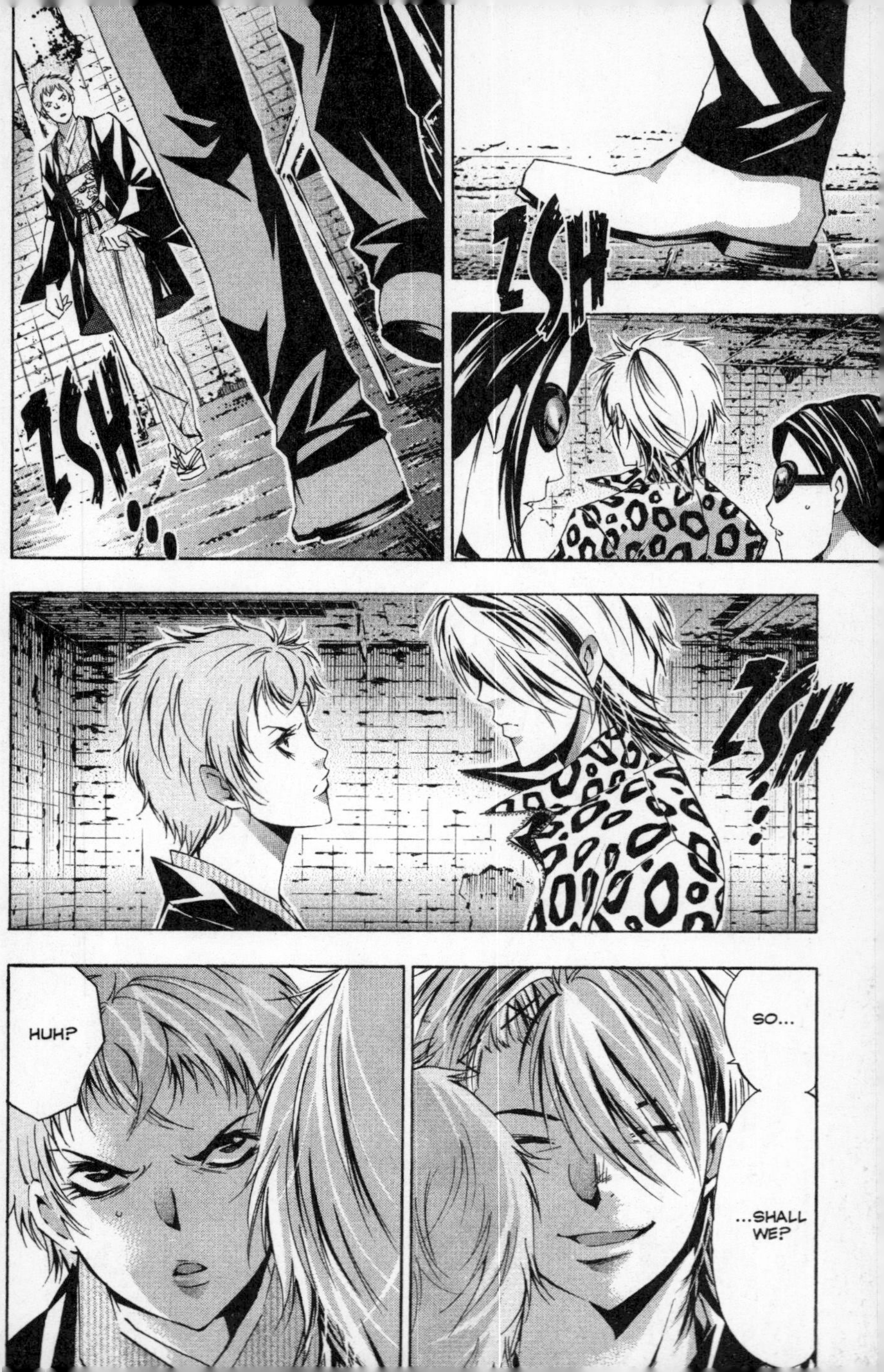
ZSH
ZSH...
ZSH...
SO...
...SHALL WE?
HUH?

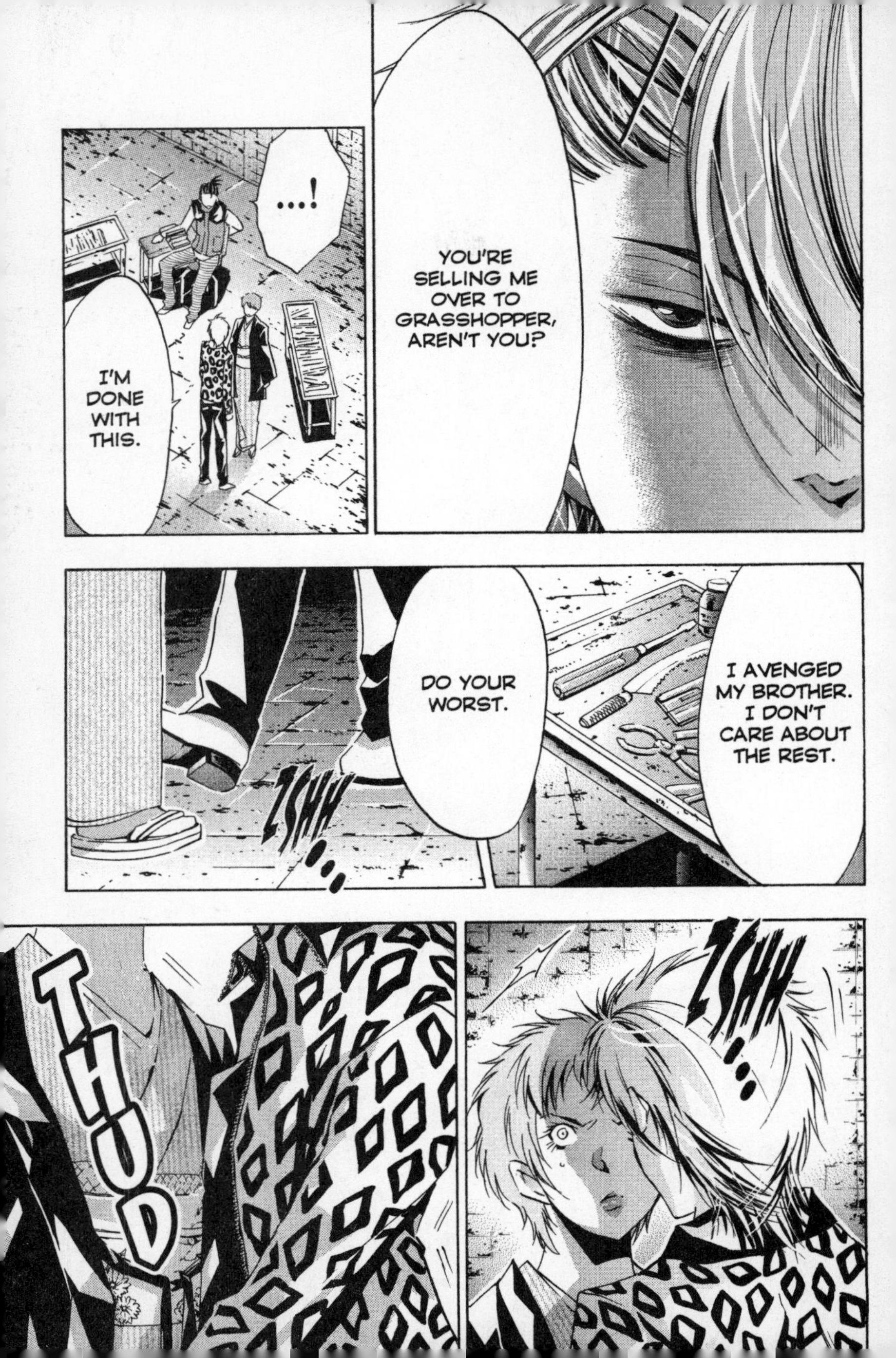
YOU'RE SELLING ME OVER TO GRASSHOPPER, AREN'T YOU?
...!
I'M DONE WITH THIS.
I AVENGED MY BROTHER. I DON'T CARE ABOUT THE REST.
DO YOUR WORST.
ZSHH...
ZSHH...
THUD

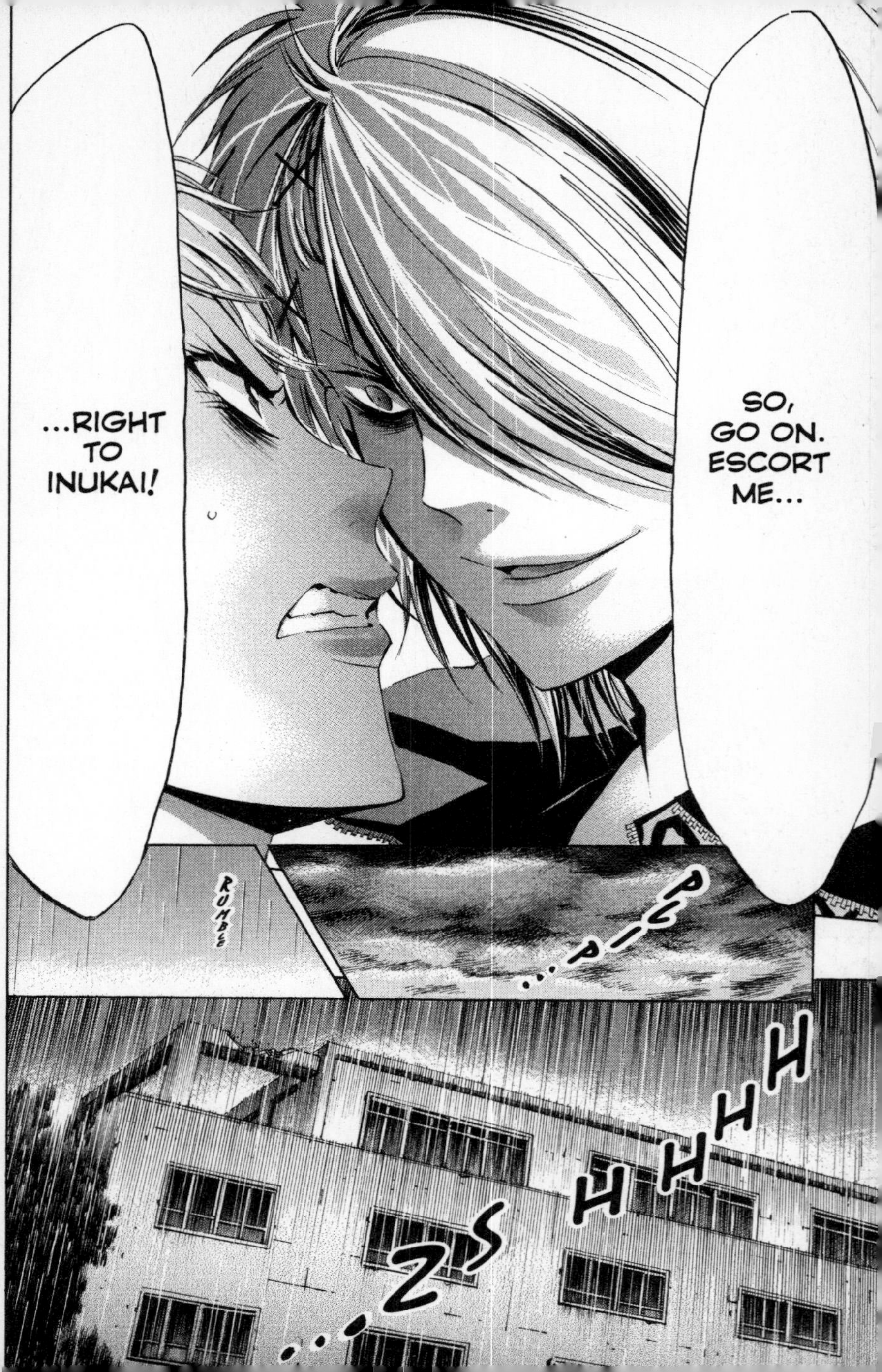
SO, GO ON. ESCORT ME...
...RIGHT TO INUKAI!
PLIP...
RUMBLE
...ZSHHHH

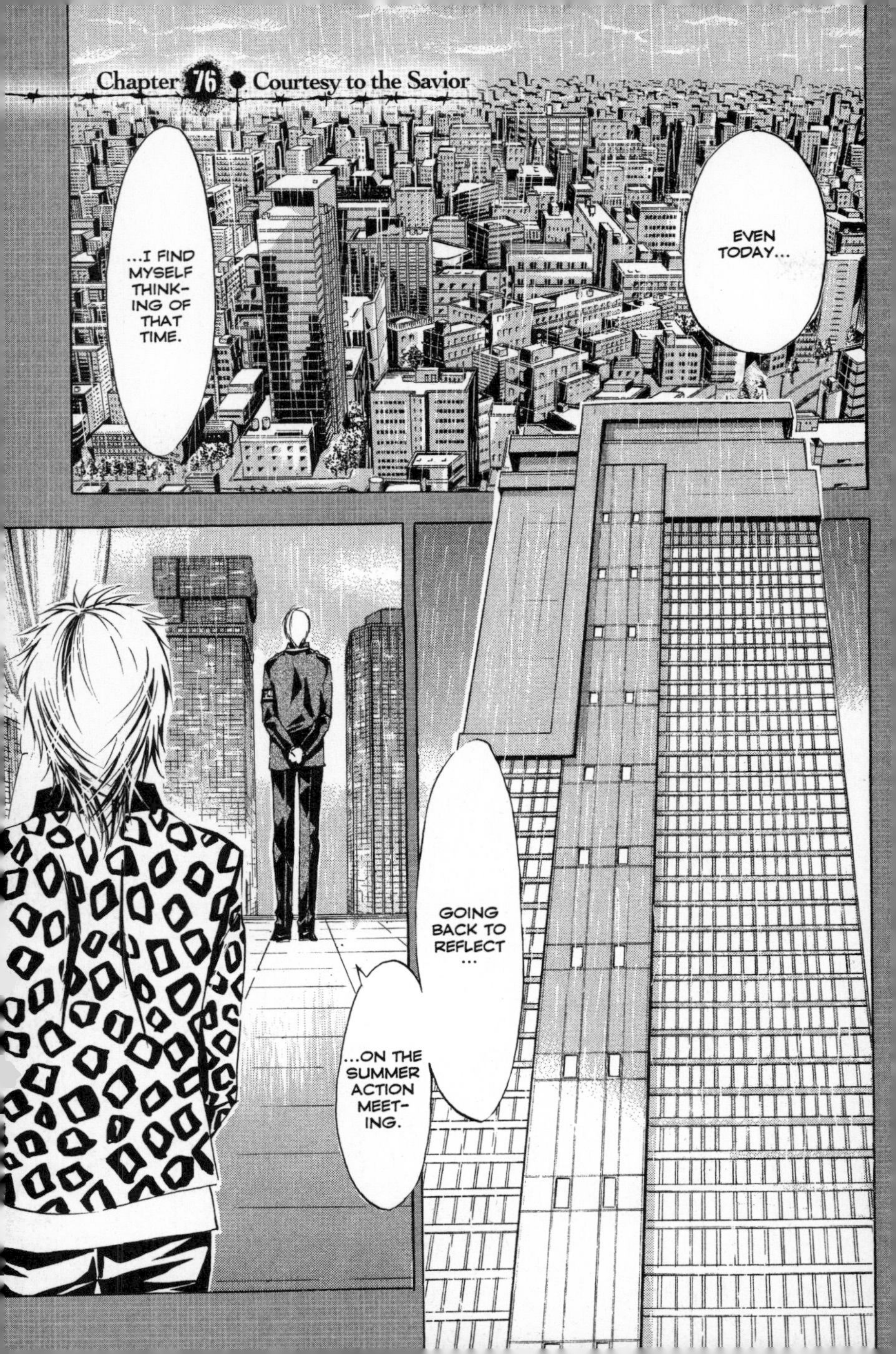
Chapter 76 Courtesy to the Savior
EVEN TODAY...
...I FIND MYSELF THINKING OF THAT TIME.
GOING BACK TO REFLECT...
...ON THE SUMMER ACTION MEETING.

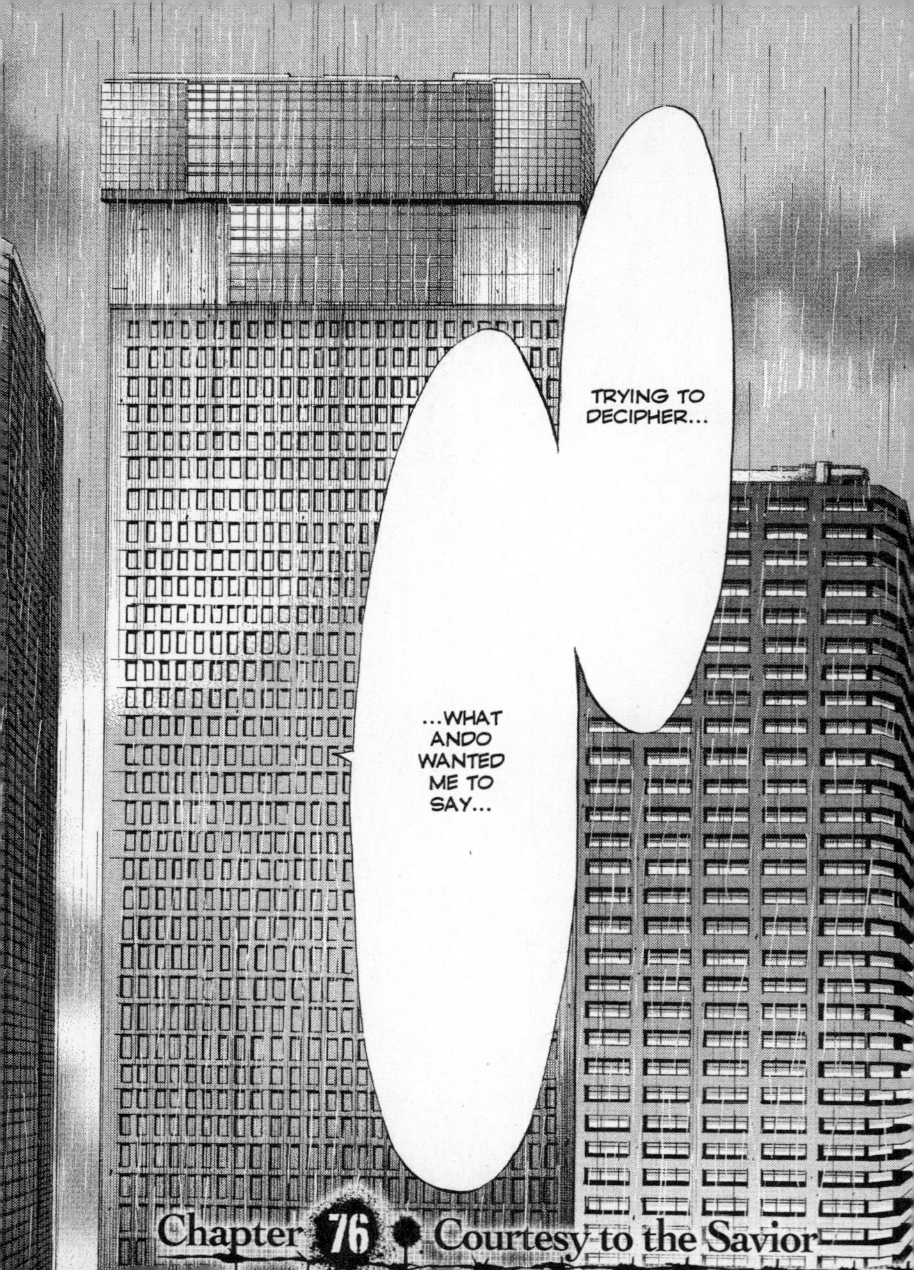
TRYING TO DECIPHER...
...WHAT ANDO WANTED ME TO SAY...
Chapter 76 • Courtesy to the Savior

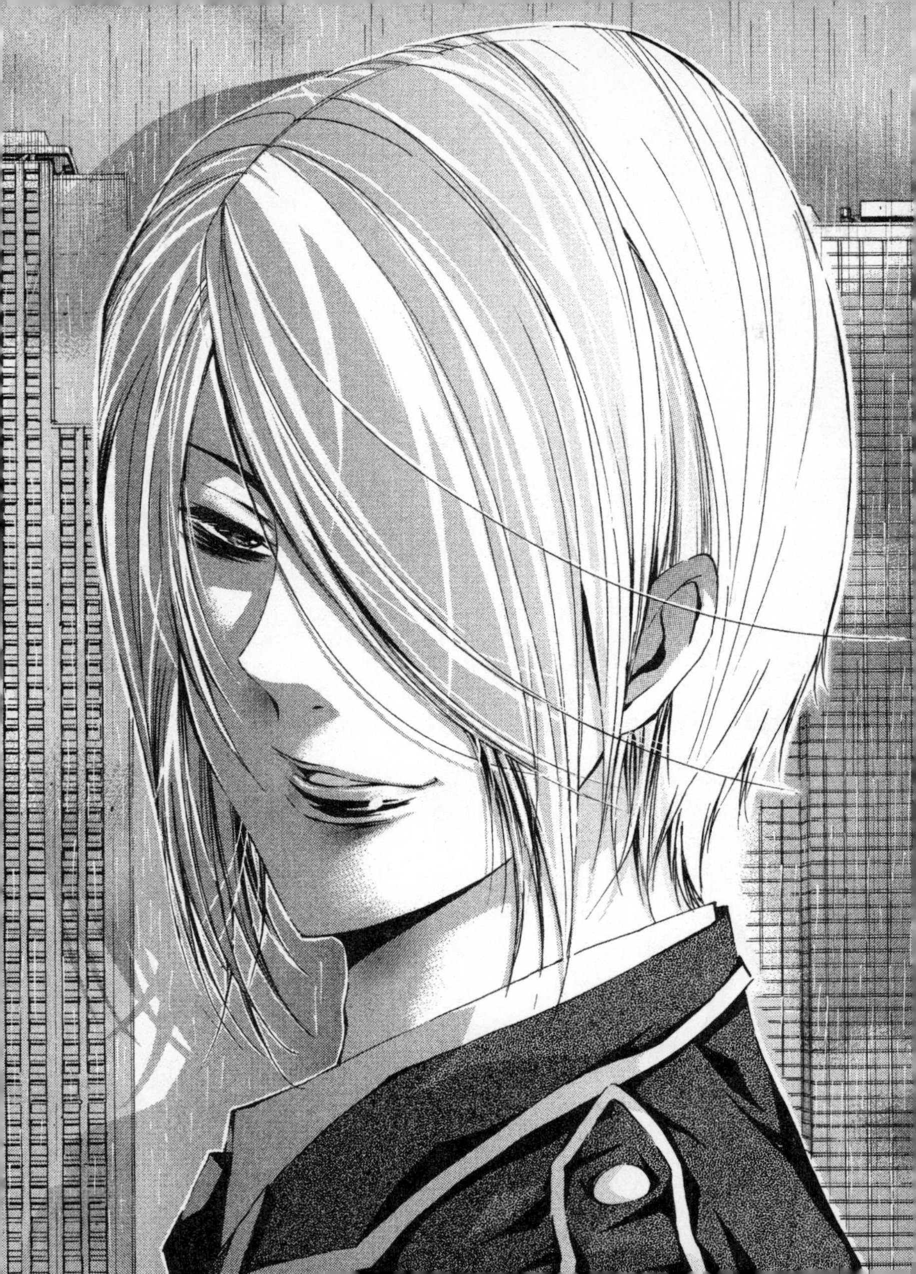

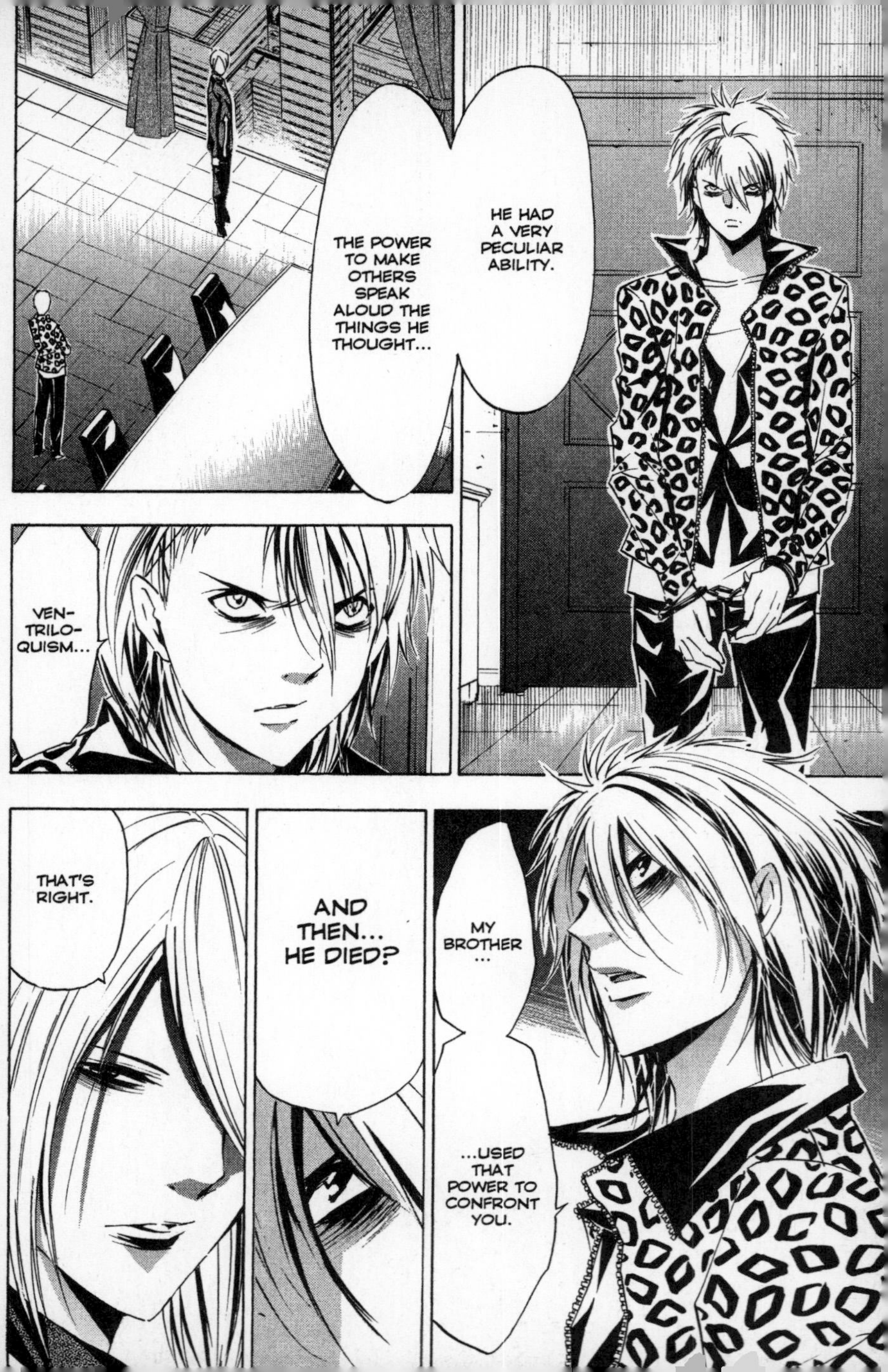
HE HAD A VERY PECULIAR ABILITY.
THE POWER TO MAKE OTHERS SPEAK ALOUD THE THINGS HE THOUGHT...
VEN-TRILO-QUISM...
MY BROTHER ...
...USED THAT POWER TO CONFRONT YOU.
AND THEN... HE DIED?
THAT'S RIGHT.

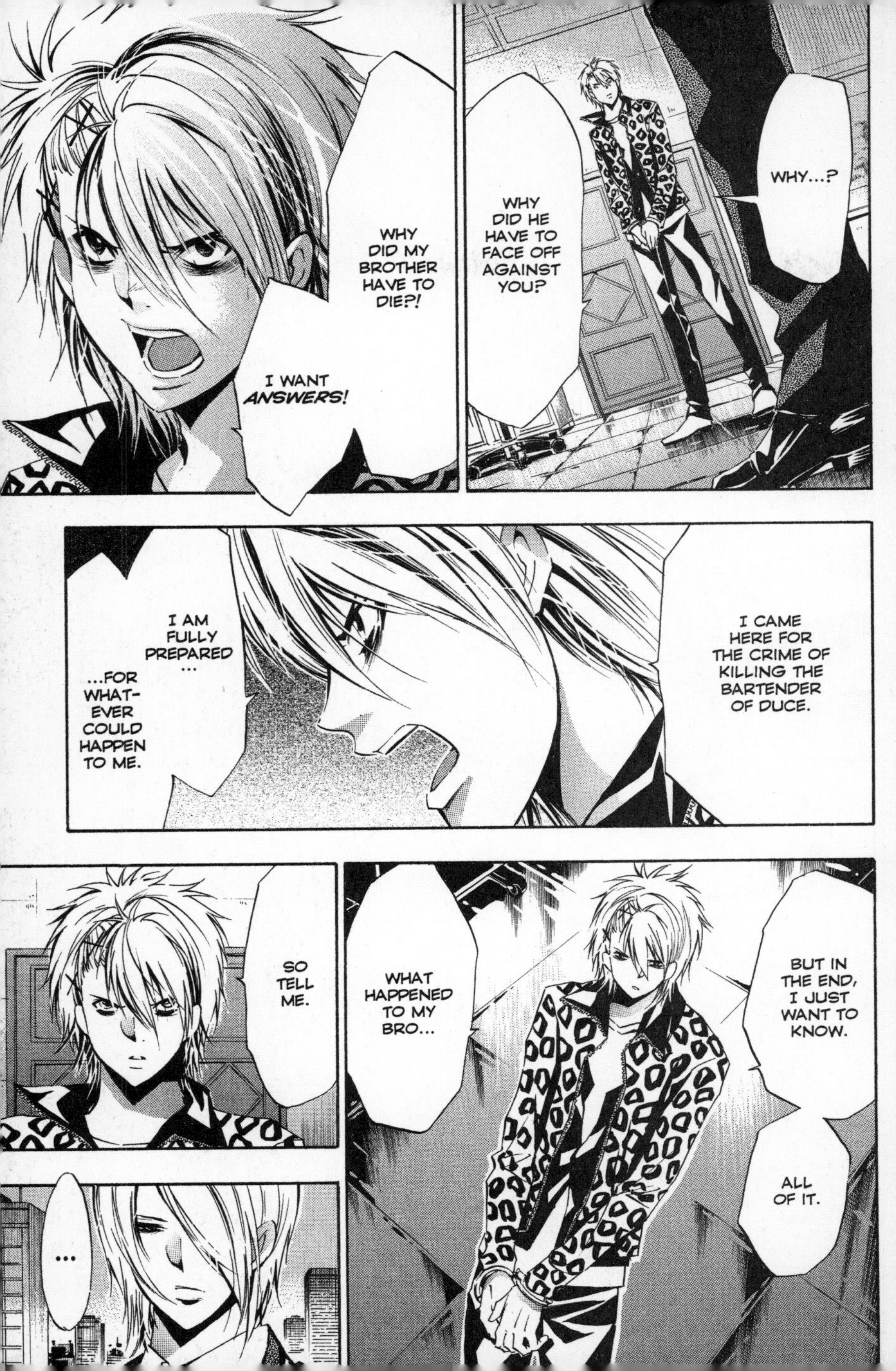
WHY...?
WHY DID HE HAVE TO FACE OFF AGAINST YOU?
WHY DID MY BROTHER HAVE TO DIE?!
I WANT *ANSWERS!*
I CAME HERE FOR THE CRIME OF KILLING THE BARTENDER OF DUCE.
I AM FULLY PREPARED...
...FOR WHAT-EVER COULD HAPPEN TO ME.
BUT IN THE END, I JUST WANT TO KNOW.
ALL OF IT.
WHAT HAPPENED TO MY BRO...
SO TELL ME.
...

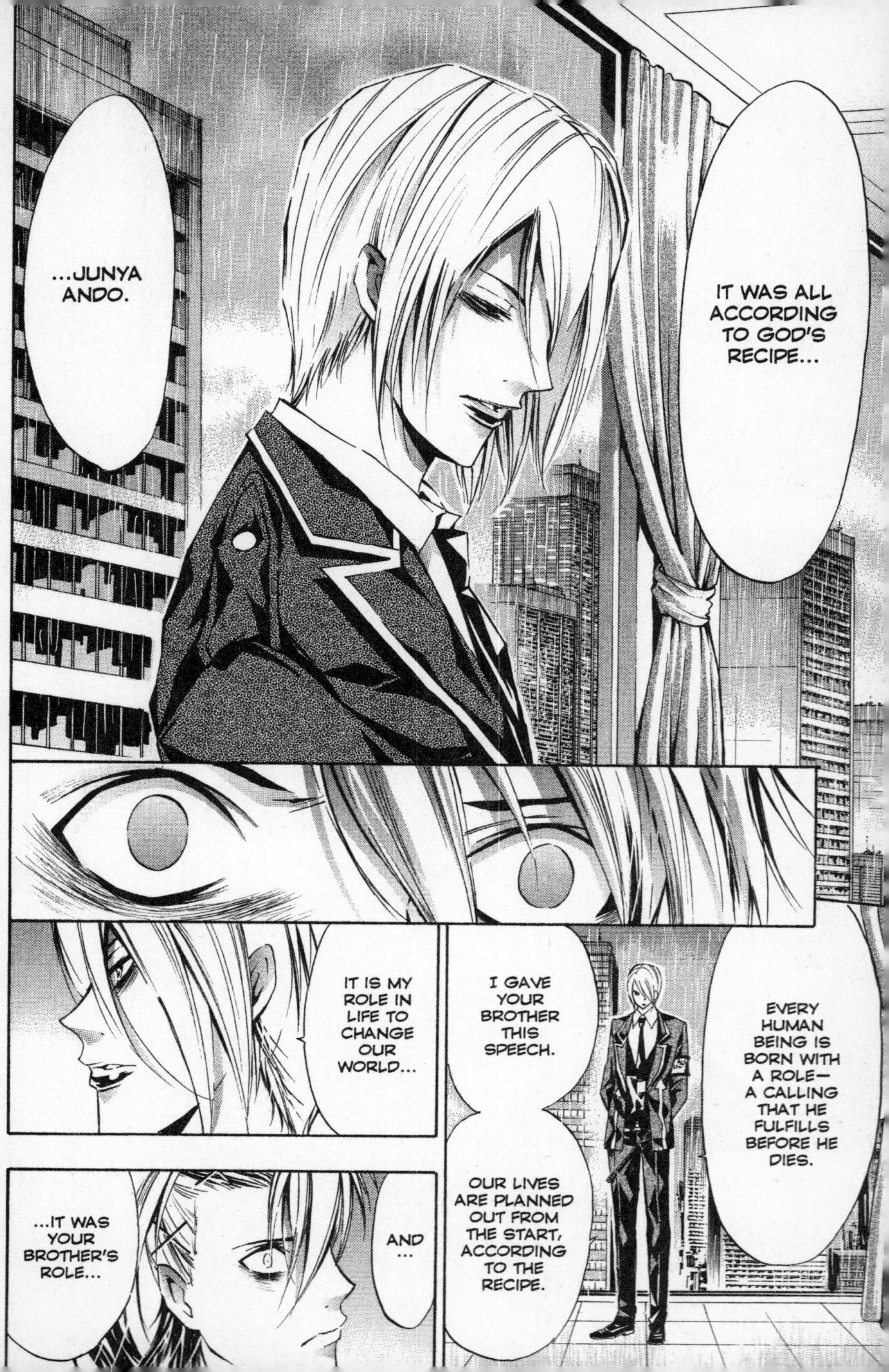
IT WAS ALL ACCORDING TO GOD'S RECIPE...
...JUNYA ANDO.
EVERY HUMAN BEING IS BORN WITH A ROLE— A CALLING THAT HE FULFILLS BEFORE HE DIES.
OUR LIVES ARE PLANNED OUT FROM THE START, ACCORDING TO THE RECIPE.
I GAVE YOUR BROTHER THIS SPEECH.
IT IS MY ROLE IN LIFE TO CHANGE OUR WORLD...
AND ...
...IT WAS YOUR BROTHER'S ROLE...

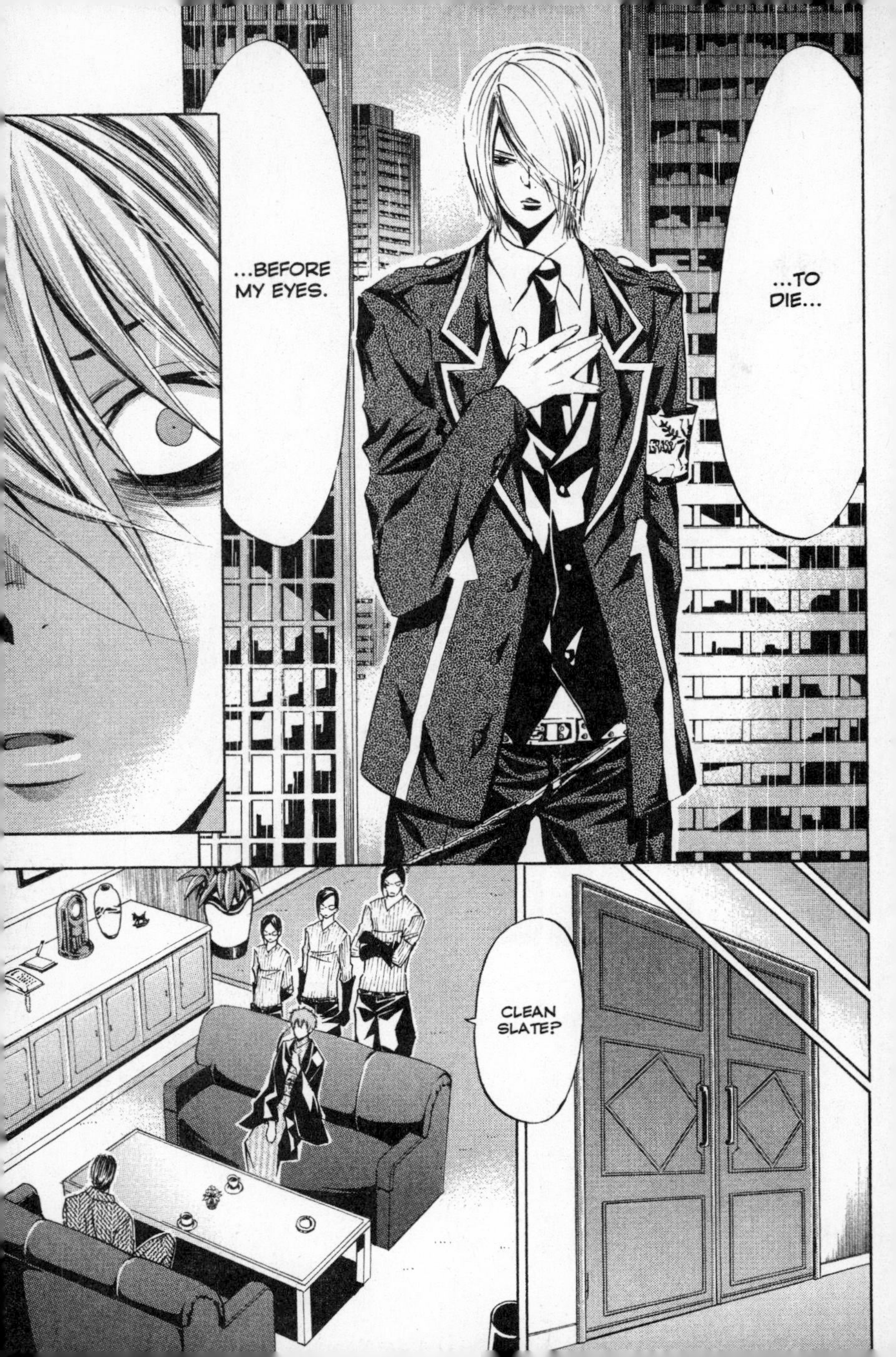
...TO DIE...
...BEFORE MY EYES.
CLEAN SLATE?

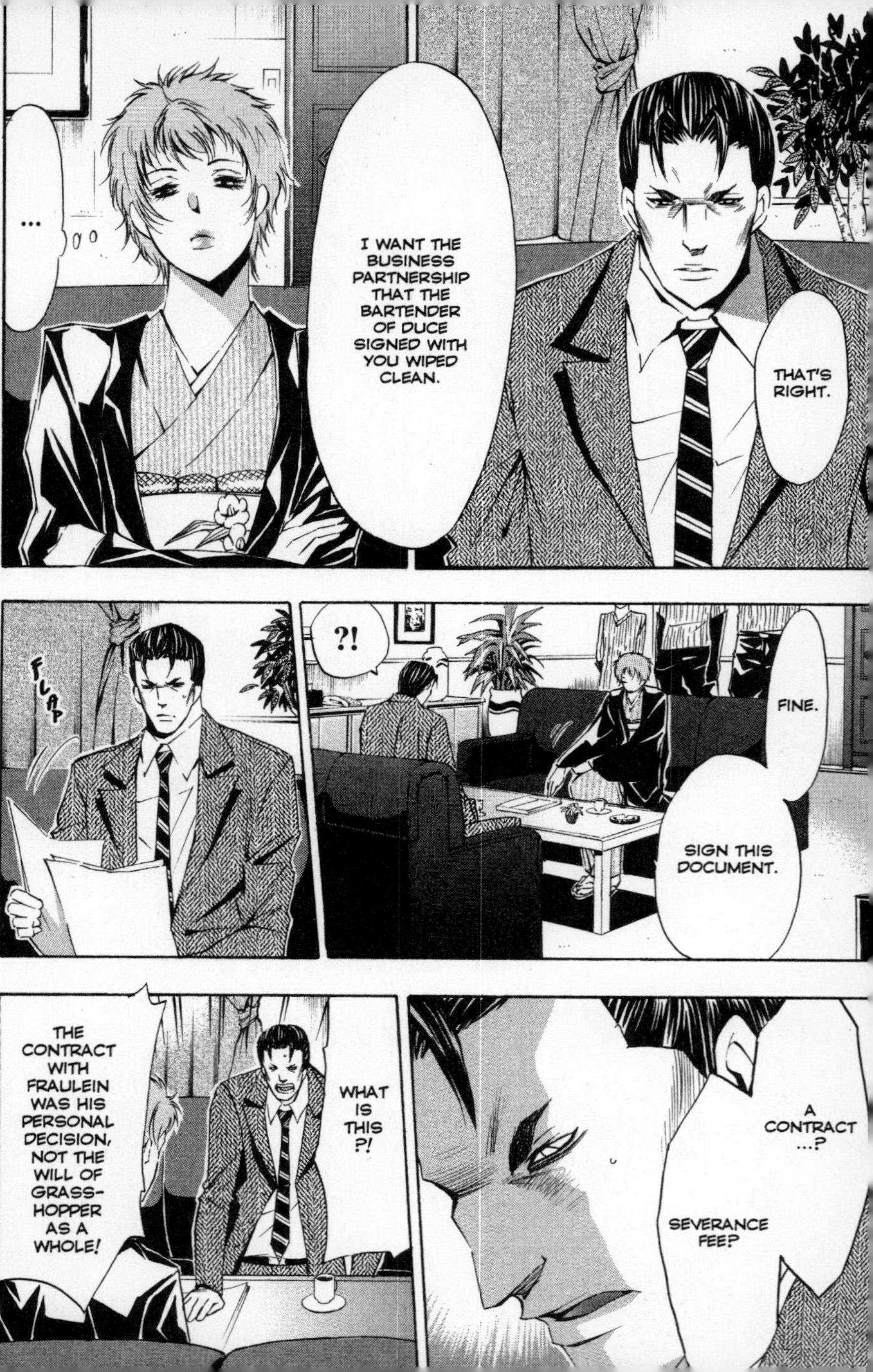
I WANT THE BUSINESS PARTNERSHIP THAT THE BARTENDER OF DUCE SIGNED WITH YOU WIPED CLEAN.
THAT'S RIGHT.
...
FINE.
SIGN THIS DOCUMENT.
?!
FLAP
A CONTRACT ...?
SEVERANCE FEE?
WHAT IS THIS ?!
THE CONTRACT WITH FRAULEIN WAS HIS PERSONAL DECISION, NOT THE WILL OF GRASS-HOPPER AS A WHOLE!

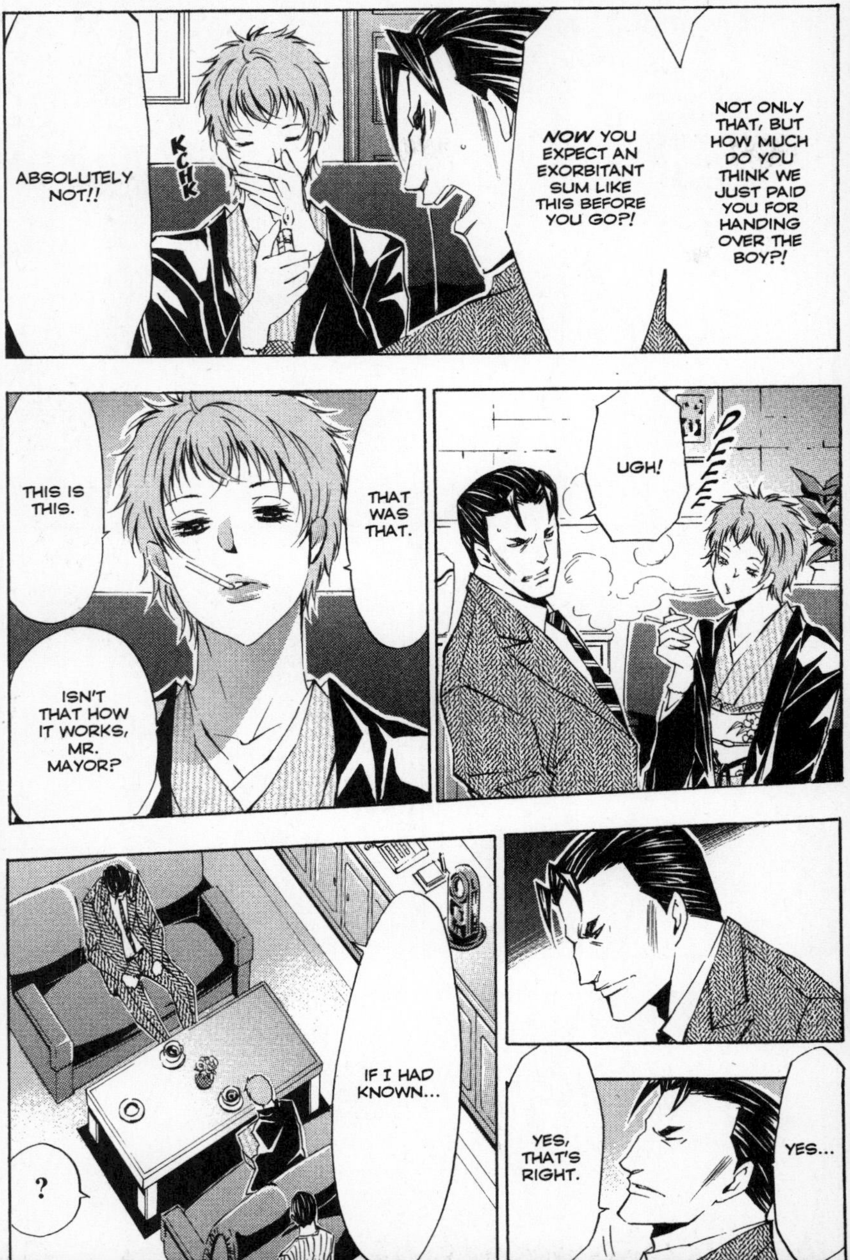
NOT ONLY THAT, BUT HOW MUCH DO YOU THINK WE JUST PAID YOU FOR HANDING OVER THE BOY?!
NOW YOU EXPECT AN EXORBITANT SUM LIKE THIS BEFORE YOU GO?!
KCHK
ABSOLUTELY NOT!!
UGH!
THAT WAS THAT.
THIS IS THIS.
ISN'T THAT HOW IT WORKS, MR. MAYOR?
YES...
YES, THAT'S RIGHT.
IF I HAD KNOWN...
?

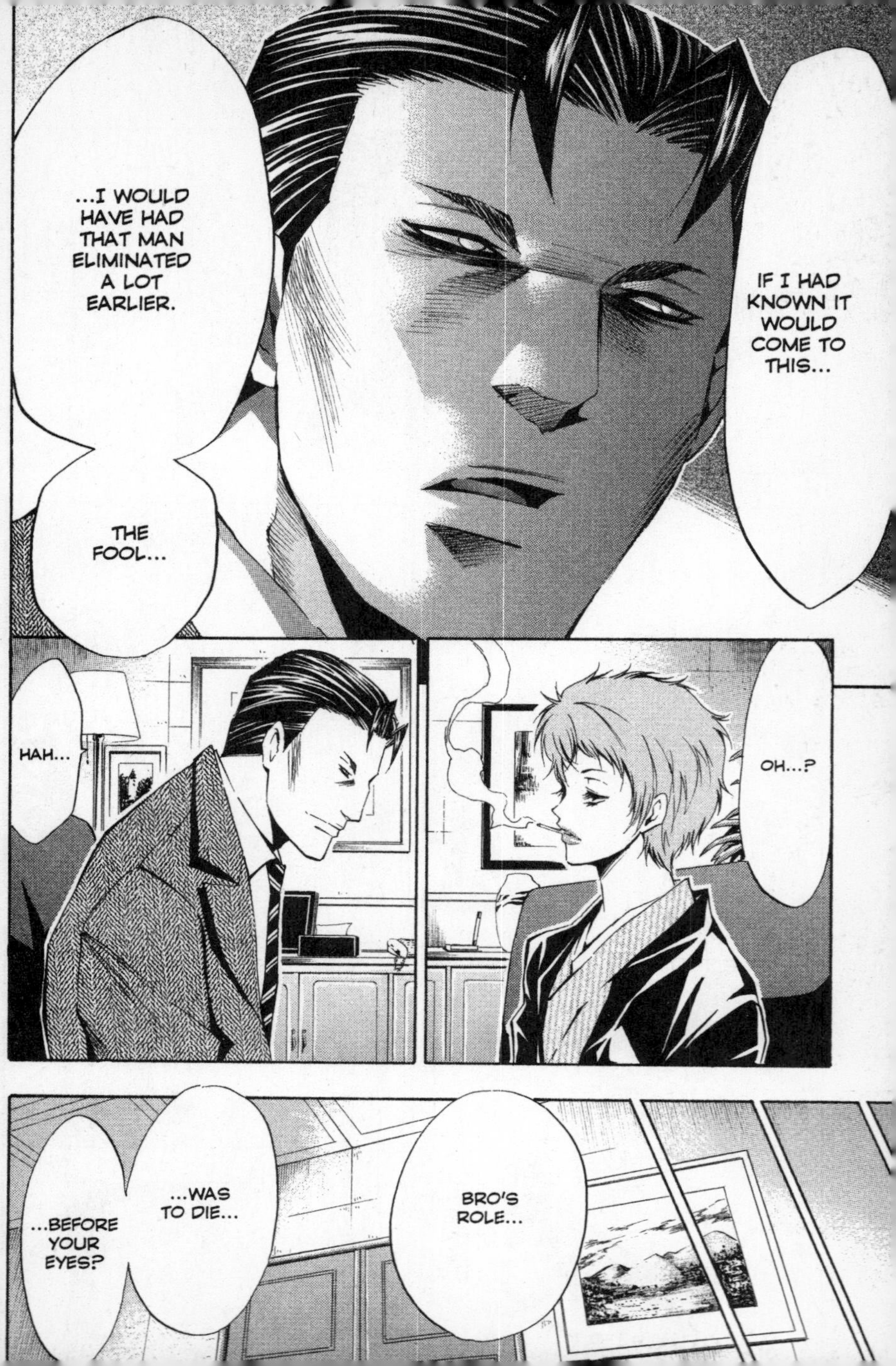
IF I HAD KNOWN IT WOULD COME TO THIS...
...I WOULD HAVE HAD THAT MAN ELIMINATED A LOT EARLIER.
THE FOOL...
OH...?
HAH...
BRO'S ROLE...
...WAS TO DIE...
...BEFORE YOUR EYES?

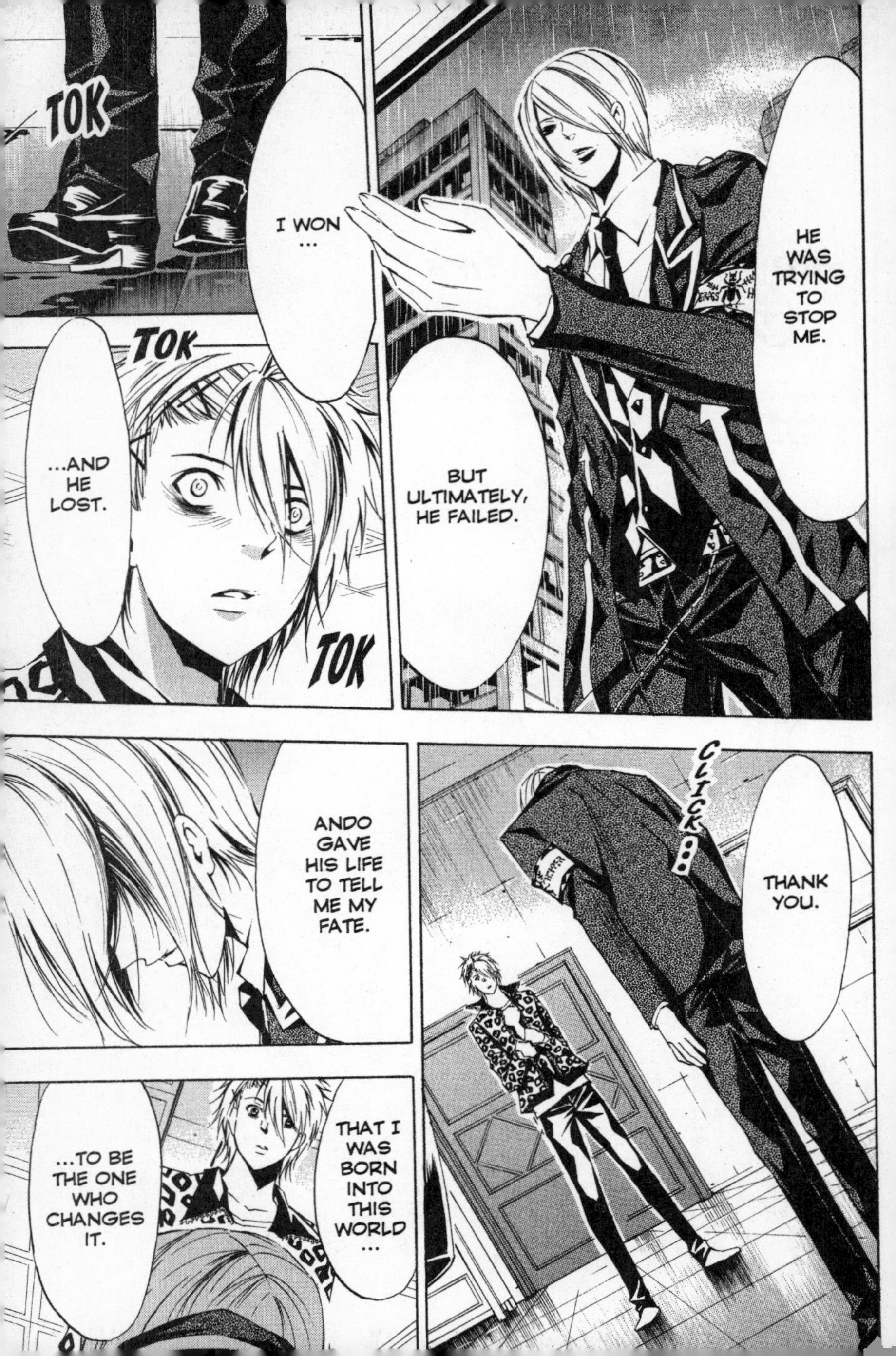
HE WAS TRYING TO STOP ME.
BUT ULTIMATELY, HE FAILED.
TOK
I WON ...
TOK
...AND HE LOST.
TOK
CLICK...
THANK YOU.
ANDO GAVE HIS LIFE TO TELL ME MY FATE.
THAT I WAS BORN INTO THIS WORLD ...
...TO BE THE ONE WHO CHANGES IT.

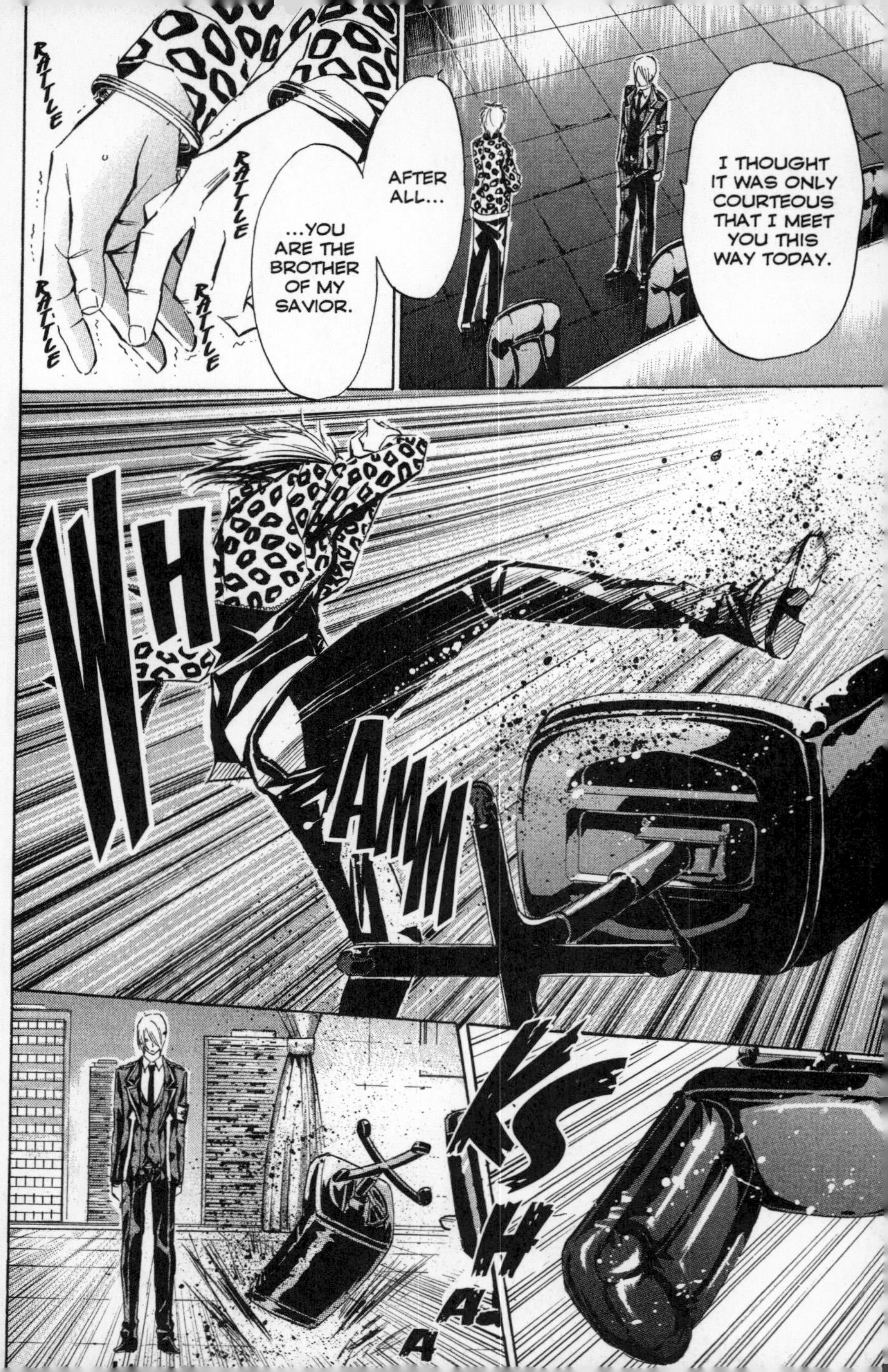
I THOUGHT IT WAS ONLY COURTEOUS THAT I MEET YOU THIS WAY TODAY.
AFTER ALL...
...YOU ARE THE BROTHER OF MY SAVIOR.
RATTLE
RATTLE
RATTLE
RATTLE
WHAMM
KSHAA

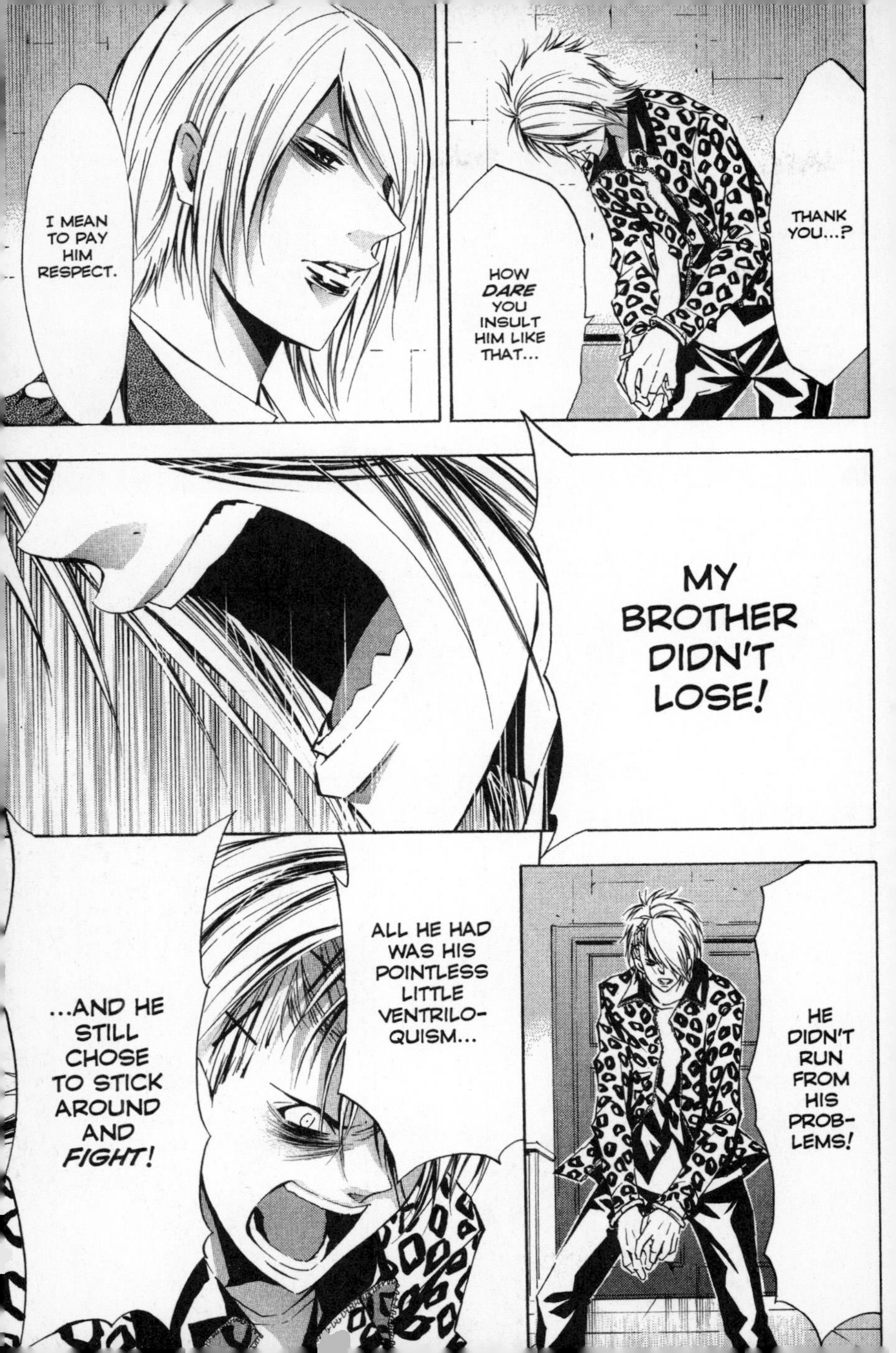
THANK YOU...?
HOW *DARE* YOU INSULT HIM LIKE THAT...
I MEAN TO PAY HIM RESPECT.
MY BROTHER DIDN'T LOSE!
HE DIDN'T RUN FROM HIS PROBLEMS!
ALL HE HAD WAS HIS POINTLESS LITTLE VENTRILOQUISM...
...AND HE STILL CHOSE TO STICK AROUND AND *FIGHT*!

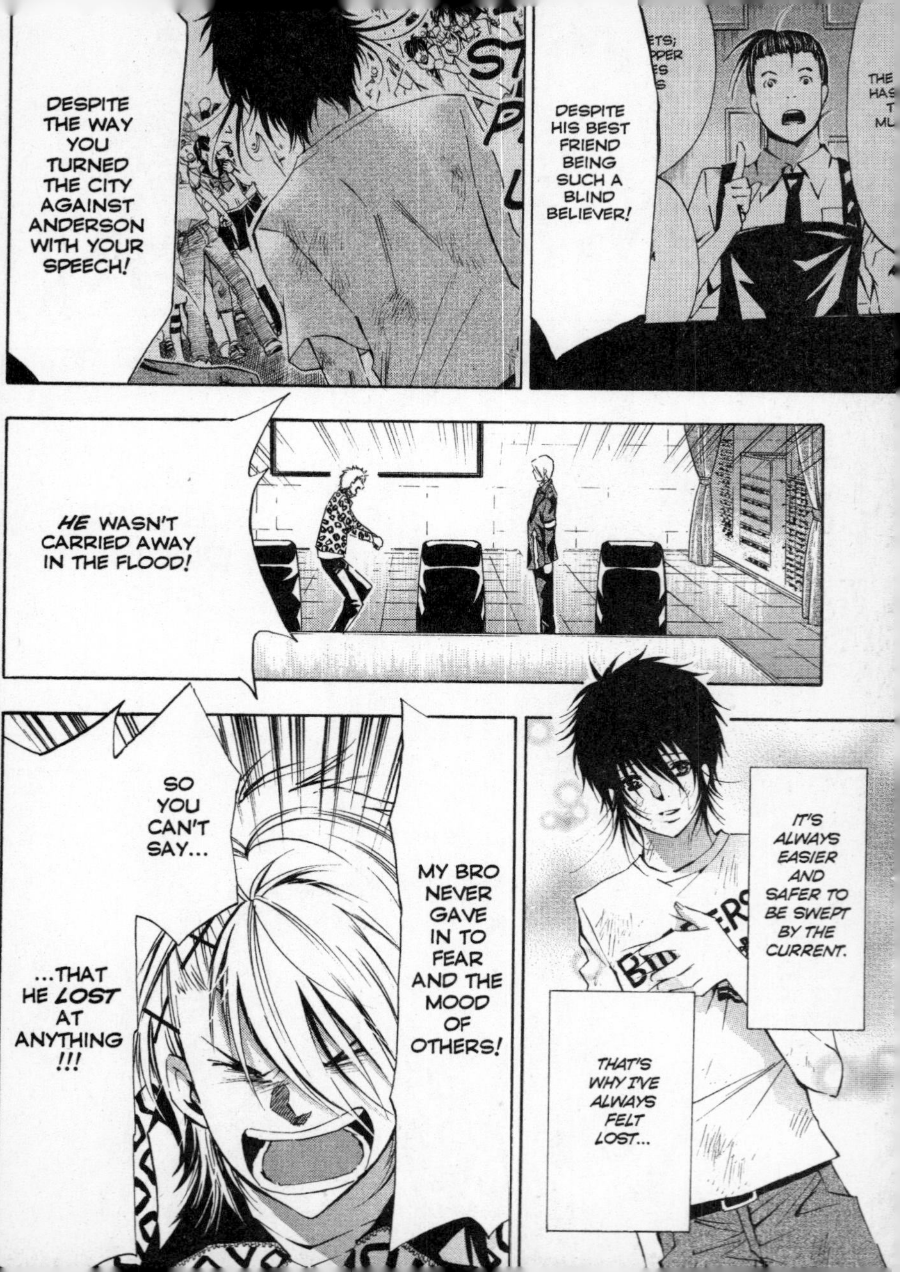
DESPITE HIS BEST FRIEND BEING SUCH A BLIND BELIEVER!
DESPITE THE WAY YOU TURNED THE CITY AGAINST ANDERSON WITH YOUR SPEECH!
HE WASN'T CARRIED AWAY IN THE FLOOD!
IT'S ALWAYS EASIER AND SAFER TO BE SWEPT BY THE CURRENT.
THAT'S WHY I'VE ALWAYS FELT LOST...
MY BRO NEVER GAVE IN TO FEAR AND THE MOOD OF OTHERS!
SO YOU CAN'T SAY...
...THAT HE LOST AT ANYTHING!!!

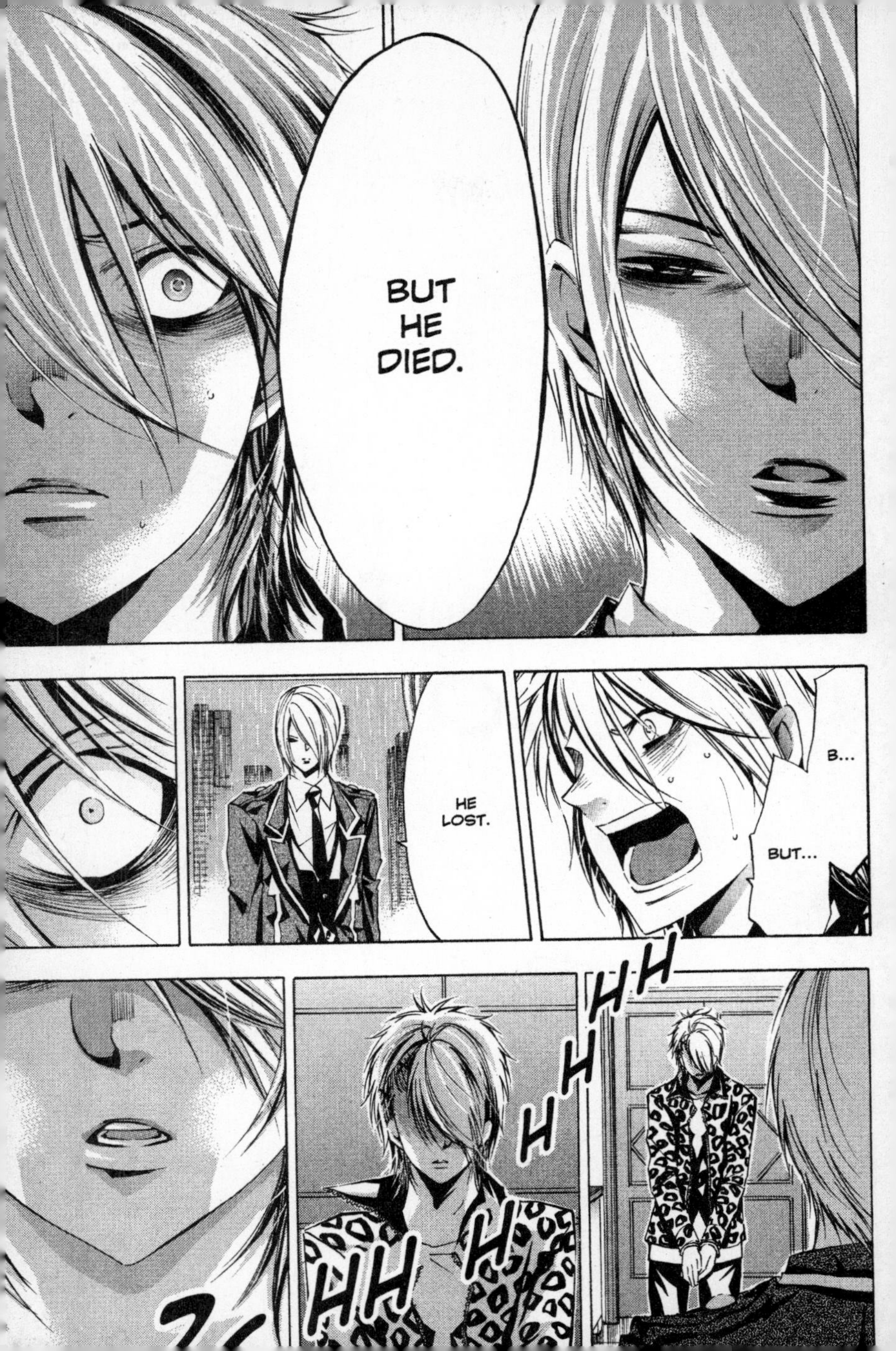
BUT HE DIED.
B...
BUT...
HE LOST.
HHHHHHHHH

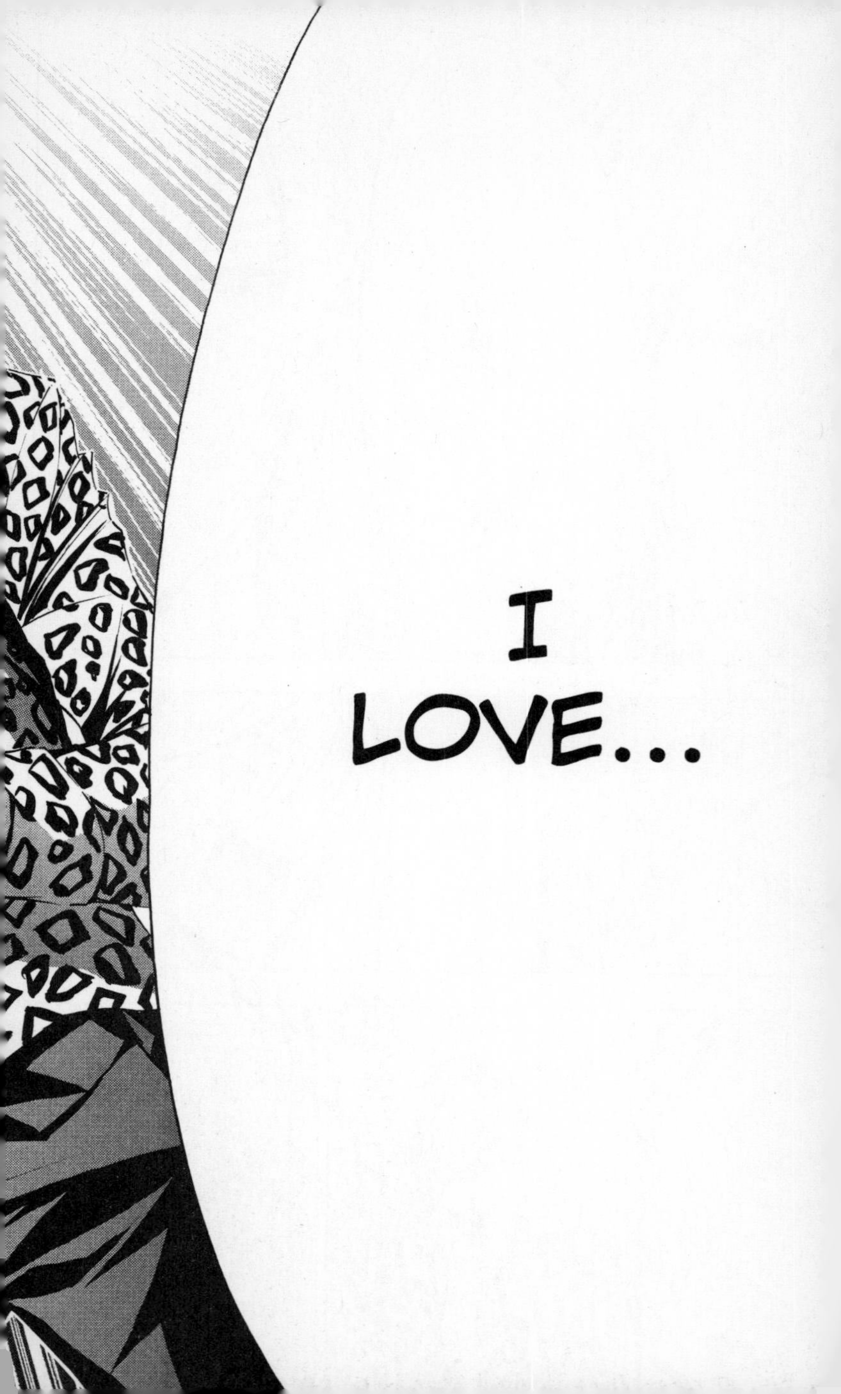
I LOVE...

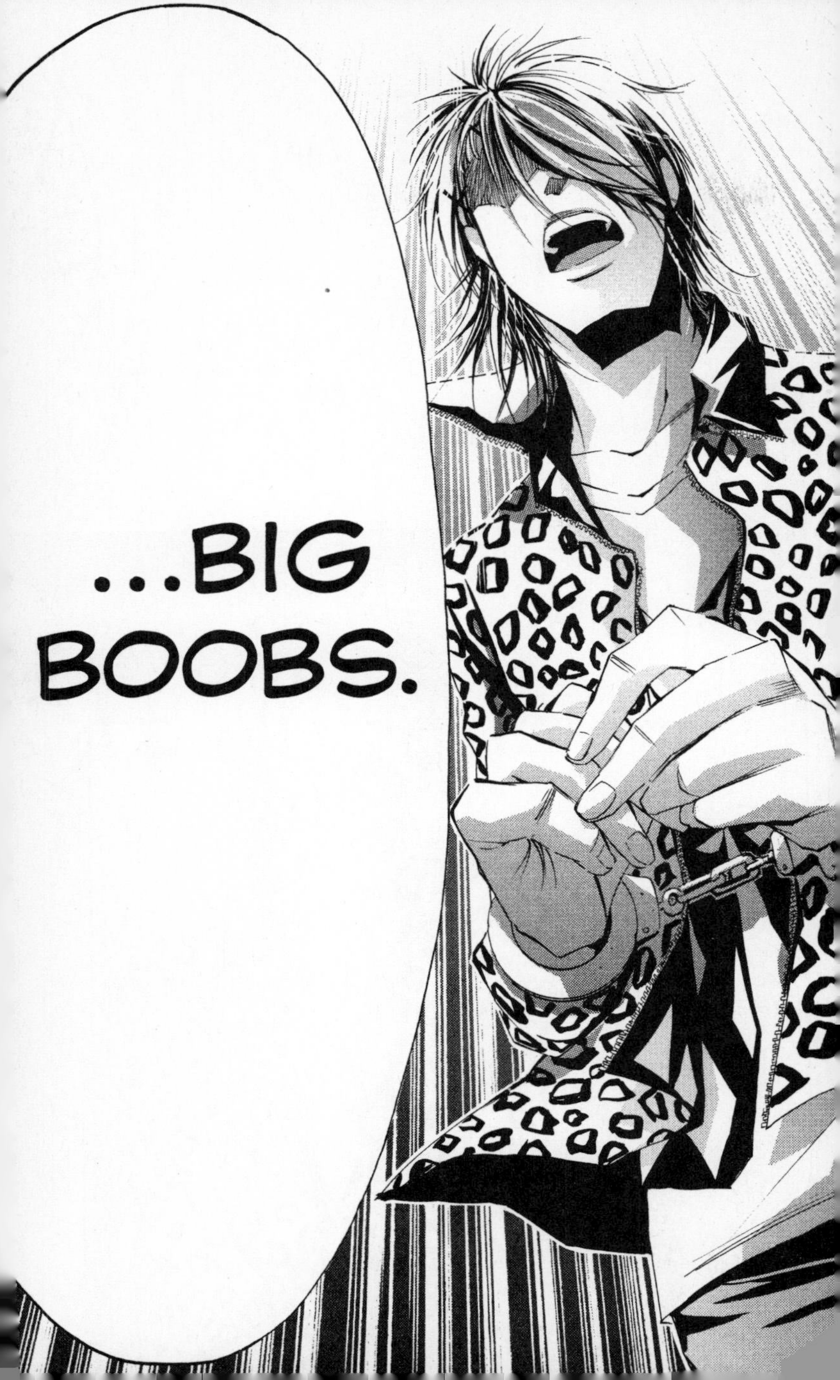
...BIG BOOBS.

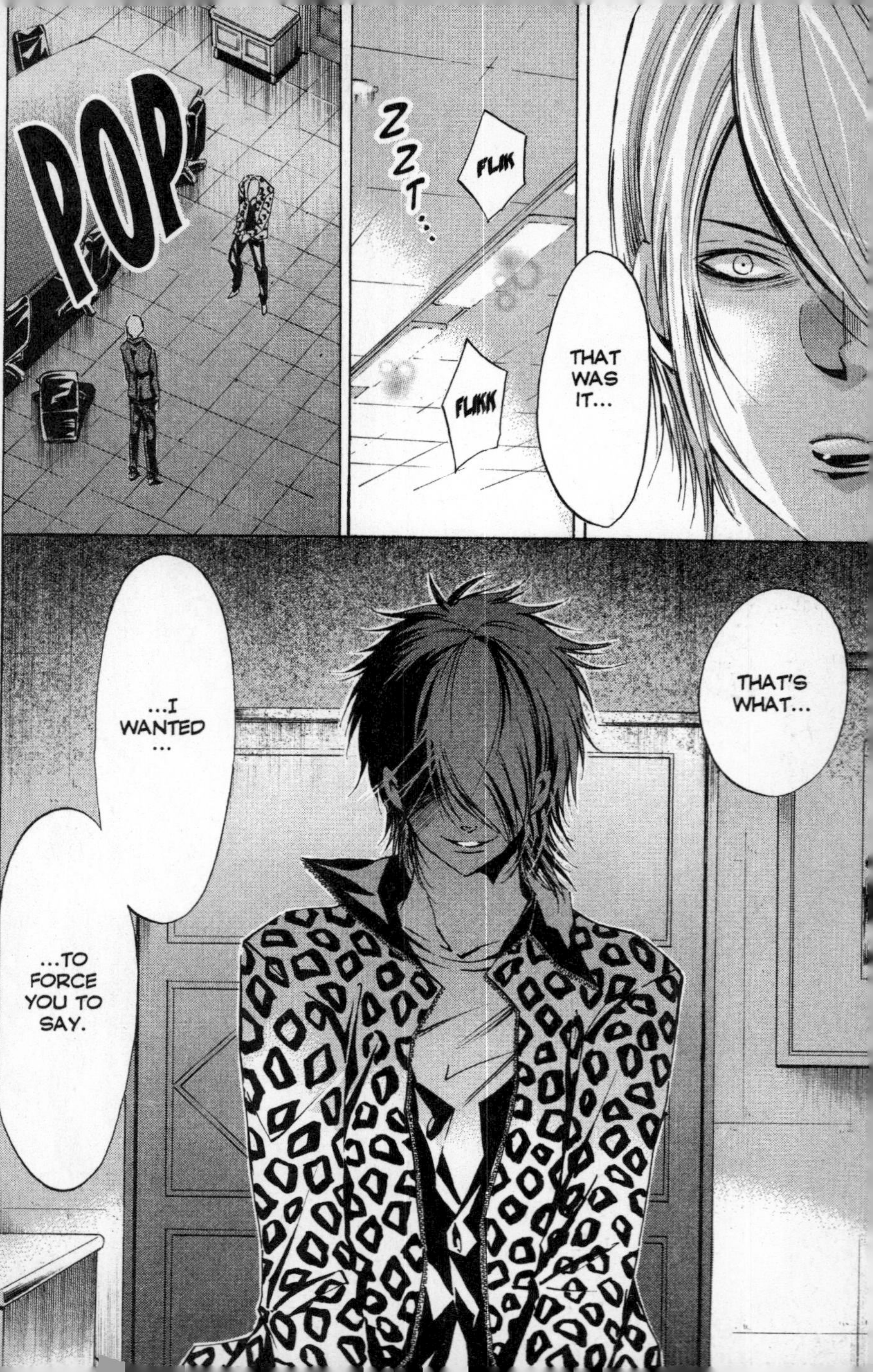
THAT WAS IT...
ZZZT...
FLIK
FLIKK
POP
THAT'S WHAT...
...I WANTED ...
...TO FORCE YOU TO SAY.

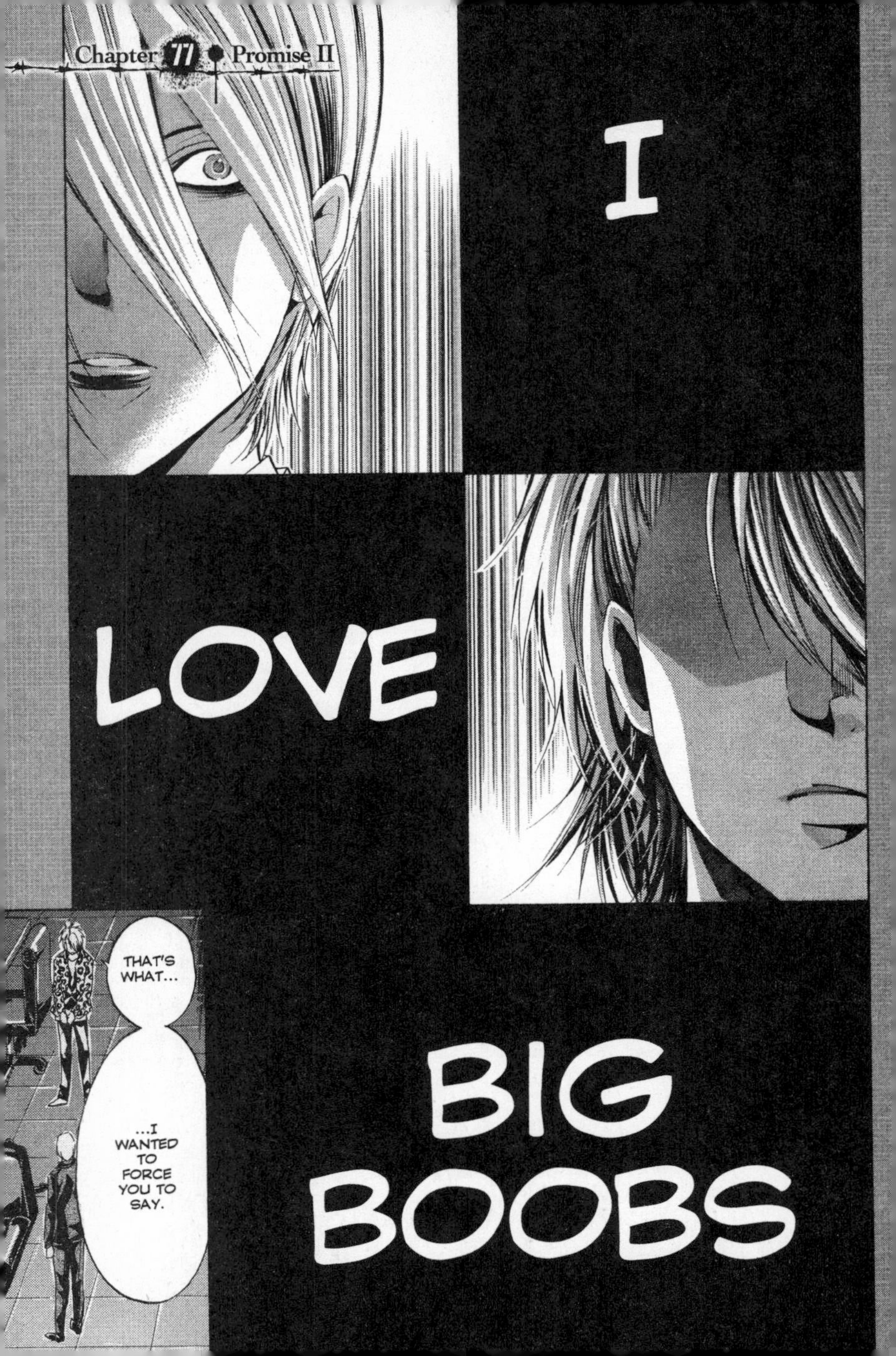
Chapter 77 Promise II
I
LOVE
BIG BOOBS
THAT'S WHAT...
...I WANTED TO FORCE YOU TO SAY.

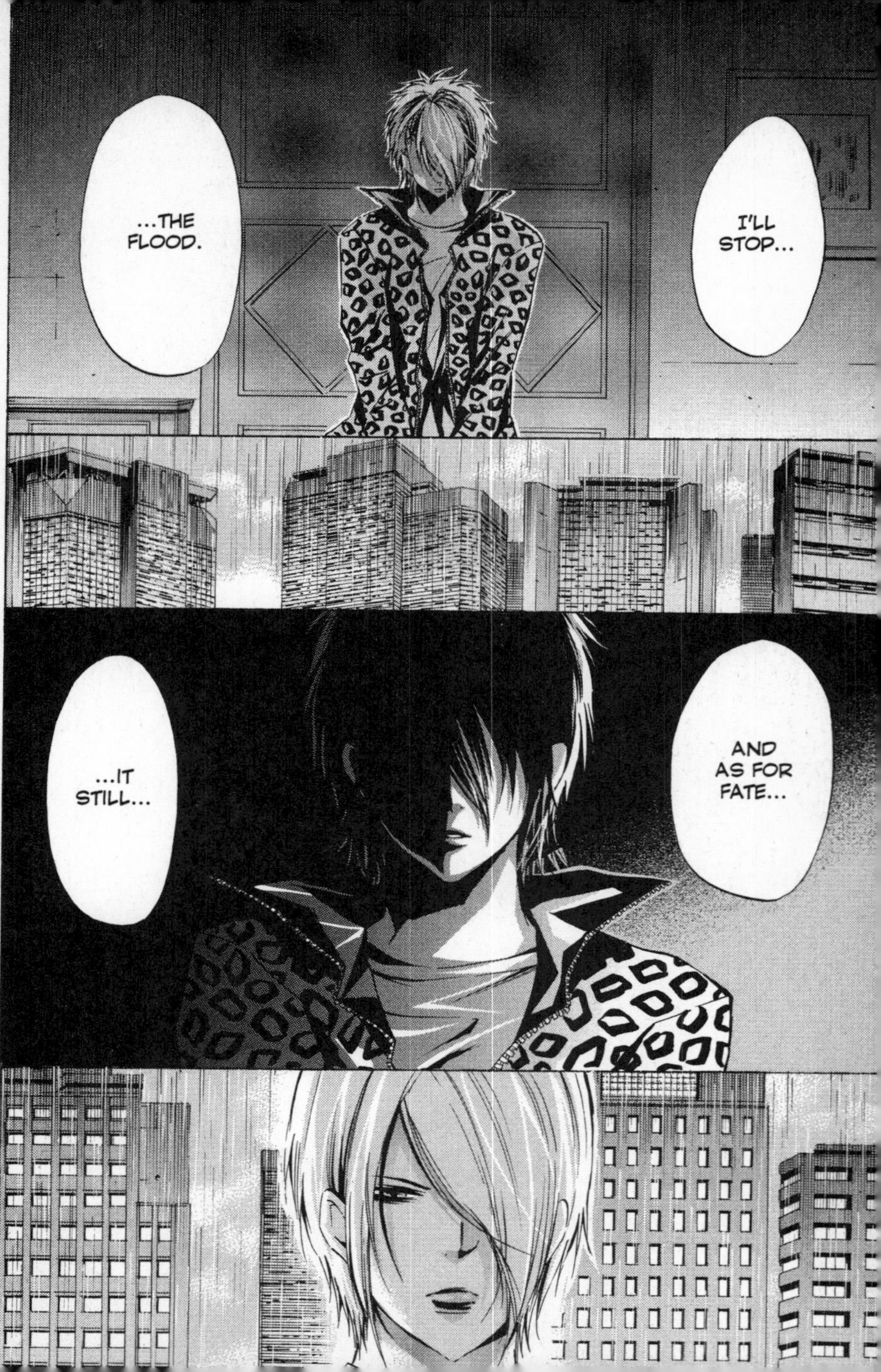
I'LL STOP...
...THE FLOOD.
AND AS FOR FATE...
...IT STILL...

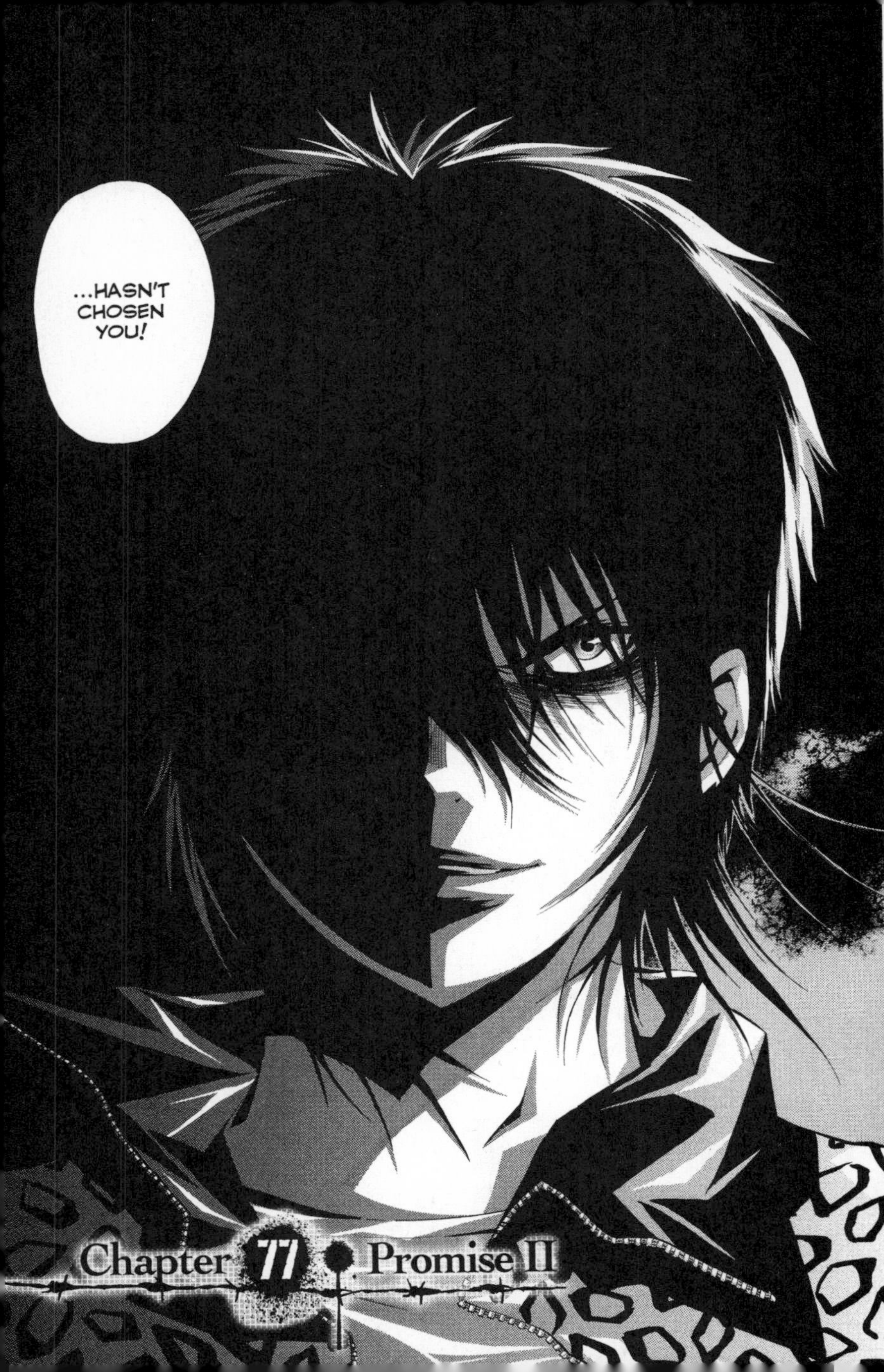
...HASN'T CHOSEN YOU!
Chapter 77 Promise II

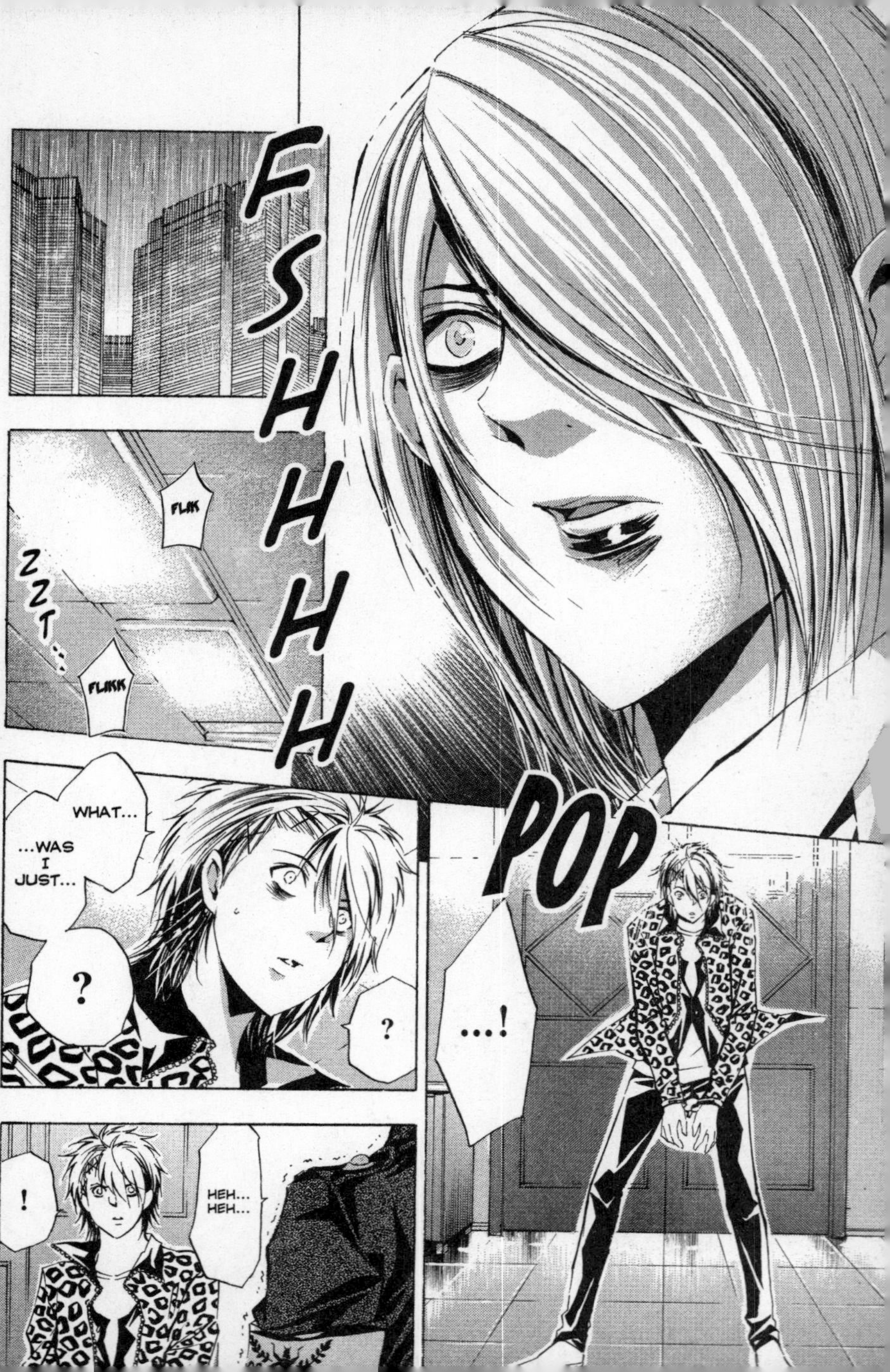
FSHHHH
FLIK
ZZT..
FLIKK
POP
...!
WHAT...
...WAS I JUST...
?
?
HEH... HEH...
!

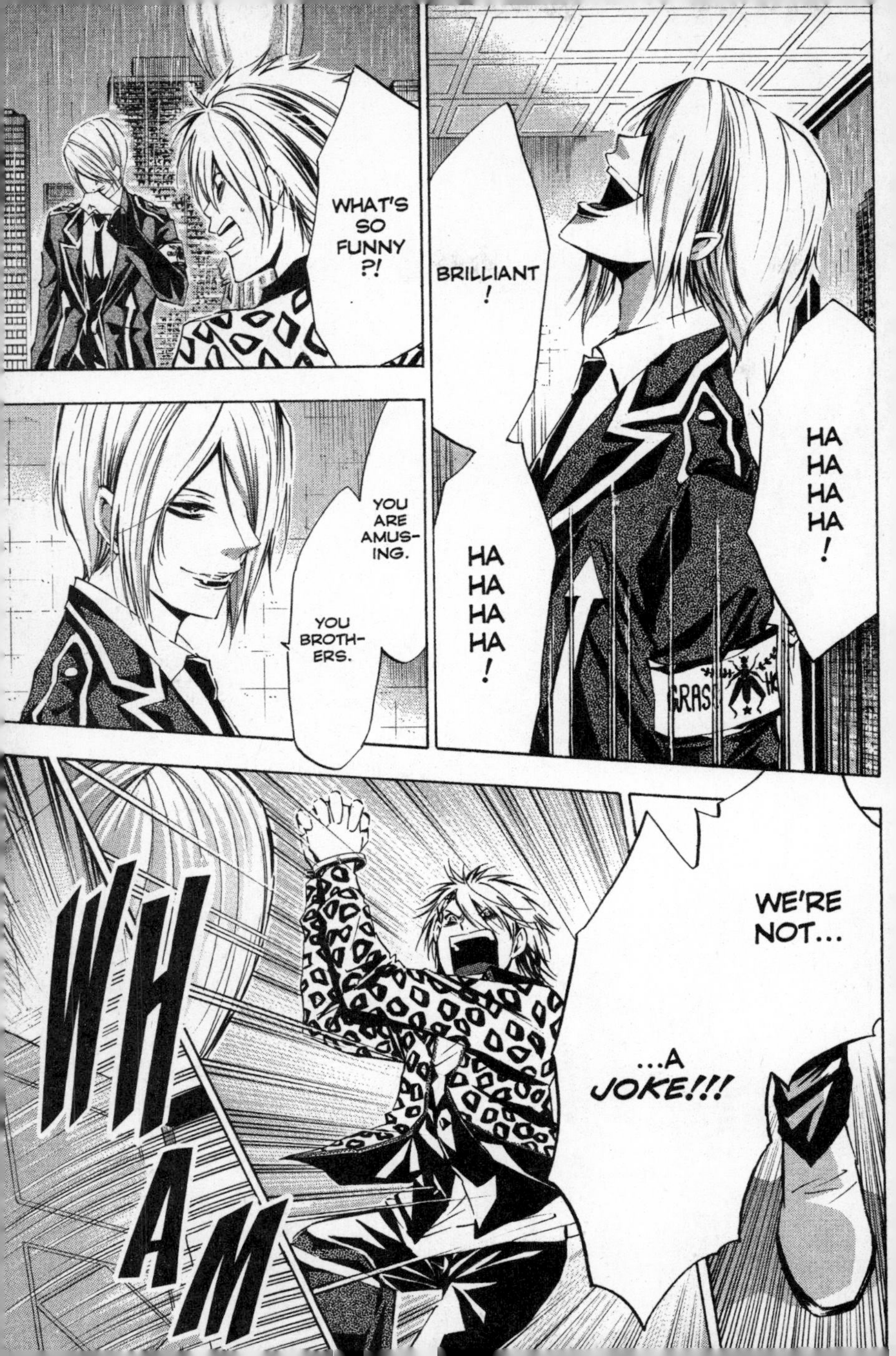

BRILLIANT!
HA HA HA HA!
HA HA HA HA!
WHAT'S SO FUNNY?!
YOU ARE AMUSING.
YOU BROTHERS.
WE'RE NOT...
...A JOKE!!!
WHAAM

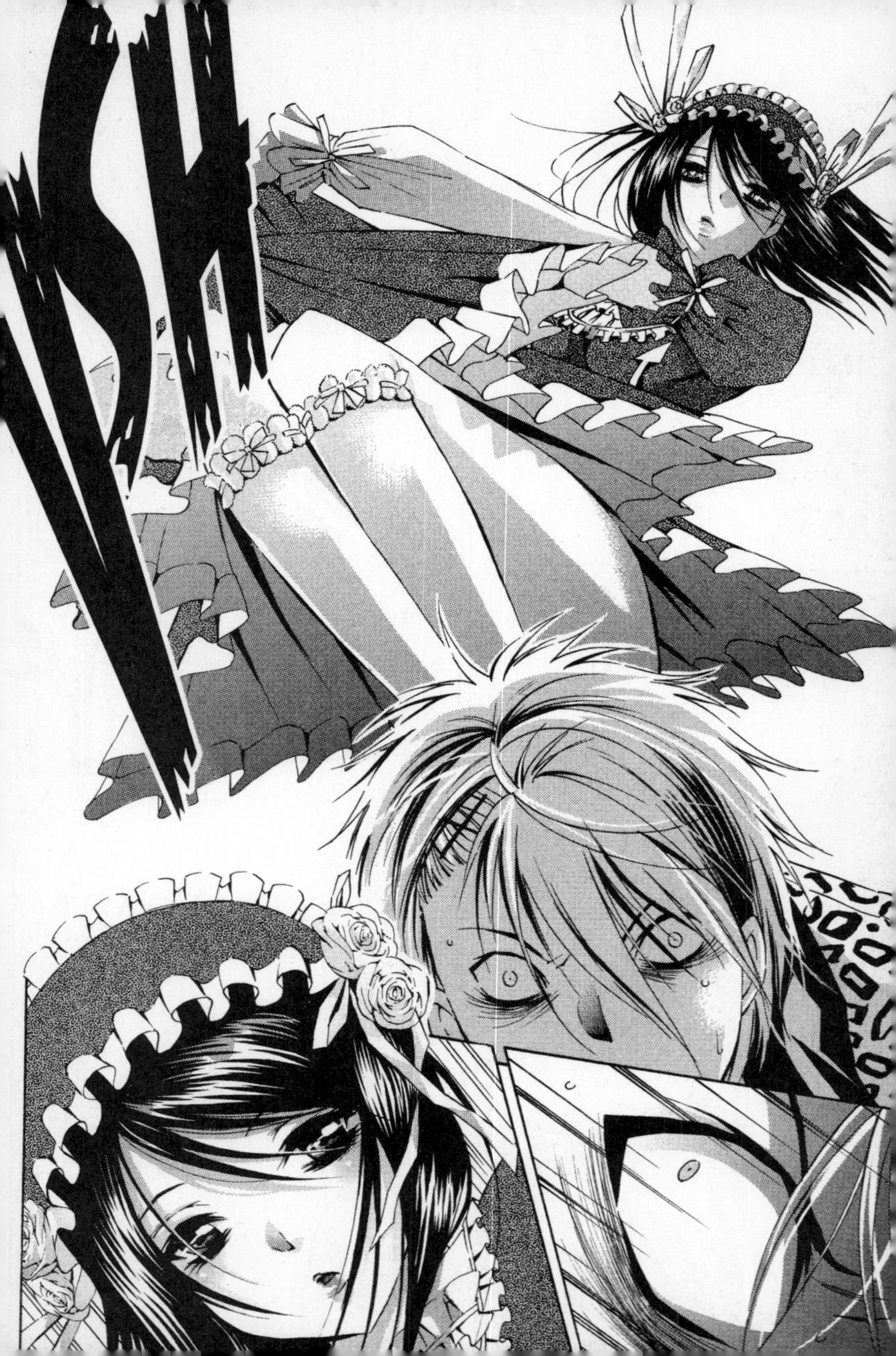

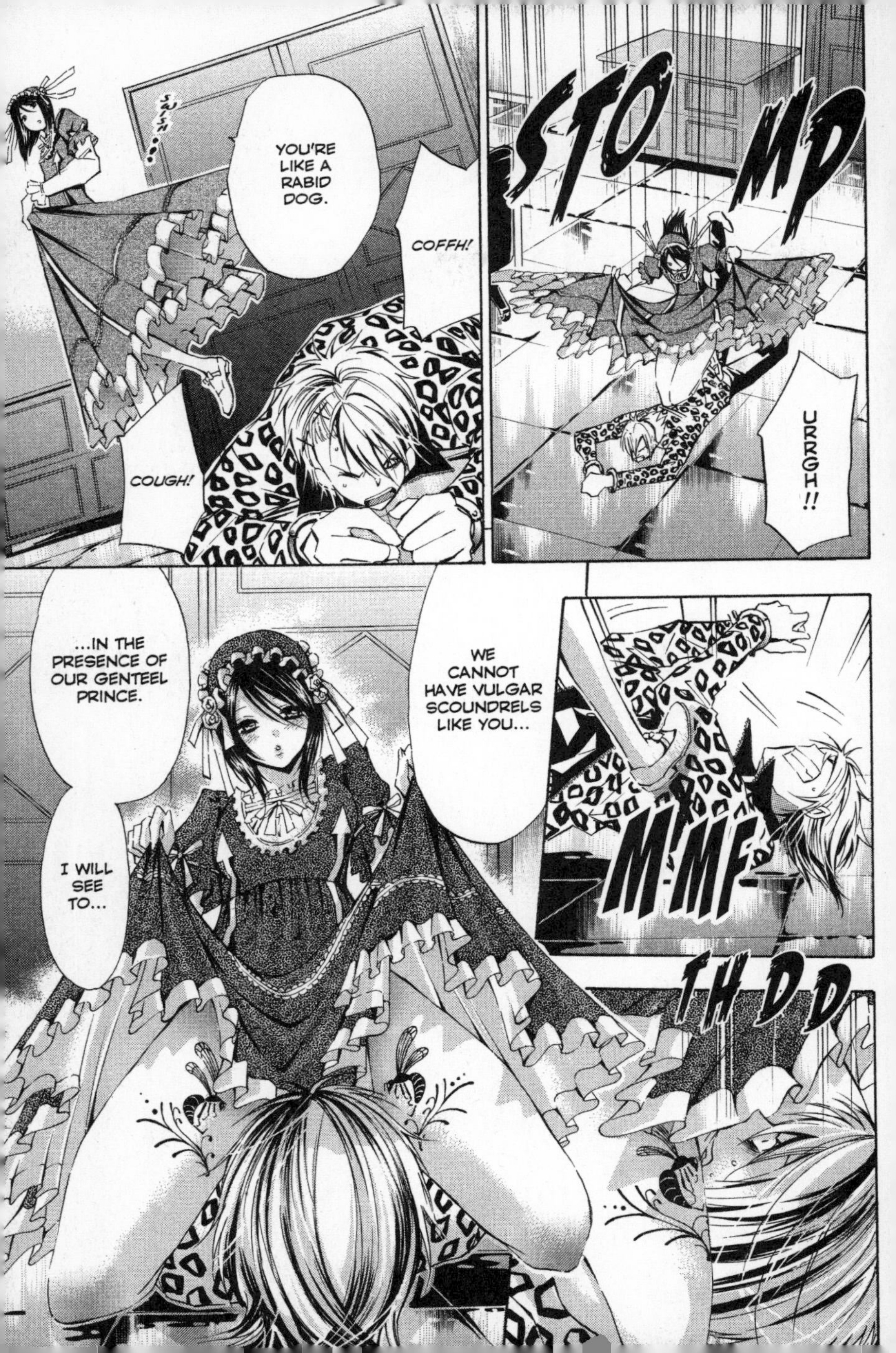
STOMP
URRGH!!
SWISH...
YOU'RE LIKE A RABID DOG.
COFFH!
COUGH!
M-MF
THDD
WE CANNOT HAVE VULGAR SCOUNDRELS LIKE YOU...
...IN THE PRESENCE OF OUR GENTEEL PRINCE.
I WILL SEE TO...

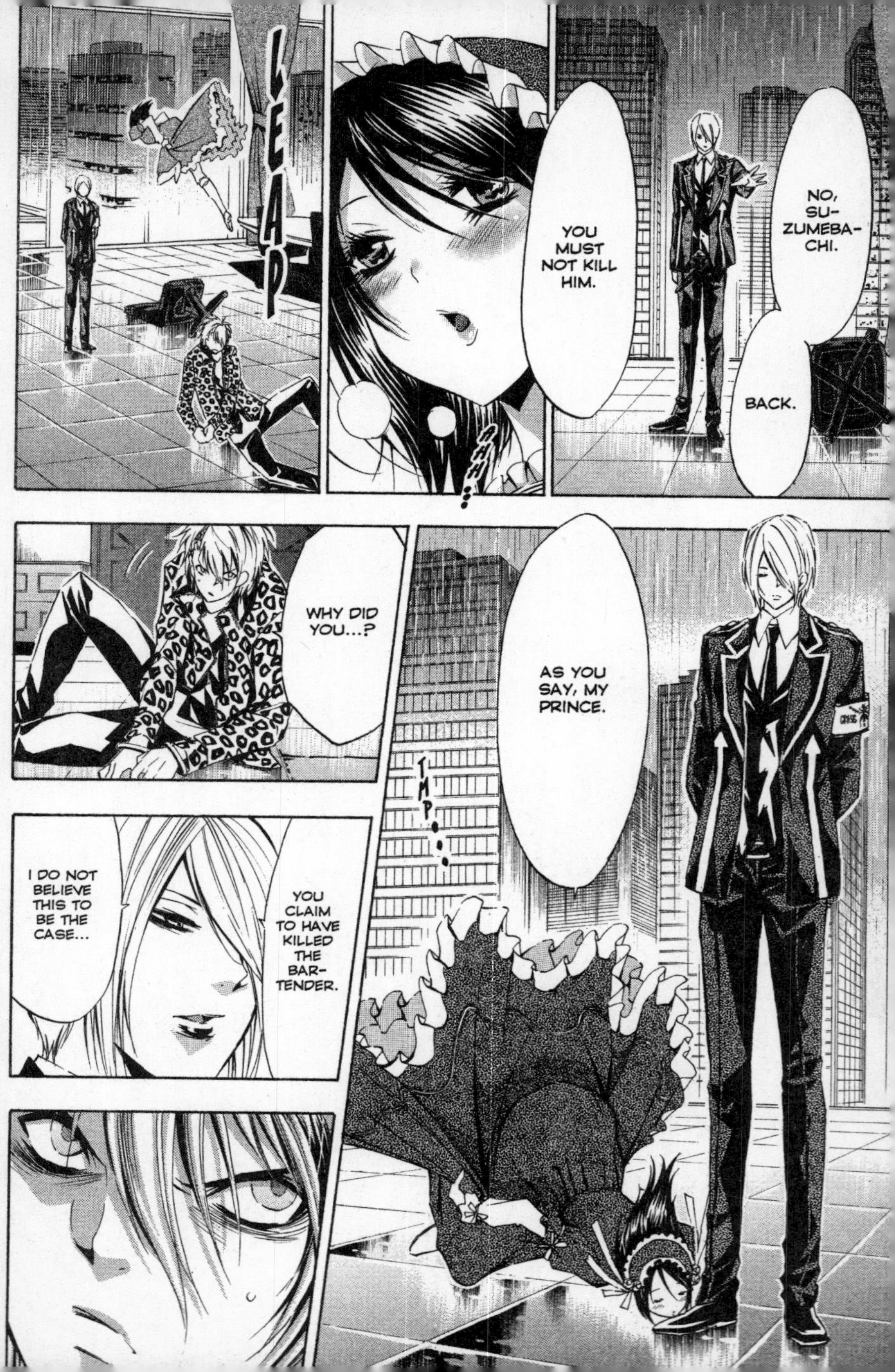
NO, SU-ZUMEBA-CHI.
BACK.
YOU MUST NOT KILL HIM.
AHH...
LEAP
AS YOU SAY, MY PRINCE.
TMP...
WHY DID YOU...?
YOU CLAIM TO HAVE KILLED THE BAR-TENDER.
I DO NOT BELIEVE THIS TO BE THE CASE...

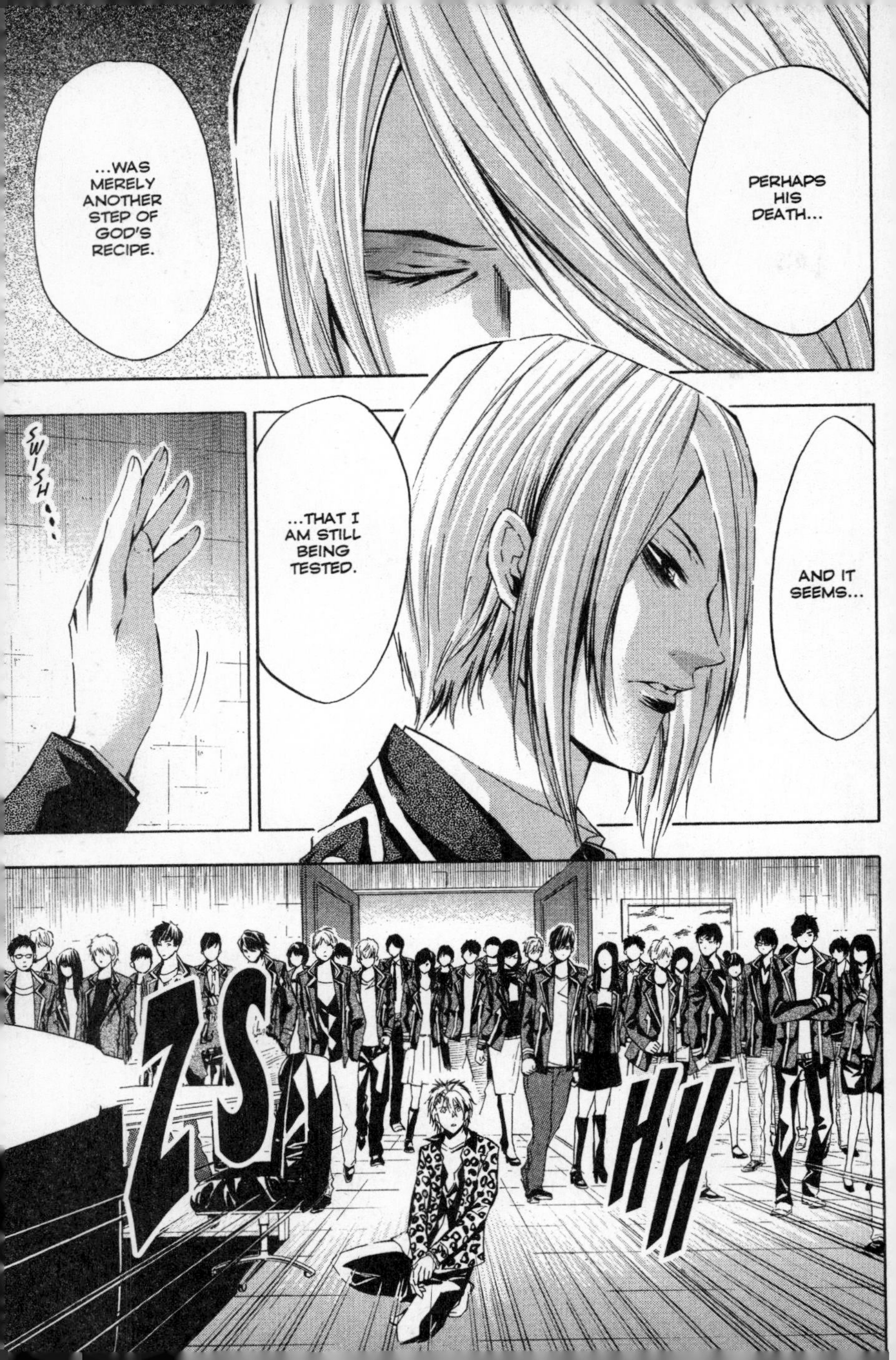
PERHAPS HIS DEATH...
...WAS MERELY ANOTHER STEP OF GOD'S RECIPE.
AND IT SEEMS...
...THAT I AM STILL BEING TESTED.
SWISH...
ZSHH

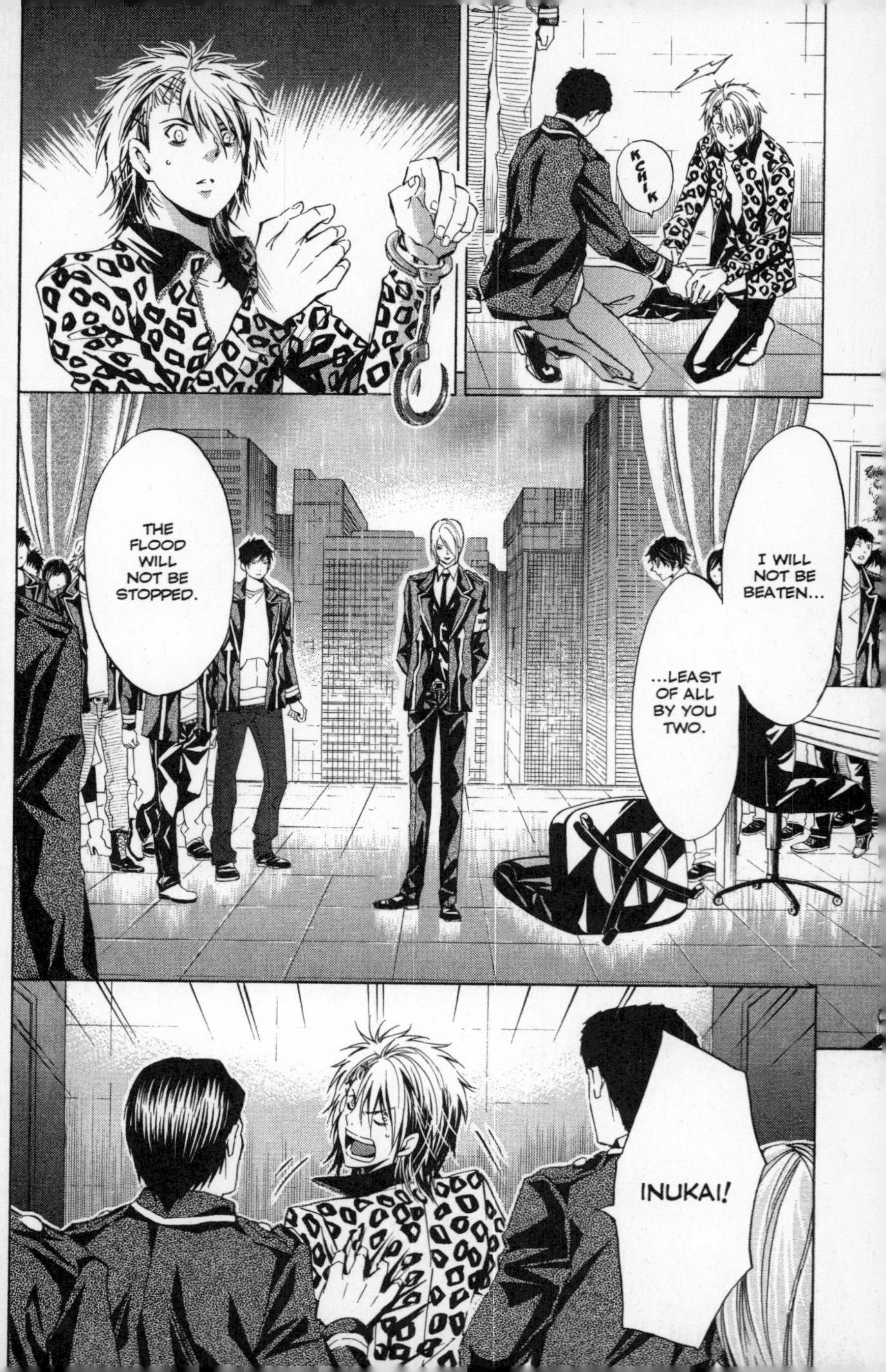
KCHIK
I WILL NOT BE BEATEN...
...LEAST OF ALL BY YOU TWO.
THE FLOOD WILL NOT BE STOPPED.
INUKAI!

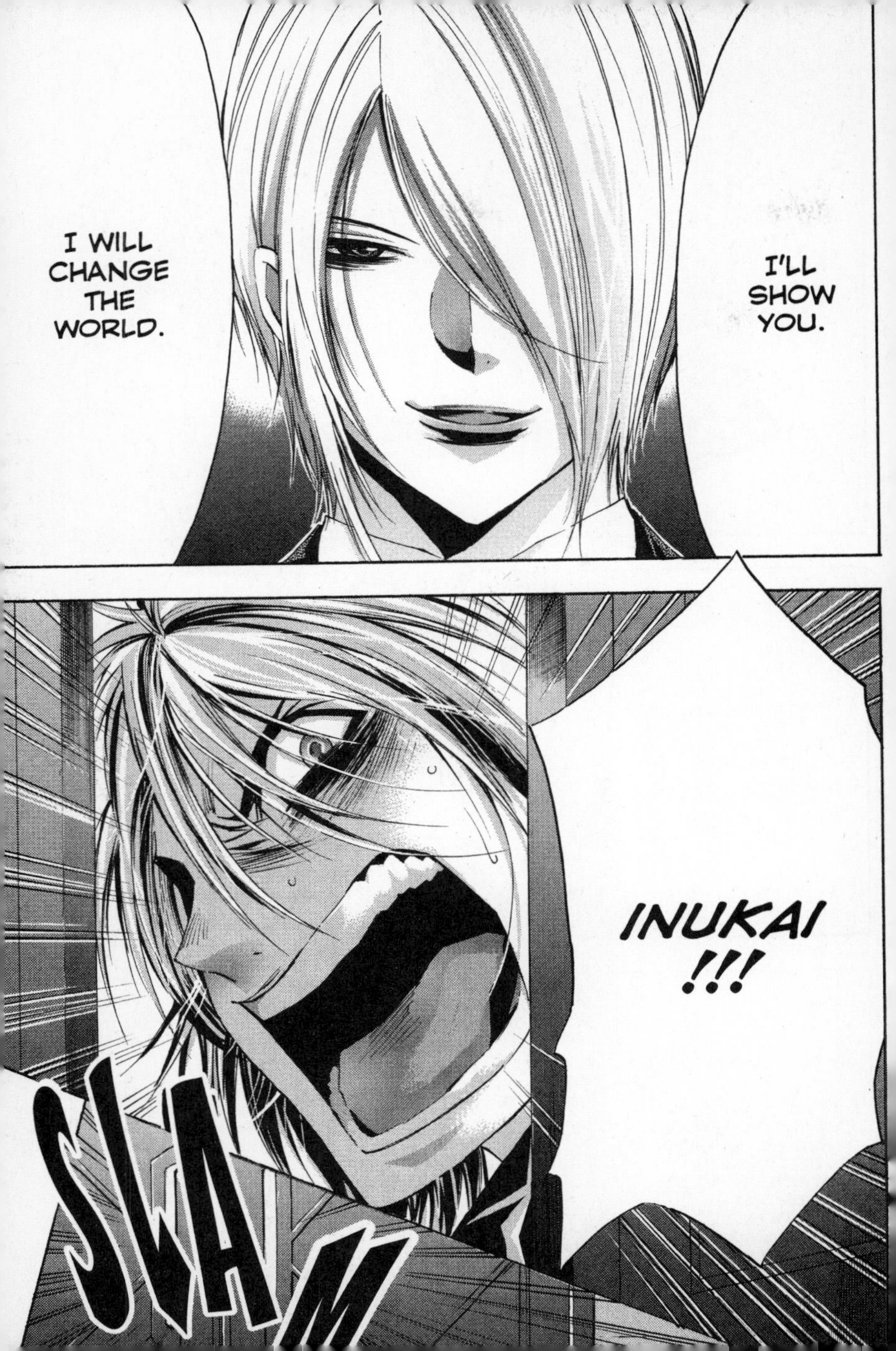
I'LL SHOW YOU.
I WILL CHANGE THE WORLD.
INUKAI !!!
SLAM

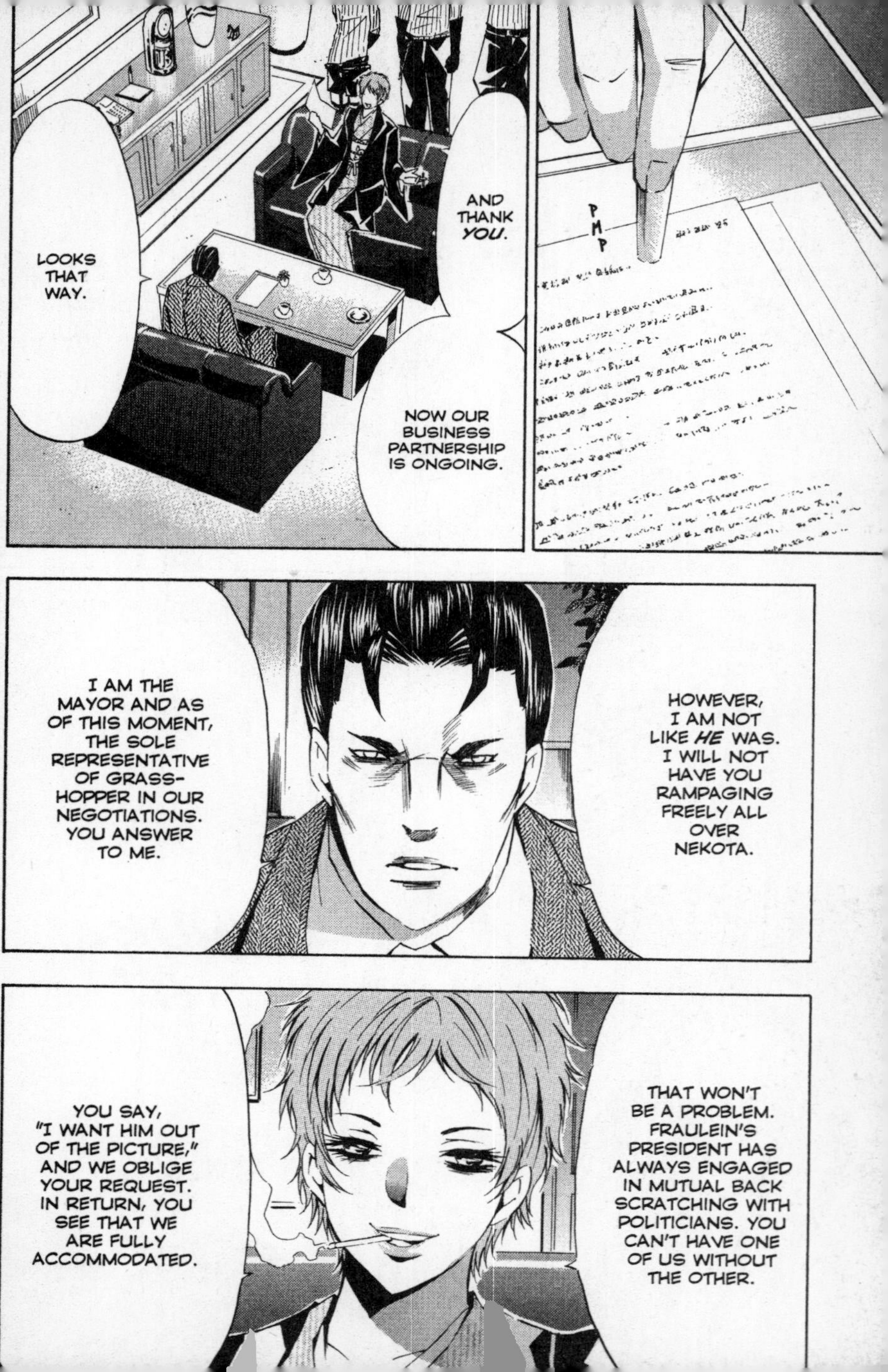
PMP
AND THANK YOU.
NOW OUR BUSINESS PARTNERSHIP IS ONGOING.
LOOKS THAT WAY.
HOWEVER, I AM NOT LIKE HE WAS. I WILL NOT HAVE YOU RAMPAGING FREELY ALL OVER NEKOTA.
I AM THE MAYOR AND AS OF THIS MOMENT, THE SOLE REPRESENTATIVE OF GRASS-HOPPER IN OUR NEGOTIATIONS. YOU ANSWER TO ME.
THAT WON'T BE A PROBLEM. FRAULEIN'S PRESIDENT HAS ALWAYS ENGAGED IN MUTUAL BACK SCRATCHING WITH POLITICIANS. YOU CAN'T HAVE ONE OF US WITHOUT THE OTHER.
YOU SAY, "I WANT HIM OUT OF THE PICTURE," AND WE OBLIGE YOUR REQUEST. IN RETURN, YOU SEE THAT WE ARE FULLY ACCOMMODATED.

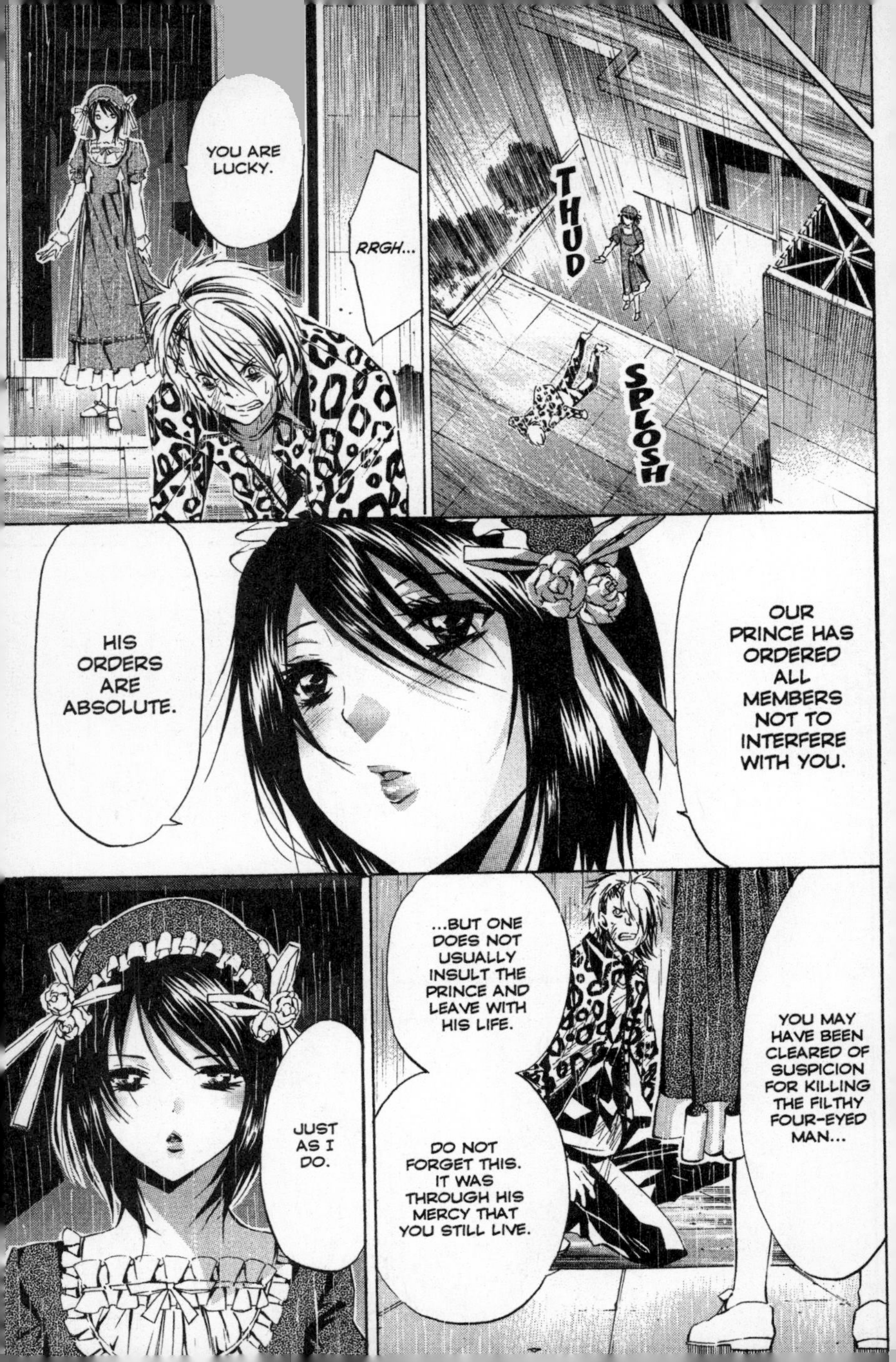
THUD
SPLOSH
RRGH...
YOU ARE LUCKY.
OUR PRINCE HAS ORDERED ALL MEMBERS NOT TO INTERFERE WITH YOU.
HIS ORDERS ARE ABSOLUTE.
YOU MAY HAVE BEEN CLEARED OF SUSPICION FOR KILLING THE FILTHY FOUR-EYED MAN...
...BUT ONE DOES NOT USUALLY INSULT THE PRINCE AND LEAVE WITH HIS LIFE.
DO NOT FORGET THIS. IT WAS THROUGH HIS MERCY THAT YOU STILL LIVE.
JUST AS I DO.

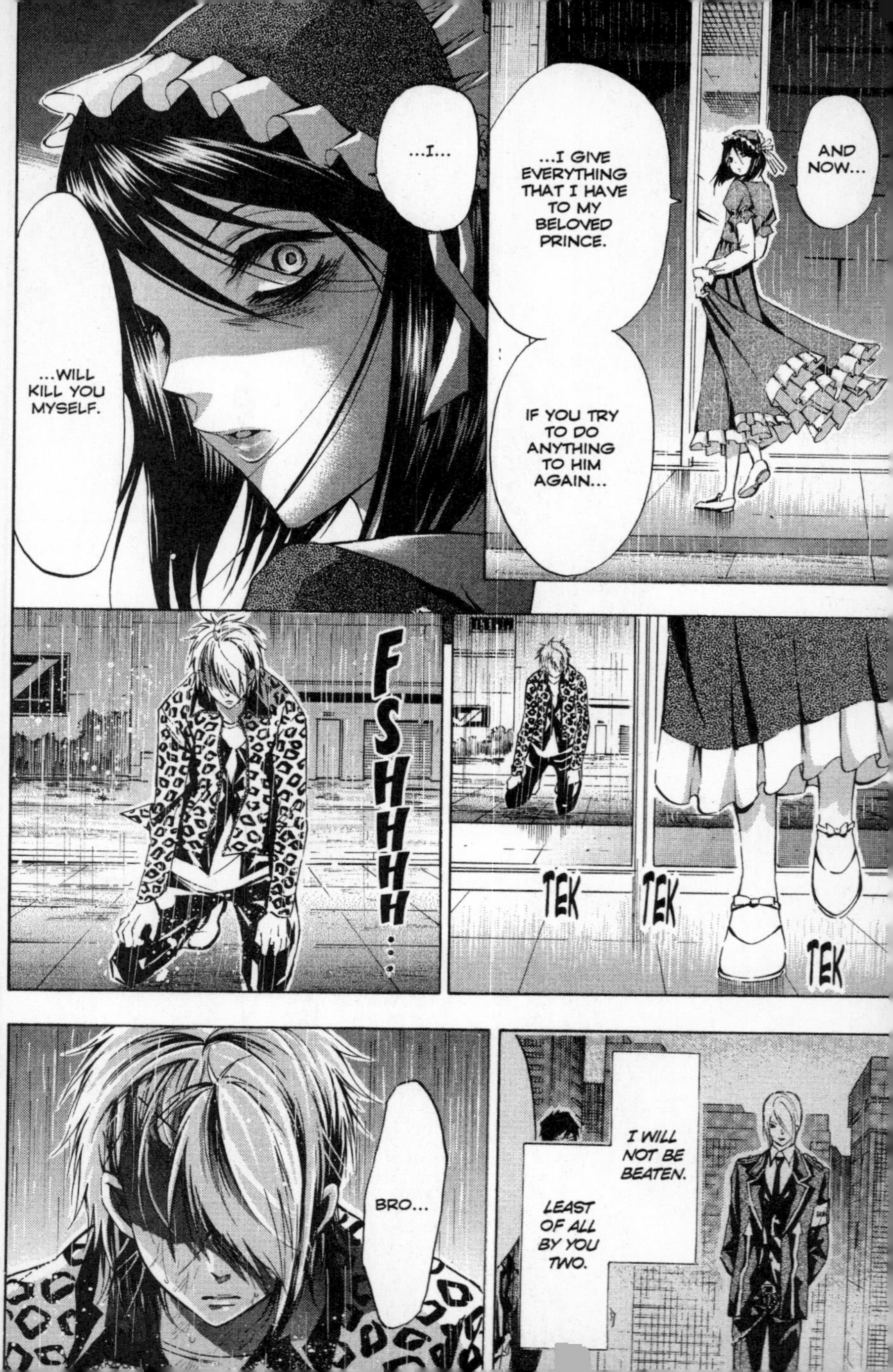
AND NOW...
...I GIVE EVERYTHING THAT I HAVE TO MY BELOVED PRINCE.
IF YOU TRY TO DO ANYTHING TO HIM AGAIN...
...I...
...WILL KILL YOU MYSELF.
TEK
TEK
TEK
FSHHHH...
I WILL NOT BE BEATEN.
LEAST OF ALL BY YOU TWO.
BRO...

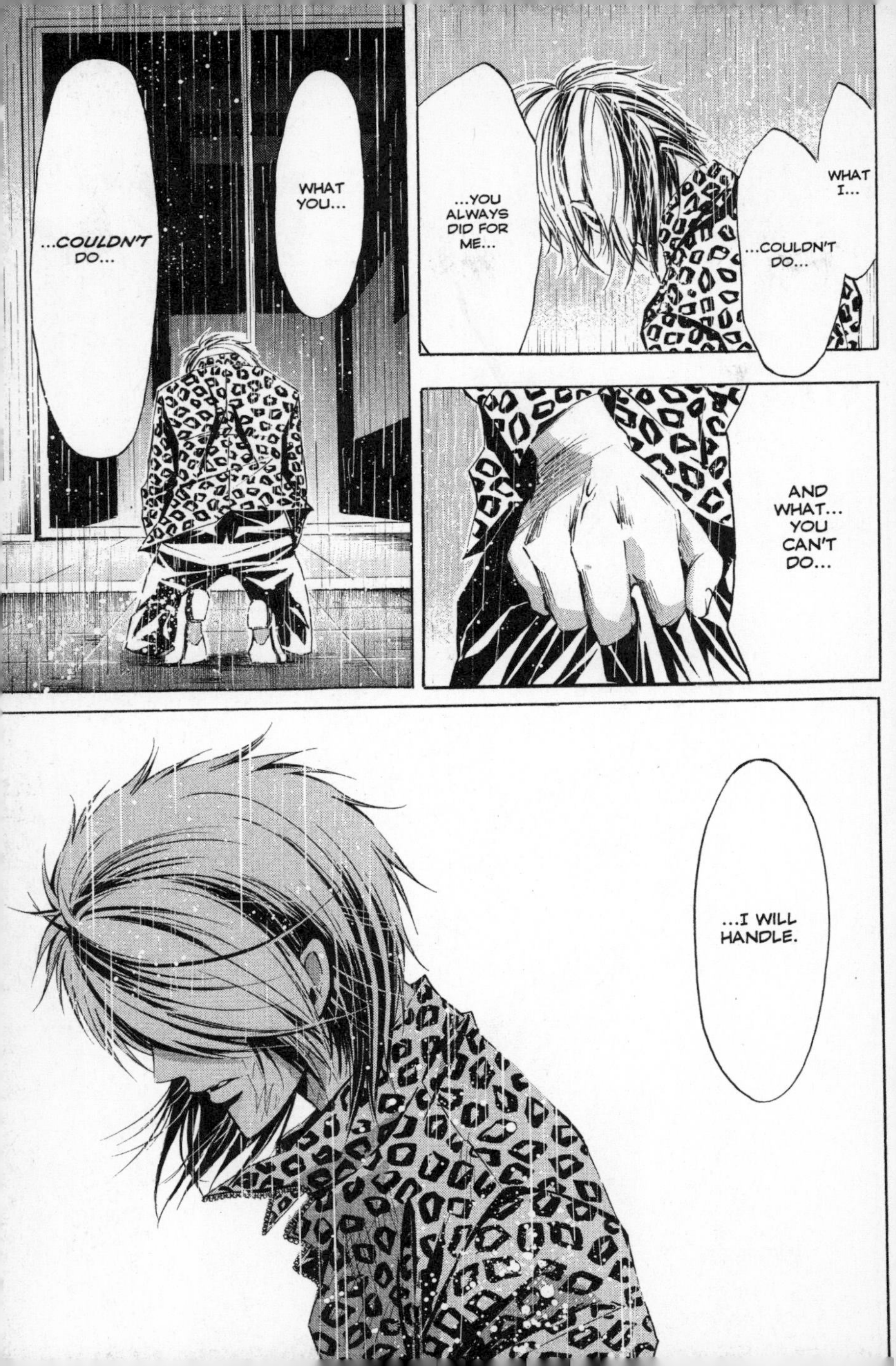
WHAT I...
...COULDN'T DO...
...YOU ALWAYS DID FOR ME...
AND WHAT... YOU CAN'T DO...
WHAT YOU...
...COULDN'T DO...
...I WILL HANDLE.

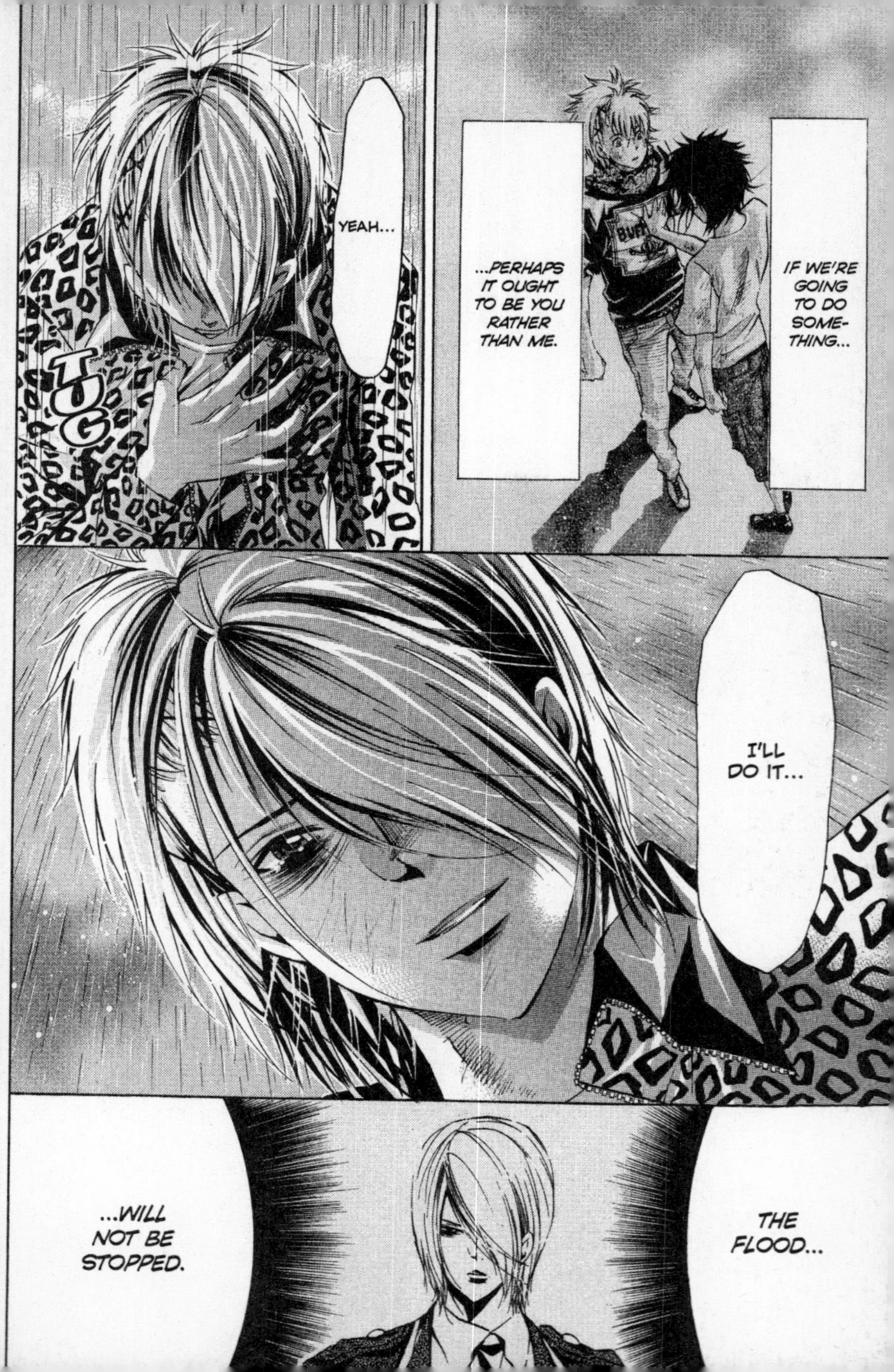
IF WE'RE GOING TO DO SOME-THING...
...PERHAPS IT OUGHT TO BE YOU RATHER THAN ME.
YEAH...
TUG
I'LL DO IT...
THE FLOOD...
...WILL NOT BE STOPPED.

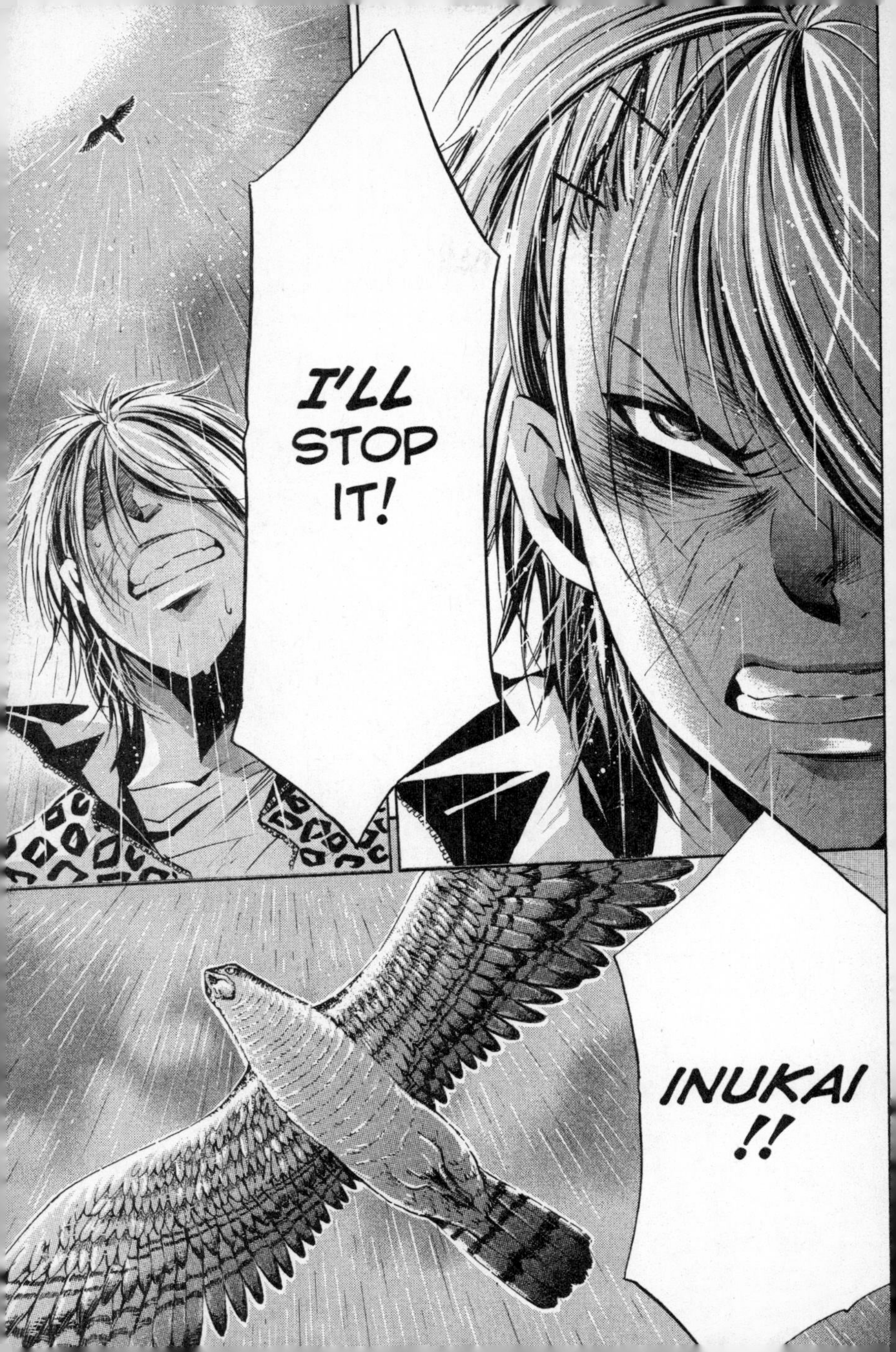
I'LL STOP IT!
INUKAI!!

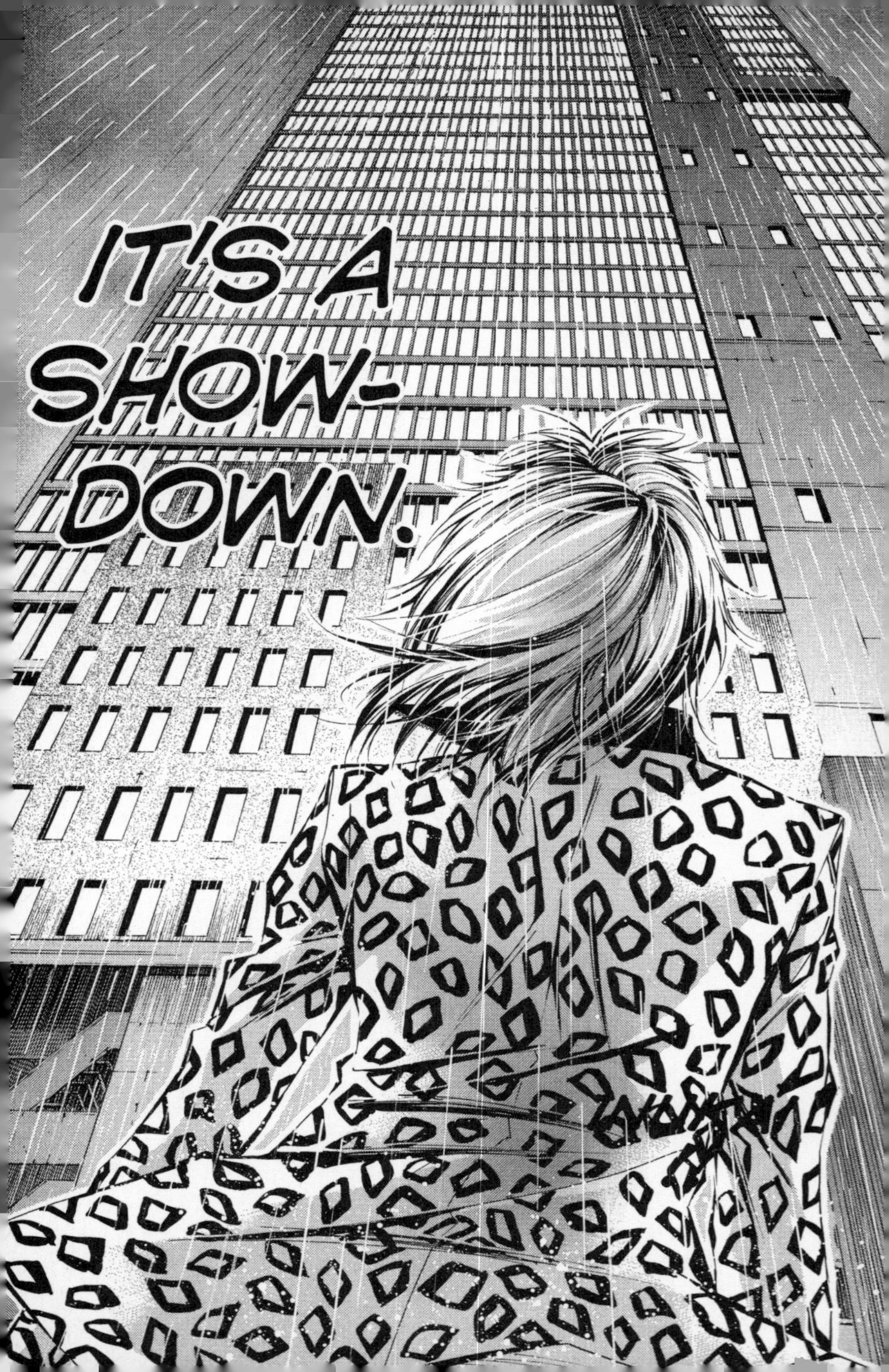
IT'S A SHOW-DOWN.

IT CONTINUES IN Vol.09

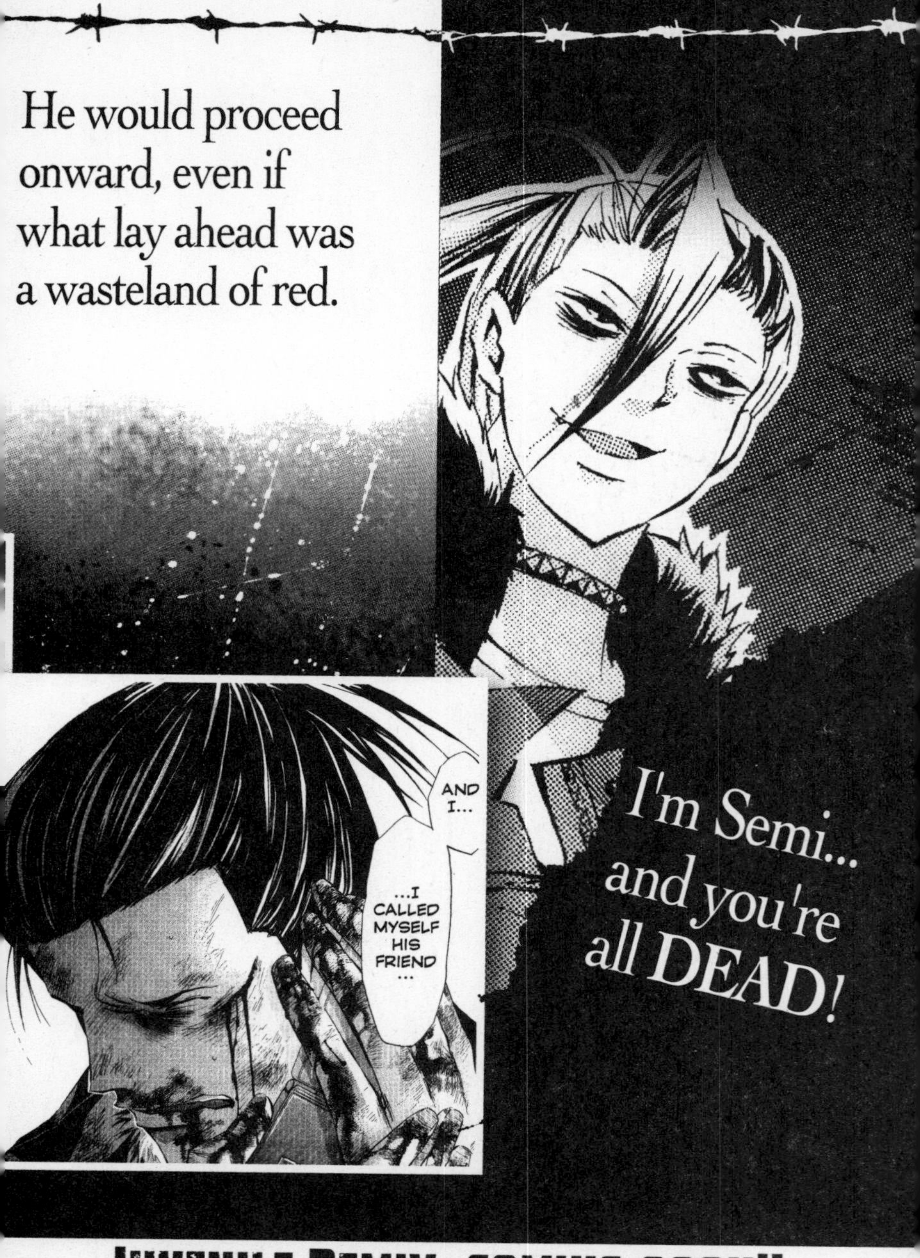
I'm Semi... and you're all DEAD!
He would proceed onward, even if what lay ahead was a wasteland of red.
AND I...
...I CALLED MYSELF HIS FRIEND...

JUVENILE REMIX, COMING SOON!!

MAOH Juvenile Remix

I'm going to WIN. No matter what it takes.

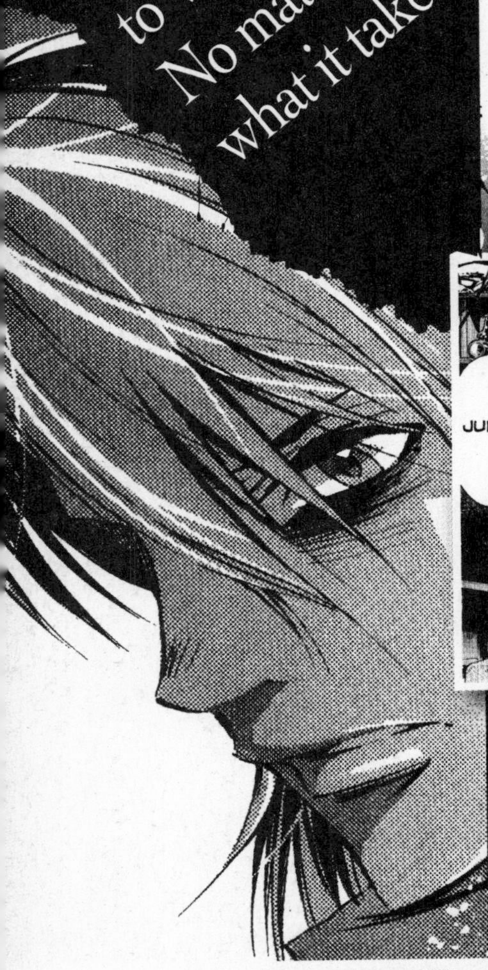

What then, is his cold, hard decision?! Finally, Junya's powers are revealed! What passes through his heart in the moment of understanding?

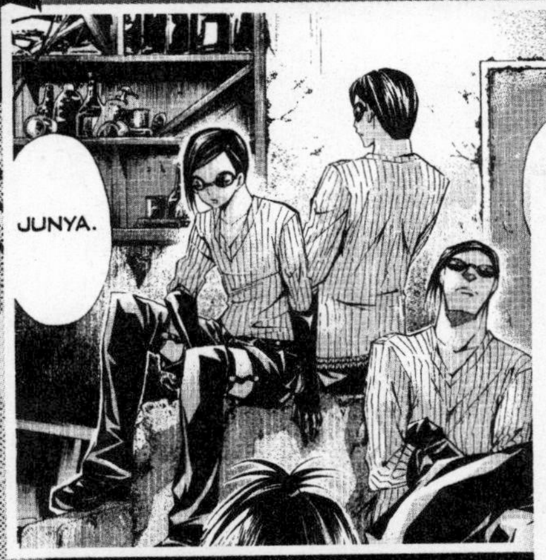
JUNYA.

THE STORY ACCELERATES! BLOOD BOILS, AND EMOTIONS RUN WILD!!!

VOLUME 9 OF MAOH:

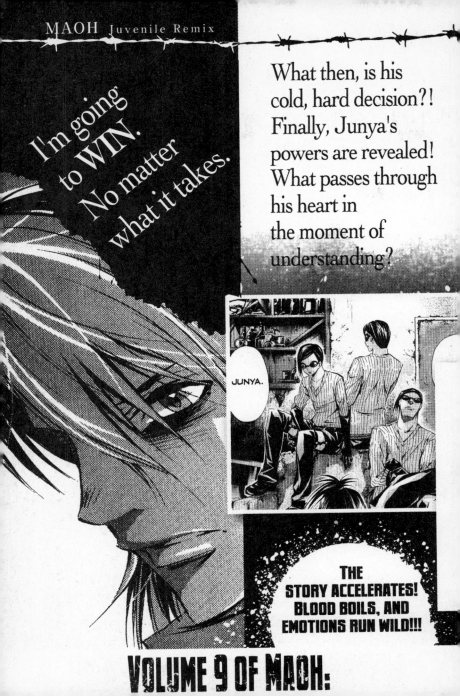

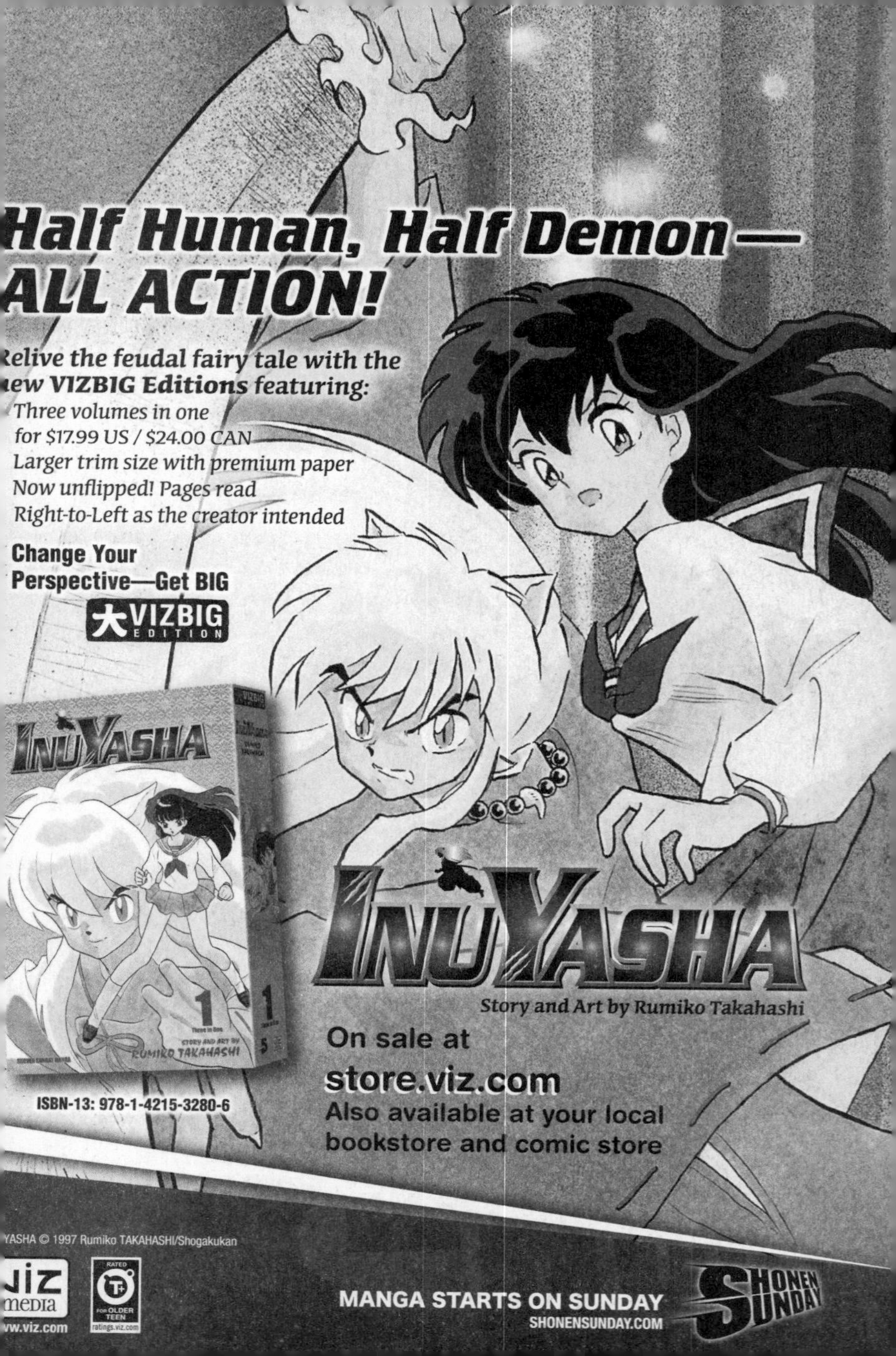
Half Human, Half Demon—
ALL ACTION!
Relive the feudal fairy tale with the new VIZBIG Editions featuring:
Three volumes in one for $17.99 US / $24.00 CAN
Larger trim size with premium paper
Now unflipped! Pages read Right-to-Left as the creator intended
Change Your Perspective—Get BIG
大 VIZBIG EDITION
INUYASHA
ISBN-13: 978-1-4215-3280-6
INUYASHA
Story and Art by Rumiko Takahashi
On sale at
store.viz.com
Also available at your local bookstore and comic store
YASHA © 1997 Rumiko TAKAHASHI/Shogakukan
viz media
ww.viz.com
RATED T+ FOR OLDER TEEN
ratings.viz.com
MANGA STARTS ON SUNDAY
SHONENSUNDAY.COM
SHONEN SUNDAY

At Your Indentured Service

Hayate's parents are bad with money, so they sell his organs to pay their debts. Hayate doesn't like this plan, so he comes up with a new one—kidnap and ransom a girl from a wealthy family. Solid plan... so how did he end up as her butler?

Find out in *Hayate the Combat Butler*— buy the manga at store.viz.com!

Kenjiro Hata

© 2005 Kenjiro HATA/Shogakukan Inc.

www.viz.com
store.viz.com